New Horizons of Critical Theory

Creative Multiverse: New Explorations in Transformative Learning and Research

There is an epochal challenge of learning from multiple experiments in self and social transformations now. *Creative Multiverse* seeks to explore and present different pathways of transformations in societies and histories around the world. It builds upon engagements in learning in different disciplines of life and academy and seeks to create a transdisciplinary space of research, dialogues and transformations.

A Series from Shipra Publications, Delhi
Email: info@shiprapublications.com
Editor: Ananta Kumar Giri,
Madras Institute of Development Studies, Chennai, India.
Email: aumkrishna@yahoo.com; Website: www.mids.ac.in/ananta.htm

International Editorial Advisory Board

New Horizons of Critical Theory

Collective Learning and Triple Contingency

Piet Strydom

SHIPRA

Price : Rs 850 US$ 42.50

ISBN: 978-81-7541-449-5

First Published in India in 2009

New Horizons of Critical Theory: Collective Learning and Triple Contingency

Published by :
SHIPRA PUBLICATIONS
115-A, Vikas Marg, Shakarpur, Delhi-110092 (India)
Tel. : 91-11-65277210, 22500954, Fax : 91-11-22458662
Email : info@shiprapublications.com
www.shipraoublications.com

This book is dedicated to
Klaus Eder
and to all those fast learners who take cues from the conflicts of our time and are working to make intercultural communication a reality.

Foreword

Oh Friend, Oh Dear Soul,
You asked, you asked
The embrace of my heart
Our questions are not only questions
Nor are they bombs nor edges of the sword
Our questions are flows—one and many
Flows of our hearts
In between flowers and hammers
Our questions are our stories
Of bathing together and searching together
Of Being Drowned and Rising Again

—A Poem originally written in Oriya by the author and self-translated into English (2008)

In the relations between the individual and the group, this constant tendency of Nature appears as the strife between two equally deep-rooted human tendencies, individualism and collectivism. On one side is the engrossing authority, perfection and development of the State, on the other the distinctive freedom, perfection and development of individual man. The State idea, the small or the vast living machine, and the human idea, the more and more distinct and luminous Person, the increasing God, stand in perpetual opposition. The size of the State makes no difference to the essence of the struggle and need make none to its characteristic circumstances. It was the family, the tribe or the city, the polis; it became the clan, the caste and the class, the kula, the gens. It is now the nation. Tomorrow or day after it may be all mankind. But even then the question will remain poised between man and humanity, between self-liberating Person and the engrossing collectivity.

Sri Aurobindo (1962), *Human Cycles*, pp. 272-273.

I have sought to draw art and craft together, because all techniques contain expressive implications. This is true of making a pot; it is also equally true of raising a child.

—Richard Sennett (2008), *The Craftsman*, p. 290.

The new social movements grapple with the problem of nature and are concomitantly posing questions about the conative underpinnings of modern society, thus problematising what motivates people, what meanings are being pursued and ultimately what human needs are being fulfilled [..] bringing about a change in the elementary cultural structures underpinning modern society, thus redefining the boundary between society and non-society, between culture and nature, and transforming our human social relationship to and appropriation of nature. Central to their endeavour, therefore, is the identification of what counts as authentic needs under contemporary conditions.

It is from this viewpoint of authentic needs that the new social movements open up the possibility of a new kind of critique. It is neither a critique of ideology nor a critique of instrumental reason and even less a critique of functionalist reason, as in the case of Marx, Horkheimer and Habermas respectively, but rather an aesthetic social critique or what I propose to call *endeetic* critique. This critique is directed at what is unquestioningly taken for granted in modern society, namely an exploitative relation to nature, and hence at the *endeetic* foundations of economics, politics, labour and social life in general – that is, foundations as determined by the prevailing definition of human needs. The outcome of this critique is the question of authentic needs which can be answered neither by science nor by the political institutions since it concerns what we really want, how we really want to live, what kind of a society we really desire, what we would really find good, and so forth. It is in this sense that the continuation of the rationalisation of modern culture and society today depends crucially on our ability to draw out the practical implications of the thrust towards the institutionalisation of an expressive form of life and to develop what amounts to an *endeetic* critique.

—Piet Strydom (2008) *New Horizons of Critical Theory: Collective Learning and Triple Contingency*

I

Piet Stydom is a creative and critical seeker of our contemporary world who has asked many questions and has also created spaces of mutual learning and collective blossoming. Strydom originally comes from South Africa and his critique of then prevailing apartheid regime made him homeless. Strydom first came to England and then settled down in Ireland where he has taught at the pre-eminent University College Cork, Ireland for more than three decades. While teaching at Cork Strydom has embodied a new mode of critique and creativity which has presented his students and fellow learners a critical and creative way of blossoming beyond the gaze of authorities and some of his students are now leading practitioners of social theory.[1] Strydom has made valuable contributions to continental traditions of critical social theory which has many insights for all of concerned seekers of knowledge and human liberation beyond the Euro-American world. It is enriching to have *New Horizons of Critical Theory: Collective Learning and Triple Contingency* in our *Creative Mutliverse* series which aims at cultivating paths of transforming learning and we are grateful to Strydom for his labor of love and to Mr. D. Kumar of Shipra Publications for generously facilitating this.

As a heart-touching teacher and fellow seeker Strydom has inspired many of us around the world to explore new horizons of learning. What is touching is the way Strydom combines critical engagement with a deep passion for emergent normativity, one which invites us to take sociological analytics to a new normative height and depth. In outlining the contours of a new socio-cognitive critique in his *Risk, Environment and Society*, Strydom pleads for a non-judgmental critical engagement: "Far from judging and condemning the ideology of a particular actor or agent [..] it is a matter of closely studying a variety of related cognitive processes and structures. Included are the frames and normative codes of all participants, despite their conflicting interpretations of it [..]" (Strydom 2002: 156). In his pioneering work, *Discourse and Knowledge: The Making of Enlightenment Sociology*, Strydom urges us to understand the limits of rights and justice frames of modernity and open ourselves to the emergent frames of co-responsibility. In his essay, "Risk communication: world creation through collective learning under complex contingent conditions," Strydom (2006) tells us how "different configurations of public spheres allow distinct learning processes" and invites us to accept the challenge of triple contingency learning: "Triple contingency learning represents the collective learning mechanism which brings us closest to the communicative self-constitution and self-organization of society. [..]

It harbors the 'cosmopolitan' promise of a transformative moment in which a 'creative combination of different forces' occurs" (2006: 9).

Continuing this inspiring spirit of a deeper normative critique and transformation, Strydom urges us to go beyond the contest of faculties, especially arts and sciences, and nurture a different relationship with science, scholarship and time. For Strydom, "Science is a much slower field than politics, not to mention economics" (2004b: 8). When science is "being steadily accelerated and stressed up well beyond its own time culture" social scientists have to contribute to the epochal need of "the unhastening or deceleration of science" (ibid).

In reflecting upon the issue of contest of faculties between arts and sciences, Strydom invites us for a new "chrono-politics." But this needs to be part of multi-dimensional strivings of cultivating a new relationship with time and generating a space of mutual nurturance and generosity. Cultivating a new relationship with time calls for appropriate self-cultivation and spaces of value formation along with structural transformations of organizations of living. It also calls for cultivating a mode of non-anxiety vis-à-vis our living and flow of time. This is not only a political process but also a spiritual process where spirituality refers to a continued quest for critique, transformation, and overcoming of boundaries which have been turned into prisons, and creation of relationships of beauty and dignity. Similarly, the emergent frames of responsibility are not only socio-political but also socio-spiritual and responsibility do not emerge only in public spheres but also involves practices of self-development and transformation which are not reducible to the public. Strydom's preference for the concept of "co-responsibility" from Karl-Otto Apel over and above over and above the more usual "collective responsibility" is "precisely to make room for the individual who also has to come to embody personally the responsibility that is required at the macro-level" (personal communication). What Strydom wrote to me recently on this issue is helpful to understand his project:

> My account [of responsibility] covers all the different dimensions, including different versions of the personal or individual, but the main point [..] is of course to argue about the new development of a macro-ethic. But the fact that it is macro does not mean that it is only macro. From the cognitive view that I hold, there is always mediation between the micro (individual, personal), meso (e.g. groups, institutions and social movements) and the macro (societal) levels. At the individual or personal level, the cognitive structures cover all the dimensions, from the intellectual (epistemic), through the moral (conscience) to the ethical/

aesthetic/conative – and at this latter level of emotional and motivational identity formation lies, in my view, the well-spring of what you call the spiritual. I've never excluded this dimension. All I haven't been doing is to explicitly elaborate, as you do, the theme of the cultivation of this dimension in itself and its relation to the other dimensions.

Strydom's plea for a non-judgmental critical theory—one which listens to all contending voices rather than quickly identifies with an apriori 'legitimationist' perspective (this is how Strydom (1999) characterizes Habermas's approach to public sphere)—resonates with a "multi-valued logic" which relates to all the participants and their truth claims as "partly true, partly false, and partly undecidable" (Mohanty 2000: 24). (cf. Mohanty 2000). Strydom's critical engagement indeed strives to go beyond a simple "either or" logic, for example the state versus social movements, in the field of risk communication. But while Strydom's "multi-logical thinking goes back to Peirce and Apel's three-place theory of signs and the ontological dimensions of firstness, secondness and thirdness" (personal communication) it can now invite a planetary border-crossing in cultivating pathways of multi-valued logic, for example, inviting the Jaina tradition of *anekanta vada* (many paths of truth), Gandhian pathways of non-violence and Husserlian pathways of overlapping contents.[2] Multi-valued logic is not solely discursive and is based upon non-violence in ontology and intersubjective relations and non-injury in modes of thinking, especially epistemic engagement. Multi-valued logic helps us in overcoming epistemic violence, the violence we inflict upon reality which is ontologically multi-dimensional where different dimensions are related to each other in a spirit of autonomy and interpenetration. Multi-valued logic is itself a work of ontological epistemology of participation where epistemic engagement with partial nature of our truth claims including attribution of falsity is accompanied by appropriate ontological preparation which facilitates such an epistemic engagement and modes of reasoning (cf. Giri 2006; Clammer et al. 2003).

II

In developing a new critical theory at the heart of which lies what he calls "socio-cognitive critique," Strydom (2002) creatively builds on both (what he calls) the new cognitive revolution and social constructivism and, at the same time, imparting to this confluence his own characteristic originality. For Strydom (2002), the cognitive turn questions "the function of norms in social action and interaction by rejecting the traditional assumptions of norms as being consistent and extending a determining influence. Instead, it emphasized the need to develop a sensitivity for and an ability to identify the whole range of culturally defined alternatives to practices and the construction and organization of society. Casualties of the change were such modernist notions as the unitary concept of modernity, the linear concept of progress, the progressivist or developmental concept of evolution, the identification of modernity and universalism and so forth" (ibid: 180). Such questioning resonates with some of the most important themes in contemporary critical theory such as contingency, disjunction between facts and norms, the work of antinomies in self, culture and society, and critique of linearity (Giri 2006; Beteille 2000). Strydom gives a cognitive thrust to social constructivism: "Constructivism, in my view, is best seen from a cognitive theoretical point of view that acknowledges both intersubjective understanding and the objectivity of reality with which we maintain pragmatic relations" (ibid: 151). Thus, with care, Strydom prepares the following pathways of "socio-cognitive critique":

a) It is based upon a 'relational conception of the social world, with the emphasis therefore being less on static substances and entities [..]' (ibid: 153);
b) It is both a 'critique of the status quo and a critique of utopianism' (ibid);
c) 'To fulfill the requirements of socio-cognitive critique, the whole network of different cognitive processes and structures is investigated.' Socio-cognitive critique advances an 'understanding of the critical task of sociology' by 'distinguishing different types of cognitive structures or models' (ibid: 157);
d) Socio-cognitive critique leads to generation of explanatory models which in turn has 'epistemic authority.' 'But the sociologist has no exclusive possession of epistemic authority. Observers and commentators as well as the observing, evaluating and judging public to the varying degrees enjoy this same privilege. In fact, often the epistemic authority of the sociologist depends on such a third point of view' (ibid)

Socio-cognitive critique is, thus related to the work of "triple contingency" in self, culture and society as well as this mode of critique itself is a mode of triple contingency learning. Triple contingency learning is a multilateral learning process in which participating actors and institutions learn from and with each other in a mutligonal way embodying an emergent self-constitution and self-organization of society. Socio-cognitive critique is thus a creative process of self-creation of society.

Further, socio-cognitive critique not only emerges out of vibrant public communication but also makes sociology public:

> The public role of sociology commences with the making visible of the whole spectrum of different experiences, perceptions, frames and knowledges. This is achieved by locating and heightening the tensions and relating the intersecting lines of creativity and conflict to each other. By adopting such a minimalist mediating role, sociology's aim is to break down the ethnocentricity of perspectives and to contribute to the development of reciprocal perspectives (ibid: 158).

"Triple Contingency" is at the core of Strydom's new critical theory which for him can take us from the "neo-classical" to the "post-classical" phase of theorizing (Strydom 2009: xxiii). For Strydom, "[..] the concept of double contingency needs to make way for a more adequate replacement—namely triple contingency. In the first scenario, two social actors, communicatively acting subjects or black boxes, A and B, face or encounter one another or enter into some relation with each other as 'I' and 'Thou.' In the basic situation of triple contingency, by contrast, there is a third perspective borne by C, who observes what A and B are saying. By so doing C has a constitutive impact on the social situation" (Strydom 1999: 8). Though this third point of view at an earlier stage of Strydom's formulation "represents society" (ibid), at a later stage it represents discursively engaged and learning public which is not just a representation of society and is not bound to a society's "internal mode of justification" (personal communication). Strydom also asks a bold question: "the third point of view: within or beyond society?" and suggests that triple contingency is a product of immanent transcendence. For Strydom, immanent transcendence refers to "the relation between immanence and transcendence as defining of the process of the constitution of social reality, and in particular transcendence as it is represented by counterfactuals" (personal communication). Furthermore, "Critical theory has a stereoscopic perspective: it never focuses only on immanence (the empirical situation), but at the same time and even more importantly on those ideas of reason, normative ideas or cultural models in the form of counterfactuals which have an immanent foothold in people's pragmatic presupposition, assumptions, expectations, anticipations, visions of what ought to be, etc., yet transcend the situation as something unrealised and even unrealisable, but as such nevertheless still structure the situation since people to varying degrees allow themselves to be led by such counterfactuals and try to live up to them and to actualise and realise them immanently" (ibid). But such a work of immanent transcendence can also involve what can be called transcendental immanence where transcendence can not be solely located within society and exists and rises from many other spheres such as Divine, Nature and in creative engagements such as art and music (cf. Giri 2004). The prophetic traditions in many religions and spiritual pathways have embodied a critique of existing society and here critique is a work of transcendental immanence and not solely that of immanent transcendence (Quarles van Ufford & Giri 2003; Toynbee 1956 & Vattimo 1999).

Strydom's pioneering concept of triple contingency urges us to explore the ontology of the third so that it again is not related to the first and the second in a dualistic mode and with an priori judgment. The third point does not represent only the observing third actor C who is observing A and B but A and B also have the need also to cultivate an observant self in their own selves. For realization of triple contingency we thus need cultivation of a third observing mode of being and becoming both within the first and the second. In this context the question that Bourdieu asks to participant observation is relevant: "How can one be both subject and object, the one who acts and the one who, as it were, watching himself acting?" (Bourdieu 2003: 282). Bourdieu himself does not address this issue as he is primarily confined within "epistemic reflexivity' without accompanying ontological nurturance. But to be able to act and observe one's own action requires cultivation of what is called *sakhi purusha* (witnessing self) in Indian spiritual traditions and what Adam Smith (1976) calls "impartial spectator." Work of triple contingency thus involves cultivation of an observant self in our own selves. It also calls for giving birth to the third in the life of first and second and in the margins in between thus heightening the need for participants in and practitioners of triple contingency to be creative mothers of an emergent third in the initial lives of the first and the second.

III

Along with explorations of collective learning and triple contingencies as fields of socio-cognitive critique, in this book, as presented in the beginning epigraph, Strydom cultivates pathways of an *endeetic* critique which has an epochal relevance for all of us as it asks the question of ends and challenges us to remain vigilant about the displacement of ends by means which constitutes a pathology of not only different paths of modernities but also in the modernization theory itself.[3] As Strydom tells us in this book in our hands, in modernity there have been different kinds of movements and what are usually labeled as counter-movements were not just irrational but were "involved in endeavorurs to realize a different or an alternative modernity."

At the contemporary juncture, Strydom urges us to realize, our explorations of alternative modernities involve questions of a new relationship between human and nature, nature and society.[4] We are invited and challenged to ask the question of our ends and be practitioners of what Strydom calls *endeetic* critique which is "directed at what is unquestioningly taken for granted in modern society, namely an exploitative relation to nature, and hence at the *endeetic* foundations of economics, politics, labour and social life in general – that is, foundations as determined by the prevailing definition of human needs." Strydom presents us some new social movements promoting a new radical expressive revolution which urges us to express ourselves authentically beyond the societal and contemporaneous definition of needs. They create a space for not only reiteration of existing needs but for the birth of new flames of aspirations in self and society. The later has a spiritual dimension which though not explored with the boundary of this name in Strydom nonetheless is suggested in his pathway of *endeetic* critique which asks questions about the meaning of our lives, the ends of our means and the nature of our needs. If we combine the paths of socio-cognitive critique and *endeetic* critique it has enormous enriching potential theoretically and practically.

Strydom's explorations of *endeetic* critique which reflects quest for meaning resonates with some of the inspiring contemporary savants of this as well as the last century. Authentic expression of self in the spaces of the public but not necessarily confined to it resonates with Victor Frankl's pathways of logotherapy where we are invited to explore and realize that "deep down man is dominated neither by the will to pleasure nor by the will to power but by will to meaning: his deep-seated striving and struggling for a higher and ultimate meaning to his existence" (1967: 117). Strydom does explore varieties of quest for meaning in our contemporary world (especially in the third part of this book) and his bringing together of cognitive, constructivist and now expressive approach to understanding and living is itself an example of remarkable quest for meaning. But this quest for meaning does meet with many shadows,[5] darkness and violence where both self and even the emergent public (not just existing crowd but participants in collective learning, social movements and observing situations of triple contingency) can and do suffer from self as well as collective delusion of what Frankl calls "collective neuroses of the present day" (ibid). Strydom's new horizons of critical theory can invite this also as an issue to cope with and transform which in turn calls for a new practice of therapy and healing where critique of self and society, and practice of sociology as creative criticism nurtured by both socio-cognitive critique and *endeetic* critique, can contribute to acknowledgement of our multiple sufferings—self as well as social—and also accompanying strivings to heal and to blossom together realizing that in between there are not only flowers but also hammers. Srydom's treatment of the public could now invite the need for realizing the delusions that the public itself can suffer from and the consequent need for enlightenment of the public as well as public healing which can come from many sources—art, social criticism as well as spiritual mobilizations.

Strydom's work also resonates with the work of some other critical and creative sociologists such as Robert Bellah who talks about a new paradigm of cultivation which seeks to heal the "split between the imaginative and the cognitive, the intellectual and the emotional [..]" (1970: 245) and pays attention to the needs of one another (Bellah et al. 1991). Resonating with Strydom's concerns about ends, attention in this paradigm of cultivation is different from "distraction" and "obsession" for example some of us being obsessed with power, money and sensual pleasure. For Bellah et al: "Attending means to concern ourselves with the larger meanings of things in the loner run, rather than with short-term pay offs" (Bellah et al. 1991: 273). And in Strydom learning this art of cultivation is itself a collective learning which involves not only the self and the other but also an observant and emergent public. At the same time it is fruitful to cultivate paths and patterns of cultivation in the spaces of what Strydom calls collective learning and triple contingency. Thus collective learning and triple contingency are also spaces and times of cultivation of attending to one another and discovering the difference between attention and distraction. This also involves compassion and confrontation, compassionately understanding as well as confronting each other and all concerned.

Strydom's *endeedtic critique*, i.e. a critique concerned with the issue of the meaning of our ends and needs also reminds us of the famous question that Maitreyee had asked about the end of our strivings thousands of years ago. Amartya Sen renders this immortal question of Maitreyee in the following way:

> It is not unusual for couples to discuss the possibility of earning more money but a conversation on this subject from around the eighth century B.C. is of special interest. As that conversation is recounted in the Sanskrit text *Brihadaranyaka Upanishad*, a woman named Maitreyee and her husband, Yajnavalkya, proceed rapidly to a bigger issue than the ways and means of becoming more wealthy: How far would wealth go to help them get what they want? Maitreyee wonders whether it could be the case that if "the whole earth, full of wealth" were to belong just to her, she

> could achieve immortality through it. "No," responds Yajnavalkya, "like the life of rich people will be your life. But there is no hope of immortality by wealth." Maitreyee remarks, "What should I do with that by which I do not become immortal? (Sen 1999: 1)

Maitreyee's question is a question of *purusartha* (ends and meaning of human lives—this is an important vision and practice of being human and realizing one's potential in society in Indian tradition) urging us to ask the question of relationship between *artha* (wealth) and *moksha* (salvation) which has layers of symbolic and worldly meaning and Sen translates its worldly meaning in this way: "If we have reasons to want more wealth, we have to ask: What are precisely these reasons, how do they work, on what are they contingent and what are the things we can 'do' with more wealth" (Sen 1999: 2). Sri Aurobindo (1957) in his *Thoughts and Aphorisms* has said there are eternities and eternities and similarly Maitreyee's concern with immortality means immortalities and immortalities which can be creatively translated to our contemporary condition of collective learning and triple contingencies. Contributing to the self-critical and public discourse of meaning and ends of human life and the public that Strydom presents with his *endeetic* critique and in the spirit of Maitreyee we can ask: What do we have to do with that kind of life, society, humanity and pursuit of wealth which does not ensure self-development, inclusion of the other and planetary blossoming?

Asking such questions about ends of lives invites us to embody both practical discourse and practical spirituality. Strydom's explorations of collective learning and triple contingencies build upon Habermas's pathways of practical discourse (albeit many further questioning to this project) and now it can also invite practical spirituality also another mother to learn from and grow together with (cf. Dallmayr 2006; Giri 2008). Practical spirituality is a multi-dimensional striving and struggle in critique, creativity and transformation which seeks to realize beauty, dignity and dialogue in lives of self, society and our Mother Earth in the midst of manifold brokenness of our world. Practical spirituality does invite us for a realizing a new end of our lives going beyond our biological and constructivist gender fixation and other role attributions. Practical spirituality invites all of us to realize that the end of our lives is to be mother of our own self (of our higher self struggling to realize itself in the midst of parts of self trying to put us in darkness) and a creative society. The new *purusartha* of practical spirituality as human blossoming, collective learning and planetary realizations calls us to be mothers including making our society and state a space of mothering where society and state provide a space for self-realization as mothers and are not only spaces of control. This involves a reconstitution of both space and time as today much of our suffering and thus needs for healing comes from an anxiety about time and being helpless victims of spaces of capital. A new *purusartha* of practical spirituality reconstitutes space and time as our mothers but this reconstitution calls for transformation of capitalism and a new spiritual realization of our own capacity to generate time as mother and not only selling our time in the media of money and market.

But the embrace of this invitation calls for further foundational self-critique and cross-cultural learning. Strydom's concluding essay in this book on cosmopolitanism and learning is an important beginning and invites us to open up critical theory itself to a cosmopolitan learning involving questioning of self and tradition, border-crossing, transforming learning and planetary conversations.[6]

Merry Christmas
December 25, 2008

Ananta Kumar Giri
Madras Institute of Development Studies
Chennai

[This foreword builds on my essay, "The Calling of a New Critical Theory: Self-Development, Inclusion of the Other and Planetary Realizations," first presented in the symposium in honor of Piet Strydom, "Critical Turns in Critical Theory," University College Cork, Ireland, April 2007. I thank Seamus Otuama for his kind invitation and to Piet Strydom and friends—Linda Connolly, Patrick O'Mahony, Gerard Delanty, Tracy Skillington, Bridget McAdam-O'Connell and Gerard Mullally—for kind and generous welcome and conversations. I also thank Piet for his comments on this foreword and him and his wife Sunette for an unforgettable evening of cooking together and weaving a poetry of life.]

REFERENCES

Bellah, Robert N. 1985 [1957]. *Tokugawa Religion*. Glencoe, NY: Free Press.

Bellah, Robert N. et al. 1991. *The Good Society*. NY: Alfred A. Knof.

Beteille, Andre. 2000. *Antinomies of Society: Essays on Ideologies and Institutions*. Delhi: Oxford U. Press.

Bourdieu, Pierre. 2003. 'Participant Objectivation.' *Journal of Royal Anthropological Institute* (N.S) 9: 281-294.

Clammer, John et al. 2003. (eds.) *Figured Worlds: Ontological Obstacles in Intercultural Relations*. Toronto: University of Toronto Press.

Dallmayr, Fred. 2006 *Small Wonder: Global Power and its Discontents*. Rowman & Littlefield.

Frankl, Victor. 1967. *Psychotherapy and Existentialism: Selected Papers on Logotherapy*. Harmondsworth: Penguin Books.

Giri, Ananta Kumar. 2002. *Conversations and Transformations: Towards a New Ethics of Self and Society*. Lanham, MD: Lexington Books.

——(2004) "Knowledge and Human Liberation: Jurgen Habermas, Sri Aurobindo and Beyond." *European Journal of Social Theory* 7 (1): 85-103.

—— (2006) "Creative Social Research: Rethinking Theories and Methods and the Calling of an Ontological Epistemology of Participation." *Dialectical Anthropology* 30: 227-271.

—— (2008a) "The Calling of a New Critical Theory: Piet Strydom's Socio-Cognitive Critique and Beyond." *Review of Development and Change* XIII (1): 77-94.

——(2008b) "The Calling of Practical Spirituality." In Makarand Paranjape (ed.), *Science, Spirituality and the Modernization of India*. Delhi: Anthem Books.

Harrington, Austin (ed.). 2005. *Modern Social Theory: An Introduction*. Oxford: Oxfored U. Press.

Mohanty, J.N. 2000. *Self and Other: Philosophical Essays*. Delhi: Oxford U. Press.

Nussbaum, Martha. 2006. *Frontiers of Justice: Disability, Nationality, Species Membership*. Cambridge, MA: Harvard U. Press.

Quarles van Ufford & Ananta K. Giri. 2003 (eds.) *A Moral Critique of Development: In Search of Global Responsibilities*. London: Routledge.

Roy, Ramashroy. 1999. *Beyond Ego's Domain: Being and Order in the Vedas*. Delhi: Shipra Publications.

Sen, Amartya. 1999. *Development as Freedom*. NY: Alred A. Knof.

Sennett, Richard. 2008. *The Craftsman*. Yale.

Smith, Adam. 1976. *A Theory of Moral Sentiments*. Oxford: Oxford U. Press.

Strydom, Piet. 1999. 'Triple Contingency: The Theoretical Problem of the Public in Communication Societies.' *Philosophy and Social Criticism* 25 (2): 1-25.

——(2000) *Discourse and Knowledge: The Making of Enlightenment Sociology*. Liverpool: Liverpool University Press.

—— (2001) 'The Problem of Triple Contingency in Habermas.' *Sociological Theory* 19: 165-188.

——(2002) *Risk, Environment and Society*. Buckingham, UK: Open University Press.

——(2004a) 'Resonance: Triggering a Dormant Dimension of the Public Sphere.' Manuscript.

—— (2004b) 'The "Contest of Faculties" and Cultures of Time: Sociological Reflections on the Relation of the Natural and Social Sciences.' Text of the paper presented to the Science Faculty Public Lecture Series, University College Cork, Ireland, Feb. 3.

——(2006) 'Risk communication as world creation through collective learning under complex contingent conditions.' Paper presented at the multidisciplinary research conference on 'New Perspectives on Risk Communication,' 31 August-2 September, Gothenburg, Sweden.

—— (2009) New Horizons of Critical Theory: Collective Learning and Triple Contingency. Delhi: Shipra.

Sri Aurobindo. 1958. *Thoughts and Aphorism*. Pondicherry: Sri Aurobindo Ashram.

—— (1962). Human Cycles. Pondicherry: Sri Aurobindo Ashram.
Toynbee, Arnold J. 1956. *A Historian's Approach to Religion*. Oxford: Oxford U. Press.
Vattimo, Giani. 1999. *Belief*. Cambridge: Polity Press.

ENDNOTES

1. The most widely known among Strydom's students is Gerard Delanty, the author of many books on social theory and the philosophy of social science, who currently teaches sociology at the University of Sussex and is the founding editor of the *European Journal of Social Theory*. But other students also continue his creative and critical work in important ways, including: Catherine Brennan, Massey University, New Zealand; John Farrell, academic translator, Frankfurt, Germany; Marie Mater, Houston Baptist University, Texas, USA; Gerard Mullally, University College Cork; Orla O'Donnell, University of Limerick, Ireland; Patrick O'Mahony, University College Cork; Séamus Ó'Tuama, University College Cork; Louise Ryan, City University, London; and Tracey Skillington, University College Cork.
2. As Mohanty tells us:

   The ethic of non-injury applied to philosophical thinking requires that one does not reject outright the other point of view without first recognizing the element of truth in it; it is based on the belief that every point of view is partly true, partly false, and partly undecidable. A simple two-valued logic requiring that a proposition must either be true or false is thereby rejected, and what the Jaina philosopher proposes is a multi-valued logic. To this multi-valued logic, I add the Husserlian idea of overlapping contents. The different perspectives on a thing are not mutually exclusive, but share some contents with each other. The different 'worlds' have shared contents, contrary to the total relativism. *If you represent them by circles, they are intersecting circles, not incommensurable, [and it is this model of] intersecting circles which can get us out of relativism on the one hand and absolutism on the other.* (Mohanty 2000: 24; emphases added)
3. What Bellah writes in his paperback edition in 1985 to his book on Tokugawa Religion first published in 1957 where he had adopted an uncritical modernization approach this context below deserves our careful consideration:

   However, the greatest weakness of the book has nothing to do with Japan but with a weakness in the modernization theory I was using: I failed to see that the endless accumulation of wealth and power does not lead to the good society but undermines the condition necessary for any viable society at all. I suffered myself from the displacement of ends by means, or the attempt to make means to ends, which is the very source of the pathology of modernization. [..] What would it mean to reverse the functionalization of religion, the reduction of the realm of ultimate ends to the status of means? What would it look like if religion set the ends, and the means—wealth and power—that have usurped the status of the ends, were reduced to the status of means again?

4. This also invites us for a more foundational critique of anthropocentrism and realization of what Martha Nussbaum calls "cross-species dignity" (cf. Nussbaum 2006).
5. In this context what Austin Harrington writes in his concluding essay, "Social Theory for the Twenty-First Century" in his edited book *Modern Social Theory* deserves our careful attention:

   There are illusions, prejudices, and lies to be purged from the spaces of our public and private lives. But we also have to accept that the answers to our problems are not always unambiguous or clearly given. When the ancient Greek philosopher Plato compared ignorance to the perception of shadows on the walls of a cave lit by a dim fire, he made an assumption of the ultimate separateness of truth and enlightenment from the daily contexts of life in which people ordinarily experience the world. Today this kind of assumption is not possible for us. Today our reality is intrinsically a reality of shadowy appearances, and shifting forms, of mediated images and messy contradictions (Harrington 2005: 314).
6. Strydom himself writes, despite all his and his co-travelers' such as Klaus Eder's critiques and transformations, "It should be emphasized, however, that whatever the theoretical dynamics exhibited by the conceptualization of the methodology of critique may be, the abiding theoretical core of critical theory, nevertheless, remains constant throughout. This core is to be found in the left- or young-Hegelian heritage which secures the uniqueness of critical theory" (2008: xx). However what Strydom writes in a recent communication deserves our careful consideration:

   Everybody and every tradition starts somewhere and is grounded somewhere. The left-Hegelian tradition had always been and still is the basic anchor point of critical theory. But the left-Hegelian tradition is not just a Continental (German) tradition represented by the left-Hegelians from Marx via Lukács to the first, second and third generations of critical theorists. The same tradition is also represented by Peirce, the founder of pragmatism or pragmaticism, as well as by

Kierkegaard who was exclusively focused on the cultivation of the self. It is much broader that the run-of-the-mill impression. Of course critical theory is open to questioning, learning, border-crossing etc., but does that mean that it has to surrender it most basic insight? That insight is 'immanent transcendence', which is precisely what allows it to mediate its own self with the transcendent Other. Surely, if the individual is to cultivate itself and thereby also becomes able to open up, then the same must hold of a tradition.

But the question here is not of surrender of insight but that of foundational interrogation, border-crossing and broadening.

But in a recent communication Strydom emphasizes that self-critique is an important part of critical theory and his project:

Critical theory started out as a critique of knowledge, e.g. Kant's critique of pure reason, Marx's critique of political economy, and so its goes on. Horkheimer's famous introduction of the very concept of critical theory was prompted by and took the form of a critique of knowledge and knowledge production processes. Habermas brought ideology critique to bear on science itself by criticising 'scientism' and, further, criticising the 'positivist' and 'scientistic' residues in critical theory itself, and in a recent book he wrote an article on 'Die Falsche im Eigenen' (On what is false in our own tradition).

Throughout my own work, I am acutely aware that critical theory has to maintain a self-critical relation to itself. In philosophy of social science materials I have always taken the view that the different philosophies have their own liabilities: if the science tradition's liability is elitism, technocracy and expertocracy, and if the interpretative tradition's is nativism, ethnocentrism and political naiveté, then *the liability of the critical tradition is dogmatism against which it must at all time guard* (emphases added).

But possibly there is still need for more foundational critique of our own self—presuppositions and traditions—and practice of transformative cross-cultural learning here

Preface and Acknowledgements

The present volume is the outcome of an invitation that Ananta Kumar Giri extended to me in April 2007 on one of his regular visits to Ireland to bring together, both published and unpublished, essays on one particular line of my thought—a line that, like various others, makes a contribution to shifting the horizon of critical theory. Accordingly, the essays collected here mark a trajectory that bore fruit in the 1980s in the wake of the appropriation of the idea of collective learning, that culminated in the introduction of the idea of triple contingency in 1990s, and along the way found application in areas of contemporary interest such as social movements, collective identity, risk, responsibility, public communication, globalization and cosmopolitanism. The majority of the essays originally appeared in leading journals between 1987 and 2008. To these I have added a number of other pieces; one a longer version of a previously published article, another published in a not easily accessible volume of conference proceedings and five further as yet unpublished pieces.

The ideas and arguments in these essays were gathered and developed in a variety of intellectual contexts and geographical locations. Lecture courses and seminars offered to undergraduates and postgraduates at University College Cork (UCC), public lectures and conference papers at home and abroad, and seminar presentations and lectures at universities abroad provided one type of context. Another was opened by research projects in a variety of areas, funded by internal UCC resources, the European Commission and the Irish Higher Education Authority, which were undertaken in an individual capacity, as responsible scientist within the framework of the Centre for European Social Research at UCC of which I, as co-founder, had been a director, and more recently as a principal investigator in intra-Arts Faculty as well as inter-Arts and Science Faculty projects at UCC. Besides my county of birth, South Africa, which I have visited on several occasions since the early 1990s, and my adopted country—Ireland—these activities have taken me to many places, some of which I have returned to several times both for shorter and longer periods. They include Belgium, the Netherlands, Germany, France, Britain, Italy, Hungary, Switzerland, the United States and Sweden. Of all the cities where I spent some time, Frankfurt in particular stands out as an intellectual beacon. I have visited it on numerous occasions and enjoyed a number of long research sojourns there, which included attendance at lectures, seminars and colloquia offered by Jürgen Habermas and Karl-Otto Apel.

As regards my relation to Frankfurt critical theory, my receptivity was sharpened by my relatively early political awakening due to regular protests against the apartheid system, and strengthened by the influence of two of my sociology teachers at the University of Stellenbosch, Dian Joubert, who often made memorable critical remarks about South African politics, and Frederik van Zijl Slabbert, later leader of the official opposition, who introduced me to the philosophy of social science. The actual starting point of my independent appropriation of critical theoretical ideas, however, was the Positivist Dispute which decisively formed and shaped my sociological consciousness in the late 1960s as an honours student in sociology. Here I first came across Apel's work which made a great impression on me, and shortly after that I started to read Habermas. By 1972 when I gained my first permanent academic appointment at the University of South Africa, I had already worked myself well into the critical theoretical frame of mind. In this context, I received invaluable encouragement from a much older colleague, Cornie Alant, who conducted his own kind of home-grown critical analyses. But it was only after having left South Africa for political reasons in 1974, during a two year stay on the Continent and in Britain, that I was able to consolidate my relations with critical theory.

In the subsequent years, after having settled in Ireland in 1976, this process was facilitated by several opportunities to attend and partake in activities in and around the University of Frankfurt and to help place my students there. In addition to the leading figures, I also gained knowledge of the work of members of the younger generation located in Frankfurt and beyond, such as Oskar Negt, Peter Bürger, Albrech Wellmer, Claus Offe, Dietrich Böhler, Klaus Eder, Max Miller, Günter Frankenberg, Ulrich Rödel, Helmut Dubiel, Alfons Söllner, Axel Honneth and Wolfgang Bonß. A crucial consolidating moment in this process was the opportunity between the early and mid-1990s for me and a number of my associates in Cork to participate in a wide-ranging European research project coordinated by Klaus Eder from the European University Institute in Florence, Italy. Since their retirement in the 1990s, I have had the privilege of enjoying the generosity, intellectual and otherwise, of Apel and to receive the occasional encouraging note from Habermas—most importantly for me being his endorsement of my concept of 'triple contingency' in 1999. I am deeply indebted to Karl-Otto-Apel, Jürgen Habermas, Klaus Eder and Max Miller in particular and I wish to express my sincere gratitude. As an outsider (which is the story of my life), however, I have had to pursue the development of my thought in relative isolation and therefore quite independently.

Besides those already mentioned, I have acquired a huge debt to so many people through exchanges, comments, criticisms and encouragement in the different lecturing and research contexts and geographical locations that it would be impossible to list them all.

I wish, therefore, to thank everyone who has helped to make possible this volume, including nurturing over years what has gone into its making. Here I have to confine myself to two categories: first, colleagues abroad who have expressed an interest in multiple aspects of my work represented by this collection of essays and encouraged me along the way and, secondly, the ex-students who participated in the developments reflected in this volume, most of whom are today well-established academics in their own right, some abroad and others colleagues of mine at UCC or elsewhere in Ireland. I mention the names chronologically as we established contact, in the case of the first group, or as they passed through my teaching, in the case of the second. The former category includes Peter Swan, Carleton University, Ottawa, Canada; José Maurício Domingues, University of Rio de Janeiro, Brazil; Tom Burns, University of Uppsala, Sweden; Ananta Kumar Giri, Madras Institute of Development Studies, Chennai, India; Åsa Boholm, Gothenburg University, Sweden; Ulrich Beck, University of Munich and Loet Leydesdorff, Amsterdam School of Communications Research, the Netherlands. I cannot leave it unmentioned that the latter has recently mathematically formalised my concept of triple contingency (Leydesdorff 2007, 2009). To the second category belong John Farrell; Catherine Brennan, Massey University, Palmerston North, New Zealand; Michael Sullivan; Gerard Delanty, Sussex University, Brighton, UK; Patrick O'Mahony, UCC; Louise Ryan, City University, London, UK; Orla McDonnell, University of Limerick, Ireland; Séamus Ó'Tuama, UCC; Gerard Mullally, UCC; Tracey Skillington, UCC; and Marie Mater, Houston Baptist University, Texas, USA. I sincerely thank each and every one of these people—and exonerate them from any responsibility for any errors of judgement or fact that remain in the text. The same applies to translation—all translations from German and French texts being my own, unless quotations derive directly from available sources.

Last but by no means the least, I wish to thank Ananta Kumar Giri as editor of the series in which this book appears for his congenial manner, persuasive power, commitment to intellectual inquiry and argumentation, penetrating yet friendly criticism, creative ideas and the perceptive opening up of a space for much needed intercultural communication.

As regards acknowledgement of the sources from which the materials in this book have been drawn, the following:

1. 'Collective Learning: Habermas's Concessions and Their Theoretical Implications' was originally published in *Philosophy and Social Criticism* 13(3), 1987, pp. 265-81, London: Sage.
2. 'The Ontogenetic Fallacy: The Immanent Critique of Habermas's Developmental-Logical Theory of Evolution' first appeared in *Theory, Culture and Society* 9(3), 1992, pp. 65-93, London: Sage.
3. 'Sociocultural Evolution or the Evolution of Practical Reason: Eder's Critique of Habermas' was first published in *Praxis International* 13(3), 1993, pp. 304-22, Oxford: Wiley-Blackwell.
4. A shorter version of 'Critical Theory and the New Social Movements: A Conflict of Interpretations', originally written in 1988-89, was published in *Telos* 85, 1990, pp. 156-64 under the title of 'Habermas and New Social Movements'.
5. 'Contemporary Social Evolutionary Theory: A New European Rapprochement' was written in the late 1990s but remained unpublished.
6. 'Triple Contingency: The Theoretical Role of the Public in Communication Societies' originally appeared in *Philosophy and Social Criticism*, 25(2), 1999, pp. 1-25, London: Sage.
7. 'The Problem of Triple Contingency in Habermas' was published in *Sociological Theory* 19(2), 2001, pp. 165-86, Oxford: Wiley-Blackwell.
8. 'Contingency: A Critique of Luhmann' was written in 2000 but remained unpublished until now.
9. 'Resonance: Triggering a Dormant Dimension of the Public Sphere' was published in Vladimir Kultygin and Vassily Zhukov (eds.) *European Social Theory: Sources and Challenges*. Moscow: Research Network on Social Theory, European Sociological Association, 2003, pp. 83-99.
10. 'Intersubjectivity: Interactionist or Discursive? Reflections on Habermas's Critique of Brandom' first appeared in *Philosophy and Social Criticism* 32(2), 2006, pp. 155-72, London: Sage.
11. 'The Construction of Collective Identity: The South African Liberation Movement as a Collective Learning Process, 1882-1987' was written in 1987 in conjunction with a lecture course delivered in the 1987-88 academic year but was never published.
12. 'Contemporary Approaches to Collective Identity: A Critical Assessment' originally formed part of an unpublished research design for the study of technological citizenship written in 1999.

13. 'The Challenge of Responsibility for Sociology' was originally published in *Current Sociology* 47(3), 1999, pp. 65-82, London: Sage.
14. 'Risk Communication: World Creation through Collective Learning under Complex Contingent Conditions' was first presented at the multi-disciplinary conference on 'New Perspectives on Risk Communication', Centre for Public Sector Research, Gothenburg University, Sweden, in 2006 and then selected for publication with other conference contributions in the *Journal of Risk Research* 11(1-2), January 2008, pp. 5-22, London: Taylor & Francis. http://www.informaworld.com
15. 'Cosmopolitanism, Globalization, and Collective Learning: Reflections on Delanty's Theory of Cosmopolitanism' was written in 2006 but is published here for the first time.

I thank Sage Publications, Wiley-Blackwell Publishing Ltd. and Taylor & Francis for extending their cooperation in granting the permission to publish the articles in this volume.

Piet Strydom

25 December, 2008
Kinsale
County Cork, Ireland

Contents

PART III
APPLICATIONS: SOCIAL MOVEMENTS, RESPONSIBILITY, RISK, COSMOPOLITANISM

Introdu

Introduction

The essays brought together in this volume were selected with the intention of highlighting one particular aspect of my thought. They mark the stages in a line of development that first came to fruition in the 1980s, underwent an enriching transformation in the 1990s, and along the way found application in a variety of areas of contemporary interest.

FROM COLLECTIVE LEARNING TO TRIPLE CONTINGENCY

During the first stage which had started already in the 1970s and yielded results in the 1980s, I appropriated the concept of 'collective learning processes' from Habermas and authors associated with him, such as Klaus Eder and Max Miller, and sought to critically clarify and develop it. During the second half of the 1980, I applied the concept in wide-ranging studies in the social movement field, particularly the South African liberation movement, and in the 1990s it still inspired my concern with the conceptualisation and analysis of the moral construct of collective or co-responsibility which has arisen in response to the problem of risk. The second stage commenced in the early 1990s and culminated in my introduction of the new concept of 'triple contingency' which appeared for the first time in published form in 1999. Not only was this concept the impetus behind my original reinterpretation of the history of sociology put forward in *Discourse and Knowledge* (2000), but over the next five years or so it provided the basis for a number of critical theoretical explorations of the basic assumptions of Habermas, Luhmann and others. The third stage was opened in the late 1990s when the insight dawned on me that there is a close link between collective learning processes and triple contingency. This connection allowed me to explore the application of this—what appeared to me—very fruitful theoretical instrument in such areas as land reform in South Africa (2008, not included here), risk communication, globalization and cosmopolitanism. At present, I am still engrossed in related research in these and other areas.

Besides this particular strand, other lines of thought that I have pursued over the past number of decades are also already announced in the early essays. Important to me, for instance, are first the epistemological-methodological line which I have taken up in *Philosophies of Social Science* (edited and introduced with Gerard Delanty, 2003) and related papers, and second especially the cognitive line which I have developed in such books as *Discourse and Knowledge* (2000), *Risk, Environment and Society* (2002) as well as in the special issue of the *European Journal of Social Theory* (10/3, 2007), which I edited on the theme of 'Social Theory after the Cognitive Revolution: Types of Contemporary Cognitive Sociology', and other related pieces (2006a, 2006c, 2006d). For some time now, in fact, the development of a new cognitive social science has been my primary focus. In the present volume, however, I leave such concerns of mine in the background in order to bring out the development running from the concept of collective learning through the concept of triple contingency to their combined application in contemporary fields of interest.

NEW HORIZONS

The horizons of critical theory adverted to in the title of this collection invoke shifts progressively achieved in the series of essays included in it—shifts, of course, which were not unrelated to contemporaneous developments in critical theory itself.

The first step involved the identification and correction of problems in Habermas's theoretical framework with a view actually to creating space for social movements as collective learning processes which he claimed to be able to accommodate but in fact did not. Whereas this advance beyond Habermas from early on allowed an appreciation that social movements as collective learning processes demanded that they be understood in terms of historically specific intersubjective contexts of experience possessing societal significance, the focus for a time remained on social movements as such. They were considered internally as intersubjective experiential contexts on the assumption that they were central to the constitution and the organization of society. The next step required insight into the limitations of such a position and a considerable broadening of perspective. Instead of confining intersubjective experiential contexts and, by extension, shared socially constructed forms to social movements themselves, the constructive process had to be transposed to the macro-level of society.

The insight had to dawn that the constructivist approach really came into its own only if it is extended to the structured relational context embracing social movements as well as the other collective agents active in the constitution and organization of society. Collective or social action that is collectively significant and makes a difference to society possesses this quality not simply of its own accord, but also because it is constructed as such in a broader framework. Habermas's insistence on the centrality of communication in the constitution of society and the significance of the public sphere in providing a social space for its staging was of course recognised as being of the greatest importance. But this is precisely where, in a further step, the broadening of the constructivist perspective compelled a differentiation of the concept of the public sphere.

Rather than one public sphere, different types of public sphere had to be identified, each of which represented a different kind of intersubjective experiential context. From this proliferation of public spheres then followed the insight that different contexts of experience make possible distinct processes of collective learning. The most decisive shift in horizon occurred, however, when it was appreciated that distinct collective learning processes borne by their own particular collective agents take place in a structured relational context which, far from being fixed beforehand, is subject to its own kind of situational contingency distinct from the contingencies of action. Due to the public communicative or, better, discursive nature of this relational context, triple contingency was finally linked to the constitutive role of the public in the kind of practical discourse representing the site of the constitution and organization of society.

As is to be expected these gradual and progressively broadening shifts in the horizon of critical theory was by no means without consequences for the most central critical theoretical concept, namely critique. Since the adoption of George Lukács's (1971) renewed Marxian idea by the early Frankfurt school, the concept of critique has undergone two transformations—the first, laying the normative foundations of critique in linguistically mediated communication and its moral potential and the second cutting deeper still to locate those foundations in the multi-level structure formation at the core of the process of the constitution of society. By the way, this emphasis on structure formation explains the central significance that collective learning and triple contingency have for my particular approach to critical theory. The first transformation took place between the 1960s and early 1980s from the 'ideology critique', 'redemptive critique' and 'critique of instrumental reason' represented by the first generation critical theorists (Horkheimer 1972, 1974; Adorno 1972, 1981; Marcuse 1972; Benjamin 1980) to the 'ideology critique' and 'critique of functionalist reason' of the second generation (Habermas 1972a, 1984a, 1987a; Apel 1984, Apel *et al.* 1971). The next transformation beyond Apel and Habermas took place in the 1980s and 1990s, involving two shifts in the horizon of critical theory that are reflected in the essays collected in this volume. These shifts are marked first by 'endeetic critique' (Strydom 1988-89, Chapter 4 in this volume), which in a sense is related to Eder's 'social critique' (1988: 275, 329, 352; 1993a: 78-80, 98-100), and then by 'socio-cognitive critique' (Strydom 1999e: 19-20, Chapter 6 in this volume; 2000: 263, 279, 301; 2002: 153-7). The former kind of critique —as the name suggests—is directed at what is unquestioningly taken for granted in modern society, namely the prevailing cultural definition of human needs as supposedly authentic needs which has a profound structuring effect on economics, politics, labour and social life in general. The latter focuses on the uncovering or exposure of the illusory side of the cultural models followed by all those involved in the constitution and organization of society, including social movements, and hence the partial use that their social practices make of the available cultural models and knowledge. This approach overcame not only Habermas's predilection to tie the normative reference point making critique possible to the moral point of view outside society, but also his tendency under criticism to revert instead to the social movement viewpoint inside society, thus losing sight of the larger relational context. It should be emphasised, however, that whatever the theoretical dynamics exhibited by the conceptualisation of the methodology of critique may be, the abiding theoretical core of critical theory, nevertheless, remains constant throughout. This core is to be found in the left- or young-Hegelian heritage which secures the uniqueness of critical theory (Fink-Eitel 1993; Honneth 2000: 88-9; Fraser and Honneth 2003: 238-45; Strydom 2009).

STRUCTURE OF THE BOOK

The first group of five essays in Part I documents the history of my critical appropriation of the concept of collective learning processes and the conclusions I drew from it, for my pursuit of critical theory. The process of appropriation started with Habermas's reconstruction of historical materialism. While the central concept of 'social movements as learning processes' (Habermas 1976b: 40; 1979a: 125) captured my attention, at the same time it left me with a feeling of unease. A close study of the writings of the younger generation of critical theorists in subsequent years assisted me in developing and articulating my critique of Habermas's position, but then the problem became one of how to move critically beyond them.

In the first essay, 'Collective Learning: Habermas's Concessions and Their Theoretical Implications', the emphasis falls squarely on the theoretical foundations of the concept of collective learning. It analyses Max Miller and Klaus Eder's criticisms of Habermas and the far-reaching concessions the latter had to make to his critics. On this basis, I then probe the theoretical implications that follow from the concessions for the concept of collective learning, the nature and place of social movements, the role of intersubjective experiential contexts, and Habermas's overall theoretical position.

The second essay, 'The Ontogenetic Fallacy: The Immanent Critique of Habermas's Developmental-Logical Theory of Evolution', focuses on the role of developmental models in the theory of evolution in order to expose the nature of Habermas's ontogenetic model and to critically assess the alternative practice-theoretical model which the younger generation of critical theorists—authors such as Johann Arnason, Axel Honneth, Hans Joas, Günter Frankenberg, Ulrich Rödel and Klaus Eder—opposed to it. On the one hand, I take the critique of Habermas together under the title of the 'ontogenetic fallacy' and, on the other, envisage a constructivist position that points beyond the practice-theoretical position of Habermas's critics.

Essay number three, 'Sociocultural Evolution or the Evolution of Practical Reason: Eder's Critique of Habermas', is a more specific consideration of Eder's proposal to reformulate the theory of evolution on the assumption that of all the younger critical theorists he has gone deepest into the theory of society. Its aim is not only to understand the change that critical theory has been undergoing, but also to enable me to develop further my own theory of the constitution and organization of society—what already in the first essay I called 'the theory of sociation' or 'the theory of societalisation' (*Theorie der Vergesellschaftung*). Communication theory, which Habermas established as central to the theory of society, is retained here yet is built into a stronger constructivist approach.

The fourth essay, 'Critical Theory and the New Social Movements: A Conflict of Interpretations', brings together and develops further core insights gained in the previous essays. Substantively, it concentrates on critical theory's approach to the new social movements against the backdrop of an elucidation of both the advantages and disadvantages of Habermas's general theoretical framework for the study of social movements. Using Stephen White's (1988) all too positive presentation of Habermas's position as a foil, it first reviews the younger critical theorists' immanent critique and innovative departures, and then extrapolates and clarifies the direction in which a critical theoretical analysis of social movements, particularly the new social movements, is pointing. Of theoretical importance is that it explores a non-linear theory of society as against Habermas's linear conception and, in conjunction with it, also a corresponding concept of critique—what I call 'endeetic critique'.

The final essay in Part I dealing with collective learning, 'Contemporary Social Evolutionary Theory: A New European

Rapprochement', is a retrospective reconstruction of the context in which my own understanding of evolutionary theory had undergone a transformation in the 1990s. It focuses on the theoretical core of social evolutionary theory by analysing the theoretical dynamics at work among three important strands of European evolutionary theory, namely, the Habermasian school represented by Klaus Eder, the Darwinian school represented by Bernhard Giesen and associates, and the Uppsala school represented by Tom Burns and associates. It finds that over time a rapprochement developed among these three originally quite different approaches. At the centre of this rapprochement, significantly, is communication theory; the introduction of which necessitated a distinction between collective learning and evolution.

The second group consisting of five essays in Part II documents my initial introduction of the concept of 'triple contingency', the subsequent critical analysis of the dependence of two leading yet diametrically opposed social theorists, Jürgen Habermas and Niklas Luhmann, on the older concept of double contingency, and finally the exploration of some of the theoretical implications of the new concept.

The sixth essay, 'Triple Contingency: The Theoretical Role of the Public in Communication Societies', advances the claim that the proposition or theorem of 'double contingency' put forward originally by Parsons, which in the 1980s and 1990s was still assumed by Habermas and Luhmann as the most basic social-theoretical concept, is in fact no longer sufficient. Today, in modes of life increasingly taking the form of communication societies, we have to reckon with 'triple contingency' instead. This conceptual innovation is then given theoretical sense by linking this more complex form of contingency to one of the most important insights gained by the social science in the recent past, namely, that the public as public is nothing less than a constitutive part of societally significant communication processes in contemporary societies. In addition to the theoretical considerations, some epistemological and methodological implications of the introduction of the third point of view into the social sciences are also explored. Epistemologically, attention is given, in particular, to constructivism which requires that plurality and difference be observed in the process of constitution of society and, correspondingly, that learning be regarded as a constructive process. The modification this demands in the concept of critique is also assessed.

Essay number seven, 'The Problem of Triple Contingency in Habermas', is a full-scale critical analysis of the discrepancy in Habermas's writings between his emphatic acceptance of the Parsonian theorem of double contingency, on the one hand, and his operation with a theoretical position that actually implies a higher degree of contingency than he recognises, on the other. It is shown that although Habermas is the originator and leading representative of the theory of the public sphere, he surprisingly neglects to theoretically capture and clarify the role of the public in communication societies in a manner fitting to this theory. This failure is accounted for by his tendency to interpret the third point of view too strongly in terms of the idealised moral point of view which has the effect of excluding or, at least, minimising contingency. Finally, some conclusions are drawn regarding the possibility that this opens up for a new situational cognitive or epistemic theory of the public and, by extension, a new theory of the evolution of situational epistemic structures beyond Habermas's theory of communicative action.

'Contingency: A Critique of Luhmann', the eighth essay, is a critical analysis of Luhmann's theory which has contingency at its very core. It focuses on his retention of the Parsonian concept of double contingency as the basic theorem of his social theory and the consequences following from this strategic decision. The investigation of his autopoietic theory of social systems shows that, although he had shifted to the more abstract level of systems theory, he continues to operate with a limited mutualistic model. Rather than triple contingency, the only possibility Luhmann sees is a multiplicity of double contingencies. It is interesting to note that in April 2007 a contribution was made to precisely the on-line 'Diskussionsforum zur soziologischen Systemtheorie Niklas Luhmanns' in which my concept of triple contingency was formalised by being cast in mathematical form and taken up into systems theory over and above the double contingency (see now Leydesdorff 2007, 2009). On the basis of both Habermas and Luhmann's debilitating attachment to double contingency, it thus becomes possible to defend the thesis that the novel concept of triple contingency can take us beyond neo-classical theory into the post-classical phase which we are at present entering.

The ninth essay, 'Resonance: Triggering a Dormant Dimension of the Public Sphere', seeks to clarify the sense of the increasingly employed yet ill-defined basic communication-theoretical concept of resonance. It adopts the viewpoint of triple contingency, in order to analyse the concept in a way that lends it more theoretical significance. The theoretical literature of the past twenty years by authors such as William Gamson, Niklas Luhmann, Jürgen Habermas and Klaus Eder certainly gives evidence of a differentiation of the concept of resonance—from cultural and system resonance through civil society and lifeworld resonance to institutional and extra-institutional resonance. By anchoring the different concepts in the resonance structures of the public sphere, however, it is shown that a concept of public resonance underpinned by triple contingency—and thus distinct from civil society or extra-institutional resonance—is nevertheless lacking. Finally, indications are given of the social research potential of the concept.

The focus of 'Intersubjectivity —Interactionist or Discursive? Reflections on Habermas's Critique of Brandom', the tenth and last essay in Part II, is Habermas's conspicuous ambivalence about adopting either an interactionist or a discursive approach to intersubjectivity and the theoretical implications entailed by it. At stake is the proper understanding of intersubjectivity, particularly the process of communication whereby it becomes established. The thrust of the argument is that Habermas fails to theorise the process of communication adequately. Although proceeding from the basic distinction between interaction and discourse, he tends to regard the process in a one-dimensional manner as involving the interactive or dialogical coordination of the intentions and actions of the participants alone. This raises the question of the missing dimension of the process, namely, the moment of synthesis of the different contributions into a collectively acceptable outcome at the discursive level which is essential for and therefore presupposed by the actual attainment of intersubjective coordination. The principal thesis is that triple contingency is the theoretical concept required to come to terms with this absent level of discursive synthesis. Without it, justice can neither be done to the temporal unfolding of communication nor to the structure formation or collective learning occurring in that medium.

The third group of five essays collected in Part III is more concerned with the application of the theoretical ideas of collective learning and triple contingency in areas of contemporary interest, yet they are by no means devoid of attempts to elaborate and refine theoretical considerations relevant to critical theory. The analyses of social movements, the construction of collective identity, risk and responsibility, risk communication, and globalization and cosmopolitanism are, therefore, interspersed with theoretical as well as methodological elaborations.

In the eleventh essay, 'The Construction of Collective Identity: The South African Liberation Movement as a Collective Learning Process, 1882-1987', the general phenomenon of social movements is refracted through the prism of the South African liberation movement. Based on available historical research and independent analysis of historical documents, it covers the period from the origination of the latter movement until the drastic transformation of South Africa to which it made a central contribution. The essay deals with the problem of collective identity construction in social movements as a process of collective learning. While this perspective in principle mediates between the structural or systemic and the action dimensions, it is confined here to the social movement as such and therefore deals with it in relative isolation for the purpose of the analysis. Its very specific focus is the unfolding, under changing conditions, of the process of internal structure formation carrying the collective identity of the movement. The general theoretical position adopted is the genetic-structuralist or interactionist-structurational one founded by Jean Piaget, but it is explored in two different versions —the more basic Oser model and the more sophisticated Starnberg model, as I call them. The former derives from Fritz Oser who is inspired by Piaget and Kohlberg, and the latter was developed under Habermas's directorship by Eder, Rödel, Frankenberg and Tugendhat at the Max Planck Institute of Social Sciences in Starnberg —both originally developed for different purposes than analysing social movements. Employing these two comparable yet quite different models, the essay reconstructs the internal developments of the South African liberation movement as a self-creative and self-organizing process taking the form of collective learning in the sense of communicative conflict resolution and, consequently, collective identity construction making possible the mediation of objective and subjective conditions and thus the coordination of action.

The twelfth essay, 'Contemporary Approaches to Collective Identity: A Critical Assessment', is devoted to a dissection of Alberto Melucci's analysis of the construction of a social movement collective identity and Shmuel Eisenstadt and Bernhard Giesen's analysis of the construction of national identity. It seeks to identify problems in their respective analyses as well as the possibilities they open up. The overall aim of the critical exercise is to find ways of taking forward the theory and analysis of collective identity construction relevant to the constitution and organization of society. Attention is paid, in particular, to the constructivist conception of the process of identity formation, which correlates with the concept of collective learning, and to the public communicative context in which such construction takes place, which brings in the concept of triple contingency.

Assuming the advances made thus far with the development of a constructivist communication and discourse theory of society, the thirteenth essay, 'The Challenge of Responsibility for Sociology', is a study in the sociology of morality that pursues a strand stretching from Durkheim to Habermas and beyond. Its focus is the new normatively relevant cultural model of collective or, better still, co-responsibility that emerged in the late 20th century through a process of collective learning from the public discourse about risk in which the environmental movement, corporations and politicians confront each other. Rather than following the process of construction as such, however, it reconstructs this new cultural model and, through an analysis of documents stemming from the 1992 UN Earth Summit in Rio de Janeiro, illuminates the structuration effect this product of collective learning has on the movement organizations, states and corporations from both the North and the South.

There are certain similarities between the last two essays which were written during roughly the same period and used similar theoretical instruments, but they involve application in two distinct areas —risk communication in the first case and cosmopolitanism in the second. Both topics are treated in a coherent manner by means of the theoretical framework developed in the preceding essays, utilising, in particular, the concepts of collective learning and triple contingency as well as critique. In a certain sense, they could thus be regarded as the culmination of the development running through the essays collected in this volume.

'Risk Communication: World Creation through Collective Learning under Complex Contingent Conditions', the penultimate essay, focuses on a phenomenon of increasing importance. The analysis takes contemporary conflicts and debates about risk as its empirical reference, but at the same time it also seeks to contribute to the filling in of the largely lacking theoretical underpinnings. Risk communication, in the full sense of the word, is regarded as a discursive event in which speakers advance claims in the face of other responding participants before a general public. The presence of the public leads the participants to evaluate what happens in moral terms, with the result that their claims obtain an unavoidable normative quality and the discursive event takes the form of a public controversy which puts pressure on the participants to coordinate their disagreements. Proceeding from the assumption of socially distributed and shared cognition, the core argument of the essay is that risk communication, in the final analysis, is a cooperative learning process in and through which a communication community constructively arrives at a diagnostic interpretation of its common situation, the challenge it faces, and possible ways of dealing with it. Since such a learning is possible only under conditions of relatively high complexity and contingency, however, its characteristic non-linear dynamic development makes uncertainty both many-sided and unavoidable. Often, however, such a collective achievement is put beyond reach, not simply because of complexity, contingency and uncertainty, but rather because the agents or groups involved follow one or other of a number of strategies which effectively block learning. Were the social sciences to contribute to the enhancement of risk communication (e.g. by facilitating value- and will-formation in the face of concrete problems), they should study the multi-levelled process of risk communication in the different interactive-discursive contexts within which it takes place with a view to clarifying the learning processes and potentials they harbour. Crucial here are the normative standards appealed to and the degree of legitimacy they allow.

Not merely the management of uncertainty depends on this, but also the very world brought into being through risk communication.

The final essay, 'Cosmopolitanism, Globalization, and Collective Learning: Reflections on Delanty's Theory of Cosmopolitanism', focuses on cosmopolitanism utilising the perspective, as in the previous essay, of collective learning and triple contingency. Starting from Gerard Delanty's innovative linking of cosmopolitanism and collective learning in the context of the process of globalization, it extrapolates the perspective thus opened up and draws out its empirically, by no means insignificant, theoretical implications. The core of the paper consists of a differentiation of the general concept of learning into a number of distinct types of social learning by placing it in the context of different intersubjective experiential frameworks and, particularly, by bringing the concept of triple contingency to bear on it. This approach makes possible the critical explosion, as it were, of the theory of globalization from the inside out by identifying the learning processes at its core that are responsible for the creation of a diversity of competing models of world openness and attempts to realise them. At the same time, the analysis of this culture of contradictions and corresponding practices, which give rise to complex collective learning processes, allows a penetrating yet differentiated and reasoned critique of cosmopolitanism.

Collected in one volume, these essays should illuminate the development running from the concept of collective learning through the concept of triple contingency to their combined application in contemporary fields of interest. From a broader perspective, the stages of this development mark what can be regarded as shifts in the horizon of critical theory.

PART I

COLLECTIVE LEARNING

1

Collective Learning: Habermas's Concessions and Their Theoretical Implications

Although the concept of collective learning was first introduced almost two decades ago and subsequently became a familiar instrument in the hands of both historians of the labour movement and political scientists concerned with protest movements,[1] the most interesting and indeed most promising development is of a recent origin. It is to be found in the writings of authors who belong to the circle around Jürgen Habermas,[2] particularly Klaus Eder and Max Miller.[3] Not only have these authors provided some urgently required clarification of the theoretical foundations of the concept, but Eder has also applied it in a wide-ranging study of the pathogenesis of political modernity in Germany. What is particularly remarkable, however, is that Miller and Eder have turned the concept against Habermas and, indeed, with such effect that the latter has felt it necessary to make certain significant concessions, yet without elaborating on the theoretical implications thereof.

In this essay, I wish to probe the theoretical implications that follow from Habermas's acceptance of the concept of collective learning. To be able to do so, I propose first to identify those problems in Habermas's learning theory which have provoked criticism, and secondly present his concessions to the critics.

1. PROBLEMS IN HABERMAS'S LEARNING THEORY

Habermas's concept of learning must first be located in the context of his theory of social evolution which, in turn, represents a reconstruction of historical materialism. The decisive question here is: What serves as the spearhead of the development of society as a whole? Whereas orthodox Marxists propose the development of the forces of production as the answer to this question, Habermas (1979a: 120, 1981aII: 464) is prepared to 'defend the thesis that the development of .... normative structures is the pacemaker of social evolution'. A second reference point for understanding Habermas's concept of learning is represented by his action-theoretical appropriation of systems theory. The decisive question in this case is: what serves as the carrier of the spearhead of social evolution? Whereas Niklas Luhmann (1984: 55-57) regards the subjectless system as vehicle and insists on the primacy of functionalistically explicable selection and stabilisation achievements, Habermas (1976b: 142) takes an action-theoretical perspective and emphasises genetically explicable moral-practical learning processes.

While these global answers give a clear indication of the general direction in which Habermas wishes to go, they do not yet reveal the specifics of his positon. We must know precisely what he understands by 'normative structures,' how they are generated, and finally which category of these structures is effectively regarded as the leading one.

As regards the question of normative structures, Habermas (1979a: 120) submits that they are represented by 'mediations of communicative action' embodied in 'mechanisms for regulating conflict, in world views, and in identity formations'. These three categories of normative structures clearly correspond to what he, in his current terminology, calls the institutional order, culture and personality in the sense of structural components of the lifeworld respectively (Habermas 1981aII: 209). As the history of social theory suggests by way of such concepts as 'world spirit' (Hegel), 'class consciousness' (Marx, Lukács) or 'collective conscience' (Durkheim), the questions of the generation of normative structures and their relations are rather more difficult to answer. Familiar strategies from the past for dealing with them are the philosophy of history and transcendental philosophy, but since both are rooted in the philosophy of consciousness and thus give rise to the mystifying fiction of a collective subject constituting a meaningful world, Habermas studiously seeks to avoid them by adopting the alternative strategy provided by the genetic approach. To understand his position, however, it is necessary to recognise that the genetic dimension can be introduced from two mutually exclusive points of view: the individualist and the interactionist.[4]

Genetic individualism does away with the fiction of a macro-subject by conceiving of normative structures as the aggregate of individual learning processes. For this purpose it proceeds on two assumptions (Miller 1986: 15-22; Eder 1985a: 55-56). The first is the uncontentious assumption that, since competences of whatever kind can be attributed only to the individual, the individual and he or she alone can be said to learn. The second assumption, which can and must be rejected from the viewpoint of a sociological learning theory, is represented by the idea that, since the individual alone is able to learn, the mechanism as well as the process of learning must be ascribed to the individual. Genetic interactionism, by contrast, focuses on collective learning. It is indeed the case that the individual alone learns, yet learning is not merely an individual process, nor does the basic mechanism of learning reside in the individual. Learning is a collective in the sense of an interactive or communicative process, and as such it is presupposed by all individual learning. Moreover, collective learning processes represent the mechanism of the genesis of normative structures.

Now, what is so remarkable is that, although Habermas rejects the philosophy of consciousness in favour of emphatically adopting the genetic interactionist or intersubjectivist communication-theoretic position, a close investigation of his learning theory reveals the presence of elements of both genetic interactionism and genetic individualism.

An analysis of his position on the evolutionarily significant learning sequence yields a pattern[5] which suggests that Habermas does not give equal emphasis to culture, institutions and personality, but rather endows the relation among them with a slanted profile. He consistently takes ontogenetic development as running ahead of societal evolutionary advances involving societal learning. In fact, he accounts for societal learning by reverting back to learning at the individual level: '*individually acquired learning abilities* and information must be latently available in world views before they can be...transposed into *societal learning processes*' (Habermas 1979a: 121). There is no doubt about the fact that Habermas shares with genetic individualism not only its first but more significantly also its second assumption. A residual individualism remains which prevents him from accomplishing the full transition to genetic interactionism.[6] The paradigm shift from the philosophy of consciousness to the philosophy of language is yet to be completed.

Habermas's inadvertent retention of a debilitating genetic individualist assumption results in his learning theory being plagued by two related problems. Their common origin is reflected in his inadequate grasp of the social dimension.

First, when one proceeds on the assumption, as does Habermas, that individual learning processes precede societal evolutionary advances, it becomes necessary to account for the connection between individual and societal learning processes (Miller 1986: 219-220). How does society become aware of and appropriate what the individual has learned? To this question Habermas has only a rather vague answer to offer. Recognising that the results of individual learning processes 'must be latently available in world views before they can be used in a socially significant way' (Habermas 1979a: 121), he however speaks of such results as only having to 'find their way into a society's collectively accessible store of knowledge' (1979a: 121, 1981aII: 464) or as having to be 'transposed into structures of world views' (1979a: 123). It remains completely unclear as to how this translation from the individual to the social level is achieved, what learning mechanism is responsible, or how world views or collective systems of interpretation come into being. Habermas in fact covers the problem when he talks of 'embodying in new institutions the rationality structures *already developed in world views*.'[7] For what could this possibly mean?

When Habermas (1979a: 121) proposes, in addition, that 'there is a need for additional empirical assumptions that might explain sociologically how individual learning processes find their way into society's collectively accessible store of knowledge', he lays himself open to a basic sociological objection. Does he recognize the social dimension at all if he is willing to treat it in terms of 'additional empirical assumptions'? Does an adequate treatment of the social dimension not require stronger theoretical assumptions? It is instructive to note that a classical genetic interactionist such as the early Piaget (1967, 1968; also Harten 1977a, 1977b), instead of locating learning mechanisms on the individual level and then adding further empirical assumptions, brings the social dimension into play by theoretical means and regards collective learning processes as representing the mechanism with reference to which alone we are able to explain the genesis of world views.

Second, from the frequent references to social movements in his theory of social evolution (Habermas 1976a: 35, 40; 1979a: 98, 115; 1981aII: 468), it would seem as though Habermas gives intersubjective experiential contexts a central place in his theoretical framework. This impression is further strengthened by the fact that he directly links social movements to learning processes:

> *'Functionalism explains evolutionary advances by correlating functionally equivalent solutions to system problems. It thus steers away from the evolutionary learning processes that could alone have explanatory power. This explanatory gap (....) can be filled with a theory of social movements (....). One conceives of social movements as learning processes through which latently available structures of rationality are transposed into social practice, so that in the end they find an institutional embodiment' (Habermas 1979a: 125).*

The question thus arises: does this mean that Habermas gives intersubjective experiential contexts a central place in this theoretical scheme? Does this mean that, contrary to my claim, he actually recognises collective learning processes?

The answer to these questions are in the negative.

On studying the above-mentioned evolutionary learning sequence, it becomes apparent that 'social movements as learning processes' are assigned only a derivative role in his scheme. They are confined to the level of the selective stabilisation of latently available cultural potentialities, with the implication that they are recognised as playing a part in institutional innovation. But this includes neither the generation of new learning abilities and knowledge nor the constitution of collective interpretative systems. This means that social movements are at best only partially identified with collective learning processes.

From the genetic interactionist point of view (Harten 1977a: 186-187; Eder 1985a: 13, 54), a collectivity or intersubjective experiential context serves, on the one hand, as the objective condition of individual learning and, on the other, is simultaneously the outcome of collective learning which is able to transpose the collective effect of individual actions not only into the object but also into the medium of learning: conflicts, problems of cooperation and collective action, hence normative questions, do not represent only objects reflected upon and dealt with in intersubjective experiential contexts, but the very process of reflection upon treatment of such problems and questions becomes the medium in which the collectivity constitutes and reconstitutes itself. As regards this complex of objective and consitutive conditions of learning, Habermas (1979a: 121) writes: 'Since the cognitive development of the individual takes place under social boundary conditions, there is a circular process between societal and individual learning'. While this interesting statement might lead one to think that he accepts collective learning processes, it should be pointed out that what he actually does here is to reduce the social world as a constitutive condition of learning to a set of 'social boundary conditions,' —that is, a set of factors either facilitating or retarding individual learning.[8] It is not surprising, therefore, that social movements as collective learning processes are not appreciated as playing a constitutive role, but are instead forced to enter the scene at the tailend of the evolutionary learning sequence.

Habermas, to be fair, is not unaware of these problems and their solution through the completion of the paradigm shift to genetic interactionism.

2. HABERMAS'S CONCESSIONS TO HIS CRITICS

In his latest response to his critics, Habermas makes concessions which have a direct bearing on the question of collective learning theory. Because of its importance, I cite in full the paragraph in question. Having given a brief outline of this own understanding, inspired by Weber, the Durkheimian middle Piaget and Lévi-Strauss, of the relationship between individual cognitive strucutres of consciousness and the structures of world views, he continues:

> *'The picture painted hitherto is admittedly still too static and does not explain the social character of the corresponding, particularly moral learning processes. As regards this issue, Max Miller, connecting up with Vygotsky (and with Oevermann's concept of "objective hermeneutics"), developed a sociological learning theory which extends the approach of Kohlberg. This theory, to be sure, relates again to ontogenesis. The problem of the societal institutionalization of new structures of consciousness raised by Krüger can be resolved only by means of a theory of collective learning processes. As regards this issue, Klaus Eder has now made a remarkable proposal' (Habermas 1986a: 394, my translation; see also Habermas 1985b: 234).*

Here Habermas makes two concessions, each of which entails a self-critique and a modification of position. In the first, he self-critically focuses on his earlier unjustifiable reliance on an individualist learning theory and consequent establishment of an unmediated relation between individual structures of consciousness and world views, and acknowledges the relevance of a sociological learning theory. In the second, he engages in a self-critique relative to his earlier indefensible confinement of collectivities to stablilising already available cultural potentialities and consequent misconstrual of the relation between the generation and the institutionalisation of cultural potentialities, and acknowledges that an adequate theory of institutionalisation requires the introduction of the concept of collective learning processes.

What interests me about these two concessions is that they entail far-reaching implications for Habermas's theoretical framework which he allows to go unmentioned and unexplored.

3. THE IMPLICATIONS FOR HABERMAS'S POSITION

I propose to draw out under three headings the implications that follow from Habermas's acknowledgement of sociological learning theory and its central concept of collective learning processes: the developmental dynamics-developmental logic distinction, the macrotheoretical parametric framework, and finally the theory of action.

(1) In their respective elaborations of sociological learning theory, Eder and Miller advance illuminating criticisms of Habermas's reception of Jean Piaget's work. Miller argues that Habermas's appropriation of the early Piaget's theory of the social constitution of universalistic morality via the middle and later Piaget's concern with the developmental logic of cognitive competences at the ontogenetic level leads him to 'displace the genuine sociological concept of collective learning processes by the concept of "developmental logic"' (Miller 1986: 216, my translation). The thrust of this argument is rendered in a still more precise form by Eder (1985a: 55-56). The psychological turn exhibited by the middle and later Piaget was instrumental in tearing apart the relationship between the processes of cognitive learning and the structures of the social world which are constitutive of these processes. Cognitive structures consequently came to appear as *a priori* attributes belonging to individuals, while the social world, stripped of its dynamic interactive character, shrank to the sum of individual actions. This nexus forms the basis of the distinction between developmental dynamics and developmental logic. Habermas's appropriation of Piaget's work partakes of the above-mentioned psychological turn and the cognitive idealism or intellectualism consequent on it, and is thus characterised by the adoption of the dynamics-logic distinction.

From the point of view of the critical theoretical model of society, the place of the terms of this distinction can be clarified by means of the following diagram:

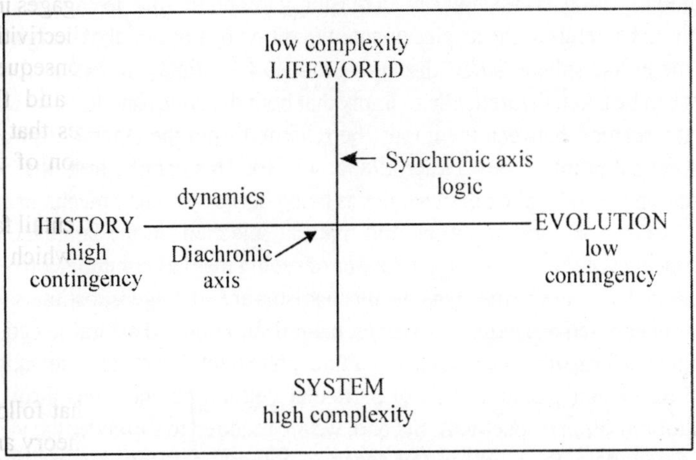

Fig. 1.1: Dynamics-Logic within the Critical Theoretical Model of Society

In so far as dynamics and logic pertain to the diachronic axis, they are the object of Habermas's theory of social evolution, the synchronic axis being the object of his theory of communicative action. Thomas McCarthy (1979: xxi) is of the opinion that the theory of social evolution represents 'the properly sociological level of Habermas's programme'. The thrust of Miller's and Eder's arguments, by contrast, is precisely that Habermas's theory of social evolution, due to its reductive approach to the social dimension, is not a properly sociological theory at all. One may sum up the position by saying that Habermas indeed incorporates the genetic dimension, yet he does so less in a sociological than in a psychological form. This sociological deficit can be corrected, according to Miller and Eder, by sociologising Habermas's theory of the development of moral consciousness. This requires the introduction of a sociological learning theory and the concept of collective learning processes on the basis of a fuller and more consistent utilisation of the communication-theoretical approach than is to be found in Habermas. Exactly how this latter task is to be achieved is a complex matter that I will attempt to make clear by means of a somewhat schematic presentation. The aim, generally speaking, is to locate collective learning processes in a position between dynamics and logic so that these processes become the mediating factor establishing and maintaining a relation between the two.

In the whole series of writings from *Strukturwandel der Öffentlichkeit* (1962) to *Theorie des kommunikativen Handelns* (1981), Habermas convincingly argues that in the course of the historical development of society communication has assumed an increasingly important role. In conjunction with such matters as the displacement of tradition by politics, the emergence of the public sphere, a new discursive mode of legitimation, and so forth, this can be taken theoretically to imply that both dynamics and logic as well as the relation between them must be regarded from the communication-theoretical point of view (Eder 1985a: 47-50). This entails, first, that we abandon the conception of dynamics as being borne by natural mechanisms, for instance 'natural variation' and 'natural selection' in the language of classical evolutionary theory, in favour of seeing them as communicatively mediated. In these terms, dynamic mechanisms are no longer substitutes for but rather based on learning processes, natural variation and natural selection taking the form of the generation of cultural potentialities through association and the selective stabilisation of particular cultural potentialities through insitutionisation respectively. Second, we are required to surrender the view of developmental logic, in the sense of internal restrictive conditions determining the direction of development, as a fixed *telos* or natural equilibrium in favour of regarding it as an intersubjective communicatively mediated self-organization of society based on social structures in the form of a normative order. On such a basis it becomes feasible to treat learning processes as being made possible by and taking place in the context of intersubjective or communicative experience, and hence as being based on presuppositions which give them direction.

The implications of such a communicative reconstitution of the diachronic axis are that not only the relation between the dynamic mechanisms of development, but also the relation between dynamics and logic are drastically changed. First, the relation between dynamic mechanisms is no longer linear or one-way, but rather reciprocal or even contradictory; the generation of cultural potentialities need not precede their selective stabilisation since association and institutionalisation now stand in a dialectical relation to one another. Second, the relation between dynamics and logic is such that the intersubjective communicative context of learning processes forms not only the basis and goal of learning, but is itself subject to change as a result of learning —for instance, the transposition of a religiously understood idea of equality (equality before God) initially into an immanent associational (equality of discourse partners) and finally into a socio-political one (political equality in a classless society).

On the whole, the relations among developmental dynamics, collective learning processes and developmental logic can thus be stated unequivocally. The developmental dynamic mechanisms of the generation and selective stabilisation of cultural potentialities, through association and institutionalisation, are based on collective learning processes, while the developmental logic, referring to the direction-giving structures established in the course of such learning and hence rooted in association and institutionalisation, is the logic of those learning processes (Eder 1985a: 98, 99). This complex of dialectical relations can diagrammatically be represented as in Figure 2 below.

Collective learning process

Developmental dynamics		Developmental Logic
Generation of cultural potentialities: association	Selective stabilisation of particular cultural postentialities: institutionalisation	Direction-giving associational and institutional structures——▶

Diachronic axis

Fig. 1.2: Communicatively Mediated Nexus of Dynamics, Learning and Logic

From what I have submitted thus far, it is clear that the acceptance of the theoretical component of collective learning compels Habermas to pursue communication theory more systematically and consistently than he has done hitherto —that is, to such an extent as to:

- give up the sharp distinction between developmental dynamics and developmental logic;
- rehabilitate the social dimension;
- rethink developmental dynamic mechanisms as the dialectically related generation and selective stabilisation of cultural potentialities through association and institutionalisation;
- rethink developmental logic as associational and institutional structures which are rooted in the developmental dynamic mechanisms; and finally
- rethink the nexus of developmental dynamics, learning processes and developmental logic as a communicatively mediated and hence dialectical one.

While these theoretical implications following from the concessions Habermas made to his critics are clear enough, they may actually be pursued much deeper by shifting from the level of the theory of social evolution to the macrotheoretical parameters framing it.

(2) By locating Habermas's theoretical position within the framework of the basic parameters of social reality and then comparing it to other macrosociological programmes, one can obtain a global grasp of the position and render it amenable to critical assessment. Taking cues from such authors as Kant, Parsons, Apel, Saussure and Habermas himself, I propose to construct a macrotheoretical parametric framework[9] and to locate Habermas's position within it as in Figure 3 below.

diachronic axis / synchronic axis	HISTORY	EVOLUTION
LIFEWORLD	Weber Barrington Moore E.P. Thompson Touraine	Hegel Marx Habermas
SYSTEM	Durkheim Elias Foucault	Parsons Luhmann

Fig. 1.3: Parametric Boundaries of Habermas's Macrosciological Programme

The nature of social reality is such that it requires of the social theortist sometimes to assume the perspective of the participant and at other times to take the point of view of the observer. This requirement is applicable to both the major parametric axes of social reality and can be satisfied by the construction of the axes according to polar opposites. In terms of the diagram, the diachronic or time axis varies between the poles of what from one viewpoint is called 'history' and 'evolution' and from another 'process' and 'structure.' The synchronic or space axis, on the other hand, varies between what in one vocabulary is called 'lifeworld' and 'system' and in another 'action' and 'structure.' Habermas, who uses the expressions 'lifeworld' and 'system' and 'history' and 'evolution,' combines the synchronic and diachronic axes in such a way that the emphasis is on lifeworld rather than on system and on evolution rather than on history. His overall position, defined as it is by these parameters, thus markedly differs from authors who locate their positions within the parameters of lifeworld and history, of system and history, or of system and evolution, as do for example Weber, Durkheim and Parsons respectively. On these same grounds, there is a basic similarity between Habermas, Hegel and Marx.

Any and every macrosociological programme unavoidably involves a theoretical choice in favour of one or the other pole of both the diachronic and synchronic axes and the establishment of a relation between them. The crucial point in now that when a theorist makes a choice in favour of a particular pole, it does not necessarily follow that the other pole of the same axis is automatically excluded. Ideally speaking, a complementary relationship should be maintained between the poles of both the axes, although the overall emphasis of a theorist falls on one rather than on the other pole. Critical theory, for example, is characterized by an emphasis on the evolution and lifeworld poles, while nevertheless relating them to the subordinate history and system poles. From this point of view, Habermas's position exhibits certain interesting features.

To begin with, there is nothing peculiar about Habermas's choice of lifeworld and system as major macrotheoretical parameters. Indeed, I am convinced with him that this is the best option open to the social theorist and analyst who wishes to approach social reality in a critical manner. What strikes one about Habermas's position, however, is that he locates himself within the parametric framework in such a way that, while system is maintained in a complementary relation to lifeworld, history is tendentially excluded rather than held in a complementary relation to evolution. In a series of publications beginning with *Legitimation Crisis* (1976, originally 1973) and culminating in *Theorie des kommunikativen Handelns* (1981), Habermas develops an argument which establishes a relation between the two poles of the synchronic axis in a complementary manner yet places lifeworld in the 'superordinate' (1976a: 14) position, thus making possible a rebuttal of the overextension of systems thinking in the guise of a 'critique of functionalist reason' (Habermas 1981aII: subtitle). What is so astonishing is that it is in respect of lifeworld and system alone he consistently emphasises the need for the establishment of an adequate relation. To be sure, he does not neglect the history-evolution distinction altogether. Combining in a reputedly complementary way the approaches of Weber and Marx, he proposes to explain the evolutionary development of societies with simultaneous reference to developmental logic and historical events (Habermas 1979b: 30-3, 1981aII: 464-8). What he does neglect to do, however, is to offer a precise analysis of this problem complex. He correctly seeks to avoid reproducing the difficulties of structuralism and the philosophy of history by proposing neither to separate history and evolution abstractly nor to set them in a direct Hegelian relation. Yet, not having developed a precise analysis of the problem, he opts for a solution that is less than adequate. Consisting of the distinction between developmental dynamics and developmental logic with an emphasis on the latter, it comes rather close to the strucuturalist immunisation of structure against history. It is doubtless the case that critical theory places greater emphasis on evolution than on history, just as it stresses lifeworld more than system. But an emphasis on evolution does not imply the exclusion of the historical dimension, just as little as the stress on lifeworld entails the screening out of system. This is precisely what Habermas's solution compels him to do: to exclude the historical pole of the diachronic axis, despite his own methodological stipulations and his criticism of Parsons to the effect that the latter's attempt to reconcile the action and system paradigms must be regarded as a failure due to the fact that no room is left for history as the medium of action and hence the change of society (Habermas 1979b: 23).

It should now be clear, I think, that the implications that follow from Habermas's acceptance of the concept of collective learning are rather thoroughgoing. The incorporation of this theoretical component challenges him to come up with a different and more adequate solution to the basic problem posed by the diachronic axis. In so far as the introduction of collective learning involves the replacement of the distinction between dynamics and logic in the sense discussed under (1) above, it further implies the reconstitution of the relation between history and evolution on the diachronic plane. Still more important, however, is that such reconstitution entails a change of emphasis within the macrotheroretical position and a redefinition of its parametric boundaries. It is not only a matter of bringing history back in and of relating it to evolution, but also one of establishing an adequate relation between the so reconstituted diachronic axis and the synchronic one.

Habermas's overall emphasis may be described as being of a synchronic-structural nature —that is, he places more emphasis on the synchronic than on the diachronic axis, and in the case of the latter he emphasises evolution or strucutre to the exclusion of history in a manner akin to strucuturalism. The acknowledgement of collective learning compels him, by contrast, to incorporate history without evolution losing its superordinate position, and to shift his main emphasis from the synchronic to the diachronic axis. This readjustment within the parametric framework represents, in my opinion, the most significant theoretical implication to follow from Habermas's concessions to his critics.[10] Just how far this implication actually reaches can be gathered, finally, from the consequences it has for his theory of action.

(3) According to Habemas (1979b: 22), sociology has been faced from the outset by the problem of the relation between two basic paradigms: action and system. Since the history of the discipline suggests that a solution to this problem lies not in the exclusion of one paradigm in favour of the other but rather in the establishment of a proper relationship between them, he proposes that 'one chooses, not system and self-steering, but lifeworld and intersubjectivity as the superordinate point of view' (Habermas 1976a: 14). This choice leads him to reject Parsons's solution and instead to accept a differentiated interpretation of Marx's position. Rather than assimilating action theory to systems theory, as does the former, the latter maintains the two paradigms in a dialectical relation which gives priority to the specifically human reality thematised by the theory of action. From this Habermas concludes that, while it is necessary to conceive society from the viewpoint of systems theory, this must be done strictly within the framework of action theory —that is, society must be regarded from the double perspective of being a social system that is most basically structured like a lifeworld.

Habermas conceives his theory of action with reference to a particular problem, namely the relation of the action and systems paradigms. This strategy immediately raises questions. Has sociology been confronted from the outset by the problem of the relation between the action and systems paradigms alone? Has it not been faced by the problem of the relation between the history and evolution paradigms also? In my opinion, the history of social theory supports a positive answer to the latter rather than to the former question. In the light of this, I am convinced that Habermas's action theoretical position is limited: it is a solution to a problem which has not been appreciated in its full complexity. Action enters the scene not only at the synchronic plane of the lifeworld, but simultaneously also at the diachronic level of history. The core of the problem addressed by the theory of action is represented not by the relation between the two poles of the synchronic axis, but rather by the considerably more complex relation between the synchronic and diachronic axes of social reality. The readjustment of emphasis within the macrotheoretical parametric framework discussed under (2) above thus calls for a basic revision of Habermas's theory of action.

CONCLUSION

In this essay, I sought (i) to describe the circumstances which compelled Habermas to make certain concessions to his critics; (ii) to present the two concessions to the effect that he acknowledges the necessity of a sociological learning theory and the concept of collective learning processes; and (iii) to draw out the most important theoretical implications following from these concessions. These implications, I argued, are so far-reaching that they require a thorough revision of both Habermas's theory of social evolution and, most fundamentally, his macrotheoretical position, and as a consequence also his theory of action.

Only once this relatively drastic modification has been carried out would Habermas be able in a grounded manner to advance the claim that he represents a genetic-strucuturalist sociology based on the interactionist or communication model (Habermas 1981aII: 554).

2

The Ontogenetic Fallacy: The Immanent Critique of Habermas's Developmental-Logical Theory of Evolution

Since the emergence of neo-evolutionism in the 1960s, various critiques of the theory of social or socio-cultural evolution have been put forward, including notably those of Immanuel Wallerstein, Alain Touraine and Anthony Giddens, all of whom decisively reject the idea of evolution. In this context, Jürgen Habermas's theory of socio-cultural evolution has also become a specific object of critique, the best known in the English-speaking world being, perhaps, Michael Schmid's (1982a) critique. While the latter is ultimately based on neo-Darwinistic assumptions (1982b, 1987) allowing a non-Marxist alternative to be pitted against Habermas's position, a significant immanent critique has been taking shape during the late 1970s and 1980s the contours of which are at present starting to become visible, despite the fact that as yet it is nowhere developed and presented in a systematic manner. I have in mind here the work of younger authors belonging to the circle around Habermas, such as Johann Arnason, Axel Honneth, Hans Joas, Günter Frankenberg, Ulrich Rödel and Klaus Eder, who have not only developed a critique of Habermas but are also engaged in developing an alternative to him within the framework of critical theory.

In this essay, I propose to present an overview of this immanent (i.e., critical theoretical) critique of Habermas's theory of socio-cultural evolution from the point of view of the basic theoretical problem that, in my opinion, is at issue in it. Allow me to briefly clarify this point of view.

In the light of debates in both theoretical biology and social theory during the last twenty to thirty years, it has become clear that development, far from resulting from and hence being secondary to evolution, has a primary and determinative influence on evolution. Development determines what kinds of change are possible and thus fixes what is evolutionarily accessible and what not. Consequently, an adequate understanding of evolution requires that a good deal of attention be paid to development. This insight explains why the problem of development has become an independent object of inquiry in both biology and sociology in the recent past.

One should not, however, allow Habermas's emphasis on the regeneration of the theory of socio-cultural evolution to mislead one into believing that development is neglected in his work. On the contrary, he is among the few contemporary authors who understand the need for concentrating on development while maintaining a firm grip on evolution rather than neglecting or even rejecting the latter in favour of the former. Thus he is able to write:

> *'Evolutionarily oriented analyses of the present...whether Marxist or non-Marxist, are forced to monitor their assumptions — assumptions that already underlie the delimitation and description of the object —on an instructive theory of social development'* (*Habermas 1979a: 126*).

Within the general context sketched thus far, the major theoretical question concerns the specific relation between development and evolution, particularly the developmental model determining evolutionary theoretical assumptions. It is this problem that, in my view, is at issue in the above-mentioned immanent critique of Habermas, centring on his developmental-logical ontogenetic model of development. The main thrust of the critique, as I see it, is that his developmental model, if not in itself problematical, is overextended: his theory of socio-cultural evolution is a developmental-logical one which, as such, rests on the employment of the ontogenetic model of development in a manner which must be regarded as involving the commitment of the ontogenetic fallacy.[1]

1. THE STARTING-POINT

Thomas McCarthy

While Hans-Christian Harten (1977a, 1977b) in the late 1970s in his studies of Jean Piaget from the viewpoint of—but also against —Habermas still uncritically proceeded, in keeping with the latter's position, from the assumption of the theoretical desirability of a close articulation of ontogenesis and socio-cultural evolution, Thomas McCarthy at about the same time expressed unease about the application of the ontogenetic model to society. Rather than concentrating on this problem, however, he saw fit to postpone its formulation and substantiation:

> *'The critical queries to which Habermas's conception of social evolution gives rise are legion...they extend to questions concerning the applicability of ontogenetic models to social*

systems —the characterization of the infrastructure of society as a network of actions certainly does not suffice to justify this transposition. For various reasons (not the least of which are my own limitations), I shall leave the formulation and substantiation of these problems to others' (*1978: 261*).

McCarthy, to be sure, did not leave it at that but proceeded to make a few brief yet pregnant suggestions which were in fact soon afterward taken up by members of the younger generation of critical theorists who developed them in a direction more critical of Habermas.

In essence, McCarthy's (1978: 261-271) argument is that Habermas's intellectual development exhibits a fundamental shift in that, whereas in his earlier work he operated with a conception of critical theory as situation-dependent and hermeneutically rich social inquiry, in his later work he adopts a much stronger theoretical programme which lays claim to validity independent of a historico-hermeneutic standpoint. The crucial point is now that this shift in emphasis is attributable to Habermas's concern with the development not only of universal or formal pragmatics, but in particular also of the theory of socio-cultural evolution. The original conception of an empirical philosophy of history with practical intent made way for the theory of socio-cultural evolution possessing the methodological status of rational reconstruction. The consequences were far-reaching. The introduction of evolutionary theory entailed, first, the replacement of the hermeneutically situation-bound character of social life as basic reference point, what Habermas (1972b: 389-392) for instance articulated as the basic experiences of modernity which accompanied the revolutionary origins of modern society, by the general state of development of humankind and, second, the weakening, if not abandonment, of the originally asserted unity of theory and practice. The practical meaning guiding the interpretation of history as well as the present was thus located not in historically and socially situated practical reason but, in a neo-Kantian turn, rather in pure practical reason.

Although the issues raised by McCarthy provided a starting point for a critical assessment of Habermas's position as it began to take shape in the 1970s, the actual elaboration of a critique of the latter's theory of socio-cultural evolution required the overcoming of certain difficulties in the interpretation put forward in *The Critical Theory of Jürgen Habermas*. The fact that David Held (1980: 281-284, 374-375) in his review and critical assessment of Habermas followed McCarthy so closely that he could not eliminate these difficulties explains why he failed to develop the critique further, despite such statements as: 'The practical implications of the theory are undeveloped' (1980: 376) and 'theoretical categorization is combined with an insufficient regard for historical analysis of evolving social relations' (1980: 378). At least three of these difficulties are worth mentioning in the present context.

First, McCarthy (1978: 253, 269) is misled by Habermas's suggestion that a fully developed theory of socio-cultural evolution involves not only a reference to systematically reconstructible patterns of development, or a developmental logic, but also an explanation in terms of developmental mechanisms or dynamics of how and why developments actually come about, and indeed to such a degree that he overlooks the developmental logical emphasis Habermas lends to his theory. In view of the fact that McCarthy not only recognises but also questions Habermas's separation of abstract evolution-theoretic explanations from substantive narrative historiographical expositions, it is incomprehensible why he overlooks this peculiar emphasis. For the separation of evolution and history and, hence, developmental logic and developmental dynamics obviously entails a partial identification of evolution and developmental logic which eventuates in an essentially developmental-logical evolutionary theory.

Second, McCarthy (1978: 236) concedes Habermas's argument that an evolutionary theory oriented towards the analysis of the present is compelled to monitor its assumptions against a guiding theory of development, but does not see that such acceptance by no means forces one to agree to the projection of a developmental-logical ontogenetic model onto socio-cultural evolution. Considering the debate about epigenetics, particularly the position of development in relation to neo-Darwinian evolutionary theory, in contemporary biological theory (e.g. Lovtrup 1974, Ho and Saunders 1979, 1982), it would seem as though Habermas's starting point possesses a good deal of plausibility, but whether a theorist is entitled to take the further step of adopting an ontogenetic model is another question —one that an increasing number of critics answer negatively.

Finally, there is a problem about the manner in which McCarthy understands the relation between the theory of socio-cultural evolution and critical theory. According to McCarthy (1978: 265, 269-270), the theory of socio-cultural evolution provides the theoretical framework for a critical historical account of the genesis of contemporary society and its pathologies. As is clear from his treatment of Habermas's critical theory of late capitalism (McCarthy 1978: 358-386), he takes this to mean that the theory of late capitalism as for instance represented in *Legitimation Crisis* (Habermas 1976) is something like an empirical appendix to a methodologically highly differentiated social philosophy or merely the application of a critical methodology. Not only does this understanding give evidence of a lack of a sufficient grasp of the structure of critical theory, but it also prevents McCarthy from seeing through the problem of the relation Habermas postulates between development and evolution. In the end, therefore, he is unable to draw appropriate conclusions from his critique of Habermas's separation of evolution and history.

Unlike Held, who followed McCarthy's account of Habermas's reconstruction of historical materialism almost verbatum and consequently failed to develop a critique of the resultant theory of socio-cultural evolution, Axel Honneth (e.g. 1981a: 162-170) simultaneously appreciated the thrust of McCarthy's various critical points and uncovered the weaknesses of his interpretation. It does not come as a surprise, therefore, that the immanent critique of Habermas's ontogenetically based developmental-logical theory of socio-cultural evolution received its first explicit formulation and substantiation in a work co-authored by Honneth (Honneth and Joas 1980, 1988). But Honneth and his co-author Hans Joas had the opportunity to also draw on the acute analysis of Habermas's reconstruction of historical materialism by Johann Arnason (1979, 1980).

Johann Arnason

In his analysis, which has been designed to highlight the differences between Habermas's reconstructed version of historical materialism and Marx's original model, Arnason (1979: 216, 211-218) does not make any mention of the ontogenetic model of development as such, yet displays a clear understanding of Habermas's relationship to the Piaget-Kohlberg tradition of cognitive psychology and the consequences the adoption of the concept of developmental logic has for the theory of socio-cultural evolution.

Approaching Habermas's reconstruction of historical materialism in a much more analytical spirit than McCarthy, he immediately sees that Habermas's theory of socio-cultural evolution is a developmental-logical theory which takes evolution to mean 'the realization of an ordered sequence of structural possibilities' (Arnason 1979: 215) and appreciates that this process is regarded as taking place, analogous to ego development, at a number of dimensions —namely worldviews, collective identity and, most important for Habermas, moral-legal structures. At the same time, however, he also identifies the basic influence cognitive psychology has had on Habermas's position. This influence, needless to say, goes back to the concept of ontogenesis as a constructive learning process undergone by a subject who develops from stage to stage through confrontation with and solution of objectively given problems. Arnason finds it exhibited by Habermas's assumption, first, of 'a certain primacy of the individual over society, and hence a priority of the relationship between man and world compared to that between man and society' (1979: 216), and, second, of systems problems bearing on moral-practical development in such a way that the emphasis is placed on 'the independence and universality of the social process' as such (1979: 212).

The theoretical implications Arnason discovered in Habermas's position are both wide-ranging and far-reaching. First, the conception of the social process as being grounded in a universal developmental logic of evolution circumscribes class struggles and social movements to such a degree that the possible historical effects of their practical projects are reduced to auxiliary functions of transmission and acceleration (1979: 213). Second, the dualistic model of the evolutionary process as an invariable correlation of system problems and logic of stages of maturation not only *a priori* excludes the discontinuous moment of evolutionary transitions which can be grasped only when attention is paid to the interlocking of the appropriation of nature and the association of people within a specific historical configuration (1979: 212-213), but by the same token also portrays 'the cumulative development of technical knowledge [as] the only possible modification of the relationship between man and nature' (1979: 217). Finally, the introduction of the concept of development logic implies 'a double closure' (1979: 217) in that it, through an instrumentalist reduction of the relation between humanity and nature and a normativistic subsumption of the relations between people in society, allows neither interference from the material context nor alternative projects.

These pernicious implications of Habermas's reconstructed version of historical materialism led Arnason to suggest the introduction of an alternative praxis theoretical position which operates with the conception of a 'pluri-dimensional and open-textured' (1979: 217) social process, involving both a more than merely instrumental or purposive-rational notion of the appropriation of nature and a notion of association admitting of alternative practical projects.

With the various suggestions and arguments put forward by McCarthy and Arnason, the agenda was set for the articulation and elaboration of the major motifs of the immanent critique of Habermas's theory of socio-cultural evolution.

2. THE CRITIQUE

Axel Honneth and Hans Joas

While Harten and McCarthy in the late 1970s accepted Habermas's postulation of a relation between ontogenesis and socio-cultural evolution, the former happily and the latter somewhat uneasily, and while Arnason without pinpointing the ontogenetic model indicated various problems in Habermas's developmental logical theory, Axel Honneth and Hans Joas as early as 1980 identified the basic difficulty of Habermas's theory of socio-cultural evolution as residing precisely in his theoretical strategy of basing the theory of socio-cultural evolution squarely on the ontogenetic model.

Whereas McCarthy permitted himself to be led astray by Habermas's suggestion that a complete evolutionary theory requires a reference to both developmental logic and developmental dynamics, thus rendering himself incapable of assuming a critical posture, Honneth and Joas (1980, 1988), like Arnason, from the start appreciated the specific character of Habermas's theory. In a brief yet penetrating analysis they clarified the role of the ontogenetic model in Habermas's conceptualisation of the theory of socio-cultural evolution, revealed the developmental-logical bias of the theory, and demonstrated the problematic nature of its implications. Central to their critical analysis is a dissection of Habermas's explanation of socio-cultural evolution in terms of developmental logic. For thereby Honneth and Joas are able to show that the ontogenetic model features in Habermas's theory not only in the sense that the development of worldviews, collective identities and moral-legal structures are conceived as being analogous to ego development, but also and in particular that his evolutionary explanation as such depends on the attempt to 'project the structure of ontogenetic learning processes onto the process of evolutionary learning' (Honneth and Joas 1988: 165). This means not only that socially mediated technical and moral learning processes follow the same pattern as the process whereby the individual subject learns from dealing with and solving problems, but also that society as a whole in its evolution advances from the primitive to the civilisational level or from archaic and developed civilisations to modernity. Evolutionary learning processes in this latter sense involve, strictly in keeping with Habermas's ontogenetic model, 'unresolved system problems that represent challenges' and 'new levels of learning' that are latently available and could be drawn upon for the purposes of solving problems threatening the continued existence of society as a whole' (Habermas 1979a: 121-122). For Honneth and Joas this position implies that 'system-threatening problems' are adduced 'in order to identify the moral learning process which........ permits the overcoming of the threat to the system and thereby the evolutionary further development of the technical-strategic system of action' (1988: 163). The manifold implications of this developmental-logical ontogenetic type of evolutionary explanation are patiently eased out by Honneth and Joas.

In the first place, an explanation that is cast in this mould necessarily abstracts from historically specific events and unique collective experiences within the framework of which social groups engage in historical action, and thus detaches itself from the real historical process (Honneth and Joas 1988: 164). Insofar as such an explanation does take the historical context into account, it does so only to ascertain formal levels of consciousness and hence ignores processes of communication guided by collective processes of interpretation and experience gained through collective learning processes. That this is indeed the line followed by the developmental-logical evolutionary explanation is borne out, for Honneth and Joas, by Habermas's rigorous separation of reconstructive developmental logic from narrative historiography. The theory of socio-cultural evolution is solely concerned with the development of structures and hence reads the historical material exclusively from the viewpoint of the logic of such development. The researcher is thus from the outset predestined to lose sight of the kind of historically innovative action which is typically represented by social movements and which does not arise in response to a problem threatening society as a social system.

Second, the ontogenetically based developmental-logical approach to socio-cultural evolution operates with an ambiguous concept of 'social learning' (Honneth and Joas 1988: 165-166). Habermas himself explicitly includes under that rubric systemic learning in the sense of the evolutionarily significant response of society as a social system to a system-threatening problem. As is suggested by historical evidence, however, moral-practical learning processes often occur within the context of social movements, the typical 'historical bearers of evolutionary learning processes' (1988: 165). The crucial point is now that social movements, typically representing a consciousness of action orientations which are socially superior and constituting a normative advance, learn not in reaction to unresolved system problems and dangers, but rather through the collective experiencing of and cooperative opposition to repression and social injustice prevailing in a society (1988: 166). Given that this is the case, Honneth and Joas insist that Habermas is compelled at all points where he wants to document historically the presence of moral learning to have recourse to social movements, which ironically, are incompatible with developmental-logical evolutionary classifications. Habermas (1981II: 468; 1987a: 316) indeed envisages as 'the major task' that remains after the developmental logical explanatory scheme had been established 'the description of evolutionary learning advances in terms of social movements and political transformations.' This position provides evidence for Honneth and Joas's (1988: 166) claim that Habermas's concept of social learning must of necessity be ambiguous to encompass within a single framework both the process of systemic learning and socially revolutionary learning processes.

The final implication Honneth and Joas discover in Habermas's introduction of the ontogenetic model into evolutionary theory links up with the theory's high degree of abstraction from everyday plexuses of meaning that renders it incapable of vindicating the critical theoretical claim of being concerned with the development of enlightening hermeneutic interpretations which have a bearing on social agents' self-understanding and help them in orienting their action (Habermas 1985b: 237). This implication, one that McCarthy failed to see, is that the developmental-logically conceived theory of socio-cultural evolution does not understand itself, as it should, as a reflexive step in substantive socio-cultural research which is by no means practically irrelevant, but rather 'pretend[s] to the status of a foundational science' (Honneth and Joas 1988: 166).

Both Honneth and Joas, each in his own way, followed up their critique in subsequent writings, and while they did not contribute much towards a further understanding of socio-cultural evolution, they nevertheless succeeded in bringing some clarity to a number of related points. On the basis of a critique of both Habermas's action theory and his adoption of functionalist systems theory, Joas (1986a: 165-6) invoked the need to recognise social order as being explicable only in terms of a theory of collective action. Following a series of essays (Honneth 1981b, 1982), reviews (1981a, 1983) and a paper (1986) in which he insisted on the centrality of social movements and their collective experience of injustice, Honneth developed a comprehensive analysis in a book in which he presents a 'critique of power' (1985, 1991) which expresses a conception of critical theory that contrasts sharply with Habermas's idea which, in turn, eventuates in a 'critique of functionalist reason' (Habermas 1981II, 1987a: subtitle).

According to Honneth, Habermas conceives the theory of evolution as being a complementary extension of universal pragmatics in the sense that, whereas the latter focuses on the reconstruction of the implicit rule systems of social action on the synchronic axis, the former seeks to reconstruct the logic of development of such rule systems on the diachronic axis, involving the determination of the necessary sequence of stages in the acquisition and establishment of rule systems under the empirical conditions of the history of the human species (Honneth 1985: 311-12). The crucial point —and this is in accord with Honneth and Joas's original insight —is now that Habermas, for the purposes of constructing his theory of evolution, made the important decision to transfer the logic of development Piaget had established for ontogenesis to the phylogenetic dimension of human history (Honneth 1985: 311). As the concept of developmental logic is but one term of a conceptual pair, this decision entails the adoption also of the second, namely developmental dynamics. But since Habermas interprets this essentially psychological distinction social- theoretically to mean that the logical dimension of the sequence of necessary stages of the rationality of action, worked up into a classification scheme, enjoys priority over the dynamic dimension of the factual process of social change, which at most possesses only narrative historiographical significance, he loses his grip on history, the dialectic of class antagonisms, social movements, and the communication-theoretical model of 'social order as an institutionally mediated communicative relation of culturally integrated groups which unfolds in the medium of conflict for as long as social power is asymmetrically distributed' (Honneth 1985: 334).

Honneth develops this by now familiar argument, although not particularly systematically, on two distinct levels. First, at the cultural level he identifies over and above the reproduction of shared background knowledge, presumably by ontogenetic learning processes, collective learning processes whereby lifeworld knowledge is expanded and changed. It is to this latter aspect that Habermas refers to as the 'rationalisation of the lifeworld,' conceiving of it as following the same logic as that postulated by Piaget for ontogenesis (Honneth 1985: 318-9). Second, for the various rationalised aspects of the lifeworld to become effective at the social level, they must in some way or another become part of social institutions and thus obtain obligatory validity. Decisive at this juncture, as Honneth (1985: 320) points out, is the model that is adopted to make sense of the implied translation of culturally rationalised structures of consciousness into institutional structures. Habermas's solution to this problem, borrowed from Weber, takes the form of a process of institutionalisation in the course of which dimensions of rationality are first differentiated into separate action domains at cultural level and only in the second instance do they have a transformative impact on social institutions; or as Honneth (1985: 320) puts it: 'the cognitive rationalisations are responsible for the emergence of institutional complexes.' Here we touch on the core of Habermas's theory of evolution: the evolution of society is possible only if the necessary institutional preconditions within the lifeworld have been established by the rationalisation of communicative action and hence advances in forms of communication (Honneth 1985: 325). If one bears in mind at this stage Honneth's basic thesis of Habermas's projection of the ontogenetically based concept of developmental logic onto the process of socio-cultural evolution, then a number of considerations assume great importance. It is not only ontogenetic and, parallel to it, collective learning processes at the cultural level that follow a three-stage logic of development, but at the same time also the process of institutionalisation at the core of socio-cultural evolution. It is in this latter respect that

Habermas represents a theory of evolution which, as Honneth (1985: 311) submits, 'investigates the development of societies with reference to its general logic.'

As I have already pointed out, Honneth objects to the concept of social evolution in this sense of the general logic of the development of societies due to the fact that it entails a historically insensitive abstract classification. Now, even if one accepts this position, which I think one should, a question still remains, namely: what exactly are the theoretical implications of a critique of the theory of socio-cultural evolution to the effect that its construction depends on an unjustifiable projection of the theory of developmental logic onto it? Honneth does not elaborate on these implications, but, like Alain Touraine (1981: 14) and Anthony Giddens (1984: 239), apparently rejects the theory of social evolution in favour of a version of the praxis theoretical position.

Günter Frankenberg and Ulrich Rödel

Problems similar to those identified by Arnason and Honneth and Joas in the theoretical context were discovered by Günter Frankenberg and Ulrich Rödel in the course of substantive research within the framework of a project concerning the development of structures of justification and conceptions of justice in modern law as a sociological problem conducted under Habermas's direction during the late 1970s and early 1980s at the Max Planck Institute in Starnberg, and reported in their book, *Von der Volkssouveränität zum Minderheitenschutz* (Frankenberg and Rödel 1981: 9-31). They speak of the 'empirical failure of the developmental-logical conception' and even of 'a general scepticism towards the fruitfulness of developmental theories of the Piagetian type' for the analysis of the history of society (1981: 18).

The basis of their research was a project designed by Klaus Eder, Frankenberg, Rödel and Ernst Tugendhat which combined a normative theory with a historical-sociological approach. The normative theoretical component, a moral philosophical construct, took the form of an ontogenetically based developmental-logical stage model, representing a reconstruction of increasingly complex justificatory structures at the level of philosophical ethical theories (Hobbes, Kant, Rawls, Habermas and Apel). Hypotheses deriving from a historical-sociological theory were then related to this strong theoretical component on the assumption that historical developments correspond to the developmental logic. As regards the question of the transition to a more complex procedure of justification, the hypothesis was introduced that, rather than taking place through mere thought or the immanent development of structures, it can empirically be determined with reference to experiences undergone in relation to changes in social reality which are translated into normative pressure by political organizations and social movements (Frankenberg and Rödel 1981: 15). The developmental logical scheme, however, was not taken as implying causal necessity in the sense of history being a progression or 'world-growth story' (Gellner cited by Giddens 1984: 237), but only as representing a certain conceptual necessity which makes it possible to derive a criterion for distinguishing between progressive and regressive changes (Frankenberg and Rödel 1981: 16).

Frankenberg and Rödel's attempt to apply this twofold (moral philosophical-historical sociological) theoretical construct to the relevant historical material, including selected doctrines of British common law and in particular legislation, judgments and political journalism bearing on the development of the freedom of political communication in the USA since the colonial period, proved to be an empirical failure, however, in that the material simply did not admit of being ordered according to the chosen viewpoint. In addition, a number of weaknesses of the developmental-logical model also became apparent. First, development is not reconstructed from the internal perspective of historical subjects and their normative evaluations, but rather *ex post* from the perspective of the external observer according to a normative standard he or she commands by virtue of disposal over a stage model. This standard has not been established by way of an analysis of historical development, but is derived *a priori* and deductively from a developmental-logical conception which clandestinely regards the contemporary normative position as the endpoint of development and adopts it as the basis of the *ex post* evaluation (Frankenberg and Rödel 1981: 19-20). Second, the developmental model, due to its emphasis on the coordination of evolutionary mechanisms from the viewpoint of the observer, leads to a reductive treatment of the complex of relations among normatively oriented historical actors and their internal perspective, institutionalised norms and system problems (1981: 20). And, finally, the model overburdens the empirical analysis with such strong theoretical presuppositions that important aspects of reality are necessarily excluded from the observer, brushed aside as theoretically insignificant, or admitted only in some reduced form (1981: 20).

It is significant that the empirical flaws of the developmental-logical model do not lead Frankenberg and Rödel in the direction of a revision of the theoretical construct, but rather points them to a skepticism towards developmental theories of the Piagetian type. It is necessary, however, to be precise about the object of this scepticism for developmental assumptions are not thrown out *in toto* (1981: 20-21). The characteristic feature of the Piagetian type of theory for Frankenberg and Rödel, as for

Honneth and Joas, obviously resides in its ontogenetic foundation as this is reflected in the twofold emphasis on the pressure of a socio-economic system problem and collective disposition over a stage specific argumentative competence which is drawn upon for the purposes of overcoming the problem. What is questionable about the ontogenetic model is whether it is meaningful at all to project its developmental-logical structure onto society in general. For the application of the ontogenetic model at this level presupposes that:

> *'societies, social groups or classes in a particular historical period —comparable to children at a particular stage of their cognitive development —are not yet able to understand and to produce arguments and justifications with reference to moral and legal norms' (Frankenberg and Rödel 1981: 18).*

This presupposition is clearly one that cannot be defended, particularly when it is seen in conjunction with the acceptance of the contemporary normative position as the endpoint of development.

Johann Arnason

What Honneth has done by way of a critique of Habermas, with reference to power, Johann Arnason (1988) seeks to do with reference to culture and the problem of interpretation. While his critique thus applies more directly to Habermas's universal pragmatics than to his theory of evolution, the latter issue comes up time and again due to the fact, as Honneth made clear, that the two theoretical components are complementary to one another. Arnason's argument is basically that Habermas's universal pragmatic communication-theoretical model, emphasising consensual principles and obligatory action orientations, is by no means the only conceivable one, and certainly not one that can conclusively put to rest the conflict of interpretations which in modern society typically results in competing socio-cultural projects, such as the mastery of nature, democracy, autonomy, a national collective identity and revolution, which nevertheless share interpretative horizons. The interesting part of Arnason's analysis is the close attention he pays to the centrepiece of the theory of communicative action which mediates between universal pragmatics and the theory of evolution in that it relates the intuitive knowledge of competent members of society and epochally valid criteria, namely the theory of forms of understanding (Arnason 1988: 187ff).

According to Arnason's interpretation, Habermas's position harbours a difficulty in that it entails the narrowing down of a fruitful perspective no sooner than it has been opened up. On the one hand, Habermas bases his theoretical programme on the dual premise of the structures of the modern understanding of the world or form of interpretation and the social relations or form of life on the assumption that they are mutually dependent and interrelated. Insofar as he assumes this position, Habermas recognises the significance and autonomy of practical reason (Arnason 1988: 266). It is not only that consistently rationalised structures of consciousness do not admit of being belatedly transposed into appropriate communicative structures, but rather can be developed at all only in conjunction with such structures; it is also that the relation between the culturally codified worldview and the historical process of the change of society exhibits tensions and deficits which require a practical critique and transformation of society.

Although Habermas thus approaches a complex concept of practical reason which applies not only to what one may call developmental collective learning processes running parallel to ontogenesis, but also to the evolution of the practically rational organization of society by way of evolutionary collective learning processes, Arnason (1988: 267) nevertheless finds that he nevertheless interprets modern structures of consciousness in a transcendental manner: they play precisely the same role in relation to the theory of communicative action as do the natural sciences in relation to Kant's critique of reason. This implies that practical reason is transposed into something *a priori* and located outside society as the standard and goal of social evolution. It is from this point of view that Habermas in *The Theory of Communicative Action* conceives of evolution as the evolution of forms of understanding (Arnason 1988: 239, 269), within the context of which the modern form enjoys a privileged position. Arnason's interpretation is supported, incidentally, by Honneth and Joas (1988: 167) who point out that in Habermas's major sociological work 'the theory of socio-cultural evolution has been left only with the function of serving as a kind of secondary theoretical affirmation of the process of the evolution of consciousness.' It is almost as though Habermas is on the verge of transposing practical reason into pure reason and of joining the ranks of the evolutionary epistemologists.

Whereas Habermas adopts his peculiar evolutionary theoretic position in order to avoid the unacceptable consequences of cultural relativism, Arnason, against the above background, comes to the significant conclusion that, if the possibility of the 'immanent self-critique' of modern society opened up by the full concept of practical reason is taken seriously, then the 'radical self-relativisation of modernity' is as little a danger as the legitimation of the self-understanding of modernity by way of 'an epoch-transcendent theory of society and history' is a viable option (Arnason 1988: 267). From this it would seem as though Arnason, unlike Honneth, would be willing to contemplate retaining the theory of evolution, yet in the form not of a universal historical and general societal theory but specifically of a theory of *social* evolution in that it focuses on the evolution of the rationality of those social practices which are decisive for the organization of society. A praxis-theoretical position is introduced which seeks to avoid the reductionism of the praxis tradition at least in this respect, namely retaining the theory of social evolution.

Klaus Eder

What remains implicit in Arnason is made into an explicit theme by Klaus Eder in *Die Vergesellschaftung der Natur* (1988). Like Arnason, he adopts a theory of praxis, but at the same time he also develops a theory of evolution which, correspondingly, takes the form of a theory of the social evolution of practical reason. Considering Eder's position as a whole, however, it is remarkable that it has undergone a drastic change in the course of some ten years or so. From being Habermas's chief theoretical collaborator in the development of the theory of socio-cultural evolution (see Eder 1976; Habermas 1979a), Eder has emerged on the side of Habermas's praxis theoretical critics, but one who, unlike Honneth, does not reject but rather fundamentally rethinks evolutionary theory. This change of position has gone through a number of clearly identifiable phases.

The first step towards distancing himself from Habermas was taken in the first part of the 1980s and culminated in his book *Geschichte als Lernprozeß?* (Eder 1985a). Inspired by Max Miller's (1986) sociological learning theory which is centred on the concept of collective learning, Eder here develops an indirect critique of Habermas's view, underpinning his essentially classical understanding of institutionalisation according to which cultural rationalisation calls forth corresponding institutions, that the rationalisation of the lifeworld is spearheaded by ontogenetic learning processes. It consists of the demonstration that everything depends instead on social or collective learning processes which are located or, at least, begin at the everyday level of the practice of life. The principles of freedom, equality and discourse were for the first time clarified and socially concretised in the political associations that increasingly formed since the 18th century and called forth learning processes in the participating individuals. Hence Eder's (1985a: 87) main empirical thesis: 'the logic of associative communalization underlies the rationalisation process of moral consciousness in the modern period.'

Although Eder's argument went to the heart of the matter, it did so only in some respects in that he at this stage still uncritically accepted Habermas's linear theory of socio-cultural evolution. This situation changed in *Die Vergesellschaftung der Natur* (1988). Eder indeed continues criticising Habermas's obliteration of collective learning processes as a result of his overextension of the ontogenetic model, as he did earlier, as for instance where he points out that Habermas actually reverses the true relationship when he depicts the connection between social structure and reason as implying that truth leads to professions and correctness to associations (Eder 1988: 302). Over and above this, however, he focuses in this work on the deformation of the theory of social evolution which occurs when the ontogenetic model is projected onto it. He thus breaks radically with Habermas's universal historical and general societal —which in effect means his developmental-logical —theory of evolution in favour of a praxis based theory of the social evolution of practical reason. Given that Eder collaborated with Habermas in the elaboration of the developmental-logical theory of evolution, it is obvious that this third step required, over and above breaking with Habermas, a radical self-critique on his own part. To his credit, Eder (1988: 33) does not attempt to conceal the radical turn-about in his thinking and the need for a far-reaching self-critique.

Eder develops a profusion of critical perspectives, both directly and indirectly, on Habermas's theory of socio-cultural evolution,[2] but it is nevertheless possible to identify a basic theoretical strategy informing his critique. It is best expressed, in my view, by the formula 'ontogenetic fallacy' (Eder 1988: 296, 310, 313). While Eder apparently draws on a different source for inspiration, namely the essays collected in Schöfthaler and Goldschmidt (1984) containing a critical discussion of Piaget's contribution from the viewpoint of the question of the relation between social structure and reason, this formula encapsulates the early insight of Honneth and Joas to the effect that the projection of the developmental-logical structure of the ontogenetic learning process onto society has theoretically profound yet undesirable consequences. Eder, however, works it out in a more differentiated although not always fully consistent manner. On the one hand, the ontogenetic fallacy consists in drawing a conclusion from ontogenesis in respect of the change and development of culture or collective symbolic systems which can be accounted for only with reference to supra-individual learning processes. At this level, therefore, the ontogenetic fallacy can be overcome by the introduction of the concept of social or collective learning processes (Eder 1988: 296-8). On the other hand, the ontogenetic fallacy is committed when one transfers the ontogenetic model to the level of evolution (1988: 313). As suggested earlier, the solution of the ontogenetic fallacy at this level demands rather more drastic intervention. On the whole, it involves a radical break with the developmental-logical conception of evolution as such. This he accomplishes in a number of steps.

First, Eder (1988: 256-7, 301) displaces the psychologically inspired distinction between developmental logic and developmental dynamics by the theory of the self-production of society, borrowed from Touraine (1977) and referred to as the theory of praxis (Eder 1988: 291-3, 300). This he does in order to fill a categorial gap he discovers in Habermas's theory under the influence of Pierre Bourdieu's (1977) theory of practice, namely a gap left by Habermas's concentration on the *opus operatum* in the sense of the effects of evolutionary changes to the detriment of the *modus operandi* in the sense of evolutionary changes and their mechanisms themselves. Second, Eder introduces a sharp distinction between ontogenetic and collective learning, on the one hand, and social evolution, on the other, in order to break the hold that developmental logic has over evolution in Habermas's work (Eder 1988: 303, 313, 316-7). Finally, these moves culminate in Eder's most drastic critical (and self-critical) step, namely radically freeing the theory of social evolution from the universal historical and general societal frame within which it is confined by Habermas, with a view to avoiding the untenable causal assumptions, schematisations, classifications and ideological implications to be found in the latter's work (Eder 1988: 33, 69, 165, 291, 325, 374).

Although various specific difficulties are to be found in Eder's proposals, a matter I propose to return to below, there is no doubt about the fact that he has succeeded in lending new impetus to the major thrust of the immanent critique of Habermas's theory of socio-cultural evolution. It is equally clear that Habermas would be able to ignore the results of this critique only at his own peril.

3. THE RESPONSE

Jürgen Habermas

It is interesting to note that a perusal of Habermas's works from the viewpoint of the question of what impact the immanent critique of his theory of socio-cultural evolution is exerting on his thinking by no means ends in a disappointment. On the contrary, his major writings from 1985 to 1988 give unequivocal if brief indications of an attempt to accommodate the major points raised by his critics.

In the fifth collection of his political writings entitled *Die neue Unübersichtlichkeit*, Habermas acknowledges Eder's critique of his assumption that ontogenetic learning processes function as pacemaker of socio-cultural evolution:

> *'He [Eder] leads innovative spurts immediately back to* social *learning processes in the framework of new forms of association, that is, to new experiences of egalitarian intercourse first in freemason lodges, secret societies and reading circles, later in the early socialist worker associations' (Habermas 1985a: 234).*

The concessions Habermas subsequently made to his critics in *Kommunikatives Handeln* (Honneth and Joas 1986: 394) by adopting in self-criticism of his earlier position, both a sociological theory of learning and the concept of social or collective learning processes, bears out the fact, however, that he did not stop at merely acknowledging the critique, but soon after was willing to embrace it —although he at this stage still neglected to spell out the implications of this step for his overall theoretical position (Strydom 1987). These concessions were preceded by an affirmative use of the concept of learning processes in *Der philosophische Diskurs der Moderne* (1985b: 394; 1987b: 339). The employment of the concept in this context, interesting to note, went together with the introduction of a new position on the aesthetic or conative component of culture: instead of an expressionist theory of art he now put forward a Heideggerian-like theory of world disclosure.

It is remarkable that in subsequent writings collected in *Eine Art Schadensabwicklung*, for instance in 'Die Idee der Universität — Lernprozesse' (1987b: 76, 79, 94, 95, 96) and 'Geschichtsbewusstsein und posttraditionale Identität' (1987b: 170), the concept of learning processes appears again and again. This same collection also contains a theoretically most interesting statement to the effect that 'it would be false to conceive of group identities as ego identities writ large —between them holds not an analogy but a complementary relationship' (1987b: 73). The question raised by Habermas's position here is: what are the implications for the ontogenetic model? Does Habermas's commitment to the ontogenetic model remain unaffected, or does this move decrease its theoretical significance? In my view, the latter of these two options applies. For the severance of the analogy or homology between ego identity and group identity implies a significant decrease in the range of application of the ontogenetic model —that is, a withdrawal from the domain of collective identity and a corresponding confinement of the model to the domain of ego identity, and a surrendering of the vacated domain to social or collective learning processes.

If my interpretation is correct, this means that by 1987 Habermas had made a remarkable transition by fully absorbing the critique Eder advanced in 1985. But this still left the universal historical employment of the ontogenetic model intact. A change of position affecting this dimension of the ontogenetic fallacy would seem to be broached, however, in Habermas's book, *Nachmetaphysisches Denken* (1988b). As in the preceding works, the concept of learning processes abounds in the philosophical essays collected in this book (1988b: 50, 101-3, 103-4, 177, 178, 191). And in this context Habermas draws a sharp distinction between ontogenetic and social or collective learning processes:

> *'Socialisation and formative processes are person dependent learning processes. From these we must distinguish supra-subjective learning effects which manifest themselves as cultural and social innovations and are sedimented in the productive forces and structures of moral consciousness'*
>
> (*Habermas 1988b: 101-3*).

It is to this latter category of social or collective learning that he refers as 'intramundane learning processes' (1987b: 339).

Of greater importance in this work than the employment of the concept of learning processes, however, are those cautious yet far-reaching steps Habermas takes toward curtailing the reach of the ontogenetic model, withdrawing it from the domain of universal history. On the whole, these steps entail a distancing from a neo-Kantian, quasi-transcendental or criteriological position in favour of a weaker theoretical stance. As against the 'idea of undamaged intersubjectivity,' given with the necessary conditions of understanding and agreement, in the sense of the totality of a reconciled form of life projected as a utopia into the future, first, Habermas introduces the conception of self-production (*Produzierens oder Selberhervorbringens*, 1988b: 186) whereby human beings in a responsible yet unintended manner through fallible and often abortive cooperative but by no means conflict-free ventures engage in the establishment of an appropriate form of life. This move entails, the introduction of the concept of 'situated reason' (1988b: 186, 48, 179). And, finally, he accepts Hilary Putnam's and Thomas McCarthy's contention, which obviously has devastating implications for his three-stage universal historical and general societal theory of socio-cultural evolution, that in cases of intercultural and historical understanding in which both rival conceptions and conflicting standards of rationality come into play, the relation between 'us' and 'them' is a symmetrical one (1988b: 177).

The various changes Habermas has made in his position between 1985 and 1988 —from the adoption of the concept of social or collective learning over and above person dependent ontogenetic learning processes, through the theory of the self-production of a form of life characterised by undamaged intersubjectivity and the related concept of situated practical reason, to symmetrical relations between intercultural and historical contexts —all provide evidence of the fact that he, in accordance with the immanent critique of his work, is discernibly freeing his theory of socio-cultural evolution from its entanglement in the woof and warp of the ontogenetic fallacy by moving away from his earlier ontogenetically based developmental-logical conception of the theory.

4. THE OUTLOOK

Considering the thrust of the immanent critique of Habermas's theory of socio-cultural evolution, as well as the latter's response to it, the major question that arises now is how the emerging new position is best further developed.

To begin with, it is certain that the emerging position involves not the rejection but rather the retention and reconstitution of the theory of socio-cultural evolution. Such authors as Alain Touraine (1981: 14) and Anthony Giddens (1984: 239) are mistaken, in my view, when they advocate that we should break with evolutionary theory in a radical way. Their common error is that they take the inflated claims of evolutionists at face value and hence as entailing the discrediting of the theory of socio-cultural evolution rather than subjecting them to a thorough critical analysis. Had they conducted such analysis and discovered the typical confusion of development and evolution and the strong naturalistic assumptions of the major evolutionary theorists, they would have realised that there is no need to reject evolutionary theory. Because of the fact that Klaus Eder sees through not only the configurationalist limitations of Touraine and Giddens's respective positions (Eder 1988: 292-5), but also the unjustifiably strong naturalistic assumptions of the classical theories of socio-cultural evolution from Spencer to Luhmann and Habermas (Eder 1988: 18, 166) and is therefore able to conduct a critical analysis of evolutionary theory in the social sciences, his *Die Vergesellschaftung der Natur* must serve as a major reference point in any discussion about the future development of the theory of socio-cultural evolution. This does not mean, however, that one would be able to adopt his proposals lock, stock and barrel. On the contrary, they display certain conceptual difficulties which would have to be eliminated before his work could become really fruitful for the development of an adequate theory of socio-cultural evolution.

The first difficulty in Eder's work pertains to his proposal to appropriate the 'theory of praxis' (1988: 291, 292) in order to conceptualise the process of the production of society which precedes and serves as the social presupposition of both the rationalisation of the lifeworld and systems building. It is possible to agree with him on the need for the introduction of a theoretical component to fill the gap left by macro communication and system theories, such as those of Habermas and Luhmann respectively, which concentrate on the *opus operatum* to the exclusion of the *modus operandi* (1988: 291). But, considering the inherent weaknesses and drawbacks of praxis philosophy (see Habermas 1982: 223-6; 1984c: 25-6; 1987b: 60-9, 75-82), it is highly questionable whether this component should be given the form of the theory of praxis. The problems Eder runs into in his attempt to do so become apparent at a number of different levels. His emphatic appropriation of the theory of praxis and simultaneous insistence that it should not be understood as an action theory due to the fact that it concerns a social reality over and above the individual (Eder 1988: 292), does not help to clarify the problematic relation between the theory of praxis and the theory of the collective production and reproduction of the constitutive structures of society. In my view, the latter can only be forced into the mould of the former with ill effects. This is borne out by the conceptual confusion surrounding his use of the term 'praxis.' Rather than lifeworld or system, Eder adopts praxis as the most basic concept which provides the root metaphor for his overarching theory of society (Eder 1988: 300). No sooner has he taken this step, however, than he proposes to treat 'praxis' as one of the terms of a conceptual pair, the other being 'poiesis' (1988: 306-7). Both 'praxis' and 'poiesis' are practices through which the potentialities made available by individual and collective learning processes are realised. Whereas the latter leads to the expansion of knowledge and control over the environment of society, the former eventuates in the rationalisation of the forms of communicative understanding and agreement. The equivocation is obvious: how could the concept of praxis be employed concurrently both as an overarching concept and as a term of a conceptual pair? A solution is obviously required which is capable of making sense both of the theory of the collective production and reproduction of society and of praxis as one of a number of social practices. I propose to return to this question in due course.

A second major difficulty in Eder's proposals resides in the status accorded to the ontogenetic model. We have already seen that Eder, with the support of Miller, elaborated on the concept of collective learning processes in order to be able to conceive of the development and change of culture or collective symbolic systems of interpretation in terms other than the development of the individual. In light of this advance, it strikes one as most peculiar when he nevertheless proposes to refer to both aspects by means of the concept of ontogenesis, thus speaking in parallel fashion of 'the ontogenesis of psychic systems' and of 'the ontogenesis of knowledge and morality' or 'the ontogenesis of society' (Eder 1988: 315, 316). While Eder was instrumental in introducing the formula of the ontogenetic fallacy for the purposes of criticizing the classical theories of socio-cultural evolution, including Habermas's, he himself, paradoxically enough, continues to commit that very fallacy in so far as he persists in thinking of the development and change of culture and society according to a model which applies strictly to the development of the individual.

The solution to the problems Eder comes up against is ready to hand in his work although without him ever realising it. It is encapsulated by the expression *Vergesellschaftung*.[3] It makes its appearance throughout Eder's work (e.g. 1988: 23, 256, 289, 290, 291, 293, 300, 307, 308, 310, 368 as well as the title), but an assessment of its varied employment shows that for him it is not a concept with a clear meaning. In the title of the book as well as at crucial points in the text (307, 308), he takes *Vergesellschaftung* to mean the human social appropriation or socialisation of nature. As such it contrasts with the production (*Herstellung*) of a social order. On another occasion, however, Eder speaks of 'the socialisation of nature' and 'the socialisation of sociality' (1988: 310) in the same breath as being subject to a particular cultural code. This code could take the form either of praxis or of poiesis, the latter representing the principles of domination and control and the former those of cooperation, understanding and agreement. This usage is in line with his perception of a need for social theory to shift from an emphasis on social order, the *opus operatum*, to the ambivalent and contradictory process of the creation or construction, the production and reproduction of society, the *modus operandi*, and that such a dynamicisation of social theory is captured by the concept of *Vergesellschaftung* (1988: 256, 290). What I find astounding is that Eder neglects to pursue and develop this latter insight. Instead of a theory of *Vergesellschaftung*, he proposes that we should adopt the theory of praxis to fulfil this requirement. The key concept of social theory or the theory of society, according to his understanding, is neither lifeworld nor system (1988: 300). The reason for this is that both of these concepts are not only incapable of grasping society as a *phénomène social total* (1988: 356), but in fact displace it. In order to grasp social reality in this sense, attention must rather be paid to the process of the collective production and reproduction of society. For Eder this means that the key concept is praxis, and that it is oriented towards the development of a constructivist macro-theory of society. In view of the inherent limitations of the praxis perspective, however, I am convinced that the concept of praxis cannot assume this function and that if it were to be retained it would have to be integrated into a more comprehensive alternative. This alternative is, in my view, represented by the theory of *Vergesellschaftung*, that is, the theory of socialisation or of sociation in both the micro and macro sense of the term.[4]

It is this theory that has to be built into the theory of socio-cultural evolution were we not only to overcome the ontogenetic fallacy and avoid its monistic impact, but also to develop evolutionary theory in an appropriately differentiated yet not eclectic manner.

3

Sociocultural Evolution or the Social Evolution of Practical Reason: Eder's Critique of Habermas

While Jürgen Habermas (1976b, 1979a) originally developed his theory of social evolution in the form of a 'reconstruction' of historical materialism, Anthony Giddens (1984: xxix, 227, 243) proposes a 'deconstruction' instead; since he is of the opinion that it is not possible 'to repair the shortcomings of either evolutionary theory in general or historical materialism in particular'. This conviction leads him (Giddens 1984: 239) to advocate, like Alain Touraine (1981: 14) before him, a radical break with evolutionary theory. Klaus Eder (1988: 292), by contrast, sees the failure of classical theories of social evolution and their consequent discrediting of the idea of social evolution itself as an opportunity to embark on 'a renewed attempt to reformulate the theory of social evolution'. This requires a critical exchange with Habermas's theory of social evolution rather than a wholesale rejection of it and at the same time retention of certain essential features of the Marxian approach. His intuition is that both Touraine and Giddens are able to discard evolution only because they take the claims of the representative authors at face value rather than analysing and criticising the confusions and erroneous assumptions undermining the classical formulations of the theory.

Having elsewhere offered a general overview (Strydom 1992) of the response of the younger critical theorists to Habermas, I wish in this essay to attend in some detail to Eder's critique of Habermas's theory of sociocultural evolution. Since this critique is available only in the form of undeveloped and unconnected suggestions, comments and criticisms, however, this requires systematisation at least up to the point where it affords us an appreciation of the developing difference between second and third generation critical theorists and, hence, of the change critical theory has been undergoing during the last decade or two. *In nuce*, this change involves a shift away from the architectonics of the communication-theoretical turn in critical theory towards an emphasis on praxis, yet without communication theory being surrendered.

In order to present the critique of Habermas's theory of sociocultural evolution in an intelligible manner, I propose first to outline Eder's change of position in relation to Habermas and the context within which this occurred, and then to review Eder's general characterisation of Habermas's theory.

1. EDER'S RADICAL TURN

As attested by at least six references to the need for a penetrating self-critique, Eder's (1988: 33, 66, 258, 288-9, 296, 347) thinking has undergone a profound change in the course of a decade, leading him from being a close collaborator of Habermas on the developmental-logical theory of sociocultural evolution to becoming one of its most acute critics. An appreciation of this radical turn is essential for understanding the critique he develops of the eminent author.

The phases through which Eder's changing position passed can be identified as relatively clear with reference to the different ways in which Habermas made use of the cognitive developmental psychology of Jean Piaget in the construction of his theory of social evolution.[1]

Eder started to move away from Habermas between the late 1970s and the early 80s and brought this step to completion in the mid-80s in his book *Geschichte als Lernprozeß?* (1985a). Under the impression of Max Miller's (1986) theory of collective learning,[2] he developed a critique of Habermas's theory of institutionalisation by showing that, over and above individual learning at ontogenetic level, the evolution of society is spearheaded by social learning processes which follow the logic of collective argumentation and are located or, at least, begin at the level of the everyday practice of life. That Eder's argument was to the point is borne out by the fact that Habermas (1985b: 234; 1986a: 394)[3] subsequently felt himself compelled not only to acknowledge the critique, but actually to make concessions to Miller and Eder on the necessity of extending the Piaget-Kohlbergian approach through the theory of collective learning in order to be able to explain the institutionalisation of new structures of consciousness. Even though this point had been driven home, the argument was not yet sufficiently comprehensive. For at this stage, Eder still uncritically accepted the universal historical and general societal applicability of Habermas's theory of social evolution. This attachment was broken for the first time in his book, *Die Vergesellschaftung der Natur* (1988).

Over and above a recapitulation of the earlier phase, Eder focuses in this work on the distortion of the theory of social evolution resulting from the projection of the ontogenetic model of developmental logic onto the evolution of society, in general. In fact, he (Eder 1988: 33) decisively radicalises the Habermasian approach to the extent that it advances the claim of possessing universal historical and general societal validity. It is interesting to note that, although completely unwilling to accept Giddens's proposal to reject the theory of social evolution out of hand, Eder (1988: 295, 299-300) was influenced in his adoption of this particular critical perspective by the former's critique of the connection made between history and evolution in social evolutionism in the context of his sociological transformation of Marx's philosophy of praxis (Giddens 1984: 236-43).[4]

2. THE THEORETICAL CONTEXT

To appreciate Eder's radical turn and to understand the thrust and direction of his critique of Habermas, however, it is necessary to locate it within the context of the debate about the theory of evolution, especially the debate concerning evolutionary hypotheses in German sociology during the 1980s. Three dimensions of this context are of particular importance: developments in evolutionary theory in biology and related disciplines, the emergence of a neo-Darwinistic theory of social evolution in German sociology, and the immanent critique of Habermas's theory of social evolution.

Developments in Evolutionary Theory

As a result of a series of theoretical advances which mitigated the most serious objections against the idea of evolution, evolutionary thinking has experienced an unexpected revival in the 20th century, from biology through anthropology and archaeology to sociology and philosophy. Proceeding from the provision of a micro-biological foundation for the classical theory and the resulting new synthetic —that is, Darwinian-Mendelian —theory, evolutionary theory was progressively linked to ecological theories and systems theories of various kinds, including non-equilibrium thermodynamic, recursive processual, self-organizational, autopoietic, hyper-cyclical, synergetic, and radical constructivist systems theories (see Schmid and Wuketits 1987). These developments are reflected in different ways in social theory, depending on the interpretive perspective employed.

At least rhetorically, the writings of major authors such as Talcott Parsons (1966, 1971, 1977a) and Niklas Luhmann (1978, 1982, 1984) are in line with the official neo-Darwinistic interpretation which gives priority to selection or external steering. Eder (1985a: 20; 1987), on the other hand, finds support for the general position he shares with Habermas in developments that are critical of the pan-selectionist approach, such as epigenetics which emphasises internal structures, learning, and the role in evolution of the organism as autonomous entity with its own development.[5] The reflexive turn implied by the concern with internal structures and learning has had the effect of putting knowledge at the centre of attention in evolutionary thinking. Here a basic option presents itself, however. On the one hand, evolutionary epistemology (Popper 1972; Campbell 1974; Plotkin 1982) seeks to explain the human mind as the result of an evolutionary process involving the adaptation of thought through mechanisms of falsification. On the other hand, Eder (1985a: 25-6, 1988: 285) is convinced that it would be possible to extricate social evolutionary theory from its rather weak position in relation to evolutionary epistemology only if it could be demonstrated that the knowledge unfolding in evolutionary processes and culminating in evolutionary epistemology is actually the outcome of societal processes.

While this first dimension of the theoretical context has a bearing more on what Eder and Habermas have in common,[6] the remaining two bring considerations into play which explain the developing differences between them.

Neo-Darwinistic Theory of Social Evolution

Inspired by the renaissance of evolutionary theory in sociology during the 1960s and 70s as well as by the emergence of socio biology in the late 1970s, German sociologists like Bernhard Giesen, Michael Schmid and Christoph Lau (Giesen and Schmid 1975; Giesen 1980a, 1980b; Giesen and Lau 1981; Lau 1981; Schmid 1982a, 1982b, 1987) embarked on the systematic development of a Darwinistic theory of social evolution. Their aim was not merely to provide a useful heuristic for the explanation of social change, but also to make a contribution to overcoming the fragmentation of sociology. Since sociological evolutionary theories, according to them (Giesen 1980b: 324; Giesen and Lau 1981: 230), typically appeal to Darwin yet under the influence of either Hegel, Marx, Comte or Spencer actually take the form of theories of general evolution which have little or nothing in common with what they pay lip service to, these authors set out to establish the Darwinistic model of evolution in all its clarity and to develop a sociological interpretation of it. On the methodological premises of rational action theory, they put forward a theory of social evolution which gives pride of place to mechanisms of selection within the scheme of variation, selection and stabilisation. From this vantage point, a wide-ranging and sometimes penetrating critique is then developed of extant versions of evolutionary theory in sociology, including the version put forward by Habermas and Eder in the 1970s.

Three related critical points which consistently recur in the writings of Giesen, Schmid and Lau are of particular importance in the present context.

The scene is set by a critique of theories of general evolution in which their usually hidden Spencerian presuppositions are first revealed and then used as a basis for an attack against their reputedly implausible explanatory assumptions, unitary or global selection criteria, insensitive taxonomic or classificatory character, and the indefensible idea of developmental trends or progress. Chief among these theories are Luhmann's systems theoretical evolutionism, in which evolution is equivalent to the growth of complexity, and Habermas and Eder's developmental-logical theory which recognises the role played by individuals yet remains attached to the conception of preformed societal development (Giesen and Schmid 1975: 403, 410; Giesen and Lau 1981: 234, 237, 252; Schmid 1982a: 175).

Second, a concerted attack is launched against Habermas and Eder's developmental-logical version of the theory of social evolution. The authors identify different category mistakes entailed by the ontogenetically based theory: an 'analogy fallacy' (Giesen ans Schmid 1975: 409) in so far as psychological arguments are used to support sociological arguments and sociogenesis and ontogenesis are thus equalised; and a 'collectivist fallacy' (Giesen and Lau 1981: 238) in so far as categories of intentionality are problematically transferred to social collectivities. Whatever the mistake, however, the proponents of the theory fail to advance detailed arguments clarifying the connection between ontogenesis and the development of worldviews; it is not sufficient to make reference to collective learning and institutionalisation, and even less to pass over the obscure empirical problem of the status of earlier societies within the framework of ontogenetic stages (Schmid 1982a: 165, 173).[7] Doubt is also expressed as to whether a structural similarity could be established between individual and socio-cultural development by way of linguistically mediated communication (Lau 1981: 38). Given these difficulties, Schmid (1982a: 174) proposes the 'radical cure' of freeing the Habermasian theory of all developmental logical connotations whatsoever.

Thirdly, the criticism is developed that the extant sociological theories of evolution postulate evolutionary sequences, such as the growth of complexity or the development of worldviews, which are not and, even worse, cannot be supported with substantive statements. Indeed, both the theories of Habermas and Luhmann have no empirical referent and thus do not admit of being related to factual evidence. Were one to achieve an empirical sequential ordering, then it would be necessary to identify an empirically locatable process of selection. The empirical vacuity of these theories, however, implies that they are devoid of explanatory power. In the case of Habermas's theory, this lack is compensated by the unacceptable strategy of having recourse to theoretical fictions (Giesen and Schmid 1975: 411; Giesen and Lau 1981: 252; Schmid 1982a: 174, 178, 179, 180).

There can be no doubt about the fact that the critique advanced by Giesen, Schmid and Lau, centring as it does around the ontogenetically based developmental nature of the Habermasian version of the theory of social evolution, found some resonance among younger critical theorists, including Eder. This is clear from the attitude they assumed towards Habermas's theory during the late 1970s and 1980s and the critique they started to develop of it.

Immanent Critique of Habermas's Theory of Social Evolution

Eder's work can be located most specifically in the framework of contemporary critical theory, particularly the immanent critique of Habermas's developmental-logical theory of social evolution, as represented by his own generation of critical theorists in his own country (e.g., Axel Honneth, Hans Joas, Günter Frankenberg and Ulrich Rödel) and abroad (e.g., Thomas McCarthy and Johann Arnason). As I have shown in detail (Strydom 1992), Eder's work fits firmly into this immanent critique. The focal point of this critique is the 'ontogenetic fallacy', that is, the theoretical error of projecting the developmental-logical structure of the ontogenetic learning process onto culture and society, and its theoretical consequences.

In the late 1970s, McCarthy (1978) and Arnason (1979) were the first critical theorists to suggest that the ontogenetic developmental model may be burdened with difficulties, and since then Honneth and Joas (1980), Frankenberg and Rödel (1981), Miller (1986), Arnason (1988), and Eder (1985a, 1988) made a systematic effort to work out the implications of this model and to correct whatever errors become apparent. The main thrust of this immanent critique was threefold. First, Honneth and Joas, but particularly Miller and, following him, Eder, clarified the problems attached to drawing conclusions from ontogenesis in respect to the change and development of culture and collective symbolic systems, and corrected the ontogenetic fallacy in this particular sense by the introduction of the concept of collective learning supported by a sociological learning theory. Next, Honneth, Frankenberg and Rödel, Arnason, and Eder exposed the implications of the ontogenetic fallacy in its second sense of extrapolating an epoch-transcendent theory of society and history from the model of ontogenetic development. Finally, the younger critical theorists each in his own way embarked on the development of a theoretical foundation to support these revisions. While they retained the Habermasian idea of the theoretical significance of communication in some form or another, this new departure invariably took the form of the philosophy or the theory of praxis, at times to the exclusion of evolution (e.g., Rödel, Frankenberg and Dubiel 1989; Honneth 1992; Joas 1992b) and at other times not.

Eder's characterisation and critique of Habermas's —and his own earlier —ontogenetically based developmental-logical theory of social evolution presupposes the three correctives introduced between 1978 and 1988 in the course of the immanent critique of the leading second generation critical theorist.

3. CHARACTERISATION OF HABERMAS'S THEORY

Evolutionary theory in contemporary sociology, to begin with, can in Eder's (1988: 287-8) view be divided into two basic types. The first assumes the form of a naturalistic theory which proceeds from the assumption that social evolution is continuous with the evolution of animal sociality and hence regards the evolution of society as an extension of the evolution of nature. The opposite category is filled by a culturalistic theory, based on the assumption of an anthropological break, according to which social evolution follows its own peculiar cultural logic, driven by specifically human learning processes, well beyond the logic of natural evolution. While Luhmann's functionalist theory of social evolution corresponds to the former description, Habermas's rationalist theory of social evolution is examplary of the latter type. What systems theory is to the functionalist version, competence theory is to the rationalist one.

Eder's (1988: 288-9) own position fits into the second category, of course, but what he finds striking from his new perspective is the fact, made clear by their protracted debate,[8] that Habermas's theoretical construction is exactly complementary to that of Luhmann. Whereas Luhmann reduces culture to the status of a co-variable of society which contributes to the autopoietic ability of society, Habermas insists on the autonomy of culture and, by extension, of the lifeworld. They thus represent two competing developmental logics between which one is able to choose only on the basis of a normative prejudgement —a prejudgement, it should be noted, which either way neutralises the problem of evolution by teleologically dissolving it. In the case of the systems theoretically conceived developmental logic, evolution is identified with structural differentiation. The competence theoretical developmental logic, by contrast, dissolves evolution by identifying it with rationalisation based on stage-bound ontogenetic development. The specificity of Habermas's culturalistic theory of social evolution, however, rests on his normativistic reconstruction of historical materialism which gives primacy to moral evolution (Eder 1988: 30-38).

In order to pinpoint the most basic limitation of Habermas's theory, however, Eder (1988: 290-1) focuses on what is accorded the role of motive force of evolution. In the case of its functionalist counterpart, differentiation qua social evolution is regarded as being driven by an implicit compulsion towards autopoiesis. In the rationalist theory, in turn, the motor of rationalisation qua social evolution is located in an implicit pressure towards learning. It is significant that both Luhmann and Habermas make the question of whether autopoiesis or learning actually occurs dependent on an investigation of the particular historical conditions, while leaving the fact that it takes place at all unaccounted for. The theoretical frameworks of both authors thus exhibit a lacuna to the extent that they have been constructed in such a way that the social presuppositions of human learning processes and of the autopoiesis of social systems are excluded. It is in order to theorise this gap that Eder finds it necessary to have recourse to the ideas of two influential contemporary social theorists, Pierre Bourdieu and Alain Touraine. The names of Giddens and Miller must also be mentioned in this context.

With the assistance of a distinction Bourdieu (1977) introduced in connection with his theory of practice, first, Eder (1988: 291) is able to establish that the theoretical position of Habermas, like that of Luhmann, is exhausted by a focus on the *opus operatum* in the sense of the effects of evolutionary changes —that is, rationalisation and differentiation —to the exclusion of the *modus operandi* in the sense of the mechanisms of evolution. The latter Eder (1988: 291, 292-5) interprets in terms of the contributions of a number of social theorists. First there are the comparable attempts of Touraine (1977, 1981) and, less importantly, Giddens (1984) to compensate the unhistorical nature of evolutionary theories by the introduction of a sociological concept of history and praxis. The mechanisms of social evolution thus include social praxis or collective practices in Touraine's sense of the production of society and in Giddens's sense of the practical structuration of social relations. Although at first sight very different from the positions of Touraine and Giddens, the learning theoretical approach of Miller (1986) in similar vein seeks, according to Eder (1988: 292, 296-9), to emphasise the historicity of social processes by conceiving of history sociologically in terms of collective learning. Collective learning is thus another major mechanism of social evolution. Even though Touraine and particularly Giddens exhibit an anti-evolutionary animus, and even though Miller tends to screen out evolution by his clearly circumscribed ontogenetic focus, all these authors elaborate on the historical, cognitive, conflictual, collective practices through which society is produced and thus, in effect, help to clarify the mechanisms of social evolution.[9]

Against this background it becomes apparent that Habermas, like Luhmann who overlooks the process of the production of society preceding the autopoiesis of systems, neglects to analyse the social praxis underlying societal learning processes. Both their theories lack a sociologically substantive concept of praxis and, by extension, of history (Eder 1988: 291). This deficiency explains why Habermas, like Luhmann, is incapable of coming up in his theory of social evolution with anything more than unspecific, epoch-transcendent, taxonomic conceptualisations and classifications which have the effect of discrediting the very idea of evolution itself in the social sciences.

Beyond this general characterisation and assessment, Eder puts forward a profusion of largely undeveloped and unconnected critical perspectives, both directly and indirectly, on Habermas's theory of social evolution. It is now necessary to provide an initial systematisation of these critical perspectives.

4. CRITIQUE OF HABERMAS

In a general sense, the culturalistic nature of Habermas's theory of social evolution goes back to the fact that he proceeds from the assumption of an anthropological break rather than of a continuity between social and natural evolution and thus conceives of the evolution of society as following its own particular cultural logic which is driven by human learning processes. Its specific character, however, it obtains from the peculiar manner in which Habermas moralises or, rather, normativistically dissolves historical materialism. Eder raises objections against this culturalistic conception of the theory of social evolution in so far as Habermas lends it an ontogenetic, a structuralist and finally a normativistic sense.

In the following pages, I concentrate in turn on these three critical points.

The Ontogenetic Dimension

The central notion of the ontogenetic conceptual strategy, to begin with, is that of a process of the formation of progressively more inclusive structures relevant to the solution of problems, the stage-bound deployment of which exhibits a developmental logic and the retardation or acceleration of which is attributable to developmental dynamics. Earlier already, Eder (1985a:

55-6) pointed out as against Habermas that the transfer of this essentially psychological idea to the sociocultural domain has pernicious consequences for the integrity of the social dimension. Since the psychological approach cuts thought and knowledge adrift from their social basis, the connection between learning processes and social structures is torn asunder, with the result that the structures of knowledge appear as *a priori* properties of the solitary individual. The separation of developmental logic, which is identified with the individual, and developmental dynamics, which is ascribed to the social environment, leads to a cognitive idealism for which the social dimension is nothing but a stimulus for the immanent development of learning processes. Habermas's tendency towards social reductionism becomes sharply focused when one considers that this psychologically inspired approach of his proceeds from the assumption, which Eder (1988: 301) finds unacceptable, that society is the result of adaptation to the developmental logic and dynamics of psychic systems. But there is also an objectionable biologistic connotation to this position (Eder 1988: 290). The ontogenetic or, more specifically, the competence-theoretical conceptualisation of the theory of social evolution consists of depicting society as the embodiment of action competences, but since the problem of the transition from action to society cannot be solved within this theoretical framework, Habermas falls back to the biological notion of the phenotypic manifestation or embodiment of genotypic characteristics, with the result that the emergent properties of society are shifted onto the systemic dimension.

To avoid the unacceptable implications of the ontogenetic conception of cultural logic, Eder in his earlier work proposed that the theory of collective learning be introduced to bridge the various divisions and get rid of all cognitive idealism. More importantly still, he now insists that social evolution does not have its own autonomous cultural logic, but must rather be regarded as forming part of society itself (Eder 1988: 387). The theory of collective learning must thus be built into the theory of praxis in the sense of the theory of the self-production of society, as he (1988: 301) calls it with Touraine. This latter theory not only takes the place of the psychological approach, but, due to the fact that praxis mediates between individual and society, at the same time also obviates the need to have recourse to biological concepts.

In the context of Habermas's theory of social evolution, however, the ontogenetic model does not remain confined to the socio-cultural dimension, but is extended to society as a whole and in general to the universal historical plane. Over and above committing the ontogenetic fallacy (Eder 1988: 296, 310, 313; also Strydom 1992) in that Habermas draws a conclusion from ontogenesis in respect of the change and development of culture or collective symbolic systems which can be accounted for only with reference to collective learning processes, therefore, he compounds this error by transferring the ontogenetic model to the level of the evolution of societies. Irrespective of the qualified manner in which Habermas presents it, the three major stages of ontogenetic development —cognitively speaking: pre-operational, concrete operational and formal operational; normatively speaking: pre-conventional, conventional and post-conventional —essentially correspond to the three universal historical stages of the evolution of society —primitive, traditional and modern society based on the organizational principles of kinship, domination and global forms of intercourse respectively. It is against this theoretical strategy that Eder (1988: 310) objects so vehemently when he insists that Habermas falls foul of the ontogenetic fallacy in trying to solve the problem of the direction of social evolution by means of the application of Piaget-Kohlbergian developmental logic. This objection is reinforced by the criticism that Habermas makes the question of the classification of societies in general at the universal historical level the central problem of the theory of social evolution (Eder 1988: 19). In Eder's own view, by contrast, the central issue is rather the degree of social practical rationality as exhibited by the relation between the appropriation of nature and collective learning processes. This means that Habermas is correct in emphasising the significance of morality in social evolution, but that he does not radically enough free evolution from universal history (Eder 1988: 33, 291). Morality is located much more subtly within social evolution than Habermas gives one to understand.

The structuralist and normativistic connotations of Habermas's theory of social evolution are closely related to the ontogenetic sense.

The Structuralist Dimension

Although all evolutionary theories can be said to be structural theories, including those of Habermas and Eder himself, Eder understands Habermas's theory as being a structural theory in a particular sense which is open to criticism. Habermas's theory is one in which social evolution is conceived in terms of an ontogenetically based cultural logic, emphasising stage-bound cultural structures with a universalistic character rather than structures which are at one and the same time the outcome, medium and object of praxis. This implies that it is a structuralist theory of a certain type —that is, a theory of structures on the level of social order from which must be distinguished very sharply a theory of structure formation on the level of the production of society. Against this background, two of Eder's more specific critical points become intelligible.

The first criticism is that Habermas's theory of social evolution is a structural theory of what has been learned, whereas the theory of social evolution should more correctly be given the form of a structural theory of the practical utilisation of what has been learned (Eder 1988: 302). Eder denies that the theory of social evolution could be exhausted by a reconstruction of the logic of the development of the structures of knowledge systems and moral representations acquired by a society, since the crucial question that follows in the wake of the introduction of the sociologically substantive concepts of praxis and history is that of the manner in which what has thus been learned is being drawn upon and used in the organization of society.

The second criticism of Habermas's peculiar structuralist bent amounts to the thesis that in the context of his theory of social evolution he presents structural models of social formations or societies instead of structural models of social praxis (Eder 1988: 303-4). Against the background of the Marxist concept of modes of production as well as influential analyses of the exchange of women, hierarchy and the social contract, Habermas (1979a: 153, 154; 1987a: 233-75) developed the theoretically central concept of societal organizational principle which is exemplified by kinship in tribal societies, domination in traditional societies and global forms of intercourse (e.g., communication and the market) in modern societies respectively. In Eder's view, these structural models pertain to the societal context of social praxis and thus leave the structure of social praxis as such unaccounted for. The logic of this conceptual strategy thus leads to social evolution being regarded as a matter of the classification and historical concatenation of crystallised forms of social order. But far from being a theory of the evolution of societies or social formations, the specificity of the social evolutionary perspective resides in treating praxis not as a result of structural models of society, but rather as the mechanism of the production and reproduction of such forms. Since structural models of praxis thus occupy the centre of attention, social evolution is conceived in relation to the change of the generative and utilisation contexts of historically given social orders. The basic question here is how, for what purpose and by whom the knowledge and moral representations established by collective learning in a given society are employed.[10]

The Normative Dimension

As regards the normativistic feature of Habermas's ontogenetically based structuralist theory of social evolution, finally, it is necessary to have in mind the nature of the developmental-logical stages he reads into culture. With Piaget and Kohlberg, he broadly assumes three ontogenetic stages, the final and most important of which is essentially an anticipation or projection of fully developed cognitive structures. These structures represent the principle of mutual understanding, agreement and cooperation, or practical reason for short, which is absolutely crucial for the humane and rational organization of society. In keeping with his assumption that social evolution is borne by the logical development of cognitive, particularly moral, representations, Habermas scans ethical systems as an indicator of the practical rationality characteristic of a society and of its evolution. In view of the fact that the principle of practical reason as conceived by Habermas could as yet not be evolutionarily stabilised so as to exert a transformative influence on the characteristic practical irrationality of modern society, however, Eder (1988: 320, 308) points out that Habermas is engaged in the construction of ideal stages of social evolution or, rather, the mere postulation of social evolutionary potentialities to the exclusion of all attempts to identify real processes of social evolution and their particular structural elements. His theory of social evolution is not a theory of historical evolutionary processes, but a normative theory about counterfactually conceived possible evolutionary processes and, as such, a utopian counter-model opposed to the reality of the evolution of modern society. In addition, Eder (1988: 372) insists that, since learning processes do not guarantee practical reason in that there typically is a marked discrepancy between what is acquired in learning processes and what actually becomes evolutionarily effective, it is possible to glean practical reason in a society neither from its everyday lifeworld nor from its institutions and even less from its ethical system.[11] All such sociocultural bearers of practical reason harbour only effects of social praxis. The conclusion is thus that a theory which is concerned with the evolution of practical reason is required instead to focus on the social praxis serving as the vehicle of practical reason, which as a rule includes the praxis of cultural, political and social movements.

Eder's (1988: 318-21, 371-2) critique of the normativistic implications of Habermas's theory of socio-cultural evolution extends to a critique of what may be called the latter's neo-Kantian apriorism, that is, his assumption of the aprioristic conditions of practical reason. Characteristic of the apriorism of the 18th and 19th century was the commitment to something objective outside society, a so-called 'metasocial guarantee' (Touraine 1981: 53, 68), 'metadiscourse' or 'grand narrative' (Lyotard 1984: xxiii), as the secure foundation of practical reason. Eder is convinced that Habermas's ontogenetically informed and cognitivistically grounded concept of developmental logic represents nothing less than a contemporary variant of this tradition of apriorism.[12] This theoretical basis allows him to devise an aprioristic and thus pre-sociological concept of practical reason beyond society. It is given the form of the standard and goal of social evolution. According to this position, ethical forms of morality represent the criterion of evolutionary advancement (e.g. Habermas 1979a: 183-88; 1984b; 1986b). At the same time, social evolution is reduced to being nothing more and nothing less than the realisation of this objective standard beyond society. As against this view, Eder (1988: 387, 302, 371) locates practical reason and its social evolution within the confines of society itself and, with some reference to Giddens's (1984: 25-8) concept of the 'duality of structure', advances the claim that ethical forms of morality, like any other cognitive structures, are not the standard and goal but rather the outcome and means or medium of social evolution. Eder (1988: 371) regards as abortive also Habermas's attempt to avoid the theoretical problems associated with apriorism by means of the introduction of the quasi-sociological conception of practical reason as the result of discourse in the sense of communication disburdened of the pressures of action (e.g. Habermas and Luhmann 1971: 213-5; Habermas 1972a: 168-72, 1984a: 42). The fact that discourse of this kind historically enjoyed only a precarious existence in the educated sections of the bourgeoisie during the early modern period and proved helpless against practical irrationality in the subsequent years, is sufficient to his mind to underline that the establishment of the conditions of practical reason is much more difficult than the apriorism Habermas inherited from the bourgeois Enlightenment would have us believe.

The criticism that Habermas's normativistic apriorism leads to a rationalistic position which subverts the theory of social evolution by transposing the telos of moral learning processes into its criterion and goal is a serious one taken on its own. But when it is reinforced by being traced back to a basic confusion of development and evolution it is difficult to see how Habermas could possibly defend his developmental-logical theory of sociocultural evolution against the onslaught from the viewpoint of the theory of the social evolution of practical reason. While noting the tendency of classical theories of evolution to lump various distinct dimensions together, what is called the 'phylocultural complex' (Sinha 1988: 77-110)[13] which dominated not only the work of Freud but also of Piaget, Eder substantively touches on this most basic difficulty of Habermas's theory of social evolution on at least two occasions. By way of the first argument, Eder (1988: 317-8) points out that social evolution is the recapitulation or repetition neither of the ontogenetic acquisition of cognitive competences on the part of the individual nor of the constitution of knowledge systems and moral representations by collective learning processes. From this point of view, he directs the critique of a 'confusion of levels' against the argument in favour of an ontogenetic heuristics or of an isomorphy —Habermas (1979a: 99-116) speaks of 'homology' —of ontogenesis and evolution. His own answer to this difficulty consists of a strict separation of the theory of learning and the theory of social evolution. Second, Eder (1988: 370-1) argues that the premature identification of moral learning processes and social evolution has side-tracked Habermas into taking the emergence of ethicised forms of morality as the criterion of the highest level of evolutionary advancement. Before elaborating on the undesirable consequences of this, it is interesting to note that, in keeping with the above-mentioned complementarity of their respective theories of social evolution, Habermas's confusion of development and evolution as a result of the fallacious overextension of the ontogenetic model is only the counterpart of the category mistake Luhmann commits when he equally fallaciously advances the claim that the theory of the structural differentiation of social systems possesses universal historical validity.

Habermas's developmental logical theory of sociocultural evolution does not only entail untenable homological assumptions and unfortunate consequences such as temporally and spatially compressive and distortive schematisms and classifications,[14] but Eder (1988: 373-5) also discovers unsavoury implications such as an 'evolution-theoretic myth' and, to be sure, grave ideological overtones. In accordance with the phylocultural complex which dominated evolutionary thought at the turn of the century, classical theorists such as Hobhouse and his successor Ginsberg (Ginsberg 1956, 1970; Wilson 1985) in the early 20th century identified evolutionary trends which were presented as indicating progress on a universal historical and general societal scale. Habermas acutely sees through these trends as being nothing but assumptions about learning processes which lead to increased individuation, the generalisation of moral rules and the increasing abstractness of moral judgements, but, as his discussion of the so-called 'normative import of modernity'[15] shows, he continues the practice of his predecessors of falsely applying those assumptions (Eder 1988: 375-6). Modernity is depicted as the telos of moral evolution —or this is the implication, at least, as long as moral development is stretched over a universal historical and general societal framework. To the extent that Habermas holds to the conception of moral evolution as culminating in modernity, Eder (1988: 373) accuses him of entertaining an evolutionary theoretical myth.[16] Indeed, in so far as this involves the uncritical adoption of the self-description of modern society[17] and, hence, the employment of an affirmative concept of social evolution, he regards Habermas's theory as possessing definite ideological overtones (Eder 1988: 373, 374-5, 377). The key question here is whether a society, when it claims to possess a higher form of morality than another, does not in effect advance a power claim. Or more precisely: When a society tries to monopolise universalistic morality, claiming that it and it alone has achieved such a morality, is it not then engaging in an attempt to obtain a better position for itself in relation to other societies? Eder (1988: 374) takes questions such as these to be indicative of the social function of morality, something which is too often overlooked in sociological analyses of morality. In the case of Habermas, he sees this oversight as eventuating in a transformation of *The Dialectic of Enlightenment* (Horkheimer and Adorno 1972) into a theory of the unilinear progress of reason which is not entirely free from connections with the ideology of modern society.[18] What must be appreciated, if these undesirable consequences are to be avoided, is the fact that, far from culminating in modernity, moral development takes place in all societies: modern, traditional and simple (Eder 1988: 375, 18). And that this is not a matter of rejecting the theory of social evolution, but rather one of stating it in a more differentiated way, is apparent from the circumstance that it requires, first, that social evolution be sharply distinguished from learning processes and the developments associated with them, and, second, that social evolution be retrieved from the web of universal history in which it got stuck virtually from the start —all with a view to focusing on the contexts of the utilisation of the knowledge and moral representations made available by collective learning processes.

The evolution-theoretical myth according to which modernity is the telos of moral evolution, however, has also another side (Eder 1988: 373). The account of moral evolution as progressing through stages marked by primitive, traditional and modern society respectively, proceeds from an assumption which with a single blow discloses and debunks the particular use Habermas makes of the functionalist or systems-theoretical component in his overall theoretical construction. The very description of moral evolution makes plain that this model owes much to the idea of increasing complexity and, more basically, of the logic of the functional differentiation of society as a system, the empirical assumption being: the more complex society becomes the more practical rationality is required. The fact of the matter is, however, that if practical reason cannot be said to be rational simply because it represents the highest stage of cognitive development, as little can it be claimed that complexity guarantees the social evolution of practical reason. The most that could be done, in Eder's view, is that distinct paths of such evolution be distinguished with reference to the different ways in which social praxis utilises the morality made available by collective learning processes in a society. Such an approach allows the identification not only of paths which lead to a *cul-de-sac*, but by the same token also ones characterised by a more or less high degree of practical rationality. More important still, for Eder, is that the theory of the social evolution of practical reason thus makes possible the building of the theory of social evolution into the critical theory of society.

A NEW CONCEPT OF CRITIQUE

The new concept of critique connected with this endeavour provides an opportunity for a clarification of the final point of Eder's critique of Habermas's theory of sociocultural evolution.

Eder (1988: 375, 309) puts forward the criticism that Habermas's approach loses much of its critical potential due to the fact that it involves the adoption of an affirmative concept of social evolution, but the more serious argument concerns the latter's conception of the normative foundations of critique. Eder regards Habermas's theory of socio-cultural evolution as entailing a variant of Kantian critique of reason in so far as it proceeds from the construction of ideal stages and the postulation of potentialities of social evolution, and is then exercised with reference to a standard or criterion beyond society. As such, it represents what he calls 'an aprioristic critique of practical reason' (Eder 1988: 374; see also 319-20). Within the framework of the theory of the social evolution of practical reason, however, the Kantian critique of reason is sociologised, with the result that the conditions of critique are transformed. Instead of aprioristic conditions, critique is grounded in the social employment of practical reason. Such a 'social critique of practical reason' or 'critique of society' (Eder 1988: 374, 377) thus concentrates on the utilisation contexts of practical reason with the aim of disillusioning about what claims to be and is accepted as practically rational.[19] By so doing, it continues the process of disenchantment which from the outset accompanied the historical development of modern society, but at this point in time it has become reflexive. The social critique of practical reason is 'a sociological enlightenment of the Enlightenment' (Eder 1988: 319).[20] Indeed, to the extent that this reflexive critique of society is connected with the practical critique embodied as certain of the new social movements, Eder (1988: 377) regards it as forming part of the social evolution of contemporary society. Its contribution lies in helping to open up the possibility of determining anew the relationship between collective learning processes and practical reason, thus increasing the rationality of social practices. Since Habermas in his aprioristic critique continues to concentrate on the classical themes of freedom and justice, however, he is able to find only 'obscurity' (Eder 1988: 387)[21] where this new attempt at a social evolution of practical reason is undertaken in contemporary society.

4

Critical Theory and the New Social Movements: A Conflict of Interpretations

In his introduction to Jürgen Habermas's work, Stephen K. White (1988) gives an account of the latter's position on the new social movements which, despite plausibly linking this theme to the idea of a newly founded critical theoretical research programme, leaves something to be desired. Without being unsympathetic towards Habermas, one could with some justification say that White overlooks two important points. Not only does Habermas's concept of the new social movements remain undeveloped, but his articulation of the critical theoretical approach actually precludes an adequate treatment of this phenomenon. This point has been forcefully brought home by a number of authors who belong to the younger generation of critical theorists, including Axel Honneth and Klaus Eder. According to these and other critics to Habermas's left, as he perceives them (1990b: 204), his general theory of society makes the problem of social movements into a secondary one, casts it in a historically insensitive linear mould and, finally, links it too tightly to normative concerns. Moreover, Habermas's various concessions to his critics (1985b: 234; Strydom 1987) regarding collective learning bear out the fact that these problems cannot easily be skirted. Ignoring these serious theoretical questions, White is far too optimistic when he submits that Habermas provides 'the best available framework' (1988: 124) for the study of the new social movements.

In this essay, I avail of the opportunity White provides to highlight the major deficiencies of Habermas's approach and to indicate the direction in which a critical theoretical analysis of social movements, particularly the new social movements, is pointing. I propose to do this by contrasting White's presentation of Habermas's position with the criticisms and innovative departures of younger generation critical theorists.

1. HABERMAS'S THEORETICAL FRAMEWORK IN QUESTION

At a crucial point in his presentation of Habermas's work, White sees fit to draw the following conclusion:

> *'Habermas's communicative model provides the best available framework, not only for the construction of explanations of the behaviour of the new social movements, but also for understanding why such movements have arisen, and for interpreting what, at a general level, is at stake in the struggles in which they engage. In terms of their behaviour, the communicative model is the only one complex enough to provide some comprehension of the peculiar mix of strategic, norm-guided (especially its universalistic quality) and expressive or dramaturgical action such groups engage in. In terms of understanding why such movements have arisen and interpreting what is at stake in their struggles, Habermas directs our attention to his interpretation of modernity and modernization, more particularly to the notions of systemic versus communicative sociation and of a one-sided process of societal rationalization versus a rationalized lifeworld'* (*White 1988: 124*).

The claim White advances here to the effect that Habermas's model provides the means for distinguishing among the strategic, norm-guided and expressive aspects of collective action is relatively uncontentious, although I will argue at some length that the expressive aspect is not adequately grasped by Habermas. What is more provocative and important in the present context is the further claim made with regard to the quality of Habermas's theoretical framework relative to the explanation of the genesis of the new social movements and the interpretation of their societal significance. The reason why this particular aspect attracts attention will become apparent in some detail below, but it may proleptically be said to reside in White's theoretically one-sided emphasis on Habermas's 'communicative model' and, from the view point of the problem of social movements, his subsequent theoretically vacuous linking of this model to Habermas's theory of modernity. My argument will not be that what White does is entirely wrong, but rather that what he leaves out of his account is so central to understanding particularly the weakness of Habermas's position on social movements that he is of necessity bound, by contrast with the subtleties of his exposition in other departments, to give a superficial, undifferentiated and politically naive interpretation of the German writer's treatment of the theme of the new social movements.

It goes without saying, of course, that White is correct in locating Habermas's concern with the new social movements within the context of the latter's theory of modernity. The problem is that he, despite his recognition of the overall framework-function fulfilled by Habermas's 'general theory of society' (White 1988: 23), neglects to take account of the way in which the theory of modernity is integrated into the more general theory. The root cause of this neglect can be traced back to his conception, inspired by Imre Lakatos (1970), of Habermas's philosophical-sociological contribution as representing a research programme in the social sciences, more specifically his circumscription of the 'core' (White 1988: 9) of such a research programme. It is not the Lakatosian concept as such that is to blame, to be sure, but rather White's one-sided application of it.

According to White (1988: 9, 128), the core component of Habermas's research programme is represented by the 'philosophical' or 'quasi-Kantian dimension' of the latter's work. It takes the form of a theory of rationality which constitutes a minimal intersubjectivist model of the subject. It is this dimension that he refers to as the 'communicative model'. This core component in turn informs the 'social-scientific' or 'Hegelian-Marxian dimension' (White 1988: 9, 128) of Habermas's research programme which is executed in the form of an analysis of modernity, particularly advanced capitalism. What strikes one about this presentation of Habermas's position, however, is the reduction of the core to the communicative model and to it alone. White (1988: 129-30) is aware of the fact that the core or philosophical level of Habermas's work is made up of what the latter conceives of as the 'reconstructive' theoretical component. But whereas this component in reality embraces both the reconstructive theory of communicative action on the synchronic axis and the reconstructive theory of social evolution on the diachronic axis (see Strydom 1990b: 541-2), he singles out the former to the exclusion of the latter. And that this reductionism could not possibly remain without serious consequences for his overview of Habermas's work, particularly with reference to the new social movements, is obvious.

Before exploring these consequences, it should be pointed out that it is remarkable that White, despite projections to the contrary (1988: 86), nowhere attempts to go into Habermas's theory of social evolution and thus to develop an understanding of what he refers to as the latter's general theory of society. In fact, he explicitly declines to attend to the theory of evolution. Two reasons are given for this strategy, the first of which is as curious as the second is unconvincing. The assertion that Habermas's neglect thus far to provide detailed historical and anthropological backing renders an evaluation of the theory of social evolution unfruitful (White 1988: 170) immediately prompts the question whether the same also does not apply to the theory of rationality or communicative action since, according to critics, backing is equally lacking in this regard. The second line of defence to the effect that the debate about the theory of social evolution 'yields more heat than light at this most broad and abstract level of analysis' (White 1988: 170), apart from revealing a lack of familiarity with the relevant literature, only confirms the earlier expressed suspicion that White does not bring a sufficiently penetrating theoretical vision to his analysis of Habermas's work. This is all the more noteworthy since the essential core of the theory of social evolution which Habermas developed in the 1970s has almost verbally and, to be sure, theoretically importantly, been incorporated into *The Theory of Communicative Action* (1984a, 1987a), the work to which White devotes most of his attention.

Since Thomas McCarthy's *The Critical Theory of Jürgen Habermas* (1978) and the remarks of the editors of *Telos* (39, 1979: 3) on the publication of Habermas's essay on 'History and Evolution' in that journal in the late 1970s, for instance, a critique of Habermas's ontogenetically based developmental-logical theory of social evolution has been developed by younger generation critical theorists such as Johann Arnason (1979), Axel Honneth and Hans Joas (1980, 1988), Günter Frankenberg and Ulrich Rödel (1981), and Klaus Eder (1985a).[1] At this stage, in fact, a drastically reformulated version is well underway (e.g. Eder 1988; Strydom 1992, 1993). It is significant that the major thrust of this critique and reformulation consists precisely of a demonstration that Habermas's theory of society does not allow an adequate treatment of social movements and thus, quite expectedly, of a determined effort to correct this defect by placing social movements at the very centre of the social theoretical stage. This critique clearly contradicts White's (1988: 111) assumption that Habermas's research programme does not marginalise social movements, although he is of course correct that it does not demote social movements to the status of marginal events to the same extent as rational choice theory or functionalist systems theory.

2. THE IMMANENT CRITIQUE OF HABERMAS'S THEORY OF SOCIAL MOVEMENTS

Having provided analyses of the immanent critique of Habermas's ontogenetically based developmental-logical theory of social evolution elsewhere (Strydom 1992, 1993), I propose to present a sample of arguments to illustrate the conclusions reached in the debate. On the whole, they underline the debilitating limitations Habermas imposes on the study of social movements by way of his general theory of society or, more particularly, his theory of social evolution.

Opening the debate, Thomas McCarthy (1978: 261-271) argued that Habermas's intellectual development exhibits a fundamental shift in that, whereas in his earlier work he operated with a conception of critical theory as situation-dependent and hermeneutically rich social inquiry, in his later work he adopts a much stronger theoretical programme which lays claim to validity independent of a historico-hermeneutic standpoint. The crucial point here is that this shift in emphasis is attributable to Habermas's concern with the development not only of a synchronic communicative model, but in particular also of the theory of socio-cultural evolution. The original conception of an empirical philosophy of history with practical intent made way for the theory of socio-cultural evolution possessing the methodological status of rational reconstruction. The consequences, as seen by McCarthy, were far-reaching. The introduction of evolutionary theory entailed, first, the replacement of the hermeneutically situation-bound character of social life by the general state of development of humankind as basic reference point, and second the weakening, if not abandonment, of the originally asserted unity of theory and practice. The practical meaning guiding the interpretation of history as well as the present was thus located not in a historically and socially situated practical reason but, in a Neo-Kantian turn, rather in pure practical reason.

At about the same time, Johann Arnason (1979) submitted an analysis in which he more explicitly than McCarthy teased out the implications of Habermas's position for the study of social movements. At the outset, he pinpointed the specific character of Habermas's theory of sociocultural evolution as a developmental-logical theory which takes evolution to mean 'the realization of an ordered sequence of structural possibilities'(Arnason 1979: 215). He also identified the basic influence cognitive psychology has had on its formulation which goes back to the concept of ontogenesis as a constructive learning process undergone by a subject which develops from stage to stage through confrontation with and solution of objectively given problems. Arnason discovered Habermas's position to have at least two serious theoretical implications. The first is that the conception of the social process as being grounded in a universal developmental logic of evolution circumscribes social movements to such a degree that the possible historical effects of their practical projects are reduced to auxiliary functions of transmission and acceleration (1979: 213). The second is that the introduction of the concept of development logic implies 'a double closure' (1979: 217) in that it, through an instrumentalist reduction of the relation between humans and nature and a normativistic subsumption of the relations between people in society, allows neither interference from the material context nor alternative historical projects.

In 1980, Axel Honneth and Hans Joas (1988) explicitly identified the basic difficulty of Habermas's theory of social evolution as residing in his theoretical strategy of basing the theory squarely on the ontogenetic model. In a brief yet penetrating analysis they clarified the role of this model in Habermas's conceptualisation of the theory of social evolution, revealed the developmental-logical bias of the theory, and demonstrated the problematic nature of its implications. Central to their critical analysis was a dissection of Habermas's explanation of socio-cultural evolution in terms of developmental logic whereby they were able to show that the ontogenetic model features in Habermas's theory not only in the sense that the development of worldviews, collective identities and moral-legal structures are conceived as being analogous to ego development, but also and in particular that his evolutionary explanation as such depends on the attempt to 'project the structure of ontogenetic learning processes onto the process of evolutionary learning' (Honneth and Joas 1988: 165) through which society as a whole advances from the primitive through the civilisational to the modern level. Evolutionary learning processes involve, on the one hand, unresolved system problems which represent challenges and, on the other, new levels of learning which are latently available and could be drawn upon for the purposes of solving problems threatening the continued existence of society as a whole. For Honneth and Joas, this position implies that 'system-threatening problems' are adduced 'in order to identify the moral learning process which permits the overcoming of the threat to the system and thereby further the evolutionary development of the technical-strategic system of action' (1988: 163). In drawing out the implications of this developmental-logical ontogenetic type of evolutionary explanation, Honneth and Joas emphasised specifically the question of social movements.

In the first place, an explanation that is cast in this mould necessarily abstracts from historically specific events and unique collective experiences within the framework of which social groups engage in historical action, and thus detaches itself from the real historical process (Honneth and Joas 1988: 164). In so far as such an explanation takes the historical context into account, it does so only to ascertain formal levels of consciousness and hence ignores processes of communication guided by collective processes of interpretation and experience gained through collective learning. That this is indeed the line that the developmental-logical evolutionary explanation follows is borne out, for Honneth and Joas, by Habermas's rigorous separation of reconstructive developmental logic from narrative historiography. The theory of social evolution is solely concerned with the development of structures and hence reads the historical material exclusively from the point of view of the logic of such development. The researcher is thus from the outset predestined to lose sight of the kind of historically innovative action which is typically represented by social movements and, hence, does not arise in response to a problem threatening society as a social system.

Second, the ontogenetically based developmental-logical approach to social evolution operates with an ambiguous concept of 'social learning'

(Honneth and Joas 1988: 165-66). Whereas Habermas himself explicitly includes under that rubric systemic learning in the sense of the evolutionarily significant response of society as a social system to a system-threatening problem, historical evidence suggests that moral-practical learning processes often, if not as a rule, occur within the context of social movements, the typical 'historical bearers of evolutionary learning processes' (1988: 165). The crucial point here is that social movements, typically representing a consciousness of action orientations which are socially superior and constitute a normative advance, learn not in reaction to unresolved system problems and dangers, but rather through the collective experiencing of and cooperative opposition to repression and social justice prevailing in a society. Given that this is the case, Honneth and Joas insist that Habermas is compelled at all points where he wishes to document historically the presence of moral learning to have recourse to social movements which, ironically, are incompatible with his developmental-logical evolutionary classifications. It is indeed so that Habermas (1987a: 316) envisages as a 'major task' the description of 'the evolutionary learning process in terms of social movements and political upheavals', but, to be sure, only after the historical material had been ordered according to the developmental-logical explanatory scheme. This provides evidence in support of Honneth and Joas's claim that Habermas's concept of social learning must of necessity be ambiguous to encompass within a single framework not only the process of systemic learning, but also the social or collective learning processes represented by social movements.

Problems similar to those identified by Arnason and Honneth and Joas in the theoretical context were discovered by Günter Frankenberg and Ulrich Rödel (1981) in the course of substantive research on modern law conducted under Habermas's direction during the late 1970s and early 1980s at the Max Planck Institute in Starnberg, Germany. In their research, they proceeded on the basis of a theoretical construct which combined a normative theory with a historical-sociological approach. The normative component took the form of an ontogenetically based developmental-logical stage model, representing a reconstruction of increasingly complex justificatory structures at the level of moral philosophical theories from Hobbes and Kant through Rawls to Habermas and Apel. Hypotheses deriving from a historical-sociological theory were then related to this strong theoretical component on the assumption that historical developments correspond to the developmental logic. As regards the question of the transition to a more complex procedure of justification, the hypothesis was introduced that, rather than taking place through mere thought or the immanent development of structures, it can empirically be determined with reference to experiences undergone in relation to changes in social reality which are translated into normative pressure by political and social movements. Frankenberg and Rödel's attempt to apply this construct to the relevant historical material proved to be an empirical failure, however, in that the material simply did not admit of being ordered according to the chosen viewpoint. In addition, a number of weaknesses of the developmental-logical model also came to light (Frankenberg and Rödel 1981: 19-20). First, development is not reconstructed from the internal perspective of historical subjects and their normative evaluations, but rather *ex post* from the perspective of the external observer according to a normative standard he commands by virtue of his disposal over a stage model. This standard has not been established by way of an analysis of historical development, but *a priori* and deductively derived from a developmental-logical conception which clandestinely regards the contemporary normative position as the endpoint of development and adopts it as the basis of the *ex post* evaluation. Second, the developmental model, due to its emphasis on the coordination of evolutionary mechanisms from the viewpoint of the observer, leads to a reductive treatment of the complex of relations among normatively oriented historical actors and their internal perspectives, institutionalised norms and system problems. And, finally, the model overburdens the empirical analysis with such strong theoretical presuppositions that important aspects of reality are inevitably excluded from the observer, brushed aside as theoretically insignificant, or admitted only in some reduced form or another.

In the context of his construction of a sociological learning theory, Max Miller (1986) put forward the argument that Habermas's appropriation of the early Piaget's theory of the social constitution of universalistic morality via the middle and later Piaget's concern with the developmental logic of cognitive competences at the ontogenetic level led him to 'displace the genuine sociological concept of a collective learning process by the concept of "developmental logic"' (1986: 216). Applied at the macro-sociological level of social evolution, this position eventuated in the rather problematic thesis that ontogenetic learning on the part of the individual runs ahead of societal evolutionary advances —problematic, that is, since it gave rise to the composite problem of accounting for the precise relation between individual learning and societal evolutionary learning, specifying the learning mechanism making possible the transition from the individual to the social level, and finally of explaining the genesis of collective systems of interpretation or world views.

Klaus Eder (1985a), focusing on this gap at the macro-level under influence of Miller, developed a critique of Habermas's view, underpinning his essentially classical understanding of institutionalisation according to which cultural rationalisation calls forth corresponding institutions, that ontogenetic learning processes are the pacemaker of the evolution of society. He demonstrated that the development of moral consciousness in the modern period depended crucially on 'the logic of associative communalisation' (Eder 1985a: 87) or a collective learning process which began at the everyday level of the practice of life and was borne by social movements. The implication of this position is that the assertion advanced from the classical perspective of the history of ideas to the effect that modern society came off the ground when universalistic moral thought was brought to bear on the law which Habermas shares with Parsons is mistaken since the transformation of the legal system in the modern period was itself the effect of collective learning. This learning process started at the level of the everyday practice of life in those associations which in time came to form the Enlightenment-bourgeois emancipation movement or the early modern social movement. The destruction of aristocratic privilege, authority, power and force by this movement in turn served as presupposition for the legal realisation of those modern universalistic principles of freedom, equality and discourse which had already been developed and given effect in everyday practices.

Drawing insights from the work of Miller and Eder, I (Strydom 1987) argued that one should not allow oneself to be misled by Habermas's frequent references to social movements in the context of his theory of social evolution since he by the very choice of theoretical strategy assigns them only a secondary or derivative role. While he indeed speaks of 'social movements as learning processes' (Habermas 1979a: 125; 1985b: 79-117), he does not dispose over an adequate conception of the social or collective nature of the learning involved in such contexts, with the result that he confines social movements to the level of the selective stabilisation of latently available cultural potentialities. At best, social movements are conceived in terms of institutional innovations rather than being appreciated as also playing a crucial part in the generation of new learning abilities and knowledge and in the constitution of collective interpretative systems.

Were one to encapsulate in a single formula the arguments advanced in the recent literature in criticism of Habermas's general theory of society from the viewpoint of the study of social movements, then the expression 'the ontogenetic fallacy' (Strydom 1992) readily suggests itself. It is undoubtedly the case that Habermas's failure to deal in a theoretically adequate manner with the phenomenon of social movements can be led back to his mistaken twofold projection of the developmental-logical structure of the ontogenetic learning process onto society. On the one hand, the ontogenetic fallacy consists in drawing a conclusion from ontogenesis in respect of the change and development of culture or collective symbolic systems which can be accounted for only with reference to supra-individual learning processes —an error that can be overcome by the introduction of the concept of social or collective learning processes. On the other, the ontogenetic fallacy is committed when one transfers the ontogenetic model to the level of evolution —an error the correction of which requires that the theory of social evolution be radically freed from the universal historical and general societal frame over which it had been stretched since the ascendancy of the so-called 'phylocultural complex' (Sinha 1988: 77-110) round the turn from the 19th to the 20th century.

Considering the immanent critique of Habermas, it becomes apparent that White's emphasis on Habermas's communicative model without regard for its systematic extension by the theory of social evolution amounts to an attempt to present Habermas's theory of action in a neutral manner. From the start, this strategy is bound to end in failure since the social theorist is confronted by a basic alternative at the point of transposing the theory of action into the theory of society. Whereas Habermas chooses the abstract dualistic model of lifeworld and system which loses touch with social movements, his critics demonstrate in different ways that an alternative hermeneutically sensitive model which is capable of dealing with the historical and institutional dimensions is necessary were one to make progress on a theoretically informed study of social movements (see Saretzki 1988). In addition to this spectacle of attempting to both have his cake and eat it, there is also a touch of irony in White's (1988: 123) appeal to Jean Cohen in support of his claim that Habermas's communicative model represents the best available framework for the study of social movements. There is, of course, no doubt about the fact that Cohen (1982, 1985; Cohen and Arato 1992), as a critical theorist, sympathetically seeks to secure the strengths of Habermas's position, but what White does not appreciate is the more specific context into which her work fits. He thus fails to notice that Cohen's reservations about Habermas's work stem from exactly the same foundation as the critique reviewed above, but which in her case eventuates in the formulation of the theory of civil society.[2]

3. POINTERS TOWARD A NEW CRITICAL THEORETICAL APPROACH TO SOCIAL MOVEMENTS

In the present context, it is not possible to go in any detail into the respective strategies developed by the above-mentioned authors with a view to overcoming the impediments Habermas's version of critical theory places in the way of the study of social movements. For the purpose of preparing the ground for a critical consideration of the conflicting interpretations of Habermas's position on the new social movements put forward by White, on the one hand, and the younger generation of critical theorists, on the other, I propose to venture a brief circumscription of those strategies that relate directly to the problem of social movements.

In order to circumvent the pernicious implications of Habermas's reconstructed version of historical materialism, Arnason early on suggested the introduction of an alternative praxis theoretical position which operates with the conception of a 'pluri-dimensional and open-textured' (1979: 217) social process involving both a more than merely instrumental or purposive-rational notion of the appropriation of nature and a notion of association admitting of alternative practical projects. As regards the latter aspect, Arnason (1988: 271, 275-276, 280-281) in a later work insists that Habermas's universal pragmatic communication model, emphasising consensual principles and obligatory action orientations as it does, cannot conclusively put to rest the conflict of interpretations which in modern society typically results in competing sociocultural projects, such as for instance the mastery of nature, democracy, autonomy, national collective identity and revolution —all of which nevertheless share an interpretative horizon. To be adequate, the study of social movements must be able to take into account such alternative projects. This requires that Habermas's interpretation of the modern structures of consciousness and hence practical reason be detranscendentalised or *de-apriorised* to a degree he does not seem willing to countenance.

As against Habermas's two-level model which focuses on an abstract process of social conflict between lifeworld and system and interprets it with reference to general knowledge about the conditions of domination-free communication, Honneth (1985, 1989, 1991), indeed, accepts the same initial communication theoretical premises as Habermas, but then proposes the introduction of an alternative model according to which society is seen as an institutionally mediated communicative relation among different culturally integrated groups which assumes its form in the medium of social struggle for so long as the social disposition over power is asymmetrically distributed. In the latter case, where practical struggles over the institutionalisation of a legitimate form of organization for society shift to the foreground, it is no longer a matter of general knowledge about abstract conditions that counts, but rather concrete knowledge of suffered domination and felt injustice which calls forth insight into the limits of a societal communicative relation. In Honneth's (1985: 305-6) view, moreover, the moral dynamics borne by practical exchanges and conflicts is less well served by a critique of functional reason induced by the lifeworld-system model, as represented by Habermas, than by a critique of power which makes available knowledge about specific forms of domination and thus helps to keep the process of the formation of society in motion by facilitating the elimination of socially rooted communication blockages and barriers.

In a recent work, Rödel and Frankenberg joined by Helmut Dubiel (1989) start from a positive identification with Habermas's theory of modernity as a post-traditional theory of politics, but then criticise the democratic theoretical implications of his work. Focusing on the marked difference between the early and the later Habermas, they accept the concept of democracy as having to do with human self-determination, but are sceptical of the appropriation and integration of functionalist assumptions and the overextended rejection of the philosophy of consciousness. Their critique is thus of a twofold nature. On the one hand, Habermas's shift toward functionalism leads to a 'normative sobriety' and willingness to make '"*realpolitische*" concessions' (1989: 156-7) and, on the other, the strictures against the philosophy of consciousness result in an inadequate treatment of the concept of public sphere (1989: 162). In so far as Habermas's theory of politics assumes that the state administration is under present conditions no longer subject to the necessity of the symbolic reproduction of institutions, Rödel, Frankenberg and Dubiel regard his functionalism as unacceptable. And in so far as Habermas's overreaction against the philosophy of consciousness entices him to hollow out the concept of the public sphere, they insist on the need to give positive content to it. This could be done by recognising that in their social perceptions human beings regard themselves as nodal points in a network of meaningful relations which make possible the imagination of relevant topics, themes, forms of discourse and even of the societal totality.

Measured against his initially close association with Habermas, Eder took a number of quite drastic steps during the 1980s to break with and revise the theory of social evolution and hence the theory of society he had shared with the former. Included here is the development of a theoretical approach not only to social movements, in general, but also to the new social movements, in particular. Of all the authors discussed thus far, he in fact goes furthest in formulating and realising such a programme. In what is to follow, therefore, we will have to return to his contribution to the study of social movements.

As regards breaking with Habermas, Eder first replaced the psychologically inspired distinction between developmental logic and developmental dynamics by the theory of the self-production of society, borrowed from Touraine, which represents the application of the constructivist perspective at the macro-level and is referred to as 'the theory of praxis' (Eder 1988: 256-7, 291-3, 300, 301). This was done in order to fill a categorial gap he discovers in Habermas's theory under the influence of Pierre Bourdieu's theory of practice, namely the gap left by Habermas's concentration on the *opus operatum* in the sense of the effects of evolutionary changes to the detriment of the *modus operandi* in the sense of evolutionary changes and their mechanisms. The theoretical significance of this is that society is conceived from the viewpoint not of social order but rather of the contradictory and ambivalent process of the creation of social order —which means to say, from the perspective of social movements. Second, Eder introduces a sharp distinction between ontogenetic and collective learning, on the one hand, and social evolution, on the other, in order to eliminate Habermas's confusion of development and evolution and thus to break the hold developmental logic has over evolution in the latter's work (Eder 1988: 303, 313, 316-7). This strategy represents a theoretical gain in that it allows an appreciation of the contribution of social movements not only to the constitution of collective systems of interpretation and to changes in the constitutive structures of society, but at the same time also supports a critical awareness of the discrepancy between the potential made available by collective learning and the selective use made of it in the actual organization of society.[3] Finally, Eder radically frees the theory of social evolution from the universal historical and general societal frame within which it is confined by Habermas, with a view to avoiding the untenable causal assumptions, schematisations, classifications and ideological implications to be found in the latter's work (Eder 1988: 33, 69, 165, 291, 325, 374) and thus making room for the phenomenon of social movements.

The various criticisms and positive pointers put forward by the younger generation of critical theorists do not merely correct Habermas's treatment of social movements as being of secondary importance as a result of his developmental-logical theory of social evolution and the related structuralistically backed idealistic view of institutionalisation. At the same time, they add up to at least a heuristic outline of a new differentiated critical theoretical approach to the concrete study of social movements. It is against the background of this outline that White's interpretation of Habermas's position on the new social movements appears as inadequate in many respects.

4. CONFLICTING INTERPRETATIONS OF THE NEW SOCIAL MOVEMENTS

Apart from his basic assumption that Habermas's research programme does not marginalise social movements, which is disproved by the immanent critique of the latter's theory of society, White advances a number of claims and interpretations of Habermas's position which invite comparison with the latest critical theoretical analysis of the new social movements. Before starting, however, it should be pointed out that what White (1988: 133) perceptively calls 'the two most fundamental lines of criticism which have been directed against Habermas's overall account of reason and modernity', is precisely what is articulated by the latest critical theoretical development —but with this difference, compared to the fashionable post-modernist point of view, that the critical theoretical developments neither discount the centrality of the problem of reason *tout court* nor entail the unqualified rejection of modernity in favour of postmodernity. To the extent that these new developments, however critical of Habermas, remain within the framework of critical theory, they therefore represent an immanent critique of his theoretical position. The two lines of criticism White has in mind are 'on the one hand, that Western structures of consciousness which privilege a cognitive-instrumental relation with outer nature, are ultimately to blame for environmental destruction' and, 'on the other hand, that such structures are intimately involved in the subjection of inner nature: an atrophying of our aesthetic-expressive capacities' (White 1988: 134). Like Habermas, White sees these criticisms as devolving on assumptions which ultimately derive from an indefensible subjectivist philosophy. But as against this position, it must be insisted that this is not necessarily the case. The current immanent critique of Habermas, at least, does not entail recourse without more ado to the philosophy of consciousness or of the subject, but in fact involves an elaboration of the critical theory of society which gets distorted in certain respects and covered over in others by Habermas's overly philosophical approach. At issue, indeed, are the concepts of reason and modernity.

The most convenient starting point for a critical consideration of White's (1988: 124) presentation is offered by his assertion that Habermas's theory provides the best available framework for explaining why the new social movements have arisen. According to his account, this explanation consists of linking the emergence of the new social movements as a defencive reaction to the increasing colonisation of the lifeworld by the encroaching bureaucratic state and capitalist economy. Since such colonisation represents a threat to and erosion of the social integration of society, Cohen (1985: 710) is justified in interpreting this explanation as a revival of the classical Durkheimian 'breakdown thesis'. She considers this thesis as an objectionable genetic explanation of social movements that is best avoided by developing sensitivity for the internal differentiation and plural nature of social movements. If one inquires a bit more deeply into its form, it becomes apparent that this rather crude explanation is moreover of the linear type in so far as it presupposes a developmental perspective according to which a historically new situation and concurrent structural problems give rise to a qualitatively new phenomenon such as the new social movements (Brand 1982: 50). As such, it contrasts not only with the equally rough cyclical explanation put forward by for example Peter Berger and associates (1974: 163-91) according to which the new social movements are nothing but a pendulum-like reactive reappearance of age-old anti-modern discontent and protest aimed at de-modernizing society, but also with the promising synthetic sociological theory of social movements at which one arrives when one combines the linear and cyclical approaches in a reflexive move such that the complementarities of both are incorporated into a dynamic theory focusing on the construction of society as an inherently contradictory and ambivalent process.[4]

From the perspective of such a more complex synthetic theory, the history of modernity is not merely the linear history of major progressive social movements such as the Enlightenment-bourgeois emancipation movement and the labour movement. It is rather the highly involved history of the dialectical interrelations of such major social movements and the social counter-movements which ran concurrently with and opposed them, such as the early Romantic, the Socialist Utopian, Anarchist and avant-garde art movements. Whereas the major movement, characteristic of a particular epoch, pitted an alternative project against the dominant modernising elite, the corresponding social counter-movements were not only against the modernising elite but, while in general being on the side of the alternative project, at the same time also countered the major social movement. They drew their cultural resources from a counter-model which was directed against the dominant modern trend represented by modernising elite and major social movement alike. And far from having been irrational or regressive *tout court*, as is assumed by both the linear and the cyclical approaches, such counter-movements were also concerned with the construction and defence of aspects of modernity which were screened out or even suppressed by the major movements. To that extent they were thus involved in endeavours to realise a different or an alternative modernity. Although not focusing on rational questions in the customary sense of the word, for instance emancipation, freedom or justice, they were by no means simply irrational and hence do not serve as a basis for counter-Enlightenment claims. Rather, the social counter-movements were concerned with the aesthetic-expressive foundations of society, the basic but taken-for-granted relation that social human beings establish with their world which has an elementary structuring effect on their rational, be it cognitive-instrumental or normative commitments.

In contradistinction to the assumption of a difference between traditionalism and modernity or the old and the new from which both the linear and cyclical approaches proceed, the notion of the 'dialectic of social movement and social counter-movement' (Eder 1988: 259)[5] with which the reflexive synthetic theory operates, appreciating the contradictory and ambivalent nature of the new as it does, rests on the distinction between dominant modernity and suppressed modernity. It is interesting to note that while Habermas's linear approach leads him to lose sight of social counter-movements in favour of concentrating exclusively on the major movements, he is at times compelled to reintroduce the dialectical vision, such as for instance in the form of the somewhat too abstract reflexive figure of 'the self-critique of the Enlightenment which is as old as the Enlightenment itself' (Habermas 1988c: 63). In addition to differentiating modernity into dominant and suppressed aspects, however, the synthetic theory also avoids an overemphasis on either cognitive (in the narrow sense) or normative orientation complexes by recognising the significant structuring effect the aesthetic-expressive foundations of society have on explicitly rational orientation complexes (Eder 1988: 38, 100, 103-222, 276, 279).[6]

The important point is now that the same stereoscopic view that is presented here of the old social movements and their respective social counter-movements must be applied also to the new social movements (Eder 1988: 229, 251-2, 260, 265-6, 268-82). No amount of sympathetic reading or constructive interpretation can conceal the fact, however, that Habermas's account of the new social movements does not nearly approach anything of this kind. This is borne out by White's presentation. On the one hand, Habermas's position remains essentially confined to a linear theoretical framework, notwithstanding a positive move in the direction of identifying the inherent ambiguity of modern institutions,[7] and, on the other, it remains single-mindedly focused on normative, particularly moral-political, orientations.

As regards the first point, Habermas's typology of the new social movements is particularly telling, something on which White has little to say apart from noting that Habermas's theory allows the drawing of a 'useful distinction' (1988: 124-5) between religious fundamentalism and the new social movements and unconsciously taking up Habermas's positive bias towards the feminist movement (1988: 142-3). Locating the new social movements strictly within the modern context, Habermas (1981b; 1987a: 393-6) bases his typology on the distinction between offencive or emancipation and defencive or resistance movements, the former being exemplified by the feminist movement in continuation of the classical bourgeois and socialist emancipation movements and the latter by the new social movements. Within the latter category, he introduces the subcategories of movements defending property and status, such as the middle class defending neighbourhoods against for example large-scale technical projects, parents protesting against educational arrangements for their children and tax protests, which on the whole are of less importance, and the new social movements proper, namely the particularistic defencive movements which take the form of resistance and retreat aimed at building a dyke against the encroaching forces of money and bureaucratic power emanating from the economic-administrative system. While these latter movements, focusing on green problems, complexity problems and more generally the overburdening of communicative infrastructures, are of interest to Habermas in so far as they form the core of what he calls the 'new conflict potential' (1987a: 394) and, in particular, facilitate a change in orientation from the old to the new politics, he adopts an ambivalent and indeed quite pessimistic attitude towards them. In his estimation, they at the same time also exhibit a high degree of 'confusion' (1987a: 396) and entertain a crude conception of rationality or, at least, show little understanding of communicative rationality.

It is not without reason, then, that Cohen (1985: 710-11) regards Habermas as considering it as not very likely that they would be able to transcend their particularism so as to become carriers of a progressive rationalisation process. Taking her to task for this, White asserts by contrast that, however implicitly, Habermas not only regards these 'new social movements as the best hope for a more "balanced" institutionalisation of the potential of modernity', but also appreciates 'the emergence of alternative practices in which there is an enhancement of the moral-practical and aesthetic-expressive dimensions of everyday social life', and, indeed, 'sees........the utopian...concept [of a] balanced use of the potential of cultural modernity...as grounded in some of the practices and ideas of the new social movements' (1988: 126-7, 138, 139). Earlier I have argued that this is not Habermas's position and, in fact, that his theoretical framework precludes this from becoming his position. In any case, not only for theoretical but also for political reasons, he would be unwilling to accept the claim that he entertains a utopia of a balanced society which is grounded in the practices of the new social movements. While the new social movements are potentially rational, within the context of the 'new obscurity' (Habermas 1986c) they may turn out to have the opposite impact. This becomes clear in view of Eder's (1989b) assessment that the new social movements represent a petit-embourgeoisment (*Verkleinbürgerlichung*). After all, National Socialism was also an attempt to replace bourgeois with petit-bourgeois culture. Eder (1989b: 543) interprets the new obscurity as a bourgeois reaction to precisely this late 20th-century development. This explains why Habermas (1987a: 393) locates feminism in the tradition of the classical emancipation movements, which further shows the inadequacy of his typology. In fact, the dialectics of movement and counter-movement applies also to the feminist movement—a movement consisting of various branches, the most important of which are not necessarily the ones fighting for equal rights.

This brings us to the second critical point, namely Habermas's single-minded focus on normative, particularly moral-political orientations. This normative overemphasis, to be sure, makes it virtually impossible for Habermas to deal adequately with the new social movements. In his interpretation, White tends to further exaggerate this emphasis. According to him, Habermas approaches the new social movements from the viewpoint of what he refers to as 'the enhancement of the new moral-political orientation: a communicative-ethical one associated...with distinctive understandings of universality, equality and tolerance' (1988: 139). The continued urgency of this long-standing issue does not take away from the fact, however, that recent developments concern a different issue, namely, the aesthetic-expressive one.[8] Like Habermas, White (1988: 138-9) refers to the 'aesthetic-expressive dimension of everyday life' and to the 'necessity for more flexible need interpretations', but they both do so from a restrictive viewpoint that remains stuck in the problem of normatively regulated participation belonging to an earlier level of development. It is for this reason that they cannot come to terms with the problem of the aesthetic-expressive foundations of society (Eder 1988: 275; Münch 1984: 119-26; Frank 1988: 63-4, 1989: 590-607). By focusing on the theory of forms of understanding —that is, the centrepiece of the theory of communicative action which mediates between universal pragmatics and the theory of evolution, something which White neglects —Arnason (1988: 266-81) demonstrated that Habermas overemphasises consensual principles and obligations to such an extent that he restricts the potentialities of modernity to one particular interpretation. As a result, alternative projects are automatically screened out. It is a matter of creating space not just for communicative action beyond the economic-administrative system, but also for expressivity beyond communicative action in the particular Habermasian sense. As long as this is ignored, it remains impossible to deal with today's most challenging problem and with the most radical of the new social movements. Over and above the institutionalisation of science and the business enterprise, on the one hand, and law and the political public sphere, on the other, these movements are concerned with the institutional possibilities of an expressive form of life and their implications for the rationalisation of society.

Considering this one-sided emphasis, it is pretentious to claim, as do White and many of Habermas's followers, that Habermas's position is 'a significant advance over the views of Foucault...[in so far as]...Habermas's model identifies common elements in new social movements which at least offer the promise of grounds for dialogue and collective action between them...beyond...particularistic and local resistance to normalization' (White 1988: 142). Not without justification, Foucault could be regarded as being equally able to isolate shared elements in the new social movements, yet very different ones than Habermas. It is not a matter of Foucault ineptly fumbling towards the normative foundations of society. Far from being concerned with the Kantian question in social theory, Foucault confronts the new problem of the creative activity of social groups as collective actors —what he calls the 'insurrection of subjugated knowledges' (1980: 81)[9] to which the aesthetic-expressive moment is crucial. While he admittedly does not provide a worked out position, under current conditions Foucault's approach may well be more relevant to an analysis of this novel aspect of the new social movements than Habermas's normative emphasis in his interpretation of modernity. The broader perspective beyond Habermas implied here can be clarified by briefly considering the innovations that social movements introduced in the course of the history of modernity.

Instead of determining the novelty of the new social movements from an historical perspective resulting in a sequence of movements in which the latest in time represents the new, a sociological perspective operating with an evolutionary distinction between the old and new (Eder 1988: 225-82) opens up an entirely different approach. It regards social movements in terms of what is variously called their 'practical rationality' (Eder 1988) or 'cognitive praxis' (Eyerman and Jamison 1991: 45), including their social practices, systems of interpretation and goals. In these terms, those movements are new that transcend the cultural content which the dominant forces of modernity seek to embody institutionally. This means that those practices, interpretations and goals are new which constitute a counter-society or an alternative modernity and, hence, could be incorporated in modern society only at the price of a more or less drastic evolutionary change. By contrast with the historically new which simply coincides with the latest, the evolutionarily new can thus be something historically old. Alternative practices and ideas repeat themselves in the course of history, emerging at one point and then disappearing as though being dead, only to reappear unexpectedly at a later date.

Today, neither the political question articulated by the classical emancipation movement nor the social question raised by the labour movement is radical any longer, since freedom and justice, although not yet fully realised, already have had a significant transformative impact on society. The truly new question now is that of nature and our relation to it. This is what concerns the new social movements and separates them from the old movements. Counter-movements have focused on the question of nature for the last three centuries, but only with the emergence of the new social movements has this question finally become a major concern. Now for the first time it would seem to have a chance of becoming the major point of orientation for societal developmental processes. This new problem confronts contemporary society with the alternatives of either continuing the mastery of nature, while perhaps building into it awareness of its negative consequences and a willingness to take corrective action, or of a radical evolutionary change on the basis of a non-exploitative relation to nature.

It comes as no surprise that in his explication of Habermas's position White remains throughout oblivious of this evolutionary option. Habermas's normative emphasis does not allow the specificity of the new social movements to be seriously addressed.

In so far as these movements are concerned with the question of nature rather than the political or social question, they are shifting the emphasis to a particular subset of the cultural or cognitive-symbolic foundations of society[10] —the traditionally so-called 'aesthetic' or what could also be called the conative foundations —and thus bring what is taken-for-granted out into the open, making it available for reflection, questioning, revision and change. Generally speaking, the cognitive-symbolic foundations of a collectively shared world refer to the basic orientations people representing different and even opposing forces in society have in common. The 'moral-political' or normative orientation that Habermas and, with him, White have in mind also belongs here but represents a different subset than the currently relevant aesthetic or conative one. This latter subset can be clarified by expanding on the terminology already introduced.

According to a widely used threefold classification of culture (e.g. Parsons 1964; Worsley 1984; Habermas 1984a, 1987a; Bourdieu 1986), the aesthetic-expressive or conative domain of experience, emotion and truthfulness contrasts with the cognitive (in the narrow sense) and the normative domains.[11] Relating these cultural dimensions to the social movements of modern times brings the specificity of the new social movements sharply into focus. The classical emancipation movement in struggling with the political problem succeeded in the realisation of rights which allowed the legitimate efflorescence of the capitalist economy and the mobilisation of science and technology for that purpose. By raising the social problem, the labour movement was able to introduce normative considerations which tamed capitalism by placing limitations on the unrestricted use of knowledge, science and technology. The new social movements grapple with the problem of nature and are concomitantly posing questions about the conative underpinnings of modern society, thus problematising what motivates people, what meanings are being pursued and ultimately what human needs are being fulfilled. What I propose to call 'endeetics'[12] —that is, whatever pertains to human needs —is therefore a central problematic brought to the fore by the new social movements.

The endeetic field can be socially located and elucidated by aligning the threefold classification of culture with the societal dimensions of production, distribution and consumption. Karl Marx (1974: 88-94)[13] already distinguished these latter dimensions, but whereas he concentrated on production and took into account also distribution, he regarded consumption as falling outside society, being something that refers to the individual and his or her natural needs. In the same sense that the new social movements are concerned with the conative rather than with the cognitive or the normative, they focus on consumption rather than on production or distribution. The point that emerges from this is that there is no such thing as natural individual needs since all needs are collective cognitive-symbolic constructions. This is basically what the new social movements are concerned with: bringing about a change in the elementary cultural structures underpinning modern society, thus redefining the boundary between society and non-society, between culture and nature and transforming our human social relationship to and appropriation of nature. Central to their endeavour, therefore, is the identification of what counts as authentic needs under contemporary conditions. Expressed in Habermas's (1979a: 2-3, 1984a: 36-42) terms, for them it is a matter neither of truth nor of correctness, but rather of truthfulness.

It is from this viewpoint of authentic needs that the new social movements open up the possibility of a new kind of critique. It is neither a critique of ideology nor a critique of instrumental reason and even less a critique of functionalist reason, as in the case of Marx, Horkheimer and Habermas respectively, but rather an aesthetic social critique[14] or what I propose to call endeetic critique. This critique is directed at what is unquestioningly taken for granted in modern society, namely an exploitative relation to nature, and hence at the endeetic foundations of economics, politics, labour and social life in general —that is, foundations as determined by the prevailing definition of human needs. The outcome of this critique is the question of authentic needs which can be answered neither by science nor by the political institutions since it concerns what we really want, how we really want to live, what kind of a society we really desire, what we would really find good, and so forth. It is in this sense that the continuation of the rationalisation of modern culture and society today depends crucially on our ability to draw out the practical implications of the thrust towards the institutionalisation of an expressive form of life and to develop what amounts to an endeetic critique.

The interpretation of the new social movements as most radically being engaged in transforming the cultural foundations of society throws light on the limits of White's (1988: 123-5) account of what is at issue. According to him, the most characteristic feature of the new social movements is their defencive and self-limiting radicalism in the sense that they 'do not support totalistic revolutionary programs, either for generating a traditional revolutionary ideology or for smashing the institutions of capitalism' (125). The fact that the new social movements are not 'collective revolutionary subjects speaking in the name of all of society and seeking to take over the economy and polity' (123), however, does not diminish the radical quality of their expressive revolution.[15] To the extent that they are concerned with the question of nature, the new social movements are more offencive and totalising than Habermas and many of his interpreters seem to think. To be sure, Habermas's negative image of the new social movements as being involved in an 'unending border conflict' between lifeworld and system[16] could be corrected and their potential as 'carriers of a [new] collective identity' (White 1988: 126, 139) could be recognised, but only by giving up the limiting theoretical premises. Given the inherent ambivalence of the new social movements, however, their rational potential on the aesthetic-expressive level makes it all the more imperative that we be aware of their potential for irrationality on the normative or moral-political level.

The basic issue in the critical theoretical study of the new social movements, then, is whether it is possible to answer the question of nature in the sense of establishing a new non-exploitative relation to nature without having to put up with a decrease in the rational qualities of political culture.

5

Contemporary Social Evolutionary Theory: A New European Rapprochement

The history of the theory of social evolution, which is punctuated by debate and controversy, presents a graphic profile that is best captured by the word 'vicissitudes'. Historically, the changes of fortune of social evolutionary theory are truly remarkable (e.g. Bock, 1978; Flew 1984), and today we are once again on the brink of a crucial juncture.

Against the background of early social evolutionism and the subsequent incorporation of evolutionary theory in biology, authors such as Karl Marx (1976), Herbert Spencer (1893) and Emile Durkheim (1964) sociologically adapted evolutionary ideas. Due largely to Spencer's contribution in the imperialist Victorian context, this classical line of development eventually culminated in social Darwinism, that morally and politically despicable intellectual scourge which was to a large extent responsible for discrediting evolutionary theory (Hofstadter 1955; Jones 1980; Francis 1981). It is in the wake of this latter development that such alternative expressions as 'social process' and 'social change' or the currently fashionable 'social transformation' were increasingly more widely used. After some twenty to thirty years following its decline and demise during the period between 1890 and 1930, however, the theory of evolution underwent a partial revival due to the fact that theories of progress, change and transformation by their very nature left important unavoidable theoretical questions in abeyance. Initially, this revival took the form of a faithful reproduction of 19th century social evolutionism, as in the case of Childe (1947, 1951), McIver and Page (1949) and White (1959). Soon afterward, however, the introduction of variations, particularly ones inspired by functionalism, led to the emergence of neo-classical social evolutionism in the 1960s and 70s, represented by Talcott Parsons (1961, 1964b, 1966, 1971) and Niklas Luhmann (1976, 1982, 1985) as well as on somewhat different premises by Jürgen Habermas (1979a, 1979b). The subsequent critique of the neo-classical assumption of developmentalism (e.g. Abercrombie 1972; Granovetter 1979; Touraine 1981; Giesen and Lau 1981; Schmid 1982a, 1982b; Giddens 1984; Eder 1988; Burns and

Dietz 1992a; Strydom 1992) shared by these major authors, irrespective of whether in the form of structural differentiation and functional specialisation, the increase of system complexity or the rationalisation of lifeworld communication, simultaneously pointed in two different directions. Not only did the critique coincide in the 1980s with a continuing renaissance of evolutionary theory in a wide range of disciplines, including sociology, largely based on the new Darwinian-Mendelian synthetic theory (e.g. Toulmin 1972; Campbell 1974; van den Berghe 1978; Harris 1979; Weick 1979; Giesen 1980; Giesen and Lau 1981; van Parijs 1981; Schmid 1982a; Plotkin 1982; Nelson and Winter 1982; Lopreato 1984; Schmid and Wuketits 1987). At the same time, it also provided a starting point for a more or less vociferous and widely noted denial of the relevance and outright rejection of the theory of social evolution from both an immanent sociological (Touraine 1981; Giddens 1984) and a transcendent postmodernist (Lyotard 1983) point of view.

It is the co-existence of these two contrary trends in contemporary sociology that accounts for the peculiar situation that, whereas a large number —if not the majority —of sociologists today apparently find evolution an anachronistic and unpalatable topic meriting no consideration at all, important developments in the theory of social evolution have taken place during the past few decades and are still ongoing. In this essay, I propose to focus on one of these developments, indeed, one of the most significant developments which have thus far nevertheless gone completely unnoticed. What I want to demonstrate is the emergence of a new European rapprochement among three distinct strands of social evolutionary theory during the late 1980s and 1990s: the situation-theoretical position of Klaus Eder, the selection-theoretical position of Bernard Giesen, and the rule system-theoretical position of Tom Burns and Thomas Dietz.[1] In this context, Eder's position has undergone by far the most extensive and noteworthy change, and the theoretical dynamics connecting it to the remaining positions make it pivotal to the new European rapprochement.[2] Theoretically, the overriding point is that this rapprochement points toward the availability of a new and more adequate version of the sociological theory of evolution at the beginning of the 21st century —what may be conceived as a post-classical theory of evolution.

1. THREE EUROPEAN STRANDS OF SOCIAL EVOLUTIONARY THEORY

In the context of the revitalisation of evolutionary theory in the social sciences in the 1970s and 80s (Schmid and Wuketits 1987), three distinct European strands of sociological theory gradually made their appearance.

The first is the German Habermasian (or Starnberg) school of which Klaus Eder is a representative;[3] the second is the German Darwinian school represented by Bernard Giesen and collaborators of his such as Michael Schmid and Christoph Lau; and the third is the Swedish Uppsala school represented by Tom Burns and Thomas Dietz and an associate of theirs such as Fredrick Buttel. Both the former two theoretical developments go back to the 1970s, with the internationally better known Habermasian strand being the older of the two, while the third, which is of a more recent origin, attracted attention in published form only in the early 1990s. Since their original appearance, both the two German strands have undergone some change. While Giesen has sought to respond to criticism of the Darwinian approach in sociology by giving greater emphasis to communication and culture, Eder's work gives evidence of a very remarkable change entailing among other things the surprising incorporation of the Darwinian model instead of the developmental-logical model. This thoroughgoing and far-reaching change has likewise been stimulated by criticism, indeed, a diversity of criticisms of the Habermasian theory of evolution. In fact, it is interesting that mutual criticism and influence played a central role in the development and transformation of Eder and Giesen's respective theoretical projects. Although no references to these latter two authors are to be found in the published writings of the somewhat more American oriented Uppsala school, Burns[4] and Dietz's basic awareness of both the Darwinian and the Habermasian traditions provides evidence that their theory shares a common context with the two German strands and has a subterranean link with them.

In the following paragraphs, I offer a brief contextual characterisation of each of these three strands of contemporary social evolutionary theory. This preliminary step is aimed at preparing the ground to bring out the points of contact and relations among the strands and to demonstrate a certain significant convergence of the three —what I call the new European rapprochement. Since I see the thoroughgoing, self-critical change in Eder's thinking[5] as being at the core of the theoretical dynamics informing this rapprochement, the next step requires that a fairly detailed reconstruction be offered of the development and change of Eder's theory of evolution in relation to the other two strands. Against this background, it will then be possible finally to concisely highlight the convergence among these three versions of evolutionary theory.

The Habermasian School

Klaus Eder's evolutionary theory originated within the framework of Habermas's (1979a) programme to reconstruct historical materialism by correcting its one-sided economic emphasis through the inclusion of the cultural dimension conceived as the spearhead of social evolution. Essential to this endeavour was the reconceptualisation of the stage-bound development of the forces of production in terms of cognitive and especially moral ontogenesis and, by extension, the development of normative structures and the rationalisation of lifeworld communication. According to this view, instrumental and strategic learning in the context of the forces of production are allowed to advance in the first instance through cultural innovation and the concomitant unfolding of the structures of collectively shared worldviews and the consequent change of social institutions. This original idea and innovative core of the programme was located within what Habermas (1979a: 95-129) conceived as the homological relation between ontogenesis and social evolution which he understood as turning on structures or rules whose transformation could be reconstructed in terms of how succeeding configurations logically presupposed preceding ones. It is this theoretical synthesis that enabled him to put forward a reconstructive developmental-logical theory of social evolution.

While Eder's theory of evolution gives evidence of the retention of comparable concerns (1973, 1976, 1977, 1982, 1983, 1983/84, 1984, 1985a), the development of his theory (1986, 1987, 1988, 1992, 1996a), while often stimulated by external critiques, is to a large extent a response to the inherent problems of the Habermasian programme. Despite Habermas's emphasis on communication and discourse theory, the theoretical assumption of a homology between individual cognitive and collective cultural structures above all precluded the possibility of a constructive process of relation formation and hence the phenomenon of the emergence of new structures. From early on, therefore, Eder was confronted with the problem of having to give communication, discursive processes, collective learning and conflict a centrality they did not and, indeed, could not attain heretofore. Instead of a global structural model, a general logical taxonomic perspective and the central mode of integration of societies, he was compelled to develop a focus that is more sensitive to both particularities and dynamics. By contrast with the generalising and unifying impetus of such notions as homology and ontogenetic developmental logic, several distinctions had to be introduced, while the relations between different levels had to be loosened or dimensions even had to be separated from one another.

The overall thrust of supplementing individual learning with collective learning, of restricting the ontogenetic model to the individual, of jettisoning the Spencerian view of universal history, of separating learning and evolution, and of stressing in particular public communication and discourse, including discursive conflict, as a vehicle of the construction of reality, was a thoroughgoing and far-reaching transformation not only of Habermas's but also of Eder's own evolutionary theory. This transformation followed a trajectory marked at its extremes by his initial developmentalism and his current situationalism.

The Darwinian School

Bernhard Giesen (Giesen and Schmid 1975; Giesen 1980a, 1980b) originally introduced his theory of evolution against the general background of the post-positivist turn in the philosophy of science in which, for instance, Stephen Toulmin (1972), who put forward a Darwinian theory of conceptual change, played an important part. The more specific foil was provided by the failure of classical systems theory to deal with deep-seated structural change and the unsatisfactory reaction to revert to individual historical descriptions of a structuralist or configurationalist kind instead. In the context of the search for a theory that was able to compensate for these deficient alternatives, Giesen regarded linear, progressive evolutionist theories such as, for instance, the developmental-logical theory of the representatives of the Habermasian school, as his closest opponent. His consistent critique of Eder over the course of many years becomes intelligible in this context (Giesen 1980a: 324, 1980b: 219, 1983: 252; Giesen and Schmid 1975: 411; Giesen and Lau 1981: 252, 253).

Borrowing the 'elementary grammar' (Giesen and Schmid 1975: 394) of evolutionary theory from biology, Giesen developed a position based on a sociological interpretation of the theoretical calculus of variation, selection and stabilisation (Giesen and Schmid 1975: 397-407; Giesen and Lau 1981: 234-40). It was a strictly Darwinian theory that was oriented, in particular, to Darwin's concept of selection. As such, it was a selectionist theory in terms of which social development or growth was seen as a limit case appearing only under particular conditions. This theory provided Giesen with the opportunity to apply Darwinism systematically to sociology in an attempt to integrate the different theoretical traditions which threatened to fall apart in the wake of the functionalist debate, the positivist dispute and the theoretical and methodological pluralisation of the 1960s and early 70s (Giesen 1980a: 323-8, 1980b: 76-81; Giesen and Lau 1981: 247-52). While Giesen initially submitted that Darwinian evolutionary theory represents the most general theory available (Giesen 1980a: 323, 1980b: 55), he subsequently toned down his claim by arguing that it is at best able to specify the line of questioning of various theoretical traditions and thus to mitigate the apparently irresolvable conflicts between them by facilitating inter-theoretical cooperation (Giesen and Lau 1981: 248).

Despite his intention to demonstrate the possibility of a broad and nuanced position taking into account both the micro- and macro-dimensions of social reality, Giesen ran up against difficulties at least partly because of his transferral of a formal model from biology to sociology. Although it is not a problem in principle if handled with due care, in his case it exhibited two tendencies which explain the subsequent development of his theory. On the one hand, his proposal to refer all macro-social phenomena to individual actors (e.g. Giesen and Lau 1981: 240) implied an individualistic orientation that could not fully account for the processes feeding into evolution. On the other, his central emphasis on selection betrayed a certain naturalistic orientation that could not do justice to the specificity of sociocultural evolution. These problems invited criticisms of his position as well as of the German Darwinian school more generally, including in particular sharply formulated ones by Eder (1985a: 31, 47, 495; 1988: 42, 44, 288).[6]

These criticisms, together with the more general impact of the Habermas school, led Giesen not only to incorporate the public communication dimension of the collective thematisation of social problems (1983), but also to take a much stronger interest in culture (1991a, 1991b, 1995; Giesen and Junge 1991; Giesen *et al.* 1998).[7] In his later writings, indeed, he locates what he calls 'a strictly *cultural* model of evolutionary selection' (1991a: 172) in a central position. This selection-theoretical model, which is articulated in terms of the threefold distinction among 'code' (categorial structures), 'process' (action and praxis or practical structures) and 'situation' (empirical structures and conditions), finds illuminating application in historical-sociological analyses, particularly of the collective identity formation of the German '*Kulturnation*' (Giesen 1995; Giesen and Junge 1991; Eisenstadt and Giesen 1995).[8] The basic idea here is that the uncoupling of these three moments under certain circumstances allows actions, social movements, conflicts and constructions of identities and institutions to be informed by different codes (or cultural models), with the result that competition between codes ensues which is eventually decided by selection according to situational structures and conditions.

Giesen's historical-sociological analyses in terms of this selection-theoretical model thus suggest that the general shift observable in his oeuvre can be interpreted as a redirection from a naturalistic to a culturalistic Darwinism.

The Uppsala School

The Uppsala school's version, particularly as put forward by Tom Burns and Thomas Dietz (Dietz *et al.* 1990; Burns and Dietz 1992a, 1992b;

Dietz and Burns 1992), was first introduced in the context of the revitalisation of evolutionary theory in sociology and the concurrent emergence of a new theoretical framework in the 1980s. This coincided with an efflorescence in social theory that was, on the one hand, pushed by a general discontent with classical and neo-classical tendencies favouring either a macro-sociological emphasis on teleology, over-generalisation and structural determination or a micro-sociological emphasis on action and interpretation; and, on the other, pulled by a search for comprehensive theories capable of mediating the micro- and macro-dimensions as well as structure and action or agency. Burns and Dietz (Dietz *et al.* 1990: 158, Burns and Dietz 1992a: 260-1) regard evolutionary theory as the most promising general theoretical framework or foundation for the integration of the different theoretical directions in sociology. Although they are by no means averse to historical sociology (Burns and Dietz 1997; Burns 1999), the Uppsala authors are especially interested in the relevance of evolutionary theory for the analysis of contemporary societies (Burns and Dietz 1992a: 259; 1999). For this purpose, they distance themselves from classical and neo-classical evolutionist theories, irrespective of whether of a developmental or ontogenetic kind, in order to adopt evolutionary theory instead.[9] For them, Darwinism alone is able to escape the debilitating limitations of evolutionism (Burns and Dietz 1992a: 260; Dietz and Burns 1992: 187-88).[10]

Within the space opened by the increasingly widely recognised distinction between evolutionist and evolutionary theory, however, the Uppsala authors set themselves off against both the sociological versions of the socio-biological approach (e.g. van den Berghe 1990) and the co-evolutionary approach (e.g. Lopreato 1990). Whereas socio-biology tends in a reductive direction by assuming that the social world is shaped by natural selection acting on genes, the co-evolutionary concern with the relation between genes and culture is not sociologically meaningless yet only marginally relevant (Dietz *et al.* 1990: 158-59). The nascent Darwinian approach, of which they seek to offer their own version, does not deny the importance of biology, but by contrast regards culture rather than genes as providing grist to the evolutionary mill. Consequently, the Uppsala authors give special weight to culture, social agency, social learning, institutional and cultural dynamics, and socio-cultural evolution (Dietz *et al.* 1990: 159-60; Burns and Dietz 1992a, 1992b; Dietz and Burns 1992).[11]

Since the immanent starting point of their evolutionary theory is their own rule system theory, Burns (1986; Burns and Flam 1987) and his associates locate the rules representing the basic unit of culture at the very centre of this complex of concerns.[12] Accordingly, they refer to their theory as 'evolutionary rule system theory' (Burns and Dietz 1997: 3). Adopting the Darwinian framework, Burns and Dietz understand by sociocultural evolution a number of different processes the dynamics of which have an impact on the persistence and prevalence of cultural and social rules in a given situation and thus shape manifest cultural and institutional orders.[13] These processes embrace the generation of a variety of rules, the selection of rules, and the transmission or reproduction of rules, all of which take place in a particular environment (Burns and Dietz 1992a: 263-71). Innovation or the generation of variability, which involves human agency and social learning, takes place at the micro-level.[14] This means that macro-level structures are decisively shaped by micro-level processes. On the other hand, macro-level structures in turn provide the environment within which the structural outcomes of micro-processes are selected and reproduced. The theoretical focal point of the Uppsala version of evolutionary sociology or socio-cultural Darwinism is thus the linkage between the micro- and macro-dimensions.[15]

Having offered a brief characterisation of the three theoretical strands in question, it is now possible to trace the theoretical dynamics that led to their convergence on the theoretical core of social evolutionary theory. Given the intermediate position Eder's work occupies, the convergence is followed through the changes in his theory and the concurrent connections forged with the other two strands.

2. THEORETICAL DYNAMICS AND THEORETICAL CORE: TOWARD CONVERGENCE

Eder's earliest publication on evolutionary theory dates from 1973 and was written in the context of the Max Planck Institute at Starnberg under the directorship of Habermas. As part of research proposals developed at the time, it was intended as a theoretical framework for comparative studies of historical societies. In the wake of the Habermas-Luhmann debate (Habermas and Luhmann 1971) in which he associated more strongly with the former, Eder starts from the different yet complementary positions of these two authors on the concept of evolution at the level of both general and specific evolution, and seeks to develop a more adequate 'alternative general evolutionary model' (1973: 24). At the general level making possible and delimiting the establishment of societal structures he found a complementarity between Luhmann and Habermas's respective assumptions of a universal process of the reduction of complexity and a universal process of the unfolding of formal competences. At the specific level of societal structures, Luhmann linked his functionalism to the pre-existing order of the present, whereas Habermas idealistically anticipated a future freed from domination. An analysis of the logical structure of their respective evolutionary schemes, on the one hand, led Eder to embrace both world complexity and rule competence, yet with the proviso that the presupposed evolution of operative structures as envisaged by Piaget should be explicitly included. On the other, he corrected Luhmann and Habermas's respective functionalist and idealistic vagueness by introducing the analysis of historical constellations of societal structures to determine which historical goal values proved progressive and hence of significance for general evolution. Eder's chosen theoretical strategy, which was reinforced not only by Habermas but also by Luhmann, accounts for the fact that at the outset of his career he systematically adopted a developmental-logical model rather than a Darwinian model for the purposes of elaborating the theory of evolution.

The essay under discussion marks the early stage of the cooperative endeavour between Habermas and Eder to develop a systematically worked out developmental-logical theory of sociocultural evolution that is supported by at least some comparative analyses of historical societies. In *Legitimation Crisis*, Habermas (1976: 7, note 20) appeals to this very essay as providing an outline of an adequate framework for a theory of social evolution. Eder's own thinking at this point is documented in particular by his doctoral dissertation published under the title of *Die Entstehung staatlich organisierter Gesellschaften* (1976; see also Eder 1977, 1982, 1984, and Eder and Rödel 1978). The cooperation between Habermas and Eder culminated in Habermas's book *Zur Rekonstruktion des Historischen Materialismus* (1976a), which appeared in English in somewhat different form under the title of *Communication and the Evolution of Society* (1979a). The role Eder played is indicated by Habermas's (1979a: 122, 158) avowed dependence on his historically rich evolutionary explanation of the rise of state-organised societies. Despite the fact that Eder (1976: 122, 133) made some reference to the Darwinian model in his major work of the time, his various writings from the period leave no doubt whatsoever that the Habermasian general evolutionary model was given undisputed priority. In fact, the developmental-logical theory enjoyed primacy in Eder's work throughout the 1970s and well into the 1980s. It still provided the theoretical basis of his *Habilitationsschrift* that was published as *Geschichte als Lernprozeß?* (1985a). In turn, this work proved to be the vehicle of such a consistent historical rendering of the developmental-logical theory that, besides a series of more general criticisms of representatives of the Habermasian school, including Habermas, Döbert and Eder (Giesen and Schmid 1975; Giesen 1980b; Giesen and Lau 1981; Lau 1981; Schmid 1982a, 1982b), it received a rather pointed criticism which became relatively widely shared (Ogorek 1987). It focused on the idealistically extended concept of developmental logic that led to the incorporation of learning into evolution in such a way that collective learning processes and sociocultural evolution were practically identical.

During the first phase of his evolutionary theory between 1973 and 1985, Eder drew inspiration from the developmental-logical theory for a critique of different theoretical positions. The thrust of this critique is intelligible in terms of his insistence on the necessity and significance of an internalist as against a purely externalist point of view. An adequate theoretical position must accommodate, methodologically speaking, not just the objectivistic observer perspective, but also the hermeneutic participant perspective. It must be possible to grasp the pre-theoretical knowledge of the members of society and to reconstruct the structures making possible such knowledge. In this vein, Eder (1973: 25-6) takes Luhmann to task for being unable to specify world complexity. One must know how the world is constituted prior to any knowledge about the world. Similarly, the goal state of social development cannot be defined with reference to the opportunistic or strategic reduction of complexity, as Luhmann proposes, but requires broader action competences, including the cultural and social interpretation of needs (1973: 32-4), to be taken into account. Not only Luhmann's functionalist evolutionism became an object of this form of critique, however, but also Darwinian evolutionary theory. In his work from the mid-1980s, Eder specifically targets 'sociological Darwinism' (1985a: 19-29, here 28), of which Giesen and his metatheoretical prop Schmid are leading representatives. In Eder's view, it focuses on external evolution in the sense of processes that are steered through external selection to the exclusion of internal evolution in the sense of processes that are internally regulated through the operation of cognitive structures and related individual and collective learning processes. Giesen is specifically criticised for proceeding from a behaviourist or non-cognitivist concept of learning and for at best adding *ad hoc* assumptions about sociocultural innovation to his Darwinian theory (Eder 1985a: 495, 31).[16] Were learning, particularly its cognitive and reflexive nature, by contrast incorporated systematically, then the theory of sociocultural evolution would go well beyond a strictly Darwinian position.[17]

In the light of the critical reception of *Geschichte als Lernprozeß?*, Eder was compelled to take more seriously criticisms put forward already in the early 1980s of his own work as well as that of Habermas. Of particular significance were criticisms of the developmental-logical theory formulated by Darwinian theorists from the viewpoint of evolution as a stochastic process. The most prominent among the Darwinian critics were Giesen, Schmid and Lau (Giesen 1980; Giesen and Lau 1981; Lau 1981; Schmid

1982a, 1982b). In subsequent writings, dating from the second half of the 1980s, therefore, we witness Eder engaged in a gradual process of reformulation and modification. The first step he took was to revise his habitually optimistic interpretation of social movements as playing a key part in societal developments (Eder 1986b). Rather than his initial identification with the new social movements as being central to cultural evolution, he expressly adopted an objectifying and disillusioning stance instead. The second and most obvious step he took was quite surprising, given his critique in 1985 not only of the official synthetic (i.e. Darwinian-Mendelian) theory, but also of attempts to transform it by the inclusion of epigenetics. This step consisted of a move somewhat closer to Darwinian theory by embracing the epigenetic critique of the official theory and developing the theoretical idea of 'socio-cultural epigenesis' (Eder 1987: 124). Instead of viewing it critically as being objectivistic as he did earlier, he now evaluated epigenetics as accommodating an internal point of view. Eder employed the idea of socio-cultural epigenesis, which encapsulates collective cognitive and moral learning processes and hence cultural development, in order to try to break the spell Habermas's model of developmental logic had cast over his thinking. In conjunction with the adoption of an epigenetic perspective, therefore, he sought to modify the idea of developmental logic by rejecting assumptions about innate progressivism and movement towards an end state. He even saw fit to go so far as to explicitly deny that either social relations or cultural symbols have 'a special logic' (Eder 1987: 122).[18] The concept by means of which he sought to go beyond developmental logic was that of conflict, particularly Alain Touraine's (1977, 1981) idea of conflict over cultural orientations leading the self-production of society, which was theorised in terms of Max Miller's (1986) idea of collective learning through the discursive coordination of antagonistic points of view.[19] Eder thus backtracked to the level of the constitution of society that lies behind or below developmental logic. Despite this radical stance of jettisoning developmental logic, however, at this stage he was not yet quite able to take the final step. Although being central to his argument in the publication in question, Eder's account of the relation between learning and evolution remained equivocal. On the one hand, he insisted on the necessity to 'separate' (1987: 109) learning and evolution, but on the other he continued to identify them, as when he submits that 'the specific characteristic of social evolution is that society learns' (1987: 124). It required another year for this ambivalence to become a conscious object of concern for him.

Die Vergesellschaftung der Natur (1988), which was published in English in a very different version under the title of *The Social Construction of Nature* (1996a),[20] is devoted to the development of a social evolutionary theory that studiously avoids the developmental-logical model together with its various pernicious consequences and implications. In this respect, the German Darwinian school still made its presence felt at this stage in Eder's development, although he refers to the representatives of this school only in criticism of their objectivism and naturalism (Eder 1988: 42, 44, 228). For various reasons, Eder (1988: 289, 293, 301, 318, 320, 362) is adamant that developmental-logical assumptions are unsuitable as a basis for a theory of social evolution. Theoretically, these assumptions entail the postulation of structurally available potentialities and, on that basis, the projection of ideal stages of social evolution. This is done from an unjustifiable *aprioristic* viewpoint, one beyond society that is assumed to be objective. The effect of this anachronistic theoretical choice is to neutralise evolution teleologically and thus to filter out the conditions as well as process of the constitution or the production and reproduction of society. Ultimately, then, his criticism is that developmentalism displaces both social evolution and social learning.[21]

On the question of the relation between evolution and learning, Eder now took a decisive stance, particularly in a section that has not been included in the English translation. To avoid the commission of the ontogenetic fallacy that is entailed by the extension of the developmental-logical model to evolution, Eder (1988: 313, 316, 317, 318) insists that it is crucial to observe a fundamental difference between learning and evolution and once and for all to uncouple the two from one another. Neither individual nor social learning amounts to evolution. Conversely, evolution cannot be regarded as a recapitulation of learning. A theory of learning, therefore, does not and cannot lead to a theory of evolution. Learning only provides an input into and is thus a condition of evolution.[22] For instance, learning increases the complexity of society, and complexity often yet not necessarily makes available a starting point for evolution. The crucial difference between the two, according to Eder (1988: 317, 328), resides in the fact that whereas learning concerns the ontogenetic and sociogenetic[23] development of knowledge and morality, evolution involves a change in the structural properties of the practices generating such development. It is on this basis that he envisages the elaboration of the 'theory of the social evolution of practical reason' (1988: subtitle and Part IV; 1996a: 34, 35) to which *Die Vergesellschaftung der Natur* is devoted. In a recent article, he celebrates precisely this basic achievement of his book, the separation of learning and evolution, under the suggestive title of 'Societies Learn yet the World is Hard to Change' (1999).

The idea of the social evolution of the practical reason embodied in the structural properties of the practices, whereby society is constituted, represents a significant move. It shifts the attention to the situationally generated and effective structures of rationality that for the time being fix the way in which the participants or members employ what they have learnt or practically deal with or socially make use of some relevant aspect of reality or another (Eder 1988: 263, 302, 319)—for instance, knowledge, moral representations or nature. These structural properties of practices are investigated within the practical context of generation and use (1988: 302, 304, 319, 346, 348, 376; 1996a: 50, 55). It is precisely the introduction of the practical constitution and employment or application context that allows Eder to definitively separate learning and evolution and thus finally to rid his theory of evolution of any lingering traces of developmental logic. It should be noted here that Eder simultaneously sought to pre-empt the potential reductive treatment of culture implied by the emphasis on practices and practical reason, comparable to Bourdieu's well-known difficulties (Honneth 1990; LiPuma 1993),[24] by giving more weight to culture and the codes it harbours (e.g. Eder 1988: 225-38; 1990a; 1990b; 1996a: 140-9). The theoretical choice of emphasising the practical employment of situationally generated and effective structures also accounts for the fact that he is compelled to turn away from traditionally predominant structural models of society, such as exchange, hierarchy, contract and reciprocity, toward structural models of social practice (Eder 1988: 303-5).[25] To grasp the structural features of practices, it is less helpful to consider the societal context of such practices, thus treating the latter as the outcome of the former, than it is to focus on structural models generated and reproduced by practices in historically specific constitution and application contexts. Social evolution then no longer presents itself as the universal historical and general societal unfolding of a sequence of crystallised forms of social order, but rather as the structured interrelation of contexts of constitution and application belonging to discontinuous, historically specific societies (Eder 1988: 304; Eder and Schmidtke 1997: 19).[26] What is of particular interest regarding the ideas Eder developed under the rubric of the social evolution of practical reason, however, is that it pointed towards the theoretical position of situationalism which he would develop in the course of the 1990s (Eder and Schmidtke 1997, 1998) and which would bring him in close proximity to and, indeed, contact with the German Darwinian school, specifically Giesen.

In the article on 'Contradictions and Social Evolution' published in 1992, Eder took the opportunity not only to elaborate in detail and make full use of his old strategy of backtracking to the process of the social construction and reproduction of society that precedes both the classical (e.g. Durkheim and Weber) and neo-classical (e.g. Parsons, Luhmann and Habermas) concern with differentiation and rationalisation as processes explaining social evolution. At the same time, and very significantly, he also adopts the threefold Darwinian model of mutation or variation, selection and reproductive isolation or stabilisation to systematise and consolidate the position he had been developing during the preceding years. Although this publication contains only a brief critique of Schmid's selection-theoretical position (Eder 1992: 323), it should be emphasised that here Eder moved another step closer to Darwinism. Initially, Eder (1992: 345) aligns collective learning processes with mutation or variation, social conflict with selection, and both differentiation and rationalisation with the reproductive isolation or stabilisation of society. But he also recognises that, compared to biological evolution, social evolution is more complicated in that it depends on the evolutionary interaction of these various mechanisms. Not only does this for him mean that the above-mentioned alignment is looser and more flexible, but also that an absolutely strict application of Darwinian theory is not possible in sociology (Eder 1992: 345-46). In keeping with his earlier emphasis on the context of use, however, great weight is given to conflict or struggles of classification and reclassification as marking the situational context and representing the selection environment where a starting point for subsequent institutionalisation is provided. It is the systematic statement contained in this article that provided the general framework for detailed research on ecological communication conducted in the early 1990s and presented in the third part of *The Social Construction of Nature* (1996a: 162-212).

The study of the framing and communication of environmental issues in this book is a theoretically and methodologically advanced and highly refined investigation of how collective learning and discursive conflict in public communication produce changes at one level that are at another level handled by evolutionary processes. Initially, the focus is on collective agents, such as the ecology movement, industry and the state, who are analysed in terms of the respective combinations of mutually substitutable empirical, moral and aesthetic framing devices they use to construct their own frames of nature, the way they symbolically and narratively package those frames, and the strategic manner in which they communicate those frames in public. The focus then shifts to a discourse analysis of the competition and conflict among the strategically sponsored frames of the different collective actors as mediated by the mass media in public discourse. Here special attention is given to the output of public discourse beyond the intentions of the participants, namely the master or macro-frame —in this case the 'new "post-industrial" masterframe' of 'ecology' (Eder, 1996a: 183) —that emerges from the frame competition and is collectively accepted, in keeping with the response of the public, as the common reference of agents who nevertheless occupy different social, cultural and interpretative positions. A significant concomitant change produced by this conflict and collective learning is the transformation of the late 20th-century public sphere through a restructuring of ideological cleavages and political alignments (Eder 1996a: 185; 1996b).

The various changes brought about by the learning of the collective agents and the conflict of their frames in public discourse provide a foothold for socio-cultural evolution to take its course at a different level. In this context, Eder (1996a: 194-202) analyses evolution with reference to the phenomenon of the institutionalisation of environmental protest that takes the form of the evolution of cultural classificatory categories or codes which structure social experience and organise social activities. While a genetic structuralist understanding deriving from Eder's earlier studies of Mead, Piaget, Habermas and Bourdieu undoubtedly informs this position of his, he here conceives of these cultural structures as 'rule systems' (Eder 1996a: 194-95). What is significant is that, in speaking of rule systems, he explicitly calls upon the Uppsala school's theory of rule systems (Burns 1986; Burns and Flam 1986). He also accepts, indeed in keeping with the Habermasian distinction among the theoretical-empirical, moral and aesthetic components of culture, Burns and Dietz's classification of rule systems into descriptive, prescriptive and evaluative categories. As culturally available social grammars, Eder regards these rule systems as being central to the emergence under new conditions of an intersubjectively shared social world —albeit never one that is perfect or precludes differences and disagreements. In the process of allowing a transition from a chaotic to an ordered social situation, however, these rule systems are themselves subject to evolutionary pressures. A particular configuration of rule systems, or a 'rule regime' (Eder 1996a: 198), is selected at the expense of other possible configurations and becomes stabilised in the form of a set of interrelated institutions.[27] Once again it is remarkable that when Eder conceives of the evolutionary selection of rule systems, he not only seeks support for his position in the Uppsala school's Darwinian theory of the evolution of rule systems (Burns and Dietz 1992a; Dietz and Burns 1992), but for the first time in his writings also makes positive reference to the German Darwinian school's evolutionary theory (Eder 1996a: 195). The reference in question here is a book by Giesen (1980) in which he put forward a selectionist evolutionary theory. Prior to 1996, Eder had virtually always referred only critically, sometimes even quite scathingly, to this work in particular and to the Darwinian school's selection-theoretical position more generally (Eder 1985a: 31, 495; 1987: 102-3, 111, 1988: 42, 44, 288; 1992: 323).[28]

In his research and publications of the late 1990s which deal with ethnic mobilisation, identity struggles and social exclusion, Eder is centrally concerned with the systematic development and application of what he calls 'situationalism' or a 'situation-theoretical perspective' (Eder and Schmidtke 1998). The basic idea underpinning this new perspective is that disagreement generates communication in situations that are historically produced and reproduced, so that it is necessary to take account of the close relation between the micro- and macro-dimensions, between construction processes and structuration processes, or between interactive relations and historical configurations. At the core of this perspective, therefore, is a theoretical model of situations, which he started to develop in the mid-1990, that gives priority to the variable structural properties of situations which are created and reproduced in the medium of communication, are defined by cultural codes, and are stabilised as historically new, societally significant modes of legitimation (Eder and Schmidtke 1998: 428-31). The model is a multi-level communication one that simultaneously takes into account whether individual or collective actors are involved, whether their actions are strategically or normatively coordinated, and whether a third party in the guise of an observer or the public is either present or absent. As such, it is intended to serve the analysis of processes of the construction of society taking place in the medium of communication and public discourse in which divergent culturally coded life and identity projects are caught up in competition or conflict which creates the conditions for or contributes to the production and reproduction of social structures independent of the intentions of the participants. In so far as the situation-theoretical model facilitates the realisation of this intention, it allows the treatment of the micro- and macro-dimensions as different levels of abstraction of the same phenomenon, namely situational structures making possible the construction of differences between social actors or their coordination.

On this basis, the theory of evolution can be restated in terms of the relation of social interaction logics and processes whereby modern societies are changed and reproduced (Eder and Schmidtke 1998: 434). The situation-theoretical model directs attention, on the one hand, toward communicative relations in which collectively shared definitions are constructed which initiate, facilitate or block macro-structural processes responsible for the reproduction or change of society and, on the other, toward the macro-structural properties which are thus generated, selected and stabilised. Macro-structures are contingent, yet as a rule they prove to be relatively stable over certain time-spans during which they prioritise a particular type of situation and hence a corresponding mode of cultural coding and communication. Evolutionary theory, then, makes possible the reconstruction of macro-structures as configurations of situations (Eder and Schmidtke 1997: 19), which in turn requires comparative historical-sociological research.

Eder's situation-theoretical perspective clearly resonates methodologically with Karen Knorr-Cetina's (1988: 21) 'methodological situationalism' and theoretically with Ulrich Beck's (1988: 211) 'relations of definition', yet it goes a step further precisely in so far as it is built into a broader evolutionary theory. Much more important, therefore, is its acknowledged relatedness to the German Darwinian school's —particularly Giesen's —'selection-theoretical' position (Giesen 1975: 396-407; 1980a: 324-8; 1980b: 76-81; 1987; 1991a: 173-5; 1993; 1995; Giesen and Lau 1981: 247-52; Giesen *et al.* 1998; Schmid 1982a, 1982b, 1987),[29] which the authors themselves explicitly place in the context of evolutionary theory. What is most remarkable from the point of view of a possible convergence in contemporary European social evolutionary theory, however, is that Eder does not merely make positive reference to the writings and move closer to the theoretical position of his old enemy, the Darwinian school, but actually draws on established relations of cooperation with Giesen.[30] In fact, what we witness here is the result of a process of cooperation conditioned by increasingly converging ways of dealing with social phenomena from a basically evolutionary viewpoint that goes back to the 1980s and intensified in the 1990s in relation to a shared interest in collective identity. In a recent publication, therefore, Eder explicitly acknowledges the closeness of his own situationalism to Giesen's selection-theoretical position, and even credits Giesen with having developed the theoretical idea of the objective structuredness of interaction situations which are culturally coded and communicatively reproduced (Eder and Schmidtke 1998: 427, 432). It is also clear, for instance from the same source, that the theory of collective identity formation which Giesen developed in terms of his selectionist theory became an integral part of the research on ethnic mobilisation and conflict conducted by Eder and his associates at the Humboldt University. This explains the joint authorship —that is, Klaus Eder, Bernhard Giesen, Oliver Schmidtke and Damian Tambini —of the manuscript entitled *Collective Identities in Action: A Theory of Ethnic Politics* (Eder *et al.* 2002) which was still unpublished at the time of the writing of the present essay. The cooperation between Eder and Giesen, to be sure, is not confined to this project.

3. IN LIEU OF A CONCLUSION: THE NEW EUROPEAN RAPPROCHEMENT

In the above, I have argued that a closer inspection of the revitalisation of evolutionary theory in the social sciences and different proposals to integrate sociology theoretically reveals, among other things, an interesting and in fact quite surprising new European rapprochement. Three distinct strands of social evolutionary theory in Europe, ones that emerged independently of one another, remained separate for an appreciable time and were even antagonistic toward each other, gradually moved closer to one another, recognised mutual points of contact and started to integrate in certain respects.

Eder gradually took leave of Habermasian developmental-logic theory from which he started by extrapolating its communication and discourse-theoretical component and eventually combining it with the Darwinian model of variation, selection and stabilisation. The outcome of this was a situationalist or situation-logical theory that, on the one hand, draws on a social constructivist view of collective learning and, on the other, focuses on emergent structures and institutions and the concomitant evolution of rule regimes. Giesen originally proceeded from Darwinism but felt compelled in the course of time to mitigate its inherent naturalistic tendency by reinterpreting the core concepts of evolutionary theory in terms of action, communication and culture. Thus his initial strictly Darwinian selectionist theory developed into a more appropriate sociological version that reconstructs cultural processes according to the logic of selective reproduction or of the situation. Accordingly, he conceives of his current selectionist theory also as a situationalist one. The considerable impact Eder and Giesen have had on one another accounts to a significant degree not only for the change of their respective theories in the course of time, but also for the gradual convergence between them. Coming on the scene somewhat later than the former two, Burns and Dietz from the start adopted a Darwinian inspired theory of sociocultural evolution. At its core they placed cultural rule systems that are, on the one hand, infused with variety by social learning processes and, on the other, are subject to situation-specific selection processes accounting for the evolutionary change in the prevalence of particular rules in a population. Whereas Giesen (1995: 229) saw Burns and Dietz's position as a selection-theoretical Darwinism that is directly comparable to his own version, Eder appreciated that their conception of rule systems represented a ready contact point with his own understanding inspired by Habermas, Mead, Piaget, and Bourdieu.

In the late 1990s, the convergence among these three versions of the new social evolutionary theory reached the point where their common theoretical core began to assume clear contours. Generally speaking, these contours are determined by the articulation of Darwinian evolutionary theory, particularly the threefold model of variation, selection and stabilisation or reproduction, in terms of interactionism or, differently, communication and discourse theory which, in addition, is given historical depth. It is in this sense of the combination of constructivism and selectivity, which represents a huge advance in social evolutionary theory, that we should understand such conceptual models as collective learning-discourse-evolution (Eder), code-process-situation (Giesen) and agency-selection-cultural and social rule systems (Burns and Dietz).[31]

Shunning strong naturalistic approaches,[32] such as sociobiology, all three strands focus on sociocultural evolution, which is in turn understood in evolutionary rather than in developmentalist or evolutionist terms. In this context, all the authors operate with a post-classical concept of culture. On the one hand, they recognise the relative autonomy of culture as consisting of a cognitive dimension embracing rules, codes, schemes, models or frames making possible perception, interpretation and experience; on the other, however, they appreciate the symbolically mediated social use that is made of culture by social actors or collective agents or through social practices within specific situations. Considering social actors and their interactions as providing building blocks of cultures and societies, the authors are all concerned with the dynamic processes, from conflict through social or collective learning to discursive construction, whereby such building blocks are generated, situationally selected and institutionally secured and reproduced. But, most centrally, the evolutionary question focuses on the change of the structures regulating the practices whereby social reality is constituted and reproduced. It is this series of theoretical assumptions that accounts for the fact that all three schools insist that evolutionary-theoretical reasoning must operate on the level of the linkage between the micro- and macro-dimensions of social reality.

What is significant about the rapprochement among Eder, Giesen, and Burns and Dietz is that it draws attention to the fact that at the beginning of the new millennium we have available in sociology the outlines of a new and much more adequate non-reductive theory of evolution than we have ever had. Rather than either a Darwinian selectionist or a developmentalist structural theory of a classical or neo-classical kind, we witness the emergence of a more complex post-classical situational theory. It is not unreasonable to expect, therefore, that sociologists will acquire a better understanding of evolutionary theory and that they will afford it increasing recognition and currency during the next decade or so. What many will undoubtedly realise in the process is that such a theory is necessary for an adequate theory of social change or transformation and that it is an indispensable tool both for systematic historical-sociological comparison and analyses of contemporary societies.

PART II

TRIPLE CONTINGENCY

6

Triple Contingency: The Theoretical Problem of the Public in Communication Societies

One of the most important insights gained by the social science, sociology in particular, in the recent past is that the public as public is nothing less than a constitutive part of societally significant communication processes in contemporary societies. Advancement in the social scientific understanding of observation in social processes, stimulated by developments in cybernetics and the cognitive sciences, has supported and strengthened this insight. During the 1950s and 60s, even acute and critically oriented authors such a C. Wright Mills (1956: 303) and Jürgen Habermas (1989: 249) still found it possible to work with a distinction —that is, between public and mass —that at least in effect denigrated, not unlike the mass culture critiques of the time, the larger part of the public. For some time already, this is no longer possible for we have come to recognise that the public plays an active part even at the level of mass communication. This is particularly the case in contemporary societies that are increasingly assuming the form of communication societies. Although it has been attracting more and more attention, a proper sociological understanding of the role of the public in communication societies nevertheless still seems to be lacking. The first step toward such an understanding is a theoretical translation of the above-mentioned insight. The aim of this essay is to take this tentative step by advancing the claim that the proposition or theorem of double contingency put forward by Parsons and other authors such as Habermas and Luhmann is no longer sufficient since today we have to reckon with what may be called triple contingency.[1] The implications of this more complex form of contingency, however, are not only strictly theoretical by nature. It also has a profound methodological impact. A new light is cast on the sociological perspective and hence on the self-understanding of the sociologist. Indeed, some of the most pressing current methodological debates turn precisely on this issue. In the background, of course, lurk still deeper questions concerning the epistemology of the social sciences.

In this essay, I propose first to outline the new understanding of the public, then to draw out its theoretical implications in the form of the theorem of triple contingency, and finally to follow it up with some epistemological and methodological reflections on sociology's characteristic third point of view.

1. THE PUBLIC AS CONSTITUTIVE ELEMENT OF COMMUNICATION SOCIETIES

The social phenomenon of the public made its first appearance in the context of the early modern communication revolution. In the wake of the breakdown of the religious world view and the Church's loss of monopoly over the official interpretation of reality, a socially diverse group of intelligentsia stepped into the breach whose members were compelled to appeal to the public to uphold their competing and even conflicting interpretations (Mannheim 1972: 9-11). In a period when the number of books in Europe increased from approximately 30 thousand to 9 million, the humanists of the Renaissance were the first culture producers to vie for public attention (Hauser 1951: 78-81). For their successors, the 18th-century men of letters, as well as musicians and artists, who fully experienced the shift from patronage to the market, the loss of aura of cultural objects due to their transformation into commodities and the change of personal service into an impersonal activity, the orientation towards a diffuse and unknown public became a dominant feature of their mode of existence. The rapidly growing reading, theatre-going, concert-going and art-admiring public who in the course of time acquired a new competence, aesthetic judgment, was closely related to the emergence and consolidation under conditions of mercantilism or early capitalism of a public who engaged in critical debate about the state, government and the exercise of political power and later became an ineliminable part of modern politics (Habermas 1989a, 1992).

The path followed by the public in its genesis and development, since the early modern period, particularly the 18th century, is clearly marked by legal and constitutional milestones (Habermas 1989a: 59, 70, 83; Gerhards and Neidhardt 1990: 21, 23, 25). Most important among them are the abolition of censorship, freedom of thought, the recognition of freedom of speech or expression, freedom of the press, freedom of association and assembly, freedom of demonstration, and today the nascent legal constitutionalisation of the so-called 'fourth power', the mass media (Lichtenberg 1990; Habermas 1992: 455). This trajectory, stretching as it does from an initial lifting of restrictions via the laying of institutional foundations to the contemporary protection of the public, is indicative of an increasing differentiation and organization of communicative processes. We witness, on the one extreme, the emergence of the public in the early modern communication revolution, followed by its institutional organization, and, on the other, the recognition of the authority of the public in the late 20th-century communication societies.

Talk

In the wake of the breakdown of the all-embracing 'catholic' world view, freedom of thought and freedom of speech allowed people from all sections of the population to think differently about whatever prevailed and to communicate such thought to others. Everything could be conceived differently, and through communication not only was everything now at least potentially connected with everything else, but anything could also be changed in this medium. This applied equally to human social relations. Instead of hierarchy, status and rank, supported by the correct obligatory dress code, the emphasis was now on the parity of humanity. Free individuals could now communicate with one another in an unconstrained way, engaging in social intercourse in which status was disregarded and rank replaced by social tact. People from diverse backgrounds met more or less by chance and entered into spontaneous relations which were in principle open to all potential interaction partners. The public, made up of private individuals, emerged here within the framework of interactions of an episodic nature, presupposing the presence of the interacting partners —a simple form of communication variously referred to as 'talk' (Heidegger 1967: 203-14), the 'face-to-face relation' (Schutz 1967: 167-72), 'encounters' (Goffman 1961) or '*communication au trottoir*' (Luhmann 1986: 75). Considering the development of travel, printing, armies and navies, administrative structures, markets, money, coffee houses, salons, secret societies, sexual relations, marriage, the modern European languages and national communication communities, both the micro- and macro-structural conditions of early modern 'commercial society' immensely increased the probability of such communications.[2]

Gatherings

The actual increase in talk or encounters and in particular the recognition of the rules or principles governing social intercourse made possible the deliberate organization and eventually the institutionalisation of the ability to think matters through and to communicate the results. Initially, the organization of communication took the form of gatherings, meetings, assemblies, forums or arenas such as the *soladitates* of travelling scholars, aristocratic conversational circles, learned meetings, and so forth. Later, the legal or constitutional establishment of freedom of association and of assembly definitively consolidated this new departure. The Royal Society founded on an edict of 1662 is an early example of a legally based institution, while the constitutionally based and procedurally regulated political institutions of modern times, parliaments in particular, provide another. To these could further be added the interesting instance of organizations and collective protests related to broad social movements.

In the case of gatherings at the level of organization in question here, we witness communicative arrangements which are not just public but are at the same time organized around a particular theme, problem, common concern or issue and, while drawing a self-selecting membership, are clearly structured into organizers, discussion leaders, speakers and audience. In proportion as simple, episodic interactions are generalised in a more abstract and structured form, however, the public undergoes a complementary reconstitution. The presupposition of physical presence still applies, but the role of the public develops in a more specific direction. While attendance is a matter of free choice, expressive possibilities are more limited and actual participation in the form of a contribution from the floor is circumscribed by the need to relate to the speaker and to be relevant. Besides sheer presence, effective expressive forms at the command of the public such as cheering, applause, murmuring, booing and walking out nevertheless serve as an indication of the constitutive sense it retained after its role had changed. Even the early modern executions that Foucault (1977: 75) discusses under the title of 'the spectacle of the scaffold' would not have made any sense without the presence of the public.

Communication Society

Once communication processes are uncoupled from the physical presence of the public, a completely different yet by no means untypical situation under modern conditions ensues. If institutionalised gatherings move away from talk or encounters, this new situation is characterised by a still higher degree of abstraction. This quality is explicable by reference to the absence of the public. Generalised communication processes come into operation which presuppose a complex institutional and technical infrastructure and are oriented towards an unlimited body of absent and anonymous addressees. It is not simply that abstract, anonymous interaction and communication situations increased exponentially under modern conditions. It could even be argued that the emergence of modern society, including the social sciences, sociology in particular, coincided with the appearance, as it were, of the absent, unknown, faceless collective third person, the public.[3] The institutionalisation of the absent and anonymous public profoundly changed the structure and process of public communication and thereby transformed the conditions of reproduction of modern societies. They now definitively became communication societies.

Let us look at a few examples. In law, politics, economics and science, where equality, the common good, symbolic exchange and objectivity are respectively stressed, the orientation towards the absent and anonymous public is so pervasive that those present, even family members and friends, are treated as though they were part of the public (Giesen 1995: 246). Beyond these domains which had been well-known already to the classical sociologists, however, it is mass media communication in postmodern or postsocial societies which today most graphically brings this picture home to us. Within these generalised communication processes presupposing a highly complex technical base, the communicator's role became fully professionalised and the public's role underwent a further complementary change. Its absence was made complete by having been shorn of its ability to make decisions and to act accordingly. It is on the basis of this tendency that mass society theorists and mass culture critics earlier saw fit, quite erroneously, to decry mass publics for their passivity (e.g. Rosenberg and White 1957). Since the ultimate concern is communication and not simply self-expression, implying that the number of voices clamouring for attention required regulation, the complete absence of the public is necessary to give everyone a chance to participate (Gerhards and Neidhardt 1990: 24; Fuller 1993: 294). Decisive, further, is the significance that attaches to the only remaining form of expression of the public, namely public opinion (Gerhards and Neidhardt 1990: 24; Habermas 1992: 438; Fuller 1993: 285). That public opinion is the result of a controversy in which a certain degree of agreement was attained, rather than simply a statistical quantity or an aggregate of individual opinions, reflects the fact that there are no true experts in matters concerning the public sphere. In public opinion, therefore, we see the mutual dependence of the media and the public. Whereas talk and gatherings lack general recognition unless the media provide them with a public arena and shape their themes into newsworthy items, the media depend for their impact or effect not only on their reception by the public present at episodic and organized interaction processes but also on the latter's information input and feedback. Through talk and gatherings, the public provides the media with identified and initially defined problems which admit of being made into issues, and the influence actors exercise in public communication depends in the final analysis on the resonance and acceptance or agreement of the public. Against this background, it becomes clear that allegedly passive mass publics in fact play an active role in mass communication, even if largely as recipients, whether listeners or viewers. Besides various opportunities to participate, the public possesses a certain authority in that in its own right it is an ineradicable and crucial part of generalised communication processes in contemporary societies (Gerhards and Neidhardt 1990: 34). Ultimately, the significance of the public devolves on the fact that it and it alone is constitutive of 'the internal structure of the public sphere' (Habermas 1992: 440) within which the communication processes in communication societies take place. The public renders determinate, in quite unpredictable ways, what is at first indeterminate in public communication.

2. FROM DOUBLE TO TRIPLE CONTINGENCY

Introduction of the Concept: Talcott Parsons

Parsons introduced 'double contingency' as a theoretical concept to account at a basic level for the possibility of social interaction or communication and, by extension, of social order. The focal point of the concept is provided by the differences between two social actors, ego and alter. In brief, it refers to socially undetermined situations in which social interaction remains impossible unless the lack of determination and hence the differences between social actors are overcome by those involved. Any and every instance of interaction between two social actors —two being the elementary possibility —therefore necessarily takes place under conditions of double contingency. On introducing the concept, Parsons stated the theorem or proposition of double contingency in the following form:

> *There is a* ***double contingency*** *inherent in interaction. On the one hand, ego's gratifications are contingent on his selection among available alternatives. But in turn, alter's reaction will be contingent on ego's selection and will result from a complementary selection on alter's part. Because of this double contingency, communication, which is the preoccupation of cultural patterns, could not exist without both generalization from the particularity of the specific situations (which are never identical for ego and alter) and stability of meaning which can only be assured by 'conventions' observed by both parties (Parsons and Shils 1951: 16).*[5]

Two actors encounter one another in a social situation. Whatever each does depends on what each chooses to do and on what the other does. For both, the situation is equally open in that each could choose this way or that and could decide to react this way or that. Both actors are moreover equally uncertain, for both are potentially unlimited sources of words and actions. To overcome this condition of a situation that is equally open and uncertain for both actors, that is, the condition of double contingency,[6] they need to relate to one another in such a way that each has stable meanings to have recourse to and that the situation becomes one which is common to them both. The question then becomes: What does Parsons see as the solution to the problem posed by the fact of double contingency? How do the two actors relate to one another? On what basis do the actors make a selection among available alternatives? On what basis do they react to one another?

Parsons's (1964: 37-8; 1977b: 168-9) solution to the problem of double contingency takes the form of cultural determination. Culture, which is always already available as a shared system, penetrates action orientations to such an extent that the existence of a value consensus can be assumed. This can be considered from two sides. On the one hand, culture provides shared symbols or elements of tradition which control general systems of orientation. Decisive for the solution in question, however, cultural patterns of value on the other hand are internalised and institutionalised so as to become part of personalities and interaction systems as need dispositions and role expectations respectively. Two actors, motivated by their needs, who face one another in an encounter generally delineated by cultural symbols, are thus able to relate to each other or to enter into social interaction due to the correspondence between or overlap of the role expectations or normative orientations they had acquired through socialisation.

Assimilation to Communicative Action Theory: Jürgėn Habermas

In his analysis of Parsons's work, Habermas (1987a: 213-34) seems to accept the concept of double contingency. He indeed does not confine his critique to an attack only against Parsons's proposed solution, that is, the cultural determination of action orientations, but also questions his theory of action. Yet his own alternative, the theory of communicative action, does not invalidate or jettison double contingency. In fact, central to Habermas's (1987a: 217) position is what he calls 'the problem of coordination' in the sense of the harmonisation of the plans of action of different actors, and in a later work (Habermas 1992: 173) he explicitly accepts Parsons's concept of double contingency. On Habermas's account, Parsons's theory of action remains attached to both utilitarianism and empiricism, and thus not only starts from the monadic or solitary actor but also takes the form of a monological theory. As a consequence, it takes no account of the only mechanism by means of which the problem of double contingency could be solved, the coordinating mechanism of consensus building through language or communication. Parsons does not loose sight of language completely, to be sure, but he plays down the communicative aspect of coordination in favour of a reified concept of culture. The latter is past-oriented, static, objectivist and conceived epistemologically, and stands in a static, overlapping or interpenetrative relation to institutions and personality.

Habermas lays the foundations for his own solution to the problem of coordination generated by double contingency by adopting a theory of action that gives a central role to communicative consensus formation. This theory allows him not only to regard culture as fluid and as standing in a flexible relation to institutions and personality, but also to take a constructivist view. Culture, institutions and personality are symbolic structures of the lifeworld which are reproduced in the medium of communicative action, and interaction participants construct common action orientations by using their competences interpretatively to appropriate transmitted culture and to relate it either affirmatively or critically to existing norms and institutions. Under conditions of double contingency, communicatively acting participants are compelled to construct a common definition of their situation and to arrive at some understanding of relevant themes and plans. Construction of this kind is achieved through interpretative work, argumentation, the taking of yes or no positions and criticism, while the resulting mutual understanding or agreement provides an at least temporary solution to the perennial problem of double contingency.

Systems Theoretical Appropriation: Niklas Luhmann

Luhmann (1984: 148-53) regards Parsons's theorem of double contingency as being of great theoretical importance, but he takes issue with the theoretical framework as well as the details of the American theorist's formulation. Double contingency is a basic condition of the possibility of social action and hence of social systems. Both social action and social systems depend with functional necessity on the solution of the problem of double contingency. Luhmann is critical of Parsons's solution, however. To fall back on value consensus is tantamount to banking on the past, reducing social order to a problem of socialisation, misunderstanding social evolution as a variant of socialisation, and misleading oneself into believing that the constitution of social systems depends on an always already available, pre-given, shared cultural system. Luhmann's alternative is to conceive of double contingency from the more general theoretical point of view of the constitution and continuous processing of meaning linked to systems theory. This allows him to regard double contingency as an abiding problem that cannot be solved once and for all, and to insist that, rather than action subjects, it is either psychic systems or social systems that confront one another under such conditions. Parsons anyway overlooks the fact that social actors are constituted within a social system rather than preceding and thus constituting the system. On this basis, Luhmann distinguishes his position from Parsons's by introducing temporal and modal theoretical considerations. First, rather than fixing on a pre-given consensus, a solution to double contingency could be sought in a temporal process in which a consensus is built up in a manner that is sensitive to chance. Second, contingency is a modality that excludes necessity and impossibility and thus underlines the possibility of being different or something else. These assumptions imply that in the process of encountering each other and attempting to overcome double contingency, two 'black boxes' (Luhmann 1984: 156) are not compelled to fall back on the past but could, and in reality do, reach out toward a possible future world.

In Luhmann's view, the theory of action to which Parsons remains indebted must be surrendered. Traditional formulas for dealing with the problem of double contingency, such as, for instance, 'reciprocity of perspectives', are inadequate in that they assume a symmetry model which neglects the auto-selectivity of perspectives and the ungraspability of the other. Even symbolic interactionism, which correctly stresses the use of symbols, operates with only one half of double contingency.[7] As an action theory, it lacks the means to come to terms with the structure formation entailed by the other half. At this juncture, Luhmann introduces the theory of social systems, particularly autopoietic systems theory. Within this framework, double contingency is a permanent, basic problem faced by any and every system. As an 'autocatalytically operating problem', it brings about a 'state of conditional readiness' in systems, a systems building possibility in waiting, and thus necessarily and inevitably leads to the formation of systems (Luhmann 1984: 172, 177).

Habermas and Luhmann occupy two diametrically opposed positions, yet this difference should not be allowed to cloud the similarities between them. Generally speaking, of course, their respective positions are complementary in the sense that they focus on the same matter from points of view that cannot be assumed at one and the same time. Whereas

Habermas locates himself within the theory of communicative action and seeks from that base to account for society as a system, Luhmann gives priority to systems theory and undertakes to account for action within that framework. As regards their critiques of Parsons, more specifically, their respective positions are comparable in so far as both backtrack to a more general processual and constructive point of view and stress an orientation towards the future and open possibilities. But what is more remarkable in the present context is that both, despite attacks against Parsons, accept the theorem of double contingency. In the following paragraphs, by contrast, I propose to develop an argument against this very assumption. Instead of the theorem of double contingency held in common by Parsons, Habermas and Luhmann, I am going to take up a suggestion of Klaus Eder and Oliver Schmidtke (1997: 17, 1998: 429) to argue in favour of what may be called 'triple contingency'. This brings us back, of course, to the significance of the public in contemporary communication societies.

The Observer

Habermas and Luhmann, like Parsons, are able to maintain the idea of double contingency only because they make a certain assumption that is by no means untypical in the social sciences. This assumption is more readily apparent in proponents of the theory of action, but, as Luhmann's appropriation of the concept of double contingency shows, it can even find a place in systems theory. Positively, it amounts to the basic idea that mutually related or involved actors, participants or carriers of meaning, that is, essentially no more and no less than two, represent the basic unit to which one has to revert were he or she to account for the social world. Parsons focuses on 'ego and alter', Habermas similarly prefers 'communicatively acting subjects oriented toward mutual understanding', and Luhmann insists on mutually intransparent 'black boxes', whether psychic or social systems, which are nevertheless able to relate to one another through the assumption of reciprocal determinability. Most frequently, the assumption in question is linked to the pervasive idea of social relationships in terms of which the basic building block of the social world is the dyad of 'I' and 'thou', the first person and the second person. Even Luhmann (1984: 156), who points out the limitation of this concept, understands the basic situation of double contingency simply as: 'Two black boxes, due to whatever coincidence, get involved with one another'.

Negatively, the assumption underpinning the theorem of double contingency becomes apparent from the way in which the third person, the third point of view or the observer of social life, is treated. Although both Habermas (1987a: 35-9, 150-1, 173, 182-5; 1992: 399-467; 1996b:

106-122) and Luhmann (1984: 407-11; 1992a: 68-121) generally speaking have quite sophisticated positions on the observer, the arguments by means of which they appropriate the concept of double contingency contain no evidence to suggest that they recognise this constitutive component of the social world and give it its proper due. The lack of appreciation of the role of the third point of view, or even simply the attribution of an impoverished role to it, is indicative of a serious theoretical deficiency.[8] To correct it, the concept of double contingency needs to make way for a more adequate replacement —namely triple contingency. In the first scenario, two social actors, communicatively acting subjects or black boxes, A and B, face or encounter one another and enter into some relation with each other as 'I' and 'thou'. In the basic situation of triple contingency, by contrast, there is a third perspective, borne by C, who observes what A and B are saying and doing. By so doing, C has a constitutive impact on the social situation. Indeed, this threefold configuration represents the elementary social situation rather than the former twofold one. But it also brings a higher degree of contingency with it.

In the case of double contingency, two actors, subjects or black boxes are compelled to make a selection from alternatives while taking the other into account, and thus to establish a relation between them. The inclusion of the third point of view means that the social situation in the case of triple contingency is very different and more complicated from the start. It is not simply a matter of elementary interaction which was discussed above under the title of 'talk' or 'encounter'. The observer belongs to the situation as a constitutive part of its sociality. Over and above the 'I' and 'thou', the third point of view represents society. It embodies the societal power of definition. C has a constitutive social role in that he, she or it has the power to define the situation. Whatever A and B say and do, therefore, must in principle make sense to C. From the start and throughout, A and B are subject in their interrelations to meaning as defined by society and represented by the observer. As regards contingency, A and B make their choices and take each other into account, while at the same time being relativised by a societal definition or collectively accepted representation for which the observer stands which itself becomes established only in the course of the process. What this situation of triple contingency entails becomes clearer when one considers the centrality and shaping impact of public communication in contemporary societies. Neither the racial conflict in South Africa nor apparently now the ethnic conflict in Northern Ireland could have been resolved otherwise. Public communication formed an inherent part of the dynamics of both conflicts and the definitional power brought to bear on both by international observers and more broadly the observing public proved decisive.[9]

Let us explore the theorem of triple contingency further by taking a somewhat closer look at the third point of view. Two moot points are of particular importance. The first concerns the location of the third point of view: is it context-independent or does it have a foothold in society itself? The second concerns the epistemological and methodological consequences: does the third point of view entail a legitimationist or a constructivist approach? Considering Habermas's seminal contribution to the recognition of the significance of the public and his tireless efforts to resolve the issues raised by it, the following treatment of these questions will make some reference to his work.

3. THE THIRD POINT OF VIEW: WITHIN OR BEYOND SOCIETY?

In his early work, Habermas traced the genesis in the early modern period of the public as the decisive constitutive component of the public sphere. Against the background of the growth of both a cultural and a political public in various European countries, he stressed the in principle inclusiveness of the public. Despite the exclusiveness of a public in any given instance, it could never avoid the general significance of its concerns nor could it close itself off completely and bar access to those who are able to participate (Habermas 1989a: 37). It is this basic characteristic of the public, its being in principle indefinite and unlimited, that led Habermas (1973: 24-65) to give it the normative interpretation which he would later conceive of as domination-free discourse regulated by the ideal speech situation. The idealisation involved here is akin to that proposed by his mentor, friend and collaborator Karl-Otto Apel (1980, 1981) in his transformation, based on an appropriation of Peirce, of the transcendental self-consciousness underlying Kant's philosophy into the transcendental or 'ideal communication community'. 'Transcendental' or 'ideal' here qualifies the real or empirical communication community in so far as it is governed by norms or rules (Böhme 1997: 352)—such as the acceptance of the basic rules of argumentation, the equality of discourse partners, the mutual recognition of discourse partners, and so forth. While this idealising assumption makes a good deal of philosophical sense, it can, from various points of view, be regarded as too strong. This position has been taken by many of Habermas's critics, among whom both philosophers and sociologists, even ones sympathetic to him. Recently, he has sought to meet the major thrust of these criticisms by locating what he calls the 'third perspective' within society itself. Let us briefly consider one sociologically relevant strain of criticism, and then evaluate this response of his.

The abiding strain of criticism I have in mind here, which has been stated in the 1970s and subsequently restated time and time again in varying forms,[10] can be clarified from two sides. From one angle, it is argued that Habermas essentially concentrates on reasoning about the organization of society. His interest is in the ideas that structure the perception of the organizational problems of society and argumentation about them. The underlying aim in doing so is to account for the development of the ideals that can historically be attributed to society. This approach, according to the criticism, does not explain anything, however. It detaches itself from both the real historical process and the actual organization of social relations. Theoretical categorisation combined with the perusal of philosophically formulated moral systems predominates, while historically sensitive sociological analysis of the generation of such reasoning, ideas and ideals receives insufficient attention. From another angle, it is argued that the concern with the ideals of society entails a projection beyond society itself. Habermas operates with an aprioristic and hence pre-sociological assumption regarding the conditions of practical reason. He thinks of it as a normative consensus that results from discourse or reflexive communication disburdened of external pressures and power relations — or rather, counterfactually, as the anticipated result that would issue from the process were it possible to come to a positive end. This procedure may well be philosophically fruitful and justifiable (Miller 1992a: 12; McCarthy 1994: 72; Böhme 1997: 351-63) and could even be sociologically meaningful in that it provides reconstructive analysis with a guideline (Habermas 1992: 35, 94, 105, 349), but the critics doubt whether it leaves any room for a negative criterion and hence for a historical universal such as hegemony, not to mention exclusion.

In order to counter this criticism, Habermas (1988b) has submitted that his position is a 'postmetaphysical' one. Due to the collapse of the religious-metaphysical world view and the concurrent transition to a pluralistic society, moral obligations can since the 18th century no longer be publicly justified by recourse to the transcendent point of view of God. Under current conditions, the place of this standpoint, which lies beyond the world, is taken by the moral point of view that represents a reconstruction within the world of the lost unity. In a recent work, Habermas (1996b: 16, 106, 109, 125) has restated this position of 'internal transcendence' and gave the moral point of view a remarkable twist by conceiving of it as a 'third point of view' which is located 'in society itself'. According to him, this is 'the moral point of view in terms of which modern societies are criticised by their own social movements' (Habermas 1996b: 125). This means further that 'an affirmative attitude can only be taken toward the negative potential in societal tendencies which leads to an unrelenting self-critique' (1996b: 126). As against his critics, particularly the sociologists among them, it is obvious that Habermas here suggests that to ascribe to him a concern with reasoning which entails a purely positive aprioristic assumption beyond society is mistaken. The question is, however, whether he will be able to uphold this stance. Is the third point of view he defends actually located within rather than beyond society? And if it is located in society, in what sense is this the case?

Recently, Habermas (1996b: 95-127) has put forward an interesting critique of John Rawls that is all the more significant in the present context in that it manifests an unacknowledged shift from double to triple contingency. In Rawls's understanding, agreement in the political domain depends on the citizens adopting two different perspectives: the perspective of participants entailed by their adherence to some worldview or another, and the perspective of observers who register the convergence of the different worldviews and the establishment of an overarching consensus. Habermas objects that this construction presupposes two and only two perspectives, and hence neglects the third perspective going beyond them. This third perspective is the one that those involved together adopt and employ in public, the all-embracing public perspective that is intersubjectively shared by all those involved. This accounts for the fact that it possesses epistemic authority. It represents the demands of practical reason that are independent of the various worldviews of the participants and to which the various worldviews are therefore required to submit. Habermas also describes this epistemically authoritative third point of view variously as the impartial perspective, the perspective of impartial or critical evaluation and most often as the context-independent moral point of view.

It is here that a certain equivocation becomes apparent —one that grows more acute when Habermas attributes it to social movements. Habermas rightly insists that the third point of view dictated by the theorem of triple contingency should be regarded as coming into play and thereby goes beyond Rawls's concept of observation. But, on the one hand, it is depicted as a context-independent moral point of view presupposed by everyone and, on the other, it is portrayed as embodied by social movements. This description of the third point of view raises a number of related questions. Can the third point of view be both universalistic and tied to the collective identity of a particular participant? How could this be achieved? Is there not room for an intermediate conception that fits in more meaningfully with the notion of the public and its authoritative role in public communication? Should the third point of view not be tied to the communication process or discourse itself rather than to either incommensurable worldviews or to the universal audience as such or, as in Habermas, to both?[11]

These questions bring us to some pressing epistemological and methodological implications of the theorem of triple contingency.

4. LEGITIMATIONISM OR CONSTRUCTIVISM?

The theorem of triple contingency implies a new way in which to understand the conditions of adequacy of social knowledge. In terms of the concept of double contingency and its solution by means of cultural determination, Parsons conceived of these conditions in an *a priori* normative manner. This position can be taken as being expressive of the traditional sociological stance. What counts is whether social actors in fact know what they could be expected to know, that is, what they ought to know, about social relations and social interaction. One way of going beyond this traditional understanding, is to allow for research to uncover *a posteriori* the competences required by social actors in particular types of social situations. Habermas (1979a, 1984a), for instance, proposed a cognitivistic empirical-reconstructive approach which stresses ontogenetically acquired action competences and allows a differentiated analysis of communicative action in linguistically mediated contexts. This proposal of his is only one of a number of relatively recent contributions to what has been called the 'cognitive turn in sociology' (Fuller 1984) and is documented in an important yet somewhat neglected volume edited by Karin Knorr Cetina and Aaron Cicourel (1981).[12] The drawback of Habermas's approach, which is reflected in his retention of the concept of double contingency, despite the shift from a normative to a cognitive position, is that it is ultimately based on psychological assumptions. The cognitive is narrowly understood in terms of the individual mind rather than in terms of the more sociologically relevant phenomenon of social knowledge and cultural models.[13] In the case of triple contingency, by contrast, matters are quite different.

Instead of social actors and cognitive action competences, the concept of triple contingency calls for an emphasis on the relational setting or structured situation within which actors find themselves and within which their actions take their course. Theoretically, this requirement has been met in different ways. Eugene Rochberg-Halton (1982), for instance, speaks of 'the structured situation' with reference to the attempts of such authors as Bourdieu and Eisenstadt to bridge symbolic interactionism and structuralism. Knorr Cetina (1988) puts forward a position she calls 'situationalism' which steers a course between action theory and structuralism, between methodological individualism and collectivism.

Margaret Somers (1994) proposes an 'institutional and narrative approach' that disaggregates macro-categories or totalising metaphors and reassembles them into indeterminate clusters or configurations of cultural and institutional relationships expressed in relational metaphors. Rather than society, the focus is on the relational setting in the sense of a patterned matrix of relations through which social actors as well as power and organizations are contingently connected and positioned. Eder and Schmidtke (1997, 1998), in turn, argue in favour of a 'situation theoretic model' that is relational and structure-oriented. While it takes a plurality of actors, value orientations, actions, motives, rational calculations and so forth into account, it proceeds from the structuralist assumption that there are rules operative in social situations that coordinate action events independently of the motives, intentions and goals of the actors. They link these rules to collectively shared representations or cultural codes that are communicated within the context of public communication.

In communication societies, social action that makes a difference depends for its effect not on the subjective meaning, intention or goal of the actors involved, but rather on being objectively defined in the social situation as significant action. The constructive context provided by the relational setting or structured situation creates a web of relations which makes it possible for those observing the actors involved and commenting on them to make a decisive contribution to the definition of the meaning of their actions. In communication societies, the constructive context takes the form of the context of public communication or the public sphere. The actors and observers are all components of this public domain, and these components are all related to each other through the communication taking place within that context. This occurs by being made a medium of communication or being thematised and thus being co-ordinated with one another. A crucial effect of this tendency, which helps to account for the centrality and authority of the public in communication societies, is that in proportion as actions and relations are coordinated by communication power becomes dependent on the acceptance of definitions of reality (Eder 1993: 12). The more communication becomes the mechanism of coordination, the more power accrues to the public who is in the most propitious position to accept or reject the meanings communicated by the participants and thus to fix the collectively accepted definition of reality.

What is collectively accepted, however, is a consensus only in the ideal case. The meanings, symbols or codes which are communicated, struggled over and finally accepted are shot through with power, with the result that what is collectively accepted rather amounts to a dominant definition of reality, which could involve exclusionary mechanisms but more typically now tends to taken the form of hegemony.[14] Although it is the case, as Apel (1976) and Habermas (1979a) maintain from a transcendental or universal pragmatic position, that a final consensus is necessarily and unavoidably presupposed, communication processes cannot be analysed directly and exclusively in terms of such a consensus. Neither the participants nor even the observing public, who has the power to define the meaning of the actions of the participants, know beforehand what the final collectively accepted agreement will be (Miller 1992a: 15-16). The fact that the observing public is itself divided into 'competing counterpublics' (Fraser 1997: 75) or into supporters, sympathisers, opponents and bystanders (Neidhardt and Rucht 1991: 457) exacerbates this condition of indeterminacy and uncertainty. This condition, it should be emphasised, is precisely the locus of the third moment of contingency in question in this essay. The definition of reality that is eventually accepted in the wake of an observed process of communication and struggle over meanings, which overcomes this indeterminacy and uncertainty, is a construction achieved not only by the participants but in particular also by their audience, the observing public.

Before finally returning to the constructivism that is broached above and comparing Habermas's proposal to it, it is necessary first to ferret out some of the epistemological implications. At issue here in particular are the complicated questions of the adequacy of social knowledge, the role of the observer and the epistemic authority of the sociologist. Fuller (1984: 441-3) has summarised the traditional sociological understanding in an epistemological scheme according to which the sociologist has three complementary options vis-à-vis the social actors he or she observes. The first is to think like a native, the second to pass oneself off as a native, and the final to abandon native categories in favour of theoretical categories. Interpreting this, one may say that, in the first case where social knowledge is equated with self-knowledge, the sociologist assumes an observer's role that would suit a subjective hermeneuticist. In the second, where social knowledge is taken to coincide with knowledge of the presentation of the self to others, the sociologist adopts the role of the participant observer. In the third, finally, where the conditions of adequacy of social knowledge are located beyond the social actors at a level occupied by the social scientist alone, the sociologist is an objectivist or reductionist observer either of the positivistic or quasi-positivistic type or of the systems theoretical or functionalist type. These three positions, however, do not exhaust all the possibilities. A new departure is represented, for example, by the cognitive turn in sociology. This could be interpreted as the *a posteriori* revelation by means of indices (Fuller 1984: 443) or the 'reconstruction' (Habermas 1979: 9) of action competences. In this case, the sociologist is a cognitivist observer who equates social knowledge with the level of competence demanded of social actors in given social situations. A different interpretation, entailed by the theorem of triple contingency, becomes available when one does not confine oneself to social actors and their competences but over and above them take seriously the social knowledge and cultural models which are embodied in the observing public or, differently, are collectively accepted in a given context. Here the epistemic authority of the sociological observer derives from the observing public who places the sociologist in a position to identify and specify the collective definitions that are empirically operative and effective in the context under observation.[15] The sociologist remains a cognitivist observer, however, in that he or she focuses on cognitive or knowledge structures. The competences of actors are by no means irrelevant since they have to be considered in terms of how they enter into the construction of the collective knowledge that is eventually accepted by the public. But most important are the cultural models embodied by the public or collectively accepted knowledge.[16]

In various sociological traditions, both old and new, the constructivist approach has remained confined to the level of action. This is true not only of the more obvious cases of phenomenology (Schutz 1967; Berger and Luckmann 1967) and constructivist sociology of science (Knorr Cetina 1981),[17] but also of social constructivism focusing on social processes (Van den Daele 1977) and of social movement research concentrating on collective action and collective identity (Melucci 1995). In the latter case, when shared socially constructed ideas are acknowledged, they are confined to the level of collective action, and even when public discourse is introduced it is treated as external to social movements rather than being the structured situation within which the latter are constructed (McAdam *et al.* 1996). The constructivist approach comes into its own, however, only when it is extended to the relational and structured context of social action (Eder 1993a: 14, 60; 1996a; Eder and Schmidtke 1997, 1998). Once this is done, it becomes clear that social or collective action which makes a difference or is collectively significant possesses this quality not of its own accord, but only because it was constructed as such through communication in the public domain. This particular conception of constructivism is one of the most acute yet by no means well-understood recent insights of the social sciences, and indeed one that closely articulates with the concept of triple contingency. According to it, the constructivist perspective focuses on intentions, goals, values and identities linked to social and collective action or, differently, on action structures and meanings in so far as they are transposed from the actors to the constructive context, from the individuals to the communication between them within view of the observing public. At this latter level, they become features or attributes of the relational, structured setting shared by the participants and observers alike. They are collectively accepted and valued and in the process power accrues to them. They thus acquire the role of structuring factors, features of the social situation which serve as cultural presuppositions of social action and social processes and hence exert a structuring force on all those involved.

To bring these reflections on the epistemological and methodological implications of the theorem of triple contingency to a close, I want to consider the second of two characteristic limitations of Habermas's proposal regarding the third point of view against this constructivist background. Attention was give to the first one earlier, that is, the projection of the third point of view as the transcendent, moral point of view that leads to the predilection to analyse processes of construction in terms of a final consensus rather than in terms of the sequence of attempts on the part of the participants to jointly identify and define a controversial question and to find a collectively acceptable solution to it. The second limitation turns on Habermas's locating of the moral point of view in society itself by linking it to social movements.

Constructivism, by its very nature, forbids the social scientist to adopt an identificatory procedure. It requires that the whole plural range of participants, relevant to a given constructive context, be taken into account without any tendency to favour one and hence to identify with it. To do so, would be to subvert the very constructivist perspective the social scientist claims to be upholding. It would be tantamount to taking a legitimationist rather than a constructivist position.[18] The social scientist identifies with the intentions, goals, values and identity of one of the participants and interprets the constructive process in terms of the normative code preferred and communicated by that participant rather than standing back to consider the dynamic interplay of the normative codes of all the participants within their common setting and the outcome of this dynamic as settled by what is eventually collectively accepted. Although the social scientist might tend to want to identify with a social movement struggling for a worthy cause, in the constructivist perspective the movement is only one among a plurality of participants all of whom warrant equal attention. In so far as Habermas takes the point of view of a social movement, he adopts a legitimationist rather than a constructivist approach, and in so far as he interprets the social movement's point of view in terms of the transcendent moral point of view projected beyond society rather than as part of a communicative process, he exhibits an old discredited predilection for the philosophy of history which he has as yet not fully jettisoned.

Although constructivism operates at a certain distance from the participants, this approach is not simply morally neutral or devoid of any moral sensibility and concern. Rather than maintaining an immediate relation with a transcendent normative standard, as though the social scientist knows what ought to be the case, it is a more indirect approach. Given the nature of language and communication, a constructivist analysis undeniably presupposes by pragmatic necessity a reference to an indefinite and unlimited community, but its more immediate concern is the public. From this it seeks to grasp what is collectively accepted in the particular situation, but this does not entail measuring existing reality against a necessary and unavoidable presupposition stylised as a normative standard, as Habermas (1992: 36) insists. Even if this is not a stark confrontation of ideal and reality but an identification of traces of existing reason in distorted practices, as he holds, such a procedure tends to cast theory and analysis in the form of moralising, that is, stating what ought to be and pointing out that reality does not measure up to this standard. The constructivist approach, by contrast, is more concerned with locating starting points for a new constructive learning process that could possibly move in the direction of an unlimited and indefinite public. This requires first that the normative codes of all the participants, not just that of a preferred one, be investigated as possible presuppositions for furthering constructive learning. By singling out a social movement and linking his normative standard to it, Habermas not only identifies with the movement but also renders any critique of it impossible. All the participants, social movements included, must secondly be subjected to a social critique (Eder 1988: 275, 319, 352, 374-7; 1993a: 78-80, 98-100) that focuses on the particular illusion that each entertains in its strategic communication in relation to the other participants. Rather than simply holding up the picture of a transcendent normative standard to the participants so that they can begin to appreciate how far short their own ideals fall, as does the moral philosopher, the constructivist sociologist seeks out the illusory side of these ideals in order to expose the errors that need to be corrected. In this sense, sociology is not exhausted by describing existing reality, 'facticity', in comparison with a normative standard, 'validity', as Habermas (1992: 37, 94, 105, 349) proposes, since it specifically undertakes the uncovering and exposure of illusory ideals about reality and their effects on what becomes collectively accepted in the course of public communication within a particular situation —that is, of course, if sociology takes triple contingency seriously.

7

The Problem of Triple Contingency in Habermas

The basic concept of double contingency gives expression to a widely recognised proposition in sociological theory. Talcott Parsons, building on the foundations laid by George Herbert Mead and Alfred Schutz, in the mid-20th century gave the theorem its explicit formulation. In the second half of the century, leading social theorists such as Jürgen Habermas and Niklas Luhmann reinforced its status as a basic concept by including discussions of it in their major works. In his latest major work, published in German and English as recently as in 1992 and 1996, respectively, Habermas still emphatically accepts the theorem of double contingency.

What I find remarkable is that, despite his concentration on double contingency, Habermas actually operates with a theoretical position that accommodates a higher degree of contingency. Through such matters as the public sphere, the public, the structure of communication, the system of perspectives and personal pronouns, and the third point of view, he often touches and even elaborates upon this form of contingency, yet he never acknowledges it as such, not to mention giving it a name. It is the contingency that the public as a bearer of the third point of view brings into communicative relations and hence into the social process —what may be called 'triple contingency'.[1] Thus while writing eloquently about double contingency as well as the public sphere, Habermas surprisingly neglects to capture and clarify the role of the public in communication societies in a comparably sharp and defined manner. I suspect that this may be due to the fact that in his proposed stereoscopic stress on reconstruction and empirical description, validity and facticity, or norms and facts, he tends not merely to give too much weight to the former member of the pair but to draw the distinction in such a way that he claims too much on behalf of moral philosophy. More specifically, he tends to interpret the third point of view too strongly in terms of the idealised moral point of view than is good for the public who embodies and carries it. Instead of accommodating the level of contingency inherent in communication processes, he adopts a position that excludes contingency.

In this article, I propose to focus on the problem of triple contingency in Habermas's recent major writings. I shall argue that, despite the concept of the public in his earlier and later work, Habermas's attempt to foreclose the risk of misunderstanding or disagreement raised by the doubly contingent relation of ego and alter by means of a model of communication, that is closely tied to the moral point of view, in fact entails the obliteration of the significance of the public in communicatively mediated social processes. I shall further suggest that if instead one takes seriously the public in its inherent pluralism and sees it in relation to different cultural models activated by the competing sections of the pluralistic public and the process whereby one or a single combination of these models becomes socially accepted to the exclusion or subordination of the others, then he or she must recognise the problem of triple contingency over and above that of double contingency. If one does this, a theoretical possibility beyond Habermas's theory of communicative action becomes possible that neither jettisons the key theoretical concept of communication nor reduces all structuration to contextual or empirical contingencies.[2]

To be able to pursue the intention of this essay in an intelligible way, I shall first give an overview of Habermas's appropriation and central use of the concept of double contingency, including its original sense in sociological theory. Against this background, it will then be possible to ferret out the submerged notion of triple contingency in Habermas and to analyse the difficulties that prevent him from explicitly acknowledging and developing it. Two qualifications of the aim of this article need to be made here, however, to keep expectations within bounds. While it is quite possible, first, to deal with the problem of triple contingency in less theoretical or more substantive terms than are proposed here by analysing Habermas's aporetic treatment of the public throughout his writings, I choose the theoretical route for present purposes and reserve publication of the more substantive analysis elsewhere.[3] In the course of the development of the argument below, reference will nevertheless intermittently be made to the problem of the public, both theoretically and in Habermas. Second, the demonstration of the presence of the theoretical problem of triple contingency in Habermas of course implies a solution in the sense of a theoretical revision of his position. Although I believe that I do dispose over at least the rudiments of a new situational cognitive or epistemic theory of the public and, by extension, a new theory of the evolution of situational epistemic structures to carry out such a revision, it will not be possible to present the implied theory in the present context. Where appropriate, however, indications of what it entails will nevertheless be given.[4]

1. HABERMAS'S APPROPRIATION AND USE OF DOUBLE CONTINGENCY

Habermas borrows the neoclassical concept of double contingency from Parsons, who in turn extrapolated the concept from the classical contributions of symbolic interactionism and social phenomenology. Parsons was the first to name and to give precise formulation to what he called 'the fundamental proposition of *double* contingency of interaction' (1977b: 167). This was done in 1951 in the almost simultaneously appearing *Toward a General Theory of Action*, an anthology edited with Edward Shils, and *The Social System*. He finally restated his position in 1968 in a contribution to the *International Encyclopedia of the Social Sciences* entitled 'Social Interaction', which was later included in one of his last collections, *Social Systems and the Evolution of Action Theory* (1977b). In the latter essay, Parsons offers a lucid overview of the complete history of the concept of social interaction and its theoretical context. In addition to older historical theories, special mention is made of American pragmatism and European existentialism, including phenomenology, as two very influential theoretical traditions that have shaped the field in a decisive way. What is remarkable about his account is that Parsons gives phenomenology short shrift and, despite Schutz's incisive analysis, does not refer to the Austro-American at all. That he nevertheless had Schutz in mind is suggested by the fact that he mentions Erving Goffman, who, in his opinion, has brought together 'a Meadian symbolic interactionist and a phenomenological viewpoint' (1977b: 166).[5] There can be no doubt about the fact that Mead as well as the conspicuously absent Schutz had prepared the ground for Parsons's identification and formulation of the theorem or proposition of double contingency.[6]

The Classical and the Neoclassical Background: Mead, Schutz, and Parsons

In his pursuit of the fundamental question concerning 'the basic mechanism whereby the social process goes on' (Mead 1974: 13), which he dealt with in terms of his synthesis of ideas regarding language and communication deriving from the pragmatism of Charles Sanders Peirce, on the one hand, and German idealism, particularly as represented by Hegel's concern with the dialectic of the 'I' and Dilthey's hermeneutics, on the other, George Herbert Mead gave central attention to the problem of what was only well after his death in 1931 called 'double contingency'. The problematic situation at the bottom of the social process is that two individuals who come face-to-face and are compelled to bridge the gap separating them, thus establishing an appropriate relation to one another.

Mead's (1974: 42-134, 135-226, 227-336) phylogenetic and ontogenetic investigations into the development of symbolisation at the human evolutionary level and into the formation of the self and society respectively provided the terms of his theoretical solution. Conceiving the elementary social situation as a 'speech or communication' (p. 67) situation, he regarded the language medium as, on the one hand, making available the 'significant symbol' (pp. 45-6) that calls out in the individual advancing it the same attitude towards its meaning as it calls out in the other individual participating with the first in a given social situation and thus, on the other, allowing both individuals to 'take the attitude' not only of 'the other' but simultaneously also of 'all those concerned' or 'the larger community' (pp. 270-71). The organized set of responses or expectations of society or the generally recognised social norms toward which the participating individuals ultimately orient themselves —what Mead famously called 'the generalized other' (pp. 90, 154) —thus formed the core component of his solution to the elementary problem of establishing a social relation.

Already in his early major work advancing a social phenomenology focused on intersubjectivity, Alfred Schutz gave central attention to the problem of 'double contingency', as Parsons later called it. Schutz (1967: 97-138) starts in his analysis of intersubjectivity from the situation of two individuals confronting one another and being faced with the problem of having to come to mutual understanding. His position on intersubjective understanding, particularly the problem situation of double contingency at the heart of intersubjectivity, can be reconstructed as a layered model, stretching from the 'Other-orientation' (p. 146) in the sense of the positing of the existence of the other to the establishment of a full social or 'face-to-face relationship' (pp. 167, 169). At issue at this highest level is the relational problem of two individuals who are subject and object both for themselves and for the other, on the one hand, and the nature of their relation, on the other. The problem of double contingency is given with the fact that the one's perspective on his or her relationship to the other is contingent on the other's perspective and vice versa. Were the two partners to deal adequately with this problem so as to be able to establish a felicitous social relationship, then they would have to articulate and co-ordinate two self-other complexes. That Schutz elaborates on the specific experience and knowledge of the other encountered under the risky contingent conditions of a given social situation (pp. 169, 171-2) does not deter him from stressing the crucial significance of the 'stock of knowledge' or 'interpretive schemes' learned and acquired through experience (pp. 80-

3, 162, 169) for dealing with such contingency. These schemes, which provide meaning contexts for all further experience, structure and guide the individual's expectations, interpretation of signs, and dealings with the other and the external world.

Parsons clearly regards double contingency as a theoretical concept that is necessary to account at a basic level for the possibility of social interaction or communication and, by extension, of social order. On the one hand, double contingency draws attention to the potential hazard of conflict between individuals confronting each other face-to-face, and on the other it points toward accomplishments that could lead to cooperation and sharing (1964: 48). As such he saw it as an unavoidable basic condition that generated a problem at the social level which required a solution if social action, social interaction, social order and hence society were to be possible. Assuming a dyadic relation while acknowledging that it presupposes a common culture, Parsons starts from what he regards as the two most crucial reference points for an analysis of social interaction: '(1) that each actor is *both* acting agent and object of orientation *both* to himself and to others; and (2) that, as acting agent, he orients to himself and to others and, as object, has meaning to himself and to others, in *all* of the primary modes or aspects. The actor is knower and object of cognition, utilizer of instrumental means and himself a means, emotionally attached to others and an object of attachment, evaluator and object of evaluation, interpreter of symbols and himself a symbol' (Parsons 1977b: 167). From these two reference points, which unmistakably build on Mead and Schutz's achievements but are differentiated by means of his neo-Kantian concept of culture, Parsons then derives the theorem of double contingency: 'Not only, as for isolated behaving units, animal or human, is a goal outcome contingent on successful cognition and manipulation of environmental objects by the actors, but since the most important objects involved in interaction act too, it is also contingent on *their* action or intervention in the course of events' (p. 167). As against this somewhat misleading formulation, it should be pointed out that double contingency is connected with the word 'their' italicized by Parsons, as his other explications of the concept bear out. On the original introduction of the concept in the early 1950s, Parsons stated the proposition in the following form: 'There is a *double contingency* inherent in interaction. On the one hand, ego's gratifications are contingent on his selection among available alternatives. But in turn, alter's reaction will be contingent on ego's selection and will result from a complementary selection on alter's part' (Parsons and Shils 1951: 16). In *The Social System*, he once again identified the two 'contingency factors' that result in double contingency: the contingency of what an actor actually does in the context of an elementary interaction situation, and the contingency of the other's reaction to what is being done (Parsons 1964: 94).

In *The Social System*, Parsons (1964: 10-11) underlines the centrality of double contingency by suggesting that it is closely related to the indissoluble relation between symbolisation and interaction. Let us attempt to reconstruct the suggested position. The basic reference point for Parsons is that while symbolisation is impossible without the interaction of actors, the individual actor is unable, vice versa, to acquire a symbolic system without interaction with others. Double contingency occupies the centre of this nexus in so far as it poses a problem, on the one hand, but at the same time also demands a solution, on the other. When two actors encounter one another in an indeterminate situation and ego begins to adopt an elementary orientation toward alter, then ego engages in signification or symbolisation. This means that ego is bringing into play an expectation that necessarily involves abstraction or generalisation from the particularities of the situation. The expectation that ego brings into play here in the form of symbolisation, is one that ego has acquired through interaction with others. Whence its potential transcendence of the particular situation in which ego and alter find themselves. When alter now reacts to ego in contingency on ego's proposal, alter also articulates an expectation and thus engages in a further step of symbolisation that reinforces the structuring effect of the first symbolisation step. Two actors who have acquired a symbolic system or culture in the medium of social interaction act and react in particular ways in a specific situation such that they thereby activate relatively stable and more or less shared symbolic or cultural forms that give the situation a sufficiently abstract or generalised meaning to make communication possible between the two partners.

Proceeding from this theoretical basis, Parsons gives a particular interpretation of generalisation from the particularity of the specific situation and of identity of meaning across the range of contingent alternatives available in the situation. The direction of the move he makes, which is not untypical of the sociology of the first half of the 20th century, is already suggested by his interpretation of the symbolisation-interaction relation in terms of the integration of motivation and normative culture, but it becomes fully clear when he has to find a solution to the problem posed by the fact of double contingency, that is, when he has to face such questions as: How do two actors who encounter each other in a situation of interaction relate to one another? What allows the two actors to make a selection from among the available alternatives? On what basis are their respective performative contributions interrelated and coordinated? How is communication between ego and alter possible? Parsons's solution to the problem of double contingency takes the form of cultural determination

(Parsons 1964: 11, 37-8; 1977b: 168-9). Culture, which is always already available as a shared system, penetrates action orientations to such an extent that the existence of a value consensus can be assumed. On the one hand, it provides shared symbols or elements of tradition that control general systems of orientation. On the other, cultural patterns of value are internalised and institutionalised so as to become part of personalities and interaction systems as need dispositions and role expectations respectively. When two actors, who are motivated by their culturally defined needs, face one another in a particular situation that is nevertheless generally delineated by cultural symbols, they are thus able to relate to each other or to enter into social interaction due to the correspondence between or overlap of the role expectations or normative orientations they had acquired through socialisation.

Habermas on Double Contingency

The first impression one gets on reading Habermas's (1981aII: 319-22; 1987a: 213-15) discussion of double contingency is that he rejects it as a pseudo-theoretical problem which has been generated by unacceptable empiricist, individualist and utilitarian assumptions. This, in any event, is how he interprets Parsons's introduction of the theorem with reference to elementary interaction. As the reader proceeds, however, it becomes apparent that Habermas is willing to accept it on the basis of changed presuppositions. Instead of defining double contingency in terms of the voluntaristic free choice of ego and alter, as Parsons according to him does, he regards the theorem as invoking actors who are capable of decisions in the sense of taking yes or no positions on validity claims advanced in linguistic communication —particularly important to him being the ability to say no (1987a: 74). Not only is there something such as the 'doubly contingent relation', then, but he also accepts Parsons's suggestion that it poses a problem that requires ordering accomplishments —for him, the coordination of action. What he apparently quietly took over in the course of argumentation in *The Theory of Communicative Action*, he some years later emphatically accepts: 'I assume with Parsons that social interactions linked in space and time are subject to conditions of double contingency' (Habermas 1992: 173, 1996a: 139). Here he leaves no doubt whatsoever about where he stands on the matter.

Proceeding from these observations, I would venture to submit that Habermas's theory of communicative action is a response, in extension of Mead, Schutz and Parsons, to the problem posed by double contingency. Starting from yet redefining double contingency, *The Theory of Communicative Action* (1987a) is essentially an elaboration of a solution to the problem in terms of a more fully developed version of the theory of communication than had been available to his predecessors. *Between Facts and Norms* (1996a), which is conceived as an extension of the theory of communicative action, invites a similar interpretation. It starts explicitly (1992: 33, 1996a: 18) from double contingency and seeks to develop a solution to the problem it poses in terms of modern law. At the same time, the theoretical tour de force of these works also opens up a perspective on a problem that henceforth would become virulent in his work. Given the intense concentration and the immense expenditure of energy on the working out of the coordinating and ordering accomplishments and structures required by the complex solution envisaged by him, it does not come as a surprise that Habermas overlooks this next most important problem raised by the theory of communication, namely, the problem of 'triple contingency'. *Between Facts and Norms* as well as the later *Die Einbeziehung des Anderen* (1996b) differ from *The Theory of Communicative Action* in so far as these books contain evidence that it is becoming increasingly difficult for him to ignore this problem. The fact that Habermas does not acknowledge and explicitly take up this new problem, particularly in the sociologically relevant sections of his major works, has far-reaching implications for his place in the sociological tradition and for the relation of the younger generation to him. Because of his continued search for a solution to a problem posed in the classical phase of sociology and his concomitant failure to develop the new problem that he himself raises in the course of so doing, Habermas can be classified with Parsons as being a neo-classical sociologist. The problem that he bequeaths to contemporary sociology is that of triple contingency.

Habermas's particular position on double contingency owes everything to an extrapolation and penetrating analysis of the implications of the communication-theoretical approach far beyond Mead, Schutz and Parsons. In developing this approach, he was able to draw on the long-standing concern with language in the German philosophical tradition, the 20th century linguistic turn, and in particular the inspiring interpretations of Pierce and Wittgenstein by his friend Karl-Otto Apel (Habermas 1997b: 84-97).

In his reconstruction of Mead's symbolic interactionism, Habermas follows three distinct strands that allow him to delineate the problem of contingency,[7] while pinpointing both the strengths and weaknesses of the US author's theory of communication.[8] The strands are those leading, first, from the gesture via symbolically mediated to linguistically mediated communication; second, from context-bound signs to meaning conventions securing the identity of meaning in symbolisation; and, third, from instinctual to cultural, linguistic modes of the coordination of action. By giving attention in an innovative way to the various developments, Mead succeeded in introducing a paradigm shift that deservedly earned him the status of a founder of the modern social sciences, but Habermas nevertheless discovers a number of gaps in his path-breaking analysis that weaken his theory of communication. In addition to failing to develop his concept of language in an adequately differentiated way (Habermas 1987a: 28), Mead pursued neither the significance of meaning conventions (p. 15) nor the reaching of understanding through communication far enough (p. 28). These weaknesses go back to Mead's attachment to points of view deriving from epistemology, behaviourism and psychology that blocked the full development of a communication-theoretical understanding. As regards the problem of how the actions of ego and alter confronting each other in a social situation could be coordinated, for instance, Habermas (p. 26) insists that Mead never struck on the illocutionary binding effect contained in linguistic utterances. Similarly, his significant contribution under the title of 'the generalized other' also suffers from a flaw. Not only did he fail to differentiate sufficiently the socio-cognitive and moral points of view implied by this concept (p. 36), but he was not clear enough either about the moral dimension, particularly the validity status of norms (p. 38). This weakness can be traced to Mead's neglect of the phylogenesis of moral authority (p. 44). In Habermas's view, the various lacunae in Mead's work can be filled by a communication-theoretical position that is internally adequately articulated and consistently developed at both an ontogenetic and phylogenetic level.

Habermas's (1987a: 126-34) analysis of Schutz from the point of view of his contribution to a communication-theoretical concept of the lifeworld gives him the opportunity to appropriate a concept of cultural background knowledge that provides resources for the interpretative negotiation of common definitions of action situations, on the one hand, and is in turn reproduced through the communicative action and mutual understanding such interpretative accomplishments entail, on the other.[9] A significant aspect of Schutz's work for him, therefore, is his communicative concept of action in the sense of the interpretation of a situation and the establishment of mutual understanding. The need for this concept derives from what Schutz appreciates as the fundamental problem of intersubjectivity, which Habermas accepts as relating the 'the question of how different subjects can share the same lifeworld' (1987a: 129) and of how they can avoid 'the risk of not coming to some understanding, that is, of disagreement or misunderstanding' (p. 127). In keeping with his endorsement of the concept of double contingency, Habermas acknowledges that Schutz, by way of his concern with the risk of disagreement or misunderstanding and its avoidance by the establishment of mutual understanding, is touching on a necessary condition of the social world. Despite this significant contribution, however, Schutz failed to realise the full potential of his position. The basic problem, according to Habermas (1987a: 129, 130), is that Schutz's attachment to Husserlian phenomenology, in spite of his focus on the intersubjective social world, not only kept him within the bounds of the philosophy of consciousness, but also prevented him from fully adopting the communication-theoretical approach. Consequently, his work suffered from being suspended in an ambivalent position. Were this difficulty to be eliminated, according to Habermas's proposal, then the structures of the lifeworld would have to be understood from the start and throughout in terms of the structures of intersubjectivity generated by linguistic communication.

Earlier, I have argued that Habermas takes over the theorem of double contingency from Parsons, yet not without rejecting the voluntarism, together with its empiricist, individualist and utilitarian connotations, on foot of which it had originally been introduced and replacing it by a communication-theoretical basis. Having accepted this principle, Habermas (1987a: 215-56) then fights a running battle against the ever new permutations of Parsons's solution to the problem generated by the fact of double contingency, all of which turn on the concept of culture. During the early phase of his intellectual development, Parsons argued against the heteronomy of ends and in favour of the integrity of the social by attributing cultural value standards to individual actors and demonstrating the need for their harmonisation (p. 214). It is this kind of thinking that still shaped his introduction of the fundamental proposition of double contingency. It underwent a relatively drastic change in his early middle phase, however, when cultural anthropology assisted him in developing a concept of culture that allowed him to conceive of the cultural determination of action orientations (p. 217). Common cultural patterns, which were differentiated along neo-Kantian lines into interpretative, evaluative and expressive components, were depicted as regulatives that through internalisation and institutionalisation penetrate into motives and role expectations respectively. The manner in which cultural values structure an actor's scope of choice between alternatives yet leaves open the contingency of decisions was captured by the concept of 'pattern variables'. Parsons here ascribed a special status to culture by defining it as an external, free-floating complex of meaning possessing its own coherence and consistency as well as a certain control function. Habermas (1987a: 221, 226, 254) relentlessly criticises this as a reification of culture which he accounts for with reference to Parsons' neo-Kantian predilection and his related choice of the inappropriate epistemological model. Later, when Parsons exchanged structural functionalism for systems functionalism, he retained the conception of culture as a transcendent system of semantically related values possessing validity. It was only in his last period, characterised by his acceptance of the primacy of systems theory, that he was compelled to surrender the claim of special status on behalf of culture. Instead of neo-Kantianism, systems theory now dictated that culture be regarded as one sub-system of the general action system among others. Calling cybernetics to his assistance, however, he nevertheless managed to ascribe anew a steering function to the cultural system by means of the hierarchical control that information exerts over energy expenditure. In this way, he finally believed himself once again able to secure a determining force for culture (pp. 248-9). In Habermas's estimation, a better solution to the problem following from double contingency than is offered by this epistemologically conceived, past-oriented, static, objectivist and reified concept of culture has to be sought for in the 'communication-theoretical model of speaking and acting subjects' (p. 254).

From Double to Triple Contingency

Habermas grants that in one way or another all his predecessors saw the relevance of language and communication, yet neither Mead nor Schutz and even less Parsons fully embraced this insight, not to mention fully exploited its potential. Language as the primary means for the transmission of culture as well as the communicative dimension of action coordination should be taken more seriously that any of them realised. According to his proposed communication-theoretical model, double contingency should be conceived from the start as the relational problem of communicatively acting subjects rather than human beings without a fully differentiated propositional language, as in Mead; or intuitively proceeding and overly subjectivist actors, as in Schutz; or monadic actors whose contingent choices between alternatives are regulated by preferences, as in Parsons. Mead's position on meaning conventions and the coordination of action could be improved and Parsons's reified concept of culture could be dissolved if a Schutzian view is adopted according to which the emphasis is placed on interpretative acts oriented toward mutual understanding as the means whereby transmitted culture is appropriated and common situational definitions are arrived at. For Habermas (1987a: 220) this means that the twofold function of culture should, at all times, be appreciated, that is, its context-generating function of providing the unquestioned background against which communicatively acting subjects confront each other and are compelled to construct common situation definitions; and its text-generating function of inserting individual cultural patterns into the semantic content of utterances and thus providing knowledge that is criticisable. It is particularly at this text-generating level that Habermas makes his most characteristic and most decisive contribution which goes far beyond all his predecessors. The problem of the coordination of action raised by the fact of double contingency, which opposes two communicatively acting subjects capable of taking a decision about a yes or no position on a linguistic offer, can be solved by conceiving of the participants as being oriented toward validity claims raised in their communication (p. 215). Unlike Mead, who did not sufficiently appreciate the propositionally differentiated nature of language and hence proceeded to fix on relatively vague symbols, Habermas distinguishes and clarifies the illocutionary force of the full range of linguistic utterances, from a statement of fact through giving a command to expressing a feeling. Unlike Schutz (1967: 130), who indeed recognised the importance of the reasons underlying communicative offers yet left them essentially unanalysed under the title of the 'in-order-to-motive' of communication, Habermas analyses the rationality of speaking subjects and ferrets out the full range of validity claims that they at least implicitly advance in their communication. Finally, unlike Parsons, who located validity in the consistency requirements of a free-floating, transcendent cultural realm and thus failed to plausibly explain how it could become factically effective, Habermas (1987a: 231; 1996a: 18-19) makes the far-reaching proposal to bring validity claims down from heaven and to incorporate them from the start in empirical contexts of action.

Building on his own understanding of double contingency as the relation of communicatively acting subjects who do not know whether to expect a yes or a no response from the other on making a communicative offer, Habermas develops his position by drawing on Hegel's analysis of the 'dialectics of the I' (Habermas 1974: 144-47; 1971a: 193), on Schutz's analysis of intersubjectivity in terms of reciprocally interlocked perspectives and roles within the same communicative context (Habermas 1988a: 106) and on Mead's analysis of the change in perspective accompanying the transition from play to game (Habermas 1987a: 35-36). The result is a clarification of the structure of communication that goes well beyond double contingency and the relational problem of ego and alter. It therefore also serves him as a basis for a critique of dialogical philosophy (Habermas 1997a: 133-34) in so far as it proceeds from a selective understanding of communication and exchanges the traditional epistemological subject-object relation for the communicative I-thou relation. Formally, Habermas's analysis of the structure of communication highlights the perspectives or roles, the attitudes and the system of personal pronouns involved in communication, but it is also here that he implicitly begins to raise the problem of triple contingency. This problem, to be sure, has been dormant in his writings since his first major work, *Strukturwandel der Öffentlichkeit* (1962), which became available in English in 1989 under the title *The Structural Transformation of the Public Sphere*, but it is particularly in his work, *Between Facts and Norms* (1996a) and in the later collection, *Die Einbeziehung des Anderen* (1996b, 1999a), that it begins to assert itself in what seem to be an uncontrolled manner.

In the relation of double contingency, two communicatively acting subjects, ego and alter, are faced with the problem of taking up the communicative roles of speaker and hearer. If they succeed in overcoming these contingency conditions, the interchangeable perspectives of the speaker and the hearer become intermeshed in such a way that two coordinated ego-alter circles or perspectives of participation result. The participants' awareness is not exhausted by concentrating solely on themselves and on the other opposite them, however, since at the same time both are also able to relate to the world of perceptible and manipulable objects around them. Were they not able to do so, they would not have been able to participate fully in communication. This ability implies that, in addition to the perspectives of speaker and hearer, another perspective comes into play in the development beyond the double contingency relation. This is the perspective of the observer. When this perspective enters social interaction, ego is able to take an attitude that allows him or her to divide alter's communicative role in two, the role of alter ego in the sense of a participating counterpart and the role of a neutral or non-participating onlooker or observer belonging to the group forming part of the social situation. As a consequence of this structural differentiation made possible by the adoption of an objectifying attitude in addition to a performative attitude, the perspectives of speaker and hearer are relativised vis-à-vis a third perspective. The first person who is speaking and the second person who is addressed and responds, show up against the background of the uninvolved third person. The emergence of this basic triad marks the structure of communication that takes place in a social group within a situation in the real world. Such communication is mediated by the system of personal pronouns that allows not only an 'I' to relate to a 'you' or 'thou' as well as to a 'him', 'her' or 'them', but also others in the role of second person or third person to relate to a 'me'.

For Habermas, the most important point that follows from this analysis of the structure of communication concerns the implications of the differentiation of the third person point of view for the relation to the other. This means that relations are now being touched on which implies a shift from double to triple contingency. While the new category of taking the attitude of the other that now becomes apparent is related to what

Mead called 'the generalized other', Habermas (1987a: 35-40) nevertheless criticises Mead for not grasping it in its full sense, and therefore he brings Durkheim in to support an extended version. Mead did not make a clear distinction between the socio-cognitive and moral dimensions of generalised and hence valid social norms, and as a consequence he neglected to come to grips with normative validity in the sense of the obligatory character of valid norms in a manner approaching Durkheim. The criticism of Mead also applies to Schutz, who operated with a culturalist concept of the lifeworld to the exclusion, among other things, of the question concerning the social norms at issue in institutionalisation and social solidarity (Habermas 1987a: 139).

Sociocognitively, the individual learns in the course of ontogenesis and socialisation to objectify the reciprocal interrelation of participant perspectives from the perspective of the observer and thus to adopt an objectifying attitude toward his or her own interaction with alter ego. Once the individual is able to do this, he or she distinguishes ego's and alter's system of interchangeable, interrelated participant perspectives from the particular situation in which they find themselves, and appreciates that the system of perspectives is a general one that anyone would have to adopt were he or she to take the places of ego and alter. By being generalised, a concrete pattern of action is thus transposed into a rule of conduct or a norm. At the same time, the individual also understands that the will, interests and possible sanctions that enter ego's and alter's interaction as imperative force are not particularities attaching to ego and alter, but are rather tied up with the larger collectivity or group to which they belong. It is a group-specific generalised imperative that rests on a collective choice related to the maintenance of collective interests.

Habermas (1987a: 37; 1996b: 14-15, 20-22) is critical of non-cognitivist empiricist and weak cognitivist contextual moral theories since both accept, albeit in different ways, the result of the sociocognitive development sketched above as being definitive. This leads them to emphasise the collective regulation of the choices of participants in social interaction who coordinate their actions through collectively endorsed sanctions and the reciprocal satisfaction of interests, as in empiricist ethics, or the reciprocal reproduction of strong values, as in contextual ethics. What they overlook is the obligatory character of social norms or normative validity —'the categorial validity claim of moral obligations' or 'the epistemic core of normative validity' (1996b: 15) which becomes apparent only when one recognises 'the third point of view' (1996b: 106, 109, 114, 120, 122, 125) in the sense of the moral point of view from which intentions and policies can be judged in a context-independent and impartial way. This is the Kantian position articulated earlier by Durkheim and today, albeit softened through communication, by Habermas himself. In this case, the imperativistic authority attaching to the collective will and collective choice of a particular social groups or larger unit is transformed through socialisation and individuation, and thus insight and assent, into normative authority which no longer admits of being identified with a particular social unit due to its in principle universalistic character. This coincides with Mead's 'generalized other' in its proper sense. In terms of Habermas's (1996b: 15, 39, 117, !20) approach, this moral point of view possessing epistemic and thus postmetaphysical authority is a reconstruction of the point of view that the members of post-traditional societies themselves assume when they are required under the conditions of the problematisation or breakdown of moral norms to have recourse to epistemic grounds or reasons —which, in turn, should not be confused with the actors' motives.

2. TRIPLE CONTINGENCY IN HABERMAS

I argued above that, paradoxically, Habermas inadvertently raised the problem of triple contingency in the course of his analysis of the structure of communication which was aimed at the solution of the problem posed by the fact of double contingency. The problem of the higher level contingency was brought to the fore when the analysis, in moving beyond the relation of double contingency, uncovered the differentiation of the structure of communication which led to the emergence of the third person perspective. This means that triple contingency is connected with the triadic structure of communication. Although not recognising it as such, Habermas did begin to touch on the problem through the classical contributions of Mead, Schutz and Durkheim. While the works of the former two registered the process of the structural differentiation of communication by means of the complex of sociocognitive concepts encapsulating the system of perspectives, attitudes and personal pronouns mediating communication in social units, the latter pointed toward the moral dimension. Already the fact that Habermas tends to proceed from here to emphasise the moral dimension to the exclusion of all else, thus making a choice for abstract non-contingency against contingency,[10] suggests that he does not deal with the problem of triple contingency. But when he, despite numerous difficulties prompting him to change track, continues to fail to offer a consistent approach, one begins to suspect that he does not recognise the problem as such. *The Theory of Communicative Action* gives evidence of his ambivalence, which is compounded in *Between Facts and Norms* and in *Die Einbeziehung des Anderen*. The latter is particularly interesting in so far as it contains an explicit attempt to come to grips with the proper location of 'the third point of view'.

The Concept

Before considering Habermas's difficulties in these three works, however, let us take a preliminary look at what triple contingency involves. In the case of double contingency, as we have seen, two social actors or communicatively acting subjects, A and B, face or encounter one another and enter some relation with each other as 'I' and 'thou'. In the basic situation of triple contingency, by contrast, there is a third perspective, borne by C, who observes what A and B are saying and doing. C is indeed a non-participating observer or onlooker, as Habermas submits, but C is not simply a 'neuter' (Habermas 1987a: 35) in the sense of a neutral and uninvolved third person who at best allows or compels A and B to adopt an objectifying attitude toward their own interaction. Although not participating, C does have a certain if indirect involvement. In fact, C has a constitutive significance for the social situation as such. Habermas would indeed seem to recognise this constitutive sense through Mead's 'generalized other', but why does he persist in taking the twofold I-thou relation as representing the elementary social situation whereas it is actually the threefold configuration that for the first time establishes it? Why does he start in both his two major theoretical works —*The Theory of Communicative Action* and *Between Facts and Norms* —from double contingency?

To the triadic configuration, furthermore, applies a higher degree of contingency. In the case of double contingency, two actors or subjects, A and B, are both compelled to make a selection from alternatives while taking alter ego into account, and thus to establish a relation between themselves. The inclusion of the third-person point of view, represented by C, means that the social situation in the case of triple contingency is very different and more complicated right from the start. It is not simply a matter of the aggregation of elementary interaction. To the extent that the observer, C, belongs to the situation as a constitutive part of its sociality, the third point of view standing behind or over and above A and B represents society. It embodies the societal power of definition. C has a constitutive social role in that he, she or it has the power to define the situation. Whatever A and B say and do, therefore, must in principle make sense to C. From the start and throughout, A and B are subject in their interrelations to meanings and norms as defined by society and represented by the observer. As regards contingency, A and B make their choices and take each other into account, while at the same time being relativised by a societal definition or collectively accepted representation for which C stands. Here, again, it would seem as though Habermas is not very far off the mark. He is aware of the societal power of definition associated with 'the generalized other' not only in its sociocognitive sense but also in its moral sense. Sociocognitively, C represents the collective will in the sense of a group-specific generalised imperative, and morally it represents the normative validity and normative authority associated with the moral point of view. Yet here too, as in the previous case, a subtle difference is of enormous significance. Habermas largely emphasises the moral dimension and downplays or even rejects the sociocognitive one. This approach constitutes a problem in its own right. But in *The Theory of Communicative Action* (1987a: 231) he also claims, quite to the contrary, that his position constitutes an integration of these very same two dimensions. While he still maintains the first position, he has since come to defend the second more often. This is the source of a conspicuous ambivalence in *Between Facts and Norms* and *Die Einbeziehung des Anderen*. This ambivalence indicates that, in the final analysis, Habermas does not recognise the problem of triple contingency. For this problem consists not simply in the fact that C relativises the perspectives of A and B in that the third perspective compels them to take a detour through a cognitive-symbolic structure, but in particular in the unpredictable mediation and integration of the sociocognitive and the moral in the course of a process of deliberation or discourse in a concrete context. In contemporary communication societies, what is collectively accepted as valid is neither pre-given nor an immutable transcendent, but itself becomes established only in the course of the process. The crucial marker of what is collectively accepted as valid in such a concrete context, important to note, is the role of the public.[11] This is where the problem of triple contingency asserts itself. According to the available evidence, Habermas seems neither willing nor capable of taking this bull by the horns, despite the fact that he is the one who has done most to create the conditions for the problem of triple contingency to become visible.

The Theory of Communicative Action

In his discussion of the sociocognitive and moral dimensions of the generalised other, Habermas not only underlines the importance of this distinction, but also stresses the need to focus on the moral dimension *per se*. This emphasis goes hand in hand with a demotion of the sociocognitive dimension. Although the latter actually concerns not simply the concepts of self and other acquired in the course of socialisation and individuation, but rather the empirically identifiable, historically specific sociocultural context, he nevertheless places a stricture on it. This unaccommodating treatment can be attributed to the fact that Habermas takes a position vis-à-vis the sociocultural dimension from a moral-theoretical standpoint and thus dismisses it together with 'empiricist' or 'contextual ethics' (1987a: 37). On this faulty basis, he then proceeds to introduce a series of distinctions, such as those between imperativistic and normative authority, sanction and assent or socially generalised imperatives and intersubjective recognition (1987a: 38-9), in respect of which he creates the impression as though it were possible to embrace the last member of each pair to the exclusion of the first one. Concomitantly, he tends to give the first moment an overly empiricist interpretation. In this same vein, he defends moral-theoretical formalism of a Kantian provenance which he also finds in Durkheim and Mead (1987a: 108). At the same time, however, Habermas advances a claim that is very interesting yet contrary to this position of his. He claims that his theory of communicative action is an exercise in detranscendentalisation which he circumscribes as follows: 'Through the concept of the lifeworld, the sphere of validity claims, which is, according to Parsons, located in a transcendent realm of free-floating cultural meanings, would be incorporated from the start into empirical, spatiotemporally identifiable contexts of action...If validity claims function, so to speak, as pulleys over which consensus formation and thus the symbolic reproduction of the lifeworld pass, they are, without prejudice to their normative content, installed as social facts —their facticity needs no further foundation' (1987a: 231). In this case, Habermas does not distinguish normative validity as against the sociocognitive and related phenomena and then select it in preference over the latter, but he maintains them in their interrelationship and locates them within sociocultural reality. Regarding their interrelationship as a property of that reality, he thus opens up the possibility of seeing the members of society themselves as dealing with this interrelationship, particularly the tension between the two moments, as a problem they have to confront and resolve. Taking South Africa under the apartheid regime or Northern Ireland before the Good Friday agreement as an example, one can see how the members of these societies themselves confronted the contradiction between normative validity and what is socially accepted and sanctioned in their particular sociocultural contexts, and how they sought to collectively identify, define, address and resolve their collective problem. At this point, of course, the problem of triple contingency arises, as is suggested by the fact that public communication formed an inherent part of the dynamics of both these conflicts and that the definitional power brought to bear on both by international observers and more broadly the observing public proved decisive. Through the public, epistemic structures came into operation under specific sociocultural conditions where contingencies in the given situation had to be overcome. Yet there is no evidence to suggest that the problem as such enters the purview of Habermas's work. Despite the potential of this second proposal, the first position is the one that he predominantly represents. The critique of neo-Kantianism that he levels against Parsons would seem, ironically, to apply in a certain sense to himself as well. The preoccupation with validity, earlier championed by such neo-Kantians as Heinrich Rickert and Emile Lask, undoubtedly predominates.

Between Facts and Norms

As the different titles of the German and English editions of Habermas's later major work suggest, the second of the above-mentioned two proposals is taken up so that the tension between 'facticity and validity' (Habermas 1992) or 'between facts and norms' (Habermas 1996a) becomes its main theme. This is a promising start that fills one with the expectation that the problem of triple contingency is going to be addressed directly, yet the highly interesting and instructive book, which deals with relevant topics such as discourse or deliberation, public opinion formation and will formation, decision making, and even the public, turns out to be a disappointment in this regard. Against the foil of an overview of the linguistic turn in reaction to psychologism and of his appropriation of Peirce's work for the purposes of his own theory of the communication community, Habermas (1996a: 17-27) reasserts the detranscendentalising thrust of his project. For him, the idealisations built into language through its meaning and especially validity enter the constitution of the social reality of social interactions networked in space and time through communicative action. Although being unavoidable presuppositions anticipating ideal situations, they are made effective in interaction in so far as the illocutionary binding force of speech acts is brought into play to coordinate the actions of the participants. Communicative action allows the counterfactual assumptions of the actors, who are oriented toward the validity claims raised by themselves and the other participants, to become immediately effective in the construction and maintenance of social order, which itself consists of the recognition of normative validity claims. A careful reading of the opening sections of the book reveals that Habermas is here all the time thinking of double contingency and participants in interaction seeking to overcome the 'risk of dissension' it poses, while the generalised other is relevant only as the seat of idealisations in the form of validity claims. This means that he is overlooking the problem of triple contingency. Missing from his account is the middle level, between the participants, one the one hand, and the sphere of validity, on the other. What is lacking is the third-person perspective in the guise of the public who plays a decisive role in every concrete sociocultural context in the contemporary world in determining how the validity claims take effect in public communication and what is eventually collectively accepted. Instead of addressing the problem of triple contingency directly, Habermas arrests the dynamism that the public brings into the social process, thus making its outcome less than predictable, by introducing modern law as the mechanism by means of which the tension between facticity and validity, which in the modern context multiplies the risk of dissension, is stabilised. There is of course no sense in denying the significance of law, but, considering the problem at hand in its contemporary manifestation, Habermas's solution is a conservative one that fits well into neo-classical sociology and, by the same token, ignores a central problem of contemporary sociology.

At first sight, the thesis of the missing public in Habermas seems preposterous in respect of an author who has made such a monumental contribution to the theory of *die Öffentlichkeit*, the public sphere, publicity and the public. It is by no means my intention to question the significance of his work on this topic, from the early *The Structural Transformation of the Public Sphere* (1989) through *Toward a Rational Society* (1971a, particularly Chapter 5), later to the very important *Between Facts and Norms* (1996a, particularly Chapter 7 and 8), but there is room for a subtler point to be made. To begin with, it should be noted that there is a difference between 'the public sphere' and 'the public', and that Habermas is interested in the former rather than the latter. The 'public sphere' refers to a communication structure that is generated by communicative action and takes the form of a network for the communication of positions and opinions which become synthesised in public communication as public opinion. As such, it is the social space in which public communication takes place and within which the various participants as well as the public appear. The 'public', on the other hand, is a collective noun that designates people who are recruited from the private sphere of civil society, which is complementary to the public sphere, to serve as the carrier of the public sphere. As such, the public forms the internal structure of the public sphere.

Although Habermas is less concerned with the public, he nevertheless has some interesting things to say about it (1996a: 307-8, 327-87). The public presents itself in different forms, depending on the level of differentiation of communication processes. While the presupposition of physical presence applies at the lower levels, such as encounters and simple social interaction, the public becomes progressively generalised and more abstract as the level of differentiation increases, up to the point that it is transformed into an unlimited body of absent and anonymous addressees in the case of generalised communication processes in complex societies. Under these conditions, the public is unified by the mass media on a national scale or even more globally. Irrespective of the form it takes, the public is crucial to democracy in so far as it possesses communicative power and a certain authority which are essential to the generation of the legitimacy of the formal decision-making system. While democratic opinion formation and will formation is an institutionalised process that goes far beyond the public, it is in a crucial respect dependent on an input from the informal communication or non-institutionalised spontaneous opinion formation of the public located on the periphery. This process starts with the perception, identification and thematisation of a collective problem, and is continued with the insertion of the concomitantly formed informal opinions into public communication. In this context, political actors, actors representing their own interests (e.g. industry) and actors representing the public (e.g. associations, movements, churches, and so on) take part in a controversy in the public sphere in which they struggle over definitions and political influence over what is collectively accepted as valid. While this controversy follows a collective communicative practise structured by rules, the public is of particular importance in this communicative conflict since its authority, represented by its resonance, approval, agreement or lack of it, is decisive in determining the collective definition of the problem at issue as well as which actors' influence will count in the formal decision-making process. The public opinion eventually resulting from the collective communicative and discursive working through the available proposals, information and reasons in a more or less rational way finally delineates the maneuver space of the formal decision-making system and indicates the direction to be taken.

It should be emphasised that this outline of Habermas's position on the public has been arrived at by extrapolating and bringing together a series of isolated statements that he made in the course of an extended, largely descriptive account of the role of civil society and the political public sphere in democratic processes within constitutional states. As is clear, it contains very important insights about the constitutive sense of the public within the public sphere and of its authority in the process of public opinion formation and will formation. Yet these insights are neither developed nor integrated in a systematic way into the overall account offered in *Between Facts and Norms*. So, for instance, it cannot be said that Habermas presents an analysis in which the public is given its rightful role. Nowhere does he allow it to come in between the participants in public controversy or discourse, on the one hand, and the sphere of validity which they activate through their communicative action in the public sphere, on the other. Neither its constitutive role nor its authority leaves any trace whatsoever on the recognition and acceptance of the validity claims advanced by the various participants in public communication. At no point do validity and the communicative power of the public meet and become interconnected so as to form what is collectively accepted. In effect, the public does not have any significant role to play in Habermas's overall analysis. For this reason, it could with justification be said to be missing. Although he grants that, as against the idealisations built into language, we have to reckon with 'the world we know', with 'the facticity of a world...that is *differently* organized' (1996a: 325, translation modified), his major tendency is nevertheless to argue in favour of the efficacy of these idealisations and their direct translatability into social order (1996a: 17). Although he admits that public opinion results from a collective practice interrelating institutionalised and non-institutionalised communicative processes in which proposals, information and reasons are collectively worked through in a 'more or less rational' (1996a: 362) —that is, a not entirely rational —way, he is nevertheless inclined to proceed as though communication processes to which the role of the public is central can be approached in terms of the final consensus —envisaged from the moral point of view —they presuppose. The leading image of his later major work, the Kantian-Rousseauian model of 'self-legislation' asserting an identity between the author and the addressee of the law (1996a: 33, 38, 104, 120, 126, 408, 417), together with the numerous argumentative conclusions drawn from it, is sufficient to show that Habermas has in mind a solution to the problem of double contingency that precludes the unpredictability and instability associated with triple contingency. That the complaint sounded here is not simply an empiricist one calling for a focus on facticity is made clear in the following paragraphs.[12]

The Inclusion of the Other

The main thrust of *Die Einbeziehung des Anderen*, at least of the most substantial essays from the collection, turns on what Habermas calls 'the third perspective' (1996b: 108-111; see also 15, 106, 114, 120, 122, 125). Also here a careful study of the material reveals difficulties similar to those noted above, but in this context they take on shape around the question of the precise location of the third perspective. Habermas describes the third point of view as 'a perspective which is located in society itself' (p. 122). It is an inner-worldly remainder in everyday moral intuitions of the transcendent point of view of God which was lost when the religious world view broke down in favour of the proliferation of cultural models in pluralistic societies. As such it represents something like a 'transcendence from within' (p. 16; see also Habermas 1991: 127-56, 1996a: 17). Forming part of an immanent communication structure, it is a 'public, intersubjectively shared perspective' (1996b: 106); the perspective 'from which we, the citizens, collectively and publicly deliberate about what is in the best interest of everyone' (p. 109). It is the perspective that 'the members of post-traditional societies themselves intuitively assume when the only option left to them in the face of problematic basic moral norms is to fall back upon rational grounds' (p. 15). He also describes it as 'a social perspective' (p. 39) which is embedded in the intersubjectively shared practical knowledge on which actors draw in the lifeworld. In a critique of John Rawls, he adds to this interpretation of the third point of view a surprising twist—surprising, because he takes a step beyond double contingency and effectively begins to formulate the problem of triple contingency. As against Rawls, who from his liberal position conceives of private individuals engaging in the public political use of reason and of letting their own particular motives count in the debate, Habermas takes a stance at the level of public communication as such in order to bring out the epistemic role of practical discourse (1996b 102-3, 114; see also pp. 15, 46, 60, 63). Private points of view, personal interests and values indeed enter discourse in the form of motives, but in the course of the process both their role and their meaning undergo a change. Something individual is transformed into something shared by all. Only in such a new form do motives acquire the epistemic status of rules or structures that possess the authority to regulate the situation at large. With this statement Habermas opens a vista on triple contingency —on the role not only of direct participants, but in particular also of the public, on an intersubjectively shared vocabulary for the translation of individual desires and preferences into something situationally meaningful and effective, on something collectively acceptable and collectively valid, and finally on situational epistemic structures in the form of rules or arguments regulating the situation in a generally acceptable way. But no sooner has he opened this vista than he turns away to follow his standard and by now characteristic path. Instead of maintaining a stereoscopic perspective, he casts the third perspective in the constraining mould of the philosopher's moral point of view and thus narrows it down to a one-dimensional construct that has little or nothing to do with the public. This is how he for the most part presents the third perspective.

The third perspective, in the sense of the moral point of view, is a reconstruction of the lost transcendent point of view of God or, rather, of the point of view intuitively taken by the members of post-traditional societies when they are faced with normative questions (1996b: 15, 16, 38-9, 56, 122). In conflicts, for instance, people engage in practical discourses in which they struggle against one another with reasons, even though their common substantive background consensus has broken down (pp. 27, 56, 99). Moral philosophy, particularly in the discourse ethical variant Habermas represents together with Karl-Otto Apel,[13] starts with the members of society or the citizenry, particularly with their moral intuitions, and finds its own point of view already available among them, but it is only by painstaking reconstructive analysis that it is able to purify it in the form of the moral point of view. Reconstruction involves more than simply taking on board the prevalent convictions of a population or the already existing basic consensus in liberal societies. It requires the bringing to awareness of implicit or pre-theoretical practical knowledge already available in a cultural form and in social practices. What is brought to the fore are the form and the structure of perspectives of intact intersubjective communicative relations, the structure and procedures of a process by means of which generally acceptable norms can be discovered or constructed. This reconstruction is achieved by means of a reflexive exercise that proceeds in a critical manner. The result of such a reconstruction of the intuitive practical knowledge of the members of society is the moral point of view from which alone an impartial evaluation or judgement can be made of duties, norms, obligations and, more broadly, questions of justice (pp. 40, 48, 55, 102, 117, 120, 122). It is this point of view, which discourse ethics is designed to justify (pp. 56-64), that Habermas (pp. 96, 120) is convinced must be accepted by the members of society or the citizens to the exclusion or, at least, independent of their own particular world views if they were to arrive at a shared political conception and common standard of justice. The moral point of view, and it alone, possesses the necessary epistemic authority that makes it independent of particular points of view (p. 117). Habermas consistently maintains the primacy of the moral point of view understood in this sense, and equally consistently insists that the members of society or the citizenry must adopt this point of view so as to be able to organize their society in a reasonable way. Yet he is adamant that he does not entertain or perpetuate a philosophical paternalism (pp. 119, 122). This denial is not convincing, however, and it will remain so until he revises that basic assumption of his which leads him to give priority to the moral philosophical third point of view to the exclusion of the third perspective of the members of society or the citizenry.

The basic assumption I have in mind is related generally to Habermas's indefatigable attempt to uncouple the moral point of view, which concerns the horizontal perspective in which interpersonal relations are regulated, from the ethical point of view, which concerns the vertical perspective of particular life styles and projects. More particularly, it is related to the concomitant argument that the abstract moral question transcends the context-bound ethical question (1996b: 43). The assumption that Habermas makes here is that when the members of society raise questions, they typically raise ethical questions, even when they could be expected to raise moral questions, and that if they at all raise moral questions, they do so in an intuitive, unreflective and uncritical way that requires philosophical leadership and correction. This is an untenable assumption[14] that leads Habermas astray, despite his laudable attempt to locate the third perspective in society itself. It misleads him not merely into underestimating the third perspective carried by the public, but even into philosophically appropriating the latter to such a degree that it in effect is relegated to oblivion. These difficulties would seem, in turn, to be connected with a selective utilisation of the structure of communication.

A characteristic argumentative strategy of Habermas is to draw on the structure of communication by way of the system of perspectives which is reflected in the different attitudes and personal pronouns. In these terms, he typically argues that the social world is accessible only from the performative perspective of the participants, while the objective world calls for description from the perspective of the observer (Habermas 1996b: 55). To these two Habermas adds the third perspective which he regards as 'an impartial perspective…[that]…transcends the participatory perspective of the citizens' in that it represents 'a comprehensive, intersubjectively shared perspective' (1996b: 120; see also pp. 106, 109). It is this perspective that he emphatically calls 'the moral perspective' that is the preserve of a reconstructively proceeding moral philosophy. In his critique of Rawls, Habermas (1996b: 95-127) repeatedly attacks the US author's proposal to regard the citizens as assuming both a participatory perspective and an observer's perspective from which they respectively generalise their own positions and observe that others have done the same. His objection is that Rawls recognises only two perspectives, while the third perspective still needs to be brought in. If one now recalls Habermas's own analysis of the structure of communication presented above, however, then the erroneous nature of this argument becomes immediately apparent. What is lacking in Habermas is the perspective of the public who is not directly participating but is rather observing what those participating at that time are saying and doing and who is simultaneously evaluatively responding in such a way that it provides the resonance necessary for the establishment of public opinion and what is eventually accepted as collectively accepted. This is the social observer's perspective. This is what Rawls seems to be have in mind, rather than the neutral objectivist observer's perspective that Habermas suggests Rawls is working with.[15] It must be pointed out that the third point of view is not in addition to the participants' and the observer's perspectives, but in addition to the first-person and the second-person perspectives. Habermas obliterates the public and the third perspective it embodies by assimilating it at times to the participants, as when he thinks of all the citizens taking part in deliberation, and at other times to the philosopher's moral point of view, as when he thinks of the impartial point of view that transcends the participatory perspective of the citizenry. Also here in Habermas's more recent work, in which he explicitly attempts to locate the third point of view within society itself, there is no room for the public and its characteristic third, social observer's point of view. The irony is, however, that the philosopher's third perspective is a reconstruction of the public's point of view and, therefore, owes virtually everything to it.

What is put forward here is, of course, only a supporting argument for the main argument of the paper. The latter is that Habermas, in the most central core of his very significant contribution to sociological theory, crosses the path of the problem of triple contingency several times yet fails to recognise and to deal with it.

Conclusion

Habermas proceeds in both his major works of the 1980s and 1990s containing his very considerable contribution to sociology from the theorem of double contingency which had been established by Mead and Schutz and formulated by Parsons. In fact, both *The Theory of Communicative Action* and *Between Facts and Norms* can be regarded as an attempt to clarify what the theoretical solution to the problem posed by the fact of double contingency must be if the sociologist were to be in a position to account for social order and hence for society. In the former work, the solution to the risk of dissension is conceived in terms of the communicative coordination of actions, and in the latter, where the tension between facticity and validity is seen as being superimposed on the primary risk of dissension and hence exacerbating it, the same theory is extended to law. In the cases of both coordination and law, the solution is theoretically found in the moral dimension or the dimension of normative validity. The sustained attempt to find a solution to the risk of dissension in the realms of a sociological theory of order, and thus to pursue a classically posed problem, places Habermas among the neoclassical sociologists. The solution itself also resembles the proposal of a neoclassical predecessor. There indeed is a vast difference between Parsons's emphasis on cultural determination and Habermas's alternative of a common orientation to validity claims. But if one appreciates that the key interpretative factor is their common neo-Kantian attachment, then it becomes immediately clear that Habermas's solution is tantamount to Parsons's consensus displaced to a different, somewhat more fluid level. Behind the apparent fluidity of validity claims carried in communicative action, however, lurks the paternalistic philosopher preoccupied with validity in the form of the moral point of view. It is this position, entailing a rationalistic moral philosophical or moralistic fallacy, that prevents Habermas from recognising and addressing the problem of triple contingency to which his work gives rise. It systematically leads him, while proceeding from double contingency, to jump too rapidly to the moral point of view to attend to the risk of dissension, thus overlooking the problem of triple contingency.

All along the path of the development of his core contribution to sociology, Habermas intermittently touches on the problem of triple contingency. In his analysis of double contingency, in the preparation of his own theoretical basis in the structure of communication, in his reformulation of double contingency and the elaboration of a solution to it, in his proposal to build validity claims as social fact into concrete contexts, in his analysis of the legally secured discursive process in contemporary democratic societies, in his attempt to clarify the precise location of the third point of view —in all these contexts, he on occasion presses beyond his well-entrenched position, only to withdraw to more familiar ground at that very moment that he is required to confront the problem of triple contingency. His tendency to revert to a position that reduces or even excludes contingency outweighs his willingness to countenance a degree of contingency characteristic of societal processes of communication. In more specific terms, this means that in his all too strong emphasis on the philosopher's moral point of view, he overwhelmingly tends to obliterate the role of the public as a vehicle of the third point of view and thus to arrest the dynamism, but also the unpredictability and instability, that the public brings into the communicatively deploying and discursively organized social process. As a neoclassical sociologist, Habermas may be seen as an historical figure among contemporary sociologists, but as a theorist whose work consistently points toward a problem he himself is unwilling or unable to deal with, he bequeaths a valuable asset to his successors. This is the problem of triple contingency.

As a contemporary sociological problem, triple contingency as such obviously requires basic theoretical attention, but there is also various other matters that need systematic work. The first is the role of the public in communications societies —which I take as the substantive expression of the theoretical problem of triple contingency. Another related but broader question is the unpredictable and unstable process in which what is collectively accepted as valid actually becomes established, what the role of the public is in this, and how this occurs. An important part of this work involves the detailed investigation of particular discursive situational structures or the cognitive, knowledge or epistemic structures operating in discursive situations. Instead of contenting oneself with establishing that morality has a cognitive quality or that moral statements express knowledge (Habermas 1996b: 11), it is essential to investigate precisely what this quality entails or what this knowledge is. Instead of asserting the 'epistemic core of normative validity' (Habermas 1996b: 15) from a philosophically conceived third point of view, a study of these epistemic structures needs to be conducted from a social scientifically conceived third point of view. A phenomenological analysis of the content people associate with their own moral statements in conflict situations (Habermas 1996b: 11) will not be sufficient. It demands that situational structures be much more broadly considered in their manifestation as at one and the same time micro and macro phenomena, as at one and the same time in people's statements, in social practices and in cultural models. If, for instance, the third point of view is studied sociologically in the form of such situational structures, then the moral point of view can be directly related to the role of the public in communication societies without a loss of its epistemic core. The development of such a cognitive or epistemic theory of communication is a challenging aspect of the task implied by triple contingency, but perhaps the most challenging aspect will be to reconstruct the evolution of such discursive situational structures according to the new concept of evolution that is emerging in the wake of the exposure of the fallacious nature of Habermas's developmental-logical theory of evolution (Strydom 1992, 1993; see also Eder 1999a).

8

Contingency: A Critique of Niklas Luhmann

In modern society, necessities and impossibilities no longer provide the orderly framework of the world. No longer are there any socially necessary forms for the reciprocal limitations of society's various components or even for the social coherence of the whole. It is accepted that what is assumed could be different. Everything, although not everything all at once, could be redefined and changed through communication. Modern society accepts contingencies like none other before it, so that one could venture that contingency is modern society's defining attribute. Given these conditions, sociology's own diagnosis of modern society is subject to contingency. It is on the basis of precepts such as these that Niklas Luhmann, considered by some as the Max Weber of the late 20th century, established a basic theoretical link with Talcott Parsons. Like his predecessor, he grounded his theoretical work in the problem of contingency. The specific link between the two theorists is the 'fundamental proposition' or the 'theorem of double contingency', as Parsons (Parsons and Shils 1951: 16) and Luhmann (1984: 156) respectively called it. Parsons first introduced this theoretical proposition in the early 1950s against the background of the culmination of a diversity of classical ideas in Mead and Schutz, and some thirty years later Luhmann (1984: 148-90) appropriated it as the very basis upon which to erect his autopoietic theory of social systems.[1] In view of this subterranean connection between the two, it is interesting that Luhmann nevertheless emphatically claimed that he was able to go far beyond Parsons.

The thoroughgoing critical analysis that Luhmann's theoretical assumptions and claims —including his relation to Parsons —deserve has thus far been hampered by a number of factors. For one, Luhmann and his critics have for years engaged in a global denouncement of each other and thus perpetuated a sterile contest for which both parties were equally responsible. The Habermas-Luhmann debate, which stretched over more than two decades, was a central part of this game.[2] At this stage, particularly after Luhmann's death in November 1998, however, we have certainly gained the necessary distance to appreciate the commonalities and complementarities between the two leading German theorists to take a step ahead.[3] Another factor is the hesitant, uneven and incomplete reception of Luhmann's work, particularly in the English-speaking world, which discourages the investigation of the core of his theoretical position. We are fortunate, however, that the broader literature does contain a few attempts to give some critical attention to the concept of double contingency. The results, however, are by no means startling. Of three authors who seek both to problematise Luhmann's central theoretical assumption and to push beyond him, two unsatisfactorily content themselves simply with a multiplication of double contingency (Oberdorfer 1992; Welker 1992). The third adopts a much more fruitful approach, that is, a communication and discourse theory of collective reflection or discursive processes focusing on empirically reconstructable mechanism of the coordination of perspectives (Miller 1987; see also Miller 1994),[4] but he does not pursue it far enough. Instead of muffling it, contemporary conditions demand that we theoretically expose and analyse the question of contingency.

Against this background, I propose to devote the present article to the pursuit of both a negative and a positive endeavour. Through a critical analysis of the limitations of his theoretical position, on the one hand, I argue that Luhmann, having appropriated it, does not transform the theorem of double contingency but in fact remains so fixated on its original formulation that he is unable to transcend its confines. His claim of having gone beyond Parsons already at this fundamental theoretical level, however interesting the various moves that he does make, cannot be sustained. On the other hand, I argue that the inadequacy of double contingency as a basic sociological concept can indeed be overcome, but only if one shifts to a different level to complement it by the introduction of what may be called 'triple contingency' (Strydom 1999e). This implies that Luhmann's qualified acceptance of his critics' idea of a multiplication of double contingency, as when he, for instance, speaks of the 'semantic mediation of a multiplicity of double contingencies' (Luhmann 1992: 379),[5] is itself an inadequate and hence unacceptable response to the theoretical problem that he is facing. To ground sociological theory in the problem of contingency instead leads to the recognition of the impermanence of triple contingencies.

1. APPROPRIATION OF THE THEOREM

Double contingency, for both Parsons and Luhmann, refers to a socially significant condition of indeterminacy or openness that requires the issuing or emanation of determinations or limits if the establishment of social relations and eventually of social order were to be possible at all. Double contingency is a problem that induces a solution which entails social elaboration in the form of relation building or structure formation. Parsons originally introduced the concept in the context of the theory of action in terms of social interaction. On borrowing it from Parsons, Luhmann integrated the concept into systems theory and understood it in terms of the formation of social systems. For Parsons, the 'fundamental proposition of double contingency' (Parsons and Shils 1951: 16) was a theoretical concept to account at the most basic level for the possibility of social interaction or communication and, by extension, of social order. For Luhmann, the concept is an equally basic one, as is borne out by his description of his own 'theory of social systems' as being 'built upon the problem concept of double contingency' (1984: 154). As such it is necessary to account for the incessant process of internally driven systems formation.

Originally having introduced it within the context of social interaction, Parsons (Parsons and Shils 1951: 16; Parsons 1964: 10-11, 94; 1977b: 167-68) conceived of double contingency specifically in terms of a dyadic or dialogical model. Two persons coming face to face, ego and alter, are different from each other, and the situation in which they encounter one another is socially undetermined in that social interaction remains impossible unless they are able to deal with and sufficiently overcome the differences between them as well as the lack of situational determination. Whatever each does in this open, empty, indeterminate situation depends on what each chooses to do and on what the other actually does. For both, besides their respective systems of relevance and action alternatives, the situation is equally undetermined in that each could choose this way or that and could decide to act or react this way or that. Both actors are moreover equally uncertain, for both are potentially unlimited sources of words and actions. On the one hand, then, double contingency signals the potential hazard of conflict between individuals confronting each other face-to-face, and on the other it points toward accomplishments that could lead to coordinated and cooperative action.

As such, Parsons regarded double contingency as an unavoidable basic condition that generated a problem at the social level which required a solution if social action, social interaction, social order and hence society were to be possible. In order to provide a theoretical basis for the solution to the problem of double contingency, Parsons adopted a neo-Kantian inspired value theory of culture within his overall action-theoretical framework. Accordingly, he introduced the proposition that every social situation is preceded by a shared symbolic system that makes possible a value consensus between social actors (Parsons 1964: 37-8; 1977b: 168-69).[6] Rather than simply opting for cultural determinism, the originality of Parsons's position resides in his linking of culture through internalisation and institutionalisation to personalities and interaction systems as need dispositions and role expectations respectively. He thus incorporated a normative orientation assuming value consensus from the outset in action itself.[7]

Linking with Parsons both historically and theoretically, Luhmann regards his predecessor's achievement as 'a theoretical advance that should not be squandered thoughtlessly' (1984: 149). The theorem of double contingency is of central theoretical importance in that it not only pinpoints the condition of the possibility of action, but also makes clear that the elements of systems —that is, actions —require both systems and the solution of the problem of double contingency for their constitution. This interpretation of the American theorist accounts for the fact that Luhmann (1984: 154) is willing, in quite untypical manner, to admit that the Parsonian concept provides the starting point for his own version of social systems theory.[8] To serve as an adequate basis for his theory, however, Parsons's proposal for the solution of the problem of double contingency needs to be reconceptualised, and this, needless to say, is not without implications for the concept itself.

Luhmann (1984: 150-2) rejects the assumption of a value consensus predicated on a shared symbolic system that precedes every social situation. For, as he acutely sees, it precludes a sociological understanding of both the genesis of the culture structuring social situations and such situations themselves as well as subsequent cultural and social change. Inverting Parsons's approach and raising it to a more abstract level, therefore, he instead focuses on double contingency as a special case of self-reference (Luhmann 1984: 151, 182). It has the potential both to generate a permanent, autocatalytical problem driving self-referential social systems forward and to solve it by stimulating the emergence of structures which increase systems complexity and create social order. Social systems are suspended in a temporal process that is subject to chance and, although operationally closed, they are open to possibilities which they self-creatively employ to render themselves different than they are at any given moment. Thus double contingency means that social systems are based on instability, have a core structure that collapses from moment to moment, and are consequently compelled to constantly realise themselves as autopoietic systems. This leaves them permanently in a state of conditional readiness to use every opportunity to form structures (Luhmann 1984: 167, 172).

2. ABORTIVE DEVELOPMENT OF DOUBLE CONTINGENCY

Joining with Parsons by retaining double contingency in its central and fundamental theoretical position, Luhmann not only develops the concept in an interesting manner, but also goes beyond his predecessor ın a variety of ways. For Luhmann, the unit of analysis can no longer be action carried by a subject, whether an actor or agent, who precedes the system of action entered into in relation to another such subject, as had been the case for Parsons. It has to be the social system that constitutes the subject of action in the first instance. This entails a change from a more concrete to a more abstract point of view. Rather than everyday ego-alter interaction, the emphasis now shifts theoretically to communication as the medium of constitution of social systems. Logically, this change of position allows Luhmann to conceive of contingency in terms of modal theory as something that is both temporal and beyond necessity and impossibility. Metatheoretically and epistemologically, therefore, he is able finally to leave Parsons far behind by conceiving of culture and social reality in the dynamic yet structured terms of genesis, transformation, situatedness and construction.[9]

Despite the theoretical advancement that Luhmann not without some justification claims to have achieved above and beyond Parsons, however, a close inspection of his theory of the constitution of social systems on the basis of the theorem of double contingency suggests that the distance between the two authors at a fundamental theoretical level is actually much smaller than the reader is led to believe. A brief reconstruction of his analysis of the emergence and complexity increase of social systems in terms of double contingency leaves no doubt about this.

The starting position or original situation, for Luhmann, is as follows: 'Two black boxes, due to whatever coincidence, get involved with one another' (1984: 156). If these two systems, which are intransparent and indeterminable for one another in their initial contact, were to establish a mutual relation, then each would be required to limit its own indeterminacy in view of the opposite system by 'detautologising' itself and 'making claims on the environment' (1984: 167). Initially, each system takes the partial step of attempting to determine prospectively the other system by projecting an expectation of its likely behaviour. Next, each system reacts to this act of self-determination on the part of its opposite number by incorporating in view of the other system its projected expectation as information into its own autopoietic self-determinantion.[10] Irrespective of whether the initial expectation turned out to be an illusion or not, as incorporated information it provides the basis for a system to further develop its expectations in relation to the other system. Having reached this stage, both systems have begun to reconstitute and determine themselves with a view to the other. Thus a situationally shared social dimension has been differentiated as well as two action systems with their own particular meaning and action perspectives (1984: 153, 162, 167).

Out of the unfolding contact between the two initial systems, a nexus of relations in the form of a new system emerges, an 'emergent order' or 'social system' (1984: 157), which is indeed built from the elements of the initial systems but is distinct from them and occupies a different level.

This prima facie abstract reconstruction of the original situation and process of systems formation in terms of double contingency, however, should not be allowed to conceal something rather remarkable about Luhmann's account. Although he speaks of black boxes and concomitantly attempts to transpose his theorising to the abstract level of general systems theory,[11] Luhmann throughout tends to revert to the terminology of ego and alter. This means that his claim to outpace Parsons cannot be upheld at the basic theoretical level. His attempt to salvage the neo-classical concept of double contingency and to develop it up to the point where he is able to present it as the basis of a novel, post-traditional theory of social systems patently fails. Despite his stride toward theoretical abstraction, he remains caught up in and tied down by the limited and confining conceptual possibilities of the ego-alter model underpinning the image of 'two black boxes'. That this is not entirely accidental is borne out by the fact that he at the very outset of his principal theoretical work explicitly adopts the dialogical model of I-thou communication. Postulating that double contingency involves 'multiple constitution', which he admits is known in the literature as 'dialogue' (1984: 65), he time and time again reasserts that system formation presupposes a basic dialogical or 'mutualistic organization' (1984: 67, 157, 188). Not only does Luhmann thus, contrary to his avowed intentions, reproduce Parsons's dyadic model. But by the same token, he also fails to extrapolate double contingency from the elementary level of interaction as for instance represented by two strangers meeting by chance on the pavement —what he himself on occasion called '*communication au trottoir*' (Luhmann 1986: 75) in distinction to progressively higher levels of organization such as gatherings and society.[12]

Luhmann's attachment to the dyadic model and his failure to follow its abstraction through the process of the increasing differentiation and organization of communication amount to a rather surprising lapse that quite predictably has attracted the attention of some critics. If one bears in mind the structure of communication,[13] it is not difficult to imagine what a critique of Luhmann in this case should target. Considering the sign-mediated nature of communication[14] and the full system of personal pronouns, the dialogical model operates with a selective reconstruction of the structure of communication. Replacing reflection associated with the traditional epistemological subject-object relation with communication, the dialogical model comes to focus squarely on the ego-alter or I-thou relation. As a consequence of thus prioritising the first- and second-person perspective, the dialogical model screens out the third-person perspective and covers over the significance for communication and the analysis of communication of the carrier of this non-participant yet by no means uninvolved point of view.

Both Bernd Oberdorfer and Michael Welker clearly see the elementary nature of Luhmann's dialogical model and criticise it for being too underdetermined or structurally poor to serve as an adequate basis for system formation. In comparable manner, both seek to correct the idea of 'simple double contingency' (Oberdorfer 1992: 307; Welker 1992: 356) that they ascribe to Luhmann by means of a more complex alternative. According to Oberdorfer, 'the original situation of system formation…must be conceived as a co-presence of *many* tautologically self-referential systems, so that every system is located in a field of *many* possible detautologisations' (1992: 307). Similarly, Welker proposes a 'multiple double contingency which stands in a network of relations' (1992: 361). Although Welker anticipates and seeks to disarm the counter-critique that this proposal might amount to no more than simply a 'quantitative enhancement' (1992: 361), it is difficult to see how he could avoid such a conclusion. Luhmann himself correctly rejects the notion of multiple double contingency as implying 'pure multiplication' and insists instead that doubly contingent relations require a social system which provides the necessary 'semantic mediation' (1992b: 379).[15] That Luhmann's response is still inadequate, however, is shown by the fact that what requires semantic mediation, according to him, is precisely 'a multiplicity of double contingencies' (1992b: 379). Although in qualified form, Luhmann takes on board and without much ado capitulates before his critics' well-meant yet misleading proposal. To imagine what is required to go beyond this theoretically meaningless quantitative concept of double contingency,[16] it is advisable to recall once again the three-pronged model of the full structure of communication mentioned above. This is what Miller has in mind in his potentially more fruitful critique of Luhmann.

Max Miller's principal argument is that Luhmann's attempt to establish double contingency as his basic theoretical starting point ends in failure due to the fact that the model of dialogical or mutualistic constitution already at the elementary level leads to a loss of those experiences that enjoy collective recognition (1987: 189, 203, 206).[17] Although Luhmann recognises a meaningful world dimension that allows the differentiation of distinct social perspectives and action orientations, as we have seen, according to Miller he is nevertheless unable to say how differences in the experience of meaning can be identified jointly, how expectation structures are built up and consolidated, and how social order is possible. This would require a 'coordinated understanding of differences' at the social level, which in turn presupposes that communicative relations take the form of what Miller calls 'collective processes of reflection' (1987: 203, 188, 200-1).[18] Such processes thematise and articulate the dynamics of collectively accepted knowledge, coordinate different and even conflicting perspectives, and eventuate, for instance, in collectively accepted definitions of crisis and in collectively accepted normative innovations, without obliterating differences in the interpretation of such crises and interpretations. In effect, Miller here replaces Luhmann's dialogical model of ego-alter communication tied to his basic theorem of double contingency with the more complex collective model of 'discourse or argumentation' (1987: 188).[19] On the basis of this model, he proposes to empirically reconstruct the communicative mechanisms, whether methods or structures, which are at play in the coordination of distinct and even conflicting understandings of differences.[20]

Despite this commendable theoretical advance over the concept of double contingency, however, it is remarkable that Miller himself often couches his discussion in terms of ego and alter. This tendency of his to remain at the level of ontogenesis and elementary interaction processes is reinforced by the ambiguity of his frequent references to the model of 'argumentation'. Whereas the model of argumentation leads one to think in terms of a proponent who tries to convince an opponent of a particular standpoint, a step beyond double contingency requires something entirely different. Rather than the twofold relation of ego and alter, it is necessary to focus on the threefold relation that includes also the third person —to be sure, eventually the third person in its collective manifestation. In this case, it would be more appropriate to adopt the model of discourse, particularly as exemplified by public communication, or debate and controversy in the public sphere.[21]

As against Luhmann, but also against his above-mentioned critics, I propose to grasp the possibility opened by this shift in emphasis by introducing, instead of double contingency or even multiple double contingency, the concept of triple contingency.

3. TRIPLE CONTINGENCY

In the course of his appropriation and development of the concept of double contingency, Luhmann (1984: 153-4) puts forward a pointed critique of such well-known theoretical notions as 'interaction' ('*Wechselwirkung*'), 'mirroring', 'social relationship', 'reciprocity of perspectives' and the like —all of which presuppose the assumption that the social consists of a relation between individuals. Despite thus revealing the limits of the traditional sociological idea that the social world is composed of dyadic building blocks, he nevertheless continues to understands the basic situation at the bottom of social order simply as one in which 'two black boxes, due to whatever coincidence, get involved with one another' (1984: 156). It is precisely this assumption that enables Luhmann, like Parsons before him, to give double contingency the central and fundamental theoretical position he does. Negatively, this assumption becomes apparent from the way in which the observer of social life, the third person or the third point of view is treated. Luhmann (1984: 407-11, 1992a: 68-121) certainly has quite a sophisticated position on observation which is informed by second-order cybernetics. Some authors (e.g. Eder and Schmidtke 1998: 429) regard it as an advance on what is today accepted in the social sciences and even suggest that Luhmann thereby captures a dimension that has been largely missing from sociological theory.[22] If this is actually the case, however, Luhmann does not bring it into play in the arguments by means of which he appropriates and develops the concept of double contingency. As is clear from the analysis presented earlier, these arguments contain no evidence to suggest that he recognises the third point of view as a constitutive component of the social world, not to mention giving it its proper due. This lack of appreciation of the role of the third point of view, which is a consequence of the theoretical significance he ascribes to double contingency, is indicative of a serious theoretical deficiency. It can be corrected, therefore, only if the central and fundamental theoretical location of double contingency is cleared to make way for a more complex theoretical concept. This demand is fulfilled by what I call 'triple contingency' (Strydom1999d, 1999e, 2001)[23] —a concept that is obviously not unrelated to neo-classical sociology yet is of a decidedly post-classical kind.

The employment of the model of communication mentioned above makes possible a clear distinction between double and triple contingency. In the by now well-known case of double contingency, two social actors, A and B, encounter one another and enter into some communicative relation with each other, ego or 'I' being face-to-face with alter or 'thou'. In the basic situation of triple contingency, by contrast, there is a third perspective, borne by C, who observes, evaluates and eventually even comments upon what A and B are saying and doing. The inclusion of the third point of view means that the social situation is very different and more complicated from the start than in the case of double contingency. In view of the fact that observation, evaluation and commentary unavoidably impact on A and B, C forms a constitutive part of the social situation. Indeed, the social situation cannot be reduced to the relation between A and B. Rather than the twofold one, the threefold configuration of A, B and C represents the elementary social situation. If one now makes a transition from the elementary model of communication among individuals employed thus far to its more complex form of for instance public communication, then the triple contingency scenario would not merely involve a multiplication of the doubly contingent relation between a number of As and Bs, but would include also C who assumes the collective form of the public.

The entry of C into communication processes brings a further degree of contingency over and above the double contingency with it. In the case of double contingency, two actors are compelled to make a selection from alternatives while taking each other into account, and thus to establish a communicative relation between themselves. The third person who observes, evaluates, judges and even comments, without participating directly, belongs to the situation as a constitutive part of its sociality. Over and above the first-person and the second-person participants, the third point of view represents society. It embodies the societal power of definition. C has a constitutive social role in that he, she or it has the power to define the situation. Whatever A and B say and do, therefore, must in principle make sense to C. From the start and throughout, A and B are consequently subject in their interrelations to the meaning as defined by society and represented by the third person observer, evaluator and commentator, C. In proportion as actions and relations are coordinated through communication, power becomes dependent on the acceptance of definitions or reality (Eder 1993a: 12). As regards contingency, therefore, A and B make their choices and take each other into account, while at the same time being relativised by or taken up into a societal definition which is itself not given beforehand, but becomes established only in the course of the process.

In complex communication processes, C is equivalent to the public. The public possesses epistemic authority that is vested in its ability to activate relevant cultural models in public communication in particular situations.[24] By virtue of this authority, the public plays a significant and even decisive role in defining the situation and in the collective identification and definition of both collective problems and solutions relevant to the situation. At any given point in space and time, the public is the vehicle of the acceptance of collectively or discursively formulated problems and solutions and the embodiment of the collective validity of what is thus accepted. The fact that the collective acceptance and the ascription of collective validity to a collective definition of a problem and/or solution is not given beforehand but only emerges from a discursive process due to the observational, evaluative and commentating role that the public plays in relation to the directly involved participants, is of central importance here. It underscores why one can speak of triple contingency.

Such collective acceptance establishes an attribute of society, a social form that is not necessary; yet is nevertheless required in some guise or another, which remains stable and endures for some time. To make this sense of triple contingency somewhat more palpable one could for instance recall the centrality and shaping impact of public communication in contemporary societies. For example, neither the racial conflict in South Africa nor the ethnic conflict in Northern Ireland after the Good Friday agreement would have been resolved had it not been for the role of the public. Public communication formed an inherent part of the dynamics of both conflicts and the definitional power brought to bear on both by international observers and more broadly by the observing regional and global public proved decisive. In the South African case, which offers a more mature phenomenon than Northern Ireland to reflect upon, the constitutional solution which allows a range of competing interpretations marks the outcome of the moment of triple contingency.[25]

As these examples suggest, triple contingency is not a matter of the sheer addition of three contingencies nor one of a mere threefold interdependence among the participants and observers. The solution of the problem of triple contingency in public communication takes hold of the network as a whole in the sense of representing the generalised potential to establish a particular social form and at the same time nevertheless holding open other possibilities, while accommodating the settling of the relations of tension between the active participants as well as between them and the observing, evaluating, judging and commenting public.

4. LUHMANN BEYOND DOUBLE CONTINGENCY?

Although Habermas, like Luhmann, also adopts the concept of double contingency from Parsons and makes it the theoretical basis of his theory of communicative action (Habermas 1987a: 213-34; 1996a: 139), his work does give some evidence of the fact that he reaches beyond double contingency toward triple contingency —albeit without naming it as such or developing it in its own right (Strydom 1999d, 2001). For instance, the phenomenon of the public sphere is central to both his early (1989) and later work (1996a), but within this context he gives no systematic attention to the public as such, not to mention articulating the theoretical problem of the public.[26] The question is now whether a more charitable interpretation of Luhmann is not possible than the one put forward thus far. Does Luhmann's work, despite being based on the theorem of double contingency, provide a starting point or perhaps even several for the development of a theoretical position that is able to accommodate the problem of triple contingency? In the case of Habermas, a failure to go beyond his somewhat vague and under-complex notion of lifeworld communication, for instance by developing his concept of discourse into a theory of the discursive constitution of society, prevented him from having to acknowledge and explicate the idea of triple contingency. His theory of communicative action and especially his concept of discourse nevertheless held open the possibility of doing so. The question is whether Luhmann's work contains a comparably fecund network of theoretical concepts pointing beyond itself toward the problem of triple contingency. If one takes into account Eder and Schmidtke's (1998: 429) cautionary remarks, then he or she would have to investigate the matter more closely.

Luhmann's work indeed contains various leads that could be followed up. Three of these look particularly promising. The first is his concept of 'semantic mediation' (Luhmann 1992b: 379; also 1984: 224) mentioned above, which suggests the coordination or overcoming of differences. The second, which seems directly relevant to the question of triple contingency, is his consideration of the inclusion of third parties in systems of conflict (Luhmann 1985: 540). In this case, he mentions the 'heightening of uncertainty' that follows upon the inclusion of third parties, from spectators to morally or even legally charged observers, who are at first impartial and who could potentially be swayed to support one side or the other. He also notes the significance that third parties have acquired in the regulation of conflicts by virtue of their civilizing effect on conflicting parties. The third and final possible lead towards triple contingency is his reference to the modern phenomenon of 'a regular and constant orientation toward public opinion' (Luhmann 1998: 58-9) and, hence, the potential role of the public in the collective definition of problems and corresponding solutions. Let us briefly consider each in turn.

As against the traditional anthropological and sociological —including the Parsonian —concept of culture, first, Luhmann adopts a semantic view that reflects the refraction of culture in the various sub-systems which break the unity of society down so as to differentiate functionally specific distinctions between the system and its environment.[27] By semantic mediation he thus understands the functionally specific semantics that is associated with the binary codes and programmes of each of the sub-systems, whether the economic, legal, scientific and political or the religious and educational. The mediation of contingencies he envisages thus remain confined to the differentiated sub-systems and cannot approach the level of society, which is unable to observe its own unity other than as a difference between differences. It means that theoretically, in this case, Luhmann remains inextricably tied to the concept of double contingency.

If this ends in a negative conclusion, the second lead seems to stand in stark contrast to his functionally reduced concept of mediation. It indeed appears as though Luhmann touches on triple contingency when he registers the heightened degree of uncertainty that follows upon the inclusion of third parties in conflict systems. On close inspection, however, it becomes apparent that also in the case of conflict, which he conceives in terms of a 'negative version of double contingency' (1984: 531), Luhmann persists in thinking in terms of a two-partner model. For him, conflict resolution focuses on a parasitic phenomenon within a given system, and he makes no attempt to explain how the conflicting parties are or can be brought to jointly identify their differences.[28] How could the conflicting parties establish a common universe of discourse or reference point in terms of which alone the differences between them can become intelligible to them as differences?

The evaluation of Luhmann's third and final lead concerning the public and public opinion is decisive. As regards his accommodation of a permanent orientation toward public opinion, Luhmann confines the potential role of the public in societal communication processes to a particular sub-system of society—the political system. Although he grants that government and opposition, as well as their observation, appear 'in full view of the public', he insists that public opinion 'acts like a mirror in which politicians can see how they themselves and specific issues are judged' (1998: 59). Public opinion and hence the potential role of the public, confined to the political system as they are, do not possess any broader and certainly no societal significance. The various competences of the public to observe, evaluate, judge, evoke and activate different cultural models, form an opinion and thus to collectively identify and define socially significant problems and corresponding solutions do not add up to a higher-order perspective beyond the incongruent, functionally specific perspectives of the different functional systems. Public opinion is largely a noise for the functional systems, and as such it not only does not affect society but it in fact cannot do so. The only possible conclusion, then, is that Luhmann stubbornly refuses to relinquish or, at least, relativise his basic theorem of double contingency. He thus cannot be interpreted as opening a perspective on the novel, post-classical theoretical problem of triple contingency.[29]

CONCLUSION

Luhmann regards contingency as being the defining attribute of modern society, and, since sociology's own diagnosis of the present cannot escape this contingency either, he grounds his general theory in the problem of contingency.

Following Parsons yet abstracting from his focus on interaction, he regards the most basic, sociologically relevant manifestation of the problem of contingency, which calls for solution if social order were to be possible at all, as occurring at the leve! of the relation between social systems. Like Parsons, therefore, he builds his general theory of social systems on the basic theorem of double contingency informed by a dialogical or mutualistic model. Rejecting Parsons's attempt to tame the problem raised by double contingency by an appeal to a pre-given, static, shared cultural system, Luhmann is willing to countenance a greater degree of impermanence of double contingencies. Instead of a value theoretic concept of culture, he adopts a semantic view. The various functionally specific semantics of the different social systems within which double contingency appears in refracted form mediate the problems thus raised and make them amenable to solutions which serve the emergence of systems and the increase of their complexity. In fact, double contingency is a perennial autocatalytic problem that drives social systems forward and thus in various ways serves the autopoiesis of society as the all-encompassing social system. The impermanence of the solutions devised to the problem of double contingency in the various subsystems of society, that is, the impermanence of a multiplicity of double contingencies, is what lends modern society its contingent character.

Since there is no way to render more determinate or to limit contingency at a further or higher level than that set by double contingency, according to Luhmann (1989), modern society is contingent to such a degree that is may be fatefully yet unwittingly threatening and destroying itself. Driven by the autocatalytic problem of double contingency, functionally differentiated, operationally closed, self-referential social systems are concerned with their own autopoiesis to such an extent that their continued existence can no longer be ensured. The various functional systems are so differentiated and autonomous, and their various outcomes potentially so incongruous, that they do not admit of being coordinated. At any rate, it is not possible to form a collective understanding in a common language in the public domain, say, in the form of a collective identification and definition of a societal crisis and a corresponding solution. This remains the case for Luhmann even if it is granted that such a collective understanding, far from simply making possible and allowing a plurality of competing interpretations, actually stimulates and intensifies discursive conflict.

One does not have to overvalue social movements and entertain illusory socialist or fundamentalist hopes to recognise that Luhmann's analysis is not in accord with the growth of a reflective and critical public and with the expansion and deepening of the role of the public, both locally and globally, during the past decades. His theory of social systems, based as it is on double contingency, is implausible with respect to the growth and institutionalisation in the recent past of the 'consciousness' associated with anti-apartheid, environmentalism and biotechnological patents, to mention only some of the best known examples. To argue thus is not necessarily to reject Luhmann's work out of hand. It is rather to recognise commonalities and complementarities between him and his critics and to move a step beyond both. Luhmann's idea of fracturing the unity of society and thus pluralising and dynamising it is valuable beyond dispute. This heterogenisation of the social, to which double contingency is central, cannot be turned back even by an appeal to his major critic's —that is, Habermas's—concept of lifeworld communication. Yet it must be possible to identify those weakly required attributes of society that become discursively established in historically specific situations to resolve collectively experienced, critical problems at least for the time being. Nor is the argument presented here a denial of contingency or even of the relevance of double contingency. On the contrary, it is to plead for and to provide theoretical instruments to work on a theory of contingency that is both more nuanced and more relevant to contemporary sociology under the conditions of communication societies. Taking our cues from neo-classical sociologists like Parsons and Luhmann, as well as Habermas, all of whom in some sense or another gave a central and fundamental place to double contingency, sociological theory in the post-classical phase we are entering at present has to be built on a more appropriate concept of contingency.

Once room has been made for the novel post-classical theorem of triple contingency, the focus will have to be shifted to the empirical yet critical analysis of contingency in the form of the impermanence of triple contingencies —that is, the cultural models and social forms sanctioned by the public in configurations of historically specific situations of competition and conflict in modern society which make possible the mediation of different forms and types of knowledge. Attention to these weakly required attributes of society will at the same time compel sociology to clarify the urgent question of the particular role it plays in public communication.

9

Resonance: Triggering a Dormant Dimension of the Public Sphere

During the past two decades, the concept of resonance has made its appearance quite conspicuously in a relatively wide range of social theoretic literature, yet its precise theoretical sense still remains to be clarified. At first sight, we are confronted by a confusing list of different sociological concepts of resonance and, as is to be expected under such circumstances, it is made to play a variety of disparate roles in social research. The question that this state of affairs raises is whether it is possible at this stage to clarify the different concepts, to relate them in a theoretically meaningful way to one another, and finally to assess the uses to which the concept is being put as well as could be put in social research. In the following, I propose to take a first step towards explicating the theoretical sense of the concept of resonance and to consider some possibilities that it harbours for social research.

1. RESONANCE AND THE COMMUNICATIVE FORM OF SOCIETY

Sociologically, the concept of resonance makes sense only relative to communication. The general meaning of the word, which either applies to a sound or to a body, already suggests this much. Resonance refers, in the former case, to the echoing, resounding or continuing of a sound or tone, and in the latter to the triggering by a tone of a vibration or sympathetic awakening in a body. It is unsurprising, therefore, that the major contributions made by sociologists such as William Gamson, Niklas Luhmann and Jürgen Habermas, during the past two decades, confirm this relation between resonance and communication. What is particularly interesting, however, is that the concept of resonance acquired significance for sociologists only once society itself started to assume the form of communication and thus became transformed into a communication society or discourse society.

Sociologists who are theoretical enough to think about it, of course, conceive of the communicative form of society in appreciably different ways. A comparison and contrast of Habermas and Luhmann, for example, make this immediately clear. Both proceed from the assumption that in proportion as social relations are penetrated by communication, society takes on the form of communication in the sense that it is increasingly constituted and organised in terms of the rules of communication itself. From here, however, their paths diverge sharply. The manner in which each thinks of society as a matter of communication is radically different from the other. Whereas Luhmann (1989, 1995a) regards communication as an exclusively social mode of operation whereby society as a communicative system secures its own continuation, Habermas (1979a, 1989a, 1996a) emphasises public communication and discourse and the role they play in the constitution of society. The basic difference between the two theorists, however, boils down to the fact that Luhmann insists on separating communication and cognition, while Habermas presupposes a link between them (Rusch 1999: 8, 9; Sutter and Charlton 1999; Schmidt 1999). Adopting a system theoretical approach, Luhmann (1984) focuses on the communicative process to the exclusion of the individual, actor or agent who, in his view, is relevant at best only as an environment of the system. Habermas (1984a, 1987a), who starts from action theory, more particularly the theory of communicative action, by contrast regards the system as the outcome of action which, in turn, again has a structuring effect on action.

Gamson's (1988, 1992) idea of public communication in which sponsors, the media and culture, play a role in the construction of issue cultures undoubtedly comes closer to Habermas's interpretation than Luhmann's. This is also true of the more general understanding shared in the social sciences. Here it should be remembered, however, that in so far as the concept of discourse with its relational connotations enter the work of authors such as Habermas and Gamson, a contact point is established which shrinks the distance between them and Luhmann. Likewise, it appears at first sight as though the idea of the 'communication society' (Eder 1995: 276; Strydom 1999e; Delanty 1999: 9, 14, 69) or 'discourse society' (Beck 1997: 128) to which Habermas's thought has given rise remains wholly within a Habermasian framework. It should be pointed out, however, that the implied concept of a public process of communication or discourse —that is, in the sense of a struggle of a plurality of actors or agents in the medium of public communication over the collective identification, interpretation and definition of a problem or issue —requires, over and above the linking of communication and cognition, also their separation. As a special form of problematising public communication, discourse possesses its own logic and dynamics, which, while indeed being generated by the action and communication of social actors, allow no privileged membership rights and ultimately is withdrawn from the disposal of any participant, individual or collective (Eder 1996a; Strydom 2000, 2006b; Miller 2002a).

What needs to be done to come to grips with the theoretical sense of the concept of resonance, therefore, is that Habermas and Luhmann's respective contributions be combined rather than played off against one another. The aim of this is to retain the action dimension, but at the same time to provide for the relational dimension which, under certain circumstances, brings a logic and dynamic into play over and above the heads or behind the backs of the actors or agents. Resonance cannot be theorised and analysed exclusively in action theoretical terms, but at a certain level has to be dealt with also as being part of a relational complex which transcends action. This theoretical strategy makes possible a more differentiated understanding of the relation between resonance, on the one hand, and public communication and discourse, on the other. Above all, however, it opens an exciting possibility—the possibility of developing a better grasp of the framework and situation within which public communication and discourse take place and within which resonance is to be located. The public sphere occupies the focal point here. The theoretical advantage of allowing the concept of resonance to guide the development of a new understanding of the public sphere will become apparent in the course of the argument.

2. CONCEPTS OF RESONANCE

An investigation of a sample of the relevant literature of the past two decades reveals a seemingly confusing range of different sociological concepts of resonance. They stretch from cultural resonance through system resonance, civil society resonance, lifeworld resonance and public resonance to institutional and extra-institutional resonance. In the following paragraphs, I offer a brief analysis of the different concepts in the hope that contact points between them become apparent and the possibility arises of relating them in a theoretically meaningful way to one another.

William Gamson and Kathryn Lasch (1983), as far as my knowledge goes, introduced the concept of 'cultural resonance' in the early 1980s. During the following decade, Gamson himself, or together with collaborators, reinforced it by either repeating the original formulation or developing it somewhat (Gamson 1988; Gamson and Modigliani 1989; Gamson *et al.* 1992; Gamson and Stuart 1992). Gamson's most extensive statement is contained in Chapter 8 of his book *Talking Politics* (1992). A noted essay by Anders Hansen (1991) on the social construction of the environment in public communication, in which he elaborates on the concept of cultural resonance, played some role in bringing the Gamsonian and, more generally, the American line of thinking to wider attention, especially in Europe.

According to the Gamsonian approach, cultural resonance refers to the relation between a claim advanced or an issue articulated in public communication, on the one hand, and the 'cultural givens' —as Marshall Sahlins called it—or resources in which it is anchored, on the other, which, when activated, either facilitate the incorporation of the claim or issue in public debate, media coverage and wider social elaboration or, alternatively, discourage such diffusion. Gamson conceives of the cultural resources in question as cultural themes and counter-themes such as, for example, 'progress through technology' and its dialectical opposite 'runaway technology' or 'Frankenstein monster' in the case of nuclear power, or 'America first' countered by 'global responsibility' in the case of the role of the US as superpower in the world (1992: 151-2, 141-2). The basic assumption is that when a claim or issue resonates with a widely accepted dominant cultural given, then it undergoes incorporation and elaboration much more readily than when it brings into play a less familiar one. The concept of cultural resonance is thus intended to capture the role of culture in public communication of whatever form by pinpointing how the cultural resources drawn upon or activated by such communication either facilitate or delimit the elaboration and coverage of the message.

Niklas Luhmann proposes what may be called a concept of system resonance. In his view, the concept of 'resonance', a sociological renaming of Humberto Maturana's biological concept of 'perturbation', applies to 'the relation between system and environment' (1989: 15). For the purposes of developing this concept, he takes cues from physics according to which a body resonates in response to a sound or tone only within the limits of its own frequencies. For him, this means sociologically that a differentiated system, whether society or one of its function systems, is characterised by a specific, more or less restricted 'resonance capacity' (p. 17). Resonance occurs when the system is irritated, perturbed or stimulated by its environment and the system in response then registers this affect within the range of its own resonance capacity. For instance, the economic system is able to respond to ecological problems only in terms of the binary code of payment/non-payment according to which it functions. In Luhmann's view, it is possible for a system to allow 'too little resonance' (p. 116) for the exposure of problems it faces. For example, society could ignore the perturbation emanating from ecological dangers and fail to register it in the form of resonance. On the other hand, the 'communication of the streets' (p. 36), or social movements, could generate 'too much resonance' (p. 116) through the articulation of internal demands and thus endanger society or even burst it apart. From the above it is clear that, for Luhmann, the concept of system resonance refers to the response of a system, irrespective of its type, to system relevant events or conditions in its environment. It obviously is a general concept which in principle applies to any system —but then many a social theorist would oppose what they perceive as Luhmann's overextension of system theory.

In his contribution contained in *Between Facts and Norms*, Jürgen Habermas employs the concept of resonance in the context of a complex nexus of relations and thus suggests that it has a number of different senses. Focusing on the public sphere in its anchorage in civil society and the lifeworld, he reveals two distinct yet related concepts of resonance. He singles out 'spontaneously emergent associations, organizations and movements' that enter the public sphere due to the fact that they are 'resonant' in the sense of being 'attuned to how societal problems resonate in private life spheres (Habermas 1996a: 358, 367). From this it is clear that resonance in its most original sense concerns the relation between private life spheres or lifeworlds and problems they face, and in its second apparently more derivative sense it applies to the relation between private life spheres and the associations, organizations and movements belonging to civil society that frame and communicate in the public sphere those problems in the first instance experienced in the lifeworld. In the former case, we may speak of lifeworld resonance, and in the latter of civil society resonance. In his early work on the classical modern liberal public sphere, *The Structural Transformation of the Public Sphere*, Habermas already employed the concept of resonance in these two senses. On the one hand, he identified the 'family as a sounding board (*Resonanzfläche*) for literature' (1989a: 162; 1962: 179) in the context of which the individual was able to acquire an audience-oriented subjectivity. On the other hand, he was concerned with the 'sounding board (*Resonanzboden*) of an educated stratum tutored in the public use of reason' (1989a: 175; 1962: 196). His focus in this early work was of course principally on the latter aspect, namely members of civil society or citizens who developed a critical capacity and brought it to bear on the public exercise of power, thus giving rise to the public sphere. It is obvious that the concept of civil society resonance suggested in *Between Facts and Norms* corresponds directly to his early notion of critical citizens representing the public sphere.

In the later work, however, Habermas also suggests a third concept of resonance that has a referent in the earlier work. While *The Structural Transformation of the Public Sphere* contains references to 'the public as audience' (1989a: 161), he in *Between Facts and Norms* in effect makes a distinction between active participants in the public sphere and the public audience who looks on, evaluates and makes judgments about those actors when he writes: 'But the political influence that the actors gain through public communication must *ultimately* rest on the resonance and indeed the approval of a lay public whose composition is egalitarian. The public must be *convinced* by comprehensible and broadly interesting contributions to issues it finds relevant. The public audience possesses final authority, because it is *constitutive* for the internal structure and reproduction of the public sphere, the *only* place where actors can appear. There can be no public sphere without a public' (1996a: 364, emphasis in the original). Above I have said that Habermas *in effect* makes the distinction between active participants and public audience for the reason that he does not do so in a reflected manner. As in his earlier work, also here it remains uncertain where precisely he draws the line. His focus is overwhelmingly on civil society resonance to the detriment of public resonance. In my interpretation, a significant sense of the concept of resonance refers to the relation between active participants —irrespective of whether citizens (e.g. associations, organizations and social movements), government officials, business executives or experts —who engage in public communication, on the one hand, and the observing, evaluating and judging public audience, on the other. It is resonance in this sense of the public audience responding to activities of actors participating in the public sphere, what I call public resonance, that elsewhere I have given a theoretical basis and elaborated upon by means of the concept of 'triple contingency' (Strydom 1999e, 2001), thus going critically beyond the traditional sociological assumption of double contingency which Habermas still shares with Parsons and Luhmann in particular and neo-classical sociology in general.

In a study of the Europeanisation of the public sphere, Klaus Eder (2000b) introduces a distinction between 'institutional resonance' and 'extra-institutional resonance'. The justification for this distinction lies in the fact that the network forming in this new communication society above the local yet below the global level is bound by two different resonance bases —what he calls 'resonance in the public' and 'resonance of institutions' (2000b: 178). Although he does not sketch the genealogy of these concepts, it is obvious that Habermas looms large in the background, and it is virtually certain that Luhmann also plays a role. Institutional resonance, for instance, clearly corresponds to Luhmann's system resonance, meaning the responsiveness of institutions to events or problems within the context in which they operate. On the other hand, the idea of extra-institutional resonance derives from Habermas's lifeworld and civil society resonance, as is borne out by Eder's understanding of extra-institutional resonance in its 'positive' sense. For him, positive extra-institutional resonance is equivalent to 'critical resonance' which was the ideal of the classical bourgeois public sphere (2000b: 178) —an idea, as we have seen, developed by Habermas as early as 1962 and restated thirty years later. In its 'negative' sense, by contrast, extra-institutional resonance for Eder refers to the withdrawal of resonance that typically follows when institutions are opaque and decision-making practices become too complex to be readily comprehensible.

This distinction between positive and negative resonance seems to be close to Luhmann's too little and too much resonance. Be that as it may, Eder applies it also to the institutional case. In his view, 'negative institutional resonance' (2000b: 178, 179) refers to the classical case of enlightened despotism or —we may say —paternalism where institutions hide their arcane practices behind closed doors and remain silent. This is similar to what Habermas with reference to Roger Cobb, Jennie-Keith Ross and Marc Ross (1976) describes as 'inside access' (Habermas 1996a: 379), in which case communication circulates inside the political system, while civil society is either excluded or does not have any influence on it. By contrast, positive institutional resonance designates the case where institutions become responsive by representing themselves actively in public communication. This coincides with what Habermas, once again with reference to Cobb, Ross and Ross, calls 'mobilization' (1996a: 379-80) where the political system moves outward in order to justify itself and to garner the support of the citizens to obtain formal consideration or implementation of an already adopted programme. The two distinctions —that is, between institutional and extra-institutional resonance, and between positive and negative resonance —thus allow Eder to identify four types of resonance: critical resonance, resonance withdrawal, negative institutional responsivity and, finally, positive institutional responsivity.

Despite developing an analytically acute model, it is surprising that Eder does not draw a distinction comparable to the one discussed above between lifeworld and civil society resonance, on the one hand, and public resonance on the other. Such a distinction would bring to awareness the fact that there are in fact two distinct kinds of critical resonance. The first type of critical resonance is spearheaded by the associations, organizations and social movements that emerge from civil society, whereas the second type is carried by the observing, evaluating and judging public audience. This means that the second type of critical resonance could be triggered in the public not just by representatives of institutions such as the state or corporations, but equally well by extra-institutional outgrowths of civil society such as voluntary associations and social movements. It is worth emphasising, for it is so often overlooked, that social movements themselves can trigger not only sympathetic awakening in the public, but equally well critical resonance also. Habermas, as we have seen, is not emphatic enough in drawing the distinction between active participants in the public sphere and the public audience. Considering his concept of resonance, Eder for his part seems to collapse the two into one another. This means that he effectively uses the concept of the public in the double contingency rather than the triple contingency sense (e.g. Eder 2000b, 2001; Eder and Kantner 2001). Eder thus exhibits the same tendency for which I have criticised Habermas elsewhere (Strydom 1999d, 1999e, 2001), namely tendentially reducing the full threefold structure of communication to the twofold relation between active participants —I and thou, as the traditional formula goes —in processes of public communication.[2]

3. RESONANCE STRUCTURES OF THE PUBLIC SPHERE

Given that the concept of resonance makes sense only relative to communication and that it gained sociological significance and currency only once society itself started to assume the form of communication, the best possibility for relating the different interpretations offered by Gamson, Luhmann, Habermas and Eder to one another in a meaningful way is to locate resonance within the context of public communication and discourse. Theoretically, this means that resonance is here taken to be a dimension of the public sphere and, further, that this dimension can be brought into view and made comprehensible by identifying the various resonance structures underpinning it. Resonance, in other words, is dependent on the resonance structures of the public sphere.

In the previous section, I have suggested that the relevant social theoretical literature of the recent past contains a number of concepts of resonance. Gamson put forward the concept of 'cultural resonance' and Luhmann that of system resonance, while Habermas's analysis builds on the assumption of a difference among civil society, lifeworld and public resonance, followed finally by Eder's distinction between 'institutional' and 'extra-institutional resonance', both of which could take either a positive or a negative form. What needs to be done, therefore, is that we account for these various concepts by anchoring them in corresponding resonance structures inherent in the public sphere. To identify such a range of resonance structures, it would be necessary to develop an analytical view of the public sphere as well of its embedding. For this purpose, one could start from the Habermas-Peters core-periphery model (Habermas 1996a: 341-87; see also Strydom 2002: 112-13), yet a number of steps going well beyond this model would be required.

To build up as clear a picture as possible, let us assume six concentric circles, and let us further assume that each represents an aspect of the public sphere and of the surrounding context in which it is embedded.

The smallest circle, the inside core according to the Habermas-Peters model, represents the formal political or decision making institutions. They serve as the resonance structure that makes Luhmann's system resonance possible and, by the same token, also Eder's 'institutional resonance', whether positive or negative. The second circle, the inner periphery in the Habermas-Peters model, covers institutions such as statutory bodies, foundations, universities, chambers and so forth which fulfil delegated state functions or have been granted self-administration rights. They could likewise provide the necessary basis for system or institutional resonance.

The third circle, representing civil society where it meets the public sphere, embraces a diversity of radically different social actors or agents, from active citizens, associations, organizations and social movements, on the one hand, to business organizations and corporations, on the other. Here business organizations and corporations make available the resonance structure of system or institutional resonance, while active citizens and the associations and organizations growing out of civil society serve as the structural basis of Habermas's civil society resonance and, directly corresponding to it, what Eder conceives as 'extra-institutional resonance'. The fourth concentric circle represents the lifeworld in which civil society and, by extension, the public sphere are rooted. It embraces a wide variety of private life spheres that provide the structural basis for Habermas's lifeworld resonance.

The penultimate or fifth circle contains the cultural foundations of the lifeworld, civil society and the public sphere, and as such it provides the cultural resources —that is, cultural models, schemes, codes, or Gamson's themes and counter-themes —upon which actors or agents draw and which they activate in public communication. This circle is thus the seat of the resonance structures that make possible what Gamson conceives as 'cultural resonance'. Although Gamson neglects to analyse the different layers of resonance structures, he is obviously onto something of much importance. For whether it is a matter of system/institutional resonance, extra-institutional resonance, civil society resonance or lifeworld resonance, cultural resources and hence cultural resonance in principle come into play. As Sahlins insists, 'an event is not just a happening in the world; it is a *relation* between a certain happening and a given symbolic system' (1985: 275).

The sixth and last concentric circle, however, brings to the fore a resonance structure that is of still greater significance, particularly in contemporary communication society, yet is often forgotten, perhaps because it is theoretically not well understood. It represents the public in the sense of the lay egalitarian public audience who observes the actors, agents or players in the public arena, evaluates and judges them, and thus takes a position on the relevance and value of their respective contributions to public communication. It should be emphasised that an analytical distinction should be maintained between those participating in the public sphere such as institutional actors —for instance, the state, corporations and experts —and extra-institutional actors —for instance, voluntary associations, non-governmental organizations and social movements — on the one hand, and the observing, evaluating and judging public, on the other. Here, therefore, we encounter the most basic and pervasive, in fact, the constitutive resonance structure of the public sphere. It provides the necessary basis for what I have called 'public resonance'. And as I have submitted, it must be distinguished sharply from civil society resonance. By way of its approval or disapproval, the public audience asserts its prerogative of being the final epistemic authority in public communication and thus decisively determines the relative influence of the different actors or agents participating in the process. Not only is it presupposed by the five layers of resonance structures mentioned above, but it also makes possible both their operation and eventual efficacy.

System or institutional resonance, civil society resonance and lifeworld resonance or extra-institutional resonance and finally cultural resonance —all these forms of resonance involve a twofold structure, as was apparent from the relations isolated in the first section above —for example, claim/cultural resources, system/environment, active citizens/problem, private life spheres/problem, institution/contextual conditions and extra-institutional domain/arcane institutional practices. But even more importantly, theoretically this twofold structure has always been assumed to belong within a framework which is best understood in terms of the traditional sociological concept of 'double contingency' (Parsons, 1977b: 168-69; Luhmann 1984: 148-190, 1995a: 103-36; Habermas 1996a: 18, 139).

When one considers social forms from the point of view of communication, however, it becomes apparent sooner or later that they are not constituted by dyadic, dialogical or mutualistic relations involving two individuals, 'I' and 'thou' (Parsons, Habermas), or 'two black boxes' (Luhmann), but rather by relations bringing into play the sign-mediated nature of communication and the system of personal pronouns, including over and above the first and second in particular also the third person. By contrast with the above-mentioned forms of resonance, public resonance presupposes the completion of the full threefold structure of communication, and theoretically this in turn requires articulation in terms of the concept of 'triple contingency' (Strydom 1999e, 2001). If we agree with Sahlins, as quoted above, that a communicative event is not simply an occurrence in the world involving relations between people, but is itself a relation between that particular occurrence and a cultural system involving relations between cognitive schemes and symbols,[3] then the question still remains how that relation is activated, constrained and regulated. Here enters the problem of triple contingency and, more specifically, of public resonance.

It is quite possible, then, to relate the various concepts of resonance contained in the relevant literature in a theoretically meaningful way to one another. In the preceding paragraphs, this was done by revealing their anchorage in different layers of resonance structures forming part of the public sphere and the socio-cultural framework in which it is embedded.

4. THEORETICAL SIGNIFICANCE AND RESEARCH POTENTIAL OF THE CONCEPT OF RESONANCE

The question that arises at this stage is the precise social-theoretical significance of the concept of resonance and, eventually, the role it could play in social research. A brief analysis of the different justifications offered and uses made of the concept by the authors discussed above could be of some help in searching for an answer to this question. In doing so, however, the available theoretical support should be kept in mind. The above unearthing of the anchorage points of resonance concepts in different layers of resonance structures was obviously not simply an empirical matter of the inductive identification and addition of different kinds of resonance. Nor was it simply a matter of theorising the relations in terms of double contingency, or even of 'multiple double contingency' (Welker 1992: 361) or a 'multiplicity of double contingencies' (Luhmann 1992b: 379), while focusing on the more or less complex interdependence of competing and cooperating participants. To take seriously resonance —public resonance, in particular —in terms of the theoretical perspective of triple contingency means that one appreciates such resonance as being of constitutive and systematic significance in public communication. Sight should never be lost of the fact, therefore, that resonance penetrates and takes in the whole network of active participants and their non-participant yet deeply involved observers, evaluators and judges who carry the third point of view. This means that resonance can be understood only if it is seen in a properly conceived relational framework.

In Gamson's (e.g. Gamson and Modigliani 1987) view, cultural resonance is one of three factors determining the construction of issue cultures, the remaining two being sponsor activities and media practices. From this it is obvious that he conceives of the concept on the basis of action, communication and cultural-theoretical assumptions. An issue culture is constructed not solely in the context of relations between people, but is itself related to cultural 'givens' involving relations between ideas, codes and symbols. In social research, he therefore employs the concept of resonance in the course of analysing public debates, and the purpose of doing so is to make intelligible why some issues gain currency more easily than others due to their relations to culture.

Luhmann (1989) adopts a general theoretical position when he conceives of resonance in system theoretical terms. It pertains to the relation between a system and its environment, particularly when the environment in some way or another irritates the system and thus makes it reverberate. Social systems such as society are autopoietic or self-producing systems that consist of communication, and Luhmann (1984, 1995a) understands the latter in terms of interconnectivity among the elements of the system. Accordingly, he employs the concept of resonance not just generally to show how systems and their environments relate, but in particular to further the analysis of the self-productive process whereby systems are able to continue their existence. For instance, society deals and can only deal with ecological dangers through its various functions systems, but each of these are able to process such dangers strictly only in terms of their own particular and in principle restricted resonance capacity. There is no possibility of a more general resonance concept.

Adopting an action theoretical approach to communication instead, Habermas employs the concept of resonance to refer to the sensitivity, willingness and courage of social actors, associations, organisations and social movements and thus to gain an understanding of the communicative power of citizens. His basic assumption, which contrasts sharply with Luhmann's, is that concern with public communication and hence resonance makes sense only relative to the communicative or discursive taming of the exercise of public and social power. By confining himself, neither to the analysis of messages and their reception, as does Gamson, nor to the analysis of the responsivity of systems, as does Luhmann, Habermas thus gives rise to the possibility of an approach that is both broader than Gamson's and less abstract than Luhmann's. On the one hand, the focus is on the logic, dynamics and outcomes of public communicative processes of opinion formation and will formation in which the constitution and organization of society is at stake (Habermas 1989a, 1996a). On the other, the evolution of historically specific, discursive, situational structures requires analyses of the changing structures of the lifeworld and, in particular, of the public sphere. Relevant to the investigation of the former is what he calls the 'rationalization of the lifeworld' (1987a: 145-48), and relevant to the latter for instance the shift from the 18th-century liberal bourgeois public sphere to the late 19th- and 20th-century public sphere characterised by informal 'non-public opinion', formal 'quasi-public opinion', the media's 'publicly manifested opinion', and the public relations sector's 'manufactured', 'managed' or 'staged opinion' (1989a: 244-50).

With these various authors behind him, Eder capitalises in particular on the possibility opened by Habermas. In this vein, he goes beyond the latter's concern with what may be termed the first transformation of the public sphere —that is, the transformation of the classical modern, liberal, bourgeois public sphere by the labour movement and the socialist parties —to pursue the 'second transformation of the public sphere' (Eder 1995, 1996b) which was inaugurated by the entry of the new social movements. In his conceptualisation of the transformed public sphere, however, one detects enriching traces of both Luhmann's more abstract relational understanding and of Gamson's issue-related cultural analysis. The new public sphere is regarded as taking the form of a fluid social field of self-organizing communicative conflict and discursive dynamics centred round issues and producing unexpected emergent effects. It is against this background that Eder (2000b) put forward his fourfold concept of resonance —namely, critical resonance, resonance withdrawal, negative institutional responsivity and positive institutional responsivity —which in turn provided him with the means to develop a typology of structural options: first, the currently emerging European public sphere which in terms of resonance appears as a doubly negative 'indifferent public sphere' with a high conflict potential; second, an institutionally positive but extra-institutionally negative 'staged public sphere' dominated by public relations; third, an extra-institutionally positive but institutionally negative 'modern public sphere'; and, finally, a doubly positive 'postmodern public sphere' characterised by struggles over agenda-setting and the definition of issues (2000b: 181).

Considering the contributions of these four authors, the social-theoretical sense and social research potential of the concept of resonance clearly go well beyond its undeniable utility for the analysis of particular communicative events and their cultural implications. It extends more broadly to the framework of relations in which such events take place and through which their cultural implications take effect. If the work of Gamson and his collaborators amply demonstrates the utility of the concept for communicative and cultural analysis, both Habermas and Eder's work, especially strengthened by means of insights into relationalism deriving from Luhmann, points up the potential of exploring and opening up not only the resonance structures of the socially and culturally embedded public sphere, but also the transformation of those structures and the ensuing consequences.

Of crucial importance if one were to shift the boundaries beyond Luhmann, Habermas and Eder's concepts of resonance, however, would be the much stricter observance of the threefold structure of communication. Due to his system theoretical position, which operates with a concept of communication that likens the notion of information, Luhmann, in principle, denounces the full structure of communication (1995a) or, at best, gives it only a subordinate role in his mirror theory of the role of public opinion in the political system (1998: 58-9; 1999: 22). Although Habermas and Eder in principle accept communication in its emphatic sense, they tend to neglect it in some sense or another. Habermas does not give adequate attention to all its dimensions in both his theoretical and substantive analyses.[4] Both neglect to distinguish sufficiently clearly between active participants in the public sphere and the observing, evaluating and judging public audience. By extension, they do not make clear that there are at least two distinct kinds of critical resonance. On the one hand, active participants in the public sphere could respond critically to institutions. Habermas and Eder stress this possibility throughout. On the other hand, however, the observing, evaluating and judging public audience could develop critical resonance in relation to any of the active participants in the public sphere, whether political institutions, corporations, voluntary association, civil society organizations or social movements. Neither Habermas nor Eder spells out the related concept of public resonance. The relative neglect of the latter undoubtedly has something to do with two pre-constructivist trends, the first being the neo-classical fixation on macro-theory and the second the neo-Marxist predilection to attach an uncritical, positive evaluation to social movements. Above all, however, it has a theoretical basis in the canonical acceptance in neo-classical sociology generally of Parsons's only very partially correct proposition of the '*double contingency* inherent in social interaction' (Parsons and Shils, 1951: 16, emphasis in the original).[5]

Once this theoretical limitation is acknowledged and corrected by means of the concept of triple contingency based on the full structure of communication, a whole new vista opens for the use of the concept of resonance in social research.

First, Gamson's finely grained cultural-communicative analyses of the construction of issues could be integrated in a much broader theoretical framework embracing the public sphere and its social and cultural embedding. And building on Luhmann's general theory of resonance and on Habermas and Eder's analyses of the public sphere, this framework could be differentiated and filled out, in turn, by means of a concept of resonance fine-tuned in terms of the theory of triple contingency. Promising initial steps in social research would be the pursuit beyond the existing literature of the analysis, first, of the late 20th-century transformation of the public sphere and, second, of the nature of the contemporary public sphere. Within these contexts, however, the potentially most fruitful focus would be on the non-linear dynamics of the social processes transpiring in public communication and discourse and the concurrent structure formation. Whether considered from the viewpoint of the construction of identities, issues and cultural models or of the politics of discursive relations, the different concepts of resonance, anchored as they are in distinct resonance structures, would considerably advance the transparency and intelligibility of these dynamics. At the very least, however, they would free the theoretical view from fetters deriving from both Habermas (1987a) and Bourdieu (1986) —that is, by breaking the stranglehold of the rather rigid habitus, in the latter case, and of the contingency-resistant model of communicative action, in the former.[6]

The concept of resonance makes possible the development of a model of communication and discourse that allows one to trace the dynamics and structuration of the process. Within such a process taking place under propitious conditions, the participants in the public sphere and their public audience together work through and perhaps even work off the contingencies generated by their relations and, simultaneously, develop and extend the very framework within which they are able to do so.

10

Intersubjectivity—Interactionist or Discursive? Reflections on Habermas's Critique of Brandom

In a recent essay, Jürgen Habermas (1999b, 2003b) develops a detailed analysis and differentiated critique of Robert Brandom's normative pragmatics, as presented in his major work entitled *Making It Explicit* (1994). A central aspect of Habermas's critique is directed against Brandom's alleged objectivistic understanding of discursive practice. The angle from which Habermas undertakes this critique and seeks to correct Brandom's position is represented by his intersubjectivist point of view. Rather than trying to defend Brandom, I propose to devote these reflections to a critical analysis of Habermas's position as put forward in the core part of his essay —that is, particularly section V(2) (2003b: 161-6) — focused on the structure of communication. In the following, I leave open the question whether Brandom actually takes an objectivist approach to discursive practice which derives from his metaphysical conceptual realism and the related tendency toward a neo-Hegelian objective idealism which assumes a movement of the concept over the heads and behind the backs of the participants in communication, as Habermas argues. My focus is rather the conspicuous ambivalence in Habermas regarding an interactionist or dialogical and a discursive approach to intersubjectivity and the theoretical implications flowing from it. Above all, a proper understanding of intersubjectivity, particularly the process of communication whereby it becomes established, is at stake. The central point of the argument is that Habermas fails to theorise the process of communication adequately. Although proceeding from the basic distinction between interaction or dialogue and discourse, he tends to regard the process in a one-dimensional manner as involving the interactive or dialogical coordination of the intentions and actions of the participants alone. This raises the question of the missing dimension of the process, namely the moment of synthesis of the different contributions into a collectively acceptable outcome at the discursive level which is essential for and therefore presupposed by the actual attainment of intersubjective coordination.

In order to present the argument in a comprehensible manner, I first briefly review Habermas's critique of Brandom, then characterise his proposal to correct Brandom's objectivistic tendency, and finally embark on a more detailed analysis and critique of Habermas's position.

1. HABERMAS'S CRITIQUE OF BRANDOM

In *Making It Explicit*, Brandom systematically develops an innovative pragmatic analysis of language by focusing on discursive practice in the sense of the activities of giving and asking for reasons or mutual justification on which the social life of a speech or language community depends. Accordingly, he follows the various interrelated roles of speech acts in discourse —from speakers expressing utterances or making claims and thus undertaking something and entering into commitments, via interpreters attributing claims and commitments to speakers, to all the participants mutually evaluating and assessing or keeping score of each other's position in and contribution to their common discourse.

Habermas's critique —at least, I select here the particular aspect of it as being relevant —turns on a discrepancy he discovers in Brandom's methodological approach. On the one hand, according to his own account, Brandom starts by adopting the orientation of a second person which enables him to analyse the utterances of a speaker from the perspective of an interlocutor or interpreter participating in discourse. He emphatically holds, for instance, that the basic explanatory challenge of his normative pragmatic model of discursive practice centrally involves the practical attitude of taking and treating speech acts as having the significance of claims (Brandom 1994: 141-2, also 161-5; Habermas 2003b: 134-5). Others, must hear a speech act, listen to what is being said, understand the claim it raises, and respond to it. On closer inspection, however, Habermas (2003b: 162) finds on the other hand that Brandom actually constructs the first-person–second-person or I-thou relation as a first-person–third-person relation: a first person makes an utterance and a third person, who plays the role of an observer or spectator rather than an addressee, attributes or imputes the claim implied by the utterance to the speaker and then evaluates its validity and assesses its import.

That the attribution, evaluation and assessment tasks are not carried out by a second person, as Brandom initially intimated, is borne out for Habermas by the fact that a person is able to fulfil the role of a second person only if an 'I' orients himself or herself towards him or her as a 'thou', only if a first person addresses a second person with the expectation of a reply. The shift from a first-person–second-person relation to a first-person–third-person relation instead in Brandom's actual analysis implies in Habermas's view that he not only confuses two distinct levels of communication, but also ignores the grammatical role of the second person. On the whole, then, Brandom neglects the complex interrelation of the first-, second- and third-person perspectives, which means that he operates with an inadequate concept of communication.

From this circumstance, Habermas (2003b: 160, 163-5) draws the conclusion that Brandom adopts an objectivist, theoreticist and methodological individualist approach which is unsuited to the analysis of discursive practice. The last word is given to a spectator or observer of a speech act who attributes a claim to a speaker and evaluates it, thus making possible an objectivistic description of the process of communication or discursive practice. The spectator or observer is actually assuming the role of a theoretician who regards understanding an utterance not as the hermeneutic interpretation of a text, but rather as an operation of imputing his or her own interpretation and evaluation to the speaker. The process of communication or discursive practice itself is conceived as emerging from the inferences which each individual participant draws for himself or herself based on their observation of one another, rather than as the outcome of a cooperative accomplishment.

2. HABERMAS'S CORRECTIVE PROPOSAL

Essentially, Habermas's proposal is to adopt intersubjectivism as a corrective to Brandom's objectivism.

Habermas's (2003b: 162-4) prime target is Brandom's reputed tendency to treat communication or discursive practice in terms of the relation between a first person and a third person or between a speaker and an observing interpreter. As against this particular emphasis, he insists instead on the primacy of the relation between a first person and a second person. A first person, on the one hand, is a speaker who connects an intention with an utterance and, as an interlocutor, uses his or her assertion to demand a public reply, whether positive or negative, from an addressee. Such a response is necessary to either confirm what is at stake in the intention of the speaker or to bring him or her to revise it, and thus to produce an obligation relevant to the continuation of the exchange between the two parties. A second person, on the other hand, is one who is drawn into communication by a speaker's orientation toward him or her, thus becoming an addressee who is expected to respond in a meaningful way to the speaker's utterance. Habermas stresses the status of both the first and second persons as performers who are directly involved in the interaction and whose perspectives structurally interpenetrate so that their roles are interchangeable. This contrasts sharply with third persons who are disinterested interpreters, observers or spectators who are uninvolved, at best just registering what is being said by the performing interlocutors and waiting to see what transpires between or among them.

It is this distinction between directly involved parties to an exchange or a dispute who adopt a performative attitude towards one another, on the one hand, and observing bystanders or spectators who interpret what is going on between or among interlocutors, on the other, that leads Habermas (2003b: 163) to claim that Brandom confounds two distinct dimensions of communication. Whereas the latter at first had in mind the direct communication between speakers and addressees, his emphasis shifted and then became fixed on the indirect communication between the speakers and the spectators listening to them. Habermas's intersubjectivist corrective to Brandom's alleged objectivistic tendency is to keep these two dimensions strictly apart and to regard the direct communicative relation between speaker and addressee as the paradigmatic case.

The second component of Habermas's proposal is to embed the first-person–second-person relation in the broader context serving as its carrier or substrate. As against Brandom's tendency —as reputedly exhibited by his models of baseball, court proceedings, and ballroom dancing[1] —to treat communication or discursive practice as a self-sufficient process comprised of the contributions of individuals who mutually observe, inform and evaluate each other, Habermas (2003b: 162-6) elaborates the first principle of the theory of intersubjectivity. Communication or discursive practice is a cooperative process of learning which unfolds within the limits of a social environment and the constraints of an independently existing world. Within its social environment, the process on the one hand takes place against the background of an intersubjective lifeworld or within the shared meaning horizon of a linguistically disclosed world. On the other, it is guided by a community of justification which directs it toward the goal of a discursively achieved agreement. If successful, the process culminates in a collectively accepted result which allows the coordination of the plans and actions of the independently deciding participants. For Habermas (2003b: 164, 165), the specificity of linguistically mediated communication, which according to him is not adequately appreciated by Brandom, lies in such a coordination and more generally the social integration which follows from it. For Habermas, this emphasis directs the attention toward the dependence of communication on the necessity of keeping consonant those beliefs and opinions of participants that are relevant for coordinating their plans and actions. Central to the intersubjectivist conception of the process of communication or discursive practice, then, is the possibility for the participants to converge in their recognition of the same validity claim and to come to share knowledge of that which they are communicating about.[2] It is only on this basis, according to Habermas (2003b: 166), that the intersubjective justification of a claim raised in the process of communication or discursive practice could allow the burden of the warrant for its validity to be shouldered collectively.

It is advisable in the present context, finally, to highlight an additional, albeit remarkably brief, clarification Habermas makes to his account of communication or discursive practice embedded in an intersubjective context. Despite its brevity, it is of central importance for both an understanding and a critical assessment of Habermas's critique of Brandom, as will become apparent later. The clarification concerns the structure of communication or discursive practice and its social significance. On one occasion, Habermas insists that 'the complex interconnections of the first, second and third person perspectives' (2003b: 162) must, by contrast with Brandom, be borne in mind throughout. And on another, he suggests that the 'grammatical role' (2003b: 163) of each of the three types of persons involved in communication, including the second person ignored by Brandom, need to be considered in principle. More formally, the reference here is to the linguistic system of personal pronouns which he discussed in various places in his earlier writings (e.g. Habermas and Luhmann 1971: 193-4; Habermas 1987a: 35-6, 102-5). The social significance of these structural parameters of communication or discursive practices should be obvious. The establishment of interpersonal relations within the framework of first, second and third person perspectives through the use of personal pronouns brings to the fore a whole intersubjective world by actualising a deep-seated network of relations of not just memberships but also potential memberships in a social group or communication community.

3. CRITIQUE OF HABERMAS

Habermas regards Brandom's *Making It Explicit* as an innovative, detailed and tenacious elaboration of a programme of formal pragmatics he himself among others, has been envisaging since the 1970s. Sharing a pragmatic approach, Habermas thus fully accepts Brandom's focus on the social practices of a linguistic community in which subjects capable of speech and action engage. Brandom's specific concern is what he calls 'linguistic' or 'discursive practice' and conceives as acts of communication which involve 'giving and asking for reasons' and are regulated by the participants' mutual 'scorekeeping' (1994: 5, 141). In his analysis, Habermas speaks interchangeably of discursive practice, discourse, argumentation, communication, communicative exchange, linguistic communication, everyday communication and interaction. This varied usage, which is present also in the original German version of the essay under discussion

(Habermas 1999b), at first sight looks like a case of conceptual looseness. Indeed, in my view, it is the source of a particular ambivalence and hence lack of clarity and even mismatched analysis in his critique of Brandom.

Light is shed on this conceptual imprecision by a basic theoretical distinction on which Habermas's position rests since 1970 —namely, the distinction between 'communicative action' (or interaction) and 'discourse' (e.g. Habermas and Luhmann 1971: 114-22; Habermas 1974: 16-9; 1979a: 3-4). Here discourse is conceived as a special reflexive form of communication which indeed takes place in and through the medium of communication, yet stands in a relation of opposition to ordinary everyday communication in so far as it stops the latter in its tracks, problematises it, opens it up, induces reflection on its implicit assumptions, makes the latter explicit and thus explains and clarifies communication by reference to those very assumptions (Strydom 2000: 42-9). I am convinced that this distinction between interaction and discourse is also crucial for understanding what is actually happening in Habermas's critical engagement with Brandom's work. A close examination of the relevant writings of our two authors shows, to my mind, that whereas Brandom focuses on discourse, or the 'discursive practice' of 'giving and asking for reasons' (1994: 5), Habermas for the most part criticises Brandom from the point of view of interaction. Instead of discourse, he holds to a theory of everyday communication or interaction, or one might say a theory of dialogue. Rather than a discursive intersubjectivist position, therefore, he assumes an interactionist or dialogical intersubjectivism.

In the development of his critique of Brandom's objectivist conception of the process of communication and his concurrent theoreticist attitude, Habermas seems to fall in the trap of interactionism or dialogicism due to a forgetfulness of discourse. Various pieces of evidence can be mustered to support this interpretation. His undivided attention to the first-person–second-person relation from an internal lifeworld perspective is of first importance here. Not only is the relation between the first and second person for him the essential component of communication, but he also sees the understanding by an addressee of what a speaker means, which in turn requires something like the hermeneutic interpretation of a text, as the essential quality of this relation itself and hence also of communication. In the course of the development of this relation in the process of communication, therefore, he regards the first and second person as converging in their understanding of the claim at stake up to the point where they share the same knowledge. The emphasis here is on the I-thou relation, mutual understanding through hermeneutic interpretation, convergence and sharing. There could be little criticism of this approach if communication in the sense of internal lifeworld or everyday communication were in question, but at issue between Habermas and Brandom is more than such interaction or dialogue. What is happening here is that Habermas generalises communication in the sense of interaction or dialogue to the level of discourse, with the result that he obliterates the latter and thus misses this second dimension of communication. His own axiomatic distinction which is crucial for grasping the multi-dimensionality of the process of communication falls by the wayside.

A brief analysis delivers evidence backing up this claim. Notwithstanding the assumption of a shared horizon of meaning, the interactionist or dialogical approach regards sociality or the outcome of a social situation as depending on the intentions and actions of participants. It results from the coordination of subjective perspectives and individual actions. The outcome is given shape and form by the coordination of the meanings of the communicative actions of each participant which are hermeneutically interpreted and understood by the other participants. Such coordination is a meaningfully structured process of cooperation among the participants that gathers together the different acts of understanding and agreement so as to culminate in intersubjective understanding and agreement among the participants. This could be summarised by saying that the assumption is made that a speaker communicates a meaning in such a way to an addressee that the latter understands it in a manner identical to the speaker, with the implication that the speaker could be said to control the reception of his or her meaning and its understanding by the addressee.[3]

On close inspection, however, it becomes apparent that the interactionist or dialogical account is not adequate to capture the specificity of discursive practice involving giving and asking for reasons. Habermas demands of Brandom that he takes into consideration throughout the complex interrelations of the first-, second- and third-person perspectives instead of screening out the first-person–second-person relation. But he himself then continues to reduce this complex threefold relation to the first-person–second-person relation to the virtual exclusion of the third-person perspective. It is remarkable that, in an earlier publication, Habermas (1997a: 133-4) himself presented a convincing critique of dialogical philosophy. Proceeding from the assumption of the sign-mediated nature of communication and the full system of personal pronouns, he pointed out that dialogical philosophy operates with a selective reconstruction of the full structure of communication. Replacing the reflection model of the epistemological subject-object relation with the communicative model of reciprocal self-understanding, it focuses exclusively on the I-Thou relation. The result is a narrowing of the structure of understanding to the existential-ethical experience of the participants consequent on felicitous communication. As against this reductive tendency, he insisted that communication involves more than the ego—alter relation. It presupposes the integration of the performative attitude of the participating first and second persons with the third person attitude. Here Habermas obviously went beyond the interactionist or dialogical account he offers in section V(2) of the essay on Brandom. In the earlier publication, the full threefold structure of communication and its sign-mediated nature are manifest in sharp profile —a complex which makes itself felt in particular when we shift from interaction to discourse where the participants are required to engage in public practices of justification. In the Brandom essay, by contrast, Habermas looses sight of communication in the full sense of the word as well as apparently the Peircean theory of signs which he elsewhere accepts as being presupposed by it (Habermas 1991: 9-33; 1996a: 13-4)[4]. But this still leaves the pressing question of the role of the third person.

In his critique of dialogical philosophy, Habermas (1997a: 134) regards the third-person attitude as one towards something in the objective world. Likewise in his critique of Brandom, he proposes to correct Brandom's conceptual realism by replacing it with a pragmatic realism which acknowledges the resistance of an independent objective world (Habermas 2003b: 155-9). Yet in discourse, particularly in the practical type of discourse we are familiar with in social life taking the form of public controversy, debate or dispute characterised by the practice of justification, the third-person perspective enters by no means solely in the form of the neutral attitude towards something in the objective world. The latter attitude at best brings into play only 'it', but not yet the personal pronouns 'he', 'she' or 'they'. Habermas gives an unmistakable indication of this more complex situation in a recent outline of what may be called his cognitive-epistemic model of discourse (1999a: 46-7, 102-3). According to this model, the structuration of discourse takes place in such a way that it can be said to be an epistemically steered process. Ethical and pragmatic reasons in the sense of individual participants' motives and values are not ignored, but generalised and treated as valid epistemic contributions to discourse that are intersubjectively acceptable. On the one hand, the participants create their own reality by making individual contributions to the process through which this achievement is realised and, on the other, they are all without exception subordinate to the structures of the performatively shared situation which thus become established and collectively accepted —yet leaving room for the relational structure of otherness and difference which secures the retention of both differences and the particular. What this position implies, in my estimation, is that here not just the participants assuming first- and second-person roles and a reference to the objective world are of importance, but at the same time also epistemic properties that are discursively constructed and collectively valid since they are acceptable from the third person perspective.

With this circumscription of discourse, Habermas undoubtedly goes well beyond the interactionist or dialogical position he plays out against Brandom, and simultaneously he hints, albeit rather obliquely, at the place of the third-person perspective in such a process. In his critique of Brandom, first, he fixes on the meanings remaining identical in the transition from the first person to the second person, so that every response is seen as directly connected to a speech act, while the speaker controls the addressee's understanding. In the case of his cognitive-epistemic model of discourse, by contrast, there is a certain openness or contingency of meaning that, precisely because of the epistemic role of the discursive process, allows the participants to maintain different interpretations of the same issue without precluding their potential coordination. In his critique, moveover, he is emphatic about the inclusion only of the first- and second-person perspectives embodied by the directly involved participants, but in a process of cognitive-epistemic structure formation such as a public controversy, debate or dispute there is present also others who may be only indirectly involved yet are nevertheless indispensable for the epistemic authority of the rules or structures which become established. They constitute the audience or, more properly, the public, the embodiment of the third-person perspective, to whom the participants appeal for their support in dealing with each other and who, in turn, observes the participants and evaluates, judges and comments on their communication and behaviour, thus exerting a significant influence on the definition of reality and the related decision-making emerging from the joint discursive process.[5]

It is indeed remarkable that Habermas should overlook the third person perspective in the guise of the epistemic role and authority of the public since elsewhere he is acutely aware of its significance in public discourse:

> *'But the political influence that the actors gain through public communication must* ultimately *rest on the resonance and indeed the approval of a lay public whose composition is egalitarian. The public of citizens must be* convinced *by comprehensible and broadly interesting contributions to issues it finds relevant. The public audience possesses final authority, because it is* constitutive *for the internal structure of the public sphere, the* only *place where actors appear. There can be no public sphere without a public' (1996a: 364).*

Later in *Truth and Justification*, containing the piece on Brandom, he comparably submits: 'But before it can be considered as a general interest in public discourse, every interest that is to "count" morally in case of doubt must be convincingly interpreted and grounded as well as translated into a relevant claim *from the perspective of those affected*' (2003a: 269). Here it should be pointed out in parenthesis that, taken together, the references to the 'public' and 'those affected' contain the important suggestion that, although the public in one respect embodies social validity and authority, it should not summarily be reduced to this and thus robbed of its epistemic authority and guardianship of epistemic validity. Even in his discussion of Brandom's example of a court case involving a prosecutor and a defence lawyer arguing before a judge and jury, in which an understanding of the threefold structure of communication is clearly available, Habermas (2003b: 162-63) dismisses the judge and jury as spectators who are waiting to see what happens. Instead of sensing the potential for highlighting the full structure of communication, he reads into Brandom two distinct levels of communication which need to be kept strictly apart —the communication of those directly involved and the indirect communication of the speakers with the spectators who are listening to them. It is plain to see that here Habermas completely ignores the discursive practice that is underway. Rather than being kept apart, these two dimensions obviously require to be treated as being intimately related. What happens here, theoretically speaking, is that Habermas remains a captive of the concept of the 'double contingency' (1996a: 18, 139)[6] of social interaction appropriated from the classical tradition of social theory, rather than being able, despite his theory of discourse, to make a transition to the more adequate concept of 'triple contingency', as I have called it elsewhere (Strydom 1999d, 1999e, 2001).[7] He fixes his focus on the twofold first-person–second-person relation and the problem of the contingency of meaning within that restricted framework, instead of including also the third-person perspective that would allow him to come to grips with the full threefold structure of communication and the higher level of contingency relevant to this more complex framework.

Elsewhere in *Truth and Justification* than the chapter on Brandom where he surprisingly confines himself to an interactionist or dialogical position, Habermas on various occasions discusses crucial characteristics of discourse. He indeed sees discourse as a language game, yet beyond limiting contextualist implications it is clearly a special language game for him in that it at one and the same time represents 'the forum of justification' (2003a: 102) and a process of 'construction' (2003a: 44, 47) which takes off when new issues arise, compelling the development of new norms and their justification in the light of new challenges. As such, discourse exerts a certain 'constraint' that becomes visible through the 'decentering' of the participants' perspectives or a distancing from themselves which the process in the course of its unfolding requires of them (2003a: 105, 109, 234, 270). The constraint and decentring on the part of the participants are indications that the process of the joint discursive construction of a common world is in a significant sense a learning process (2003a: 105, 161). In the interactionist or dialogical account in the Brandom essay, by contrast, the identity of meaning, the hermeneutic interpretation of the meaning of speech acts, and the control of understanding leave no room for such constraint, decentring and learning.[8] Indeed, there is something else that is still missing even here and should therefore be added to constraint, decentring and learning —namely, openness of meaning that, in keeping with the full threefold structure of communication and its sign-mediated nature, is best conceived in terms of triple contingency.

Rather than applying his insights into constraint, decentring and learning to Brandom, Habermas instead shrinks back from the consequences of thinking discourse through to the end. There are in fact indications that he is afraid of the concept of a non-linear, dynamic process which breaks through the limits of intentionality, since in his view it inevitably entails fatalistic implications. The model of such a process guiding him in *Truth and Justification* is the objective, non-human or even anti-human process represented by the currently influential forms of Quinean naturalism and Heideggerian idealism (e.g. 2003a: 22-6; 284). Perceiving a similar thrust of an impersonal process in Brandom's tendency towards Hegelian objectivism which celebrates the movement of the concept, he reacts by adopting an interactionist or dialogical rather than a discursive position. This leads him to give a foreshortened account of discursive practice in Brandom as a self-sufficient process made up of the contributions of individuals who mutually observe each other and therefore cannot arrive at intersubjective coordination of their actions. To conceive of discourse as a non-linear, dynamic process of structure formation not fully under the control of any of the participants, yet nevertheless forming part of the larger process of communication, does not imply that it necessarily falls in the category of a strong, objectivistic naturalism or idealism. Habermas indeed emphasises the centrality of the 'cooperative learning process by way of the constructive interpretations of a communication community' (2003b: 161), but neither the dynamics nor the serrated profile of the communicative process come through clearly. What he should have appreciated is that it is a temporally and hence sequentially unfolding process that starts from individual contributions and then, through joint construction involving not only cooperation but also competition and even conflict, flowers into a moment of discursive structure formation giving rise to a shared collective outcome which, while differently interpreted by the participants, eventually allows them to coordinate their actions.[9] Despite recognising elsewhere that discourse is an epistemically steered process and despite stressing that it involves a learning process exerting constraint and requiring decentring on the part of the participants, Habermas's critique of Brandom reveals a lack of a sufficiently articulated concept not only of the temporal or sequential phasing but also of the structuration of the process of communication and discursive construction.

If one considers Habermas's distinction between interaction and discourse from a processual perspective, it becomes apparent that it is impossible to operate with the concept of coordination alone. A second concept, complementary to coordination, is required to capture the different levels of operation of the communicative process as well as the range of achievements gained in its course. Whereas Habermas focuses on interaction and the coordination of individuals that becomes possible through this medium in the course of the process, he leaves the moment of synthesis achieved through joint—that is, both competitive and cooperative—discursive structure formation unnamed and unaccounted for. Previously, I have suggested that there is a certain conceptual blockage in Habermas's understanding of discourse. It can be attributed to the fact that he does not consistently embrace the full structure of communication and the threefold sign relation underpinning it. Behind this inconsistency, in my view, lies the fact that he remains attached to the classical sociological concept of the 'double contingency' of the first- and second-person perspectives in social interaction and, as a consequence, makes their 'coordination' the central focus of his theory. What he ignores, despite bringing in the public or all those potentially affected, is 'triple contingency' and hence the 'synthesis' of the inputs of the participants in the course of the joint constructive process that, by a discursive detour, in the first place provides a basis for the eventual coordination of the participants. Habermas's narrow double contingency perspective must be extended to the broader triple contingency perspective, and the coordination of the plans and actions of the directly involved participants must be seen in relation to the non-linear dynamics of the discursive synthesis of those contributions of the participants that are judged to be epistemically relevant by the public as well as by the participants themselves from the discursively activated perspective of those potentially affected. Were he to systematise his position along the suggested lines, he would eliminate the ambivalence I have identified by bridging the gap between an interactionist and a discursive concept of intersubjectivity without having to bow his knee before the objective idealism to which he thinks Brandom is prone.

CONCLUSION

I have endeavoured to show that there is a clearly identifiable ambivalence in Habermas that is conspicuously present in his analysis and critique of Brandom. I have suggested that it is most immediately fed by an unjustifiable tendency on his part to retreat from discourse into interaction or dialogue due to a not entirely mistaken apprehension regarding objective, impersonal processes —in Brandom's case, according to Habermas, the objective idealist movement of the concept. Instead of an intersubjective discursive position, Habermas on such occasions of recoil comes to represent an intersubjective dialogical position that cannot be defended. What he does not keep in mind throughout is that not all objective processes are on par. Even in our type of society where communication has been unleashed to an unprecedented degree, discourse as a concept complementary to interaction does not admit of being assimilated without more ado to cybernetic and informational processes. Like these processes, discourse also has its rightful place. Rather than falling back exclusively on interaction or dialogue, this fact has to be established unequivocally. This means that even if Habermas is correct about Brandom's objectivism, his counter-position should not have been interactionist or dialogicist, but rather one that acknowledges the discursive dimension between these two extremes. Finally, I have also sought to suggest that Habermas's strategy in dealing with Brandom is related to his apparent inclination to stop short of fully utilising his theory of communication as a process embracing not only interaction but also discursive construction.

It is only when Habermas compensates for this theoretical deficit, which would be more in line with the work of a number of younger authors inspired by him (e.g. Miller 1992a, 2002a; Eder 1996a, 2000a; Strydom 1999e, 2000, 2001, 2002; Delanty 1999a, 1999b; Trenz and Eder 2004), that he would be able to fend off the concerted and vehement attack that a whole school following Luhmann (e.g. Sutter 1997; Hörning, Ahrens and Gerhard 1997; Sutter and Charlton 1999) is at present waging against him. What both Habermas and these critics of his have in common, ironically, is the debilitating assumption of the traditional concept of double contingency.

PART III

APPLICATIONS: SOCIAL MOVEMENTS, RESPONSIBILITY, RISK, COSMOPOLITANISM

11

The Construction of Collective Identity: The South African Liberation Movement as a Collective Learning Process, 1882-1987

During the late 1960s and early 1970s, it became increasingly apparent that not only the functionalist approach to social movements had run into difficulties which were bound to remain irresolvable unless a new perspective is introduced, but also the Marxist one. Although the former emphasises generalised beliefs and the latter contradictions or crises, they share a basic limiting assumption, namely the dualism of action and structure. In the course of the 1970s, various attempts were made to overcome the debilitating core assumption of the two otherwise diametrically opposed classical theoretical approaches. From the viewpoint of the theory of social movements, the contributions of Jürgen Habermas (1976a, 1979a, 1984a, 1987a) and Alain Touraine (1971, 1977, 1981) to a new, more complex paradigm are of particular importance. Each in his own particular way, these two theorists developed a theoretical position which mediates the structural or systemic and the action perspectives in such a way that collective action could at one and the same time be considered with reference to the internal and external relations constituting it. On the basis of the suggestive outline that emerged from Habermas's theory of social evolution and Touraine's concern with the identity of a social movement, it became possible in the 1980s to start moving tentatively toward what one may call a theory of social movements as collective learning processes.

It should be pointed out, of course, that the respective conceptions of these two theorists are characterised by their own peculiar limitations. While the concept of collective learning is absent from Touraine's work so that the theory of social movements in these terms remains undeveloped, Habermas's explicit reference to 'social movements as learning processes' does not fulfil the promise it contains.[1] Authors whose writings exhibit the first steps in the direction indicated, although the concept of collective learning is not always explicitly employed, include Alberto Melucci (1980, 1984, 1985), Klaus Japp (1984), Jean Cohen (1985) and particularly Kaus

Eder (1982, 1985a, 1985b). Interesting older works from which a good deal is still to be learned, despite their respective shortcomings, are those of Michael Vester (1970) as well as Oskar Negt and Alexander Kluge (1972).

While much still remains to be done to bring the insights of these various authors together in a theory of social movements as collective learning processes, the major dimensions of such a theory can nevertheless be gleaned from them against the background of the failure of the classical approaches because of their emphasis on irrationality (functionalist theory of collective behaviour) and the logic of capitalism (Marxism) respectively. The blind spot of these approaches is threefold, namely the process whereby a social movement emerges and its internal articulation, the process of development of a social movement in relation to its environment, and finally the forms through which collective action passes in relation to the strategies of collective action adopted. The theory of collective learning focuses precisely on these three problem complexes screened out by the classical approaches. From this novel point of view, they are seen in the following light: first, as regards its genesis and internal development, a social movement represents a self-creative and self-organizing process taking the form of collective learning in the sense of communicative conflict resolution and, consequently, collective identity construction making possible the mediation of objective and subjective conditions and hence the coordination of action; second, as regards its relation to its environment, a social movement represents a cyclical learning process taking the form of a feedback loop between theory and practice or between latent protest potential and manifest action; and, finally, as regards the specific order in which it adopts alternative strategies in the course of its development, a social movement represents a progressively deepening learning process—under appropriate conditions—taking the form of a justificatory regress or, better, reflex according to which it passes from the normal level of negotiation, through the second order level of political and/or legal institutions and the still constitutional level of protest and civil disobedience, eventually to the extra-constitutional level of resistance and violence.

In this present context, I propose to concentrate on the first of these three dimensions through a brief reconstruction of the South African liberation movement. For the present purposes, however, I further exclude treatment of the question of the initial emergence and establishment of the movement in favour of confining myself to a consideration of the internal process of the construction of its collective identity. My aim, therefore, cannot be to provide an exhaustive historical account of this process, but by relying where possible on the extant historical research and where necessary independently consulting historical documents to structure the available material from the theoretical point of view of the theory of collective learning. The task of ordering historical events relevant to collective identity construction according to such a theoretical perspective is made all the more urgent by the failure of the predominant theoretical traditions in South Africa—the liberal and the Marxist[2]—to develop an adequate account of the liberation movement.

1. THE COLLECTIVE LEARNING APPROACH

The theory of collective learning represents a specifically sociological perspective in that it recognises objective and subjective factors (for instance, structural contradictions and experiences of deprivation or grievances) only as necessary conditions of collective action and, then, on the basis of the assumption of the primacy of social actors engaged in communication, proceeds to concentrate, as sufficient condition, on the collective learning process whereby the objective and subjective dimensions are related to one another in such a manner that a self-creative and self-organizing social movement capable of collective action makes its appearance and undergoes internal development. In these terms, the genesis and development of a social movement relates most directly neither to structural conditions, changes or strains nor to subjective experiences of deprivation or grievances, but rather to the self-creative, self-organizing mechanism whereby people come together and group themselves into a collective actor. This mechanism is represented by 'practical discourse' (Habermas 1987a), 'moral discussion' (Blatt and Kohlberg 1975; Berkowitz 1981) or 'moral argumentation' (Miller 1986) in the sense of 'communicative conflict resolution' (Eder 1985b) taking the form of a collective learning process. Matters of different kinds enter into such a process—from particular interests, through moral or normative considerations such as problems of disagreement, conflict, cooperation and coordination, to rules or norms and principles of conduct. In order to resolve such moral or normative questions and problems, those involved are compelled to engage in communication to deal with their differences and to relate their actions to one another. A communicatively mediated collective learning process in this sense is responsible not only for the genesis of a social movement but, being its defining characteristic (Eder 1985b: 886), also for its internal development, that is, for the construction or formation of its collective identity.

When one embarks on a study of the internal development of a social movement in the above sense, it becomes clear sooner or later that there are various theoretical developments on which one could call for assistance.

Whatever their differences, which will be considered in due course, the most promising ones are in some way or another related to genetic-structuralism based on an interaction or communication model and are attached to the basic idea at the core of the theory of collective learning (Strydom 1987): that in morally complex situations in which human beings engage in discourse or argumentation about conflicts, intersubjective experiential contexts come to the fore which can be discerned through cognitive structures pertaining to the collectively as a whole, such as collective norms, modes of discourse and collective identities, and that these cognitive structures and thus intersubjective experiential contexts exhibit a determinable development if certain minimal conditions continue to apply over time.

Starting points for this kind of an approach are to be found in the writings of classical authors such as Emile Durkheim (1976) and George Herbert Mead (1974), but of particular importance, as intimated above, is Jean Piaget. His early work, *The Moral Judgement of the Child* (1968), has lost hardly any of its original significance despite its first publication as far back as 1932, while his contribution to sociology, *Etudes Sociologiques* (1967), also contains important insights. In the former work, Piaget argues convincingly that a universalistic morality is socially constituted, that is, through cooperation (1968: 190-314), and is thus the outcome of a collective learning process. And in the latter work, he shows that the cognitive structures represented by such a universalistic morality, far from being the sum or aggregate of individual judgements, are shared structures forming 'a system of relations each of which engenders, in so far as it is itself a relation, a transformation of the terms which it relates' (Piaget 1967: 29).[3]

The writings of a number of authors inspired by the American psychologist-educationist Lawrence Kohlberg, and of course the writings of the latter himself, are of immediate relevance. The development of Kohlberg's work exhibits a clear movement towards complementing the concern with the individual's moral judgement by the introduction of a community concept which represents the judgement structure of a whole group, also referred to as the 'moral atmosphere' of the group, but what could perhaps better be called a community of justification. Within this framework, Clark Power (Power and Reimer 1978; Power 1981), one of Kohlberg's associates, and subsequently Kohlberg (1976, 1985, 1986) himself, started to give explicit attention to the formation of collective norms and collective identity. The Swiss writer Fritz Oser, however, feels that although Kohlberg and his associates have come to employ the community concept, they nevertheless concern themselves largely with the moral judgement of individuals rather than concentrating, in true

Piagetian fashion, on the interrelations or the system of their moral judgements. In order to render this neglected structural dimension amenable to investigation, Oser returns to Piaget to develop what he calls 'a cognitive theory of interaction' (1981: 19, 95) which specifies the 'cognitive stages of intersubjectivity' or, more fully, the 'cognitive stages of interaction in moral discourse' (1984, title).[4] In due course I shall come back to Oser's contribution from the point of view of the reconstruction of the formation of the collective identity of a social movement.

A second important related yet distinct theoretical development is based on the work of Karl-Otto Apel (e.g. 1976, 1978) and Jürgen Habermas (e.g. 1978, 1979a, 1983), particularly the latter's empirical transformation of the normativity problem by the development of a material discourse ethic within the framework of a reconstruction of historical materialism. Aspects of it which are of particular relevance from the present point of view were elaborated upon within the context of a research project on the sociology of morality, law and justice executed under Habermas's direction at the Max Planck Institute in Starnberg, Germany, in the late 1970s and early 1980s by Klaus Eder, Günter Frankenberg, Ulrich Rödel and Ernst Tugendhat under the title of 'Die Entwicklung von Begründungsstrukturen und Gerechtigkeitsvorstellungen im modernen recht als soziologisches Problem'. This research project culminated in a series of fascinating publications, including works by Tugendhat (1980), Frankenberg and Rödel (1981), and Eder (1982, 1985a). It is interesting to note that another writer engaged in research at the Starnberg Institute at the time, whose name is not officially connected with this project, nevertheless made an important contribution towards rendering explicit the assumptions concerning collective learning that went into it. I have in mind Max Miller (1986), who revitalised the early Piaget under the influence of the long-standing critic of Habermas, the Frankfurt sociologist and proponent of so-called 'objective hermeneutics', Ulrich Overmann (1976, 1983; Overmann and Habermas 1979). A close perusal of the writings of the representatives of this second major theoretical development brings to light a sophisticated theoretical model that, like Oser's, can be employed for the reconstruction of the formation of the collective identity of a social movement.

Before embarking on the application of Fritz Oser's Piaget-Kohlbergian model of cognitive stages of interaction or intersubjectivity and the Piaget-Habermasian Starnberg model of practical discourse to the South African liberation movement, it should be pointed out that the two theoretical models, despite significant differences, have a basic precept deriving from the theory of collective learning in common. It is as follows: a collectivity comes into being when a number of individuals get together on the basis of mutual interpretations, understandings and commitments to pursue common goals and ideals.[5] Upon forming a collectivity, the participants enter into agreements, without necessarily renouncing their differences, which regulate their intentions and coordinate their actions, thus forming the common core of the collectivity and integrating it. These collective rules are generated by the communication of the participants, the more so to the extent that the collectivity is democratic by nature, and in the course of time these collective rules as well as the mode of communication about them undergo development. Under propitious conditions, the collective cognitive core could become increasingly more universalistic, while concurrently the discourse could become increasingly more open towards direct participation. This basic idea potentially applies to a wide range of collectivities, if not all collectivities, including social movements. Although they have not been designed for this purpose, I propose to apply both the Oser model and Starnberg model—as I propose to call them—to a social movement, in this case the South African liberation movement.

2. RECONSTRUCTION OF THE COLLECTIVE IDENTITY OF THE SOUTH AFRICAN LIBERATION MOVEMENT

The Oser Model

Fritz Oser (1981: 29; 1984: 162-3) developed the basic idea of the theory of collective learning into a four stage model of cognitive stages of interaction or intersubjectivity. Proceeding from the assumption that the process of communicative conflict resolution in a collectivity gives rise to collective cognitive structures which undergo internal modification in the course of time and thus gives evidence of a 'learning process' on the part of the collectivity, he identifies on the basis of protocols of 120 discussion groups distinct 'levels of interaction' or 'cognitive stages of moral discourse' (1981: 23) which stand in a developmental—in the sense of a hierarchical and sequential—relation to one another. Each of these levels or stages is the expression of a certain degree of cognitive, specifically moral, complexity attained in a collectivity at a certain point in its development and represents a way in which the collective structures are articulated, communication is coordinated, and a strategy for the solution of moral dilemmas forms the perspective of justice prevailing in the collectively.

The first and least complex level of interaction, what Oser calls the 'functional level', is characterised by complete instrumentalism in that the participants consider and propose solutions without taking into account their moral legitimacy or rightness. The second so-called 'analytical level' obtains its name from the tendency of the participants to concentrate virtually exclusively on facts in the belief that factual knowledge will guarantee the correctness and acceptability of the solution to the moral dilemma at hand. At the third so-called 'normative level', the question of moral justice for the first time enters in that the participants come to the realisation that the interpretation of facts varies with the rules, values and norms adopted. The fourth and final 'authentic moral level' represents the stage where the collectivity devises solutions to moral dilemmas on the basis of universalistic principles which are ethico-philosophically understood and interpreted with reference to their application and the ensuing consequences.

As social interaction or communication unfolds and collective cognitive structures develop from one stage to the next, the lower level is not discarded but integrated into the next higher one. In proportion as this occurs, the cooperative coordination of the action and interaction of the participants and hence the mode of integration of the collectively as a whole undergo a corresponding qualitative change. The four stages of interaction or intersubjectivity thus stand in the following relation to one another:

Stage 4

authentic moral

Stage 3

normative

Stage 2

analytical

Stage 1

functional

Fig. 11.1: Internal Relation of Stages of Interaction or Intersubjectivity[6]

The scene is now set for the application of Oser's model of cognitive stages of interaction or intersubjectivity to the development of the South African liberation movement, from its beginnings in 1882 right up to the late 1980s just prior to the dramatic change in the political dispensation of the country.

In this context, the first stage in Oser's model, the functional stage, can be interpreted as referring to cognitive structures which are oriented towards the defence, but also the securing under new conditions, of the interests and form of life of the participants in the movement. Here it is a matter of being result-oriented and hence of focusing narrowly on a possible solution, without giving much consideration to intentions, causal relationships, additional facts and consequences. At issue, first of all, is the consolidation of communal identities and solidarities in the face of mercantile and industrial capitalist colonial conquest and the corresponding experiences of the erosion and loss of tribal-traditional resources, such as cattle and land, and of colonial administrative-legal repression. This development culminated in attempts to defend and restore the tribal-traditional territory and form of life and to resist further encroachment by military means (Roux 1964; Thompson 1969).

The last instance of this had taken place in 1906 in the Colony of Natal and came to be known as the Bambata Rebellion after the minor Zulu chief who led the resistance (Roux 1964: 87-100; Marks 1970; Kuper 1971), but later incidents exhibiting similar characteristics may also be cited. These include, first, the millenarian separatist sect, the Israelites, who in 1921 used primitive weapons at Bulhoek in the Cape Province to resist police efforts to move them from the land they occupied and, second, the South-West African (or later Namibian) Bondelswarts tribe who in 1922 challenged the imposition of new taxes by the authorities (Roux 1964: 135-142). The core instance of this collective self-conception of tribal-traditional resistance, however, is represented by the independent separatist church movement which started in 1884 with the establishment of the Tembu national church and by 1892 culminated in the founding of Ethiopianism (Shepperson 1953; Roux 1964: 77-86; Kuper 1971: 434-6). Here we witness an embryonic African exclusiveness and nationalism which would later gain importance in connection with the so-called 'Africa for Africans' movement.

With the progressive closure of the avenues of resistance, the wars of dispossession and disarmament having been concluded in 1878 and 1881 respectively, the instrumentally oriented functionalist collective cognitive structures of the South African liberation movement were transferred to the new context defined by the completion of the imposition of the White system of economic exploitation and administrative-legal domination. This was the case, particularly in the Cape Colony, where constitutional development, in the form of responsible government and a qualified non-racial franchise granted in 1872 had been most advanced. Here, specifically in the Eastern Cape with its high concentration of Africans, the first African political organization, Imbumba Yama Africa, was set up in 1882, while the Native Education Association and the Native Electoral Association were both founded in 1884 with a view to rendering its members capable of participating in and thus maximising the realisation of their particular interests within the framework of the existing political system (Forman 1959: 9-10; Kuper 1971: 426-8; Karis and Carter 1987, I: 4-5, Document 1). These political and educational ventures were supported by the publication of the first African-edited newspaper, 'Imvo Zabantsundu', in Kingwilliamstown (Forman 1959: 10-11; Roux 1964: 53-77; Kuper 1971: 428; Karis and Carter 1987, I: 5-7, 12-17). Concentrating on electoral politics, particularly the franchise question, John Tengo Jabavu for many years used his position as editor to advance the interests of the Africans, leading opposition to new legislation and sending petitions and deputations to Cape Town to present the African case.

The South African liberation movement, in terms of the Oser model, reached its second or analytical stage for the first time around 1894 when 'Mahatma' Mohandas K. Gandhi started the Natal and South African Indian Congress, and it lasted unopposed until 1912 with the founding of the South African Native National Congress, the organization which was renamed in 1923 as the African National Congress (ANC). During the intervening years, some six more regional political organizations of the same type were established, one for Coloureds in the Cape, separate African ones in the Eastern Cape, the Transvaal and the Crown Colony of Natal, and two apparently rival ones in the Orange River Colony (Forman 1959: 12-23; Kuper 1971: 428-33; Karis and Carter 1987, I: 8-11, 61-8). A close scrutiny of the historical documents brought together by Karis and Carter bearing witness to the proliferation of Indian, African and Coloured political organizations during these years shows clearly the overwhelming concern of the liberation movement with unequivocally establishing and representing in public the facts pertaining to the situation of its members and articulating with their corresponding needs. The obsession with solutions and results characteristic of the functional stage made way for a systematic analysis of broader matters such as the intentions of the various parties, general causal connections, and the consequences of actions and policies. Instead of comparing and contrasting solutions, arguments were now being weighed. The statement issued by the executives of the South African Native National Congress in 1903, ranging analytically in the above sense over such issues as religion, education, law, administration, the franchise, labour, residential areas, and so forth, is exemplary in this respect (Karis and Carter 1987, I: 18-29 and Document 7). Even with the founding of a national African political organization, the South African Native National Congress, in 1912, two years after the unification of South

Africa, it is still possible to discern the perpetuation of the analytical stage in the construction of the collective identity of the South African movement. From this point in time, however, the normative stage started to assume increasing importance as the movement matured until it became predominant in the 1920s, remaining in this position up to the early 1940s.

Characteristic of the third or normative stage in the development of the cognitive structures of the South African liberation movement, in terms of the Oser model, is the centrality neither of solutions nor of the analysis of facts and needs, but rather of moral norms and principles considered as constitutive of a group's socio-moral form of life. Whatever analysis is conducted and whatever solutions proposed, they are consistently seen in relation to constitutive moral norms and principles. At this stage in the case of the South African movement, the critique of moral norms and principles became prevalent to a degree unknown before, and attempts were also made to universalise moral perspectives, although its full achievement had to await the next authentic moral stage.

Particularly the International Socialist League, founded in 1915 as a splinter group from the pro-war South African Labour Party, but later also the Communist Party of South Africa, established in 1921, played a significant part in bringing about a transition from the analytical to the normative stage in the liberation movement. Working class organizations such as the Industrial Workers of Africa (1917), the Industrial and Commercial Union (1919) and the Industrial and Commercial Workers Union of South Africa (1920) should also be mentioned here (Forman 1959: 24-30; Roux 1964: 122-135, 153-217; Kuper 1971: 447-8; Karis and Carter 1987, I: 145-157 and Documents 49a1-49b6). From the start, the International Socialist League, being characteristically concerned with the universality of its internationalist appeal, campaigned for the recognition of the rights of Africans, yet the inherent limitations of the South African Socialist view would for a long time prevent the exhaustion of the universalistic implications of its position. In an editorial following May Day 1916, for example, its mouthpiece 'International' symptomatically adverted to 'an ethnological tendency....which makes for the natural apartness of white and black' and hailed 'industrial cooperation.........(as)... the way to healthy segregation' (cited in Forman 1959: 21).[7] Initially, the Communist Party of South Africa concentrated on the organization of white labour, while shunning contact with the so-called 'bourgeois' ANC. However, from 1924 it gradually became active in the education and organization of black labour in the Industrial and Commercial Union and in legally unregisterable African trade unions of its own as well as adult education in the form of informal night schools, and from 1926 it also got involved in the ANC (Roux 1964: 198-217). As in the case of the International Socialist League, the Communist Party of South Africa was nevertheless unable to pursue the implications of the normative problematic it was articulating to their logical conclusions. This was due to its apparently indissoluble attachment, indicative of the normative stage of development, to the legitimacy, if not permanency, of skin pigmentation as a principle of socio-political organization. This is borne out not only by its policy of 'an independent native republic' (Roux 1964: 256; Kuper 1971: 448; Sizwe 1979: 50) envisaging a separate black state or, alternatively, Africans as the national majority in relation to Whites, coloureds and Indians as national minorities, but also by its acceptance at one time or another of the authoritative views of Stalin, Trotsky and the Fourth International—all of which, ironically, reinforced the identification of different cultural and colour groups with permanently distinct national groups (Roux 1964: 311-13; Sizwe 1979: 50-3). It is interesting to note that this position, far from being unique, represented a particular version of the same assumption which led liberals, on the one hand, to recognise the existence of four different 'peoples' in South Africa (Legassick 1976: 224-239; Dubow 1987: 71-94)[8] and Dr. A.B. Xuma, later president of the ANC, on the other hand, in 1930 to dissociate Africans summarily from both Coloureds and Indians (Karis and Carter 1987, I: 219).

As for the Coloureds and Indians, the former through their African Political (later People's) Organization, for many years under the presidency of Dr. A. Abdurahman, exhibited an unmistakable aspirant white orientation and preoccupied themselves with preventing Coloureds from being degraded to the level of Africans. The Indians, fearing the alienation of the right of intervention on their behalf on the part of the Indian government, were for long reluctant to throw in their lot with the Africans (Kuper 1971: 449; Karis and Carter 1987, I: 219, 261-2). The virtual impossibility at this stage of establishing a durable basis for mutual consultation, cooperation and coordination of political activity among Africans, Coloureds and Indians because of fears and unwillingness of their respective organizations to yield their separate independence, is amply demonstrated by a series of Non-European Conferences of the years 1927, 1930, 1931 and 1934 (Kuper 1971: 450; Karis and Carter 1987, I: 257-90),[9] which for all purposes and intents could have been regarded as abortive had it not been for the small basis they did lay for future cooperation. This positive aspect of the Non-European Conferences made itself felt in the All-African Convention held in 1935 which not only brought together Africans from all quarters of the country, but also allowed Coloureds and Indians to participate in the proceedings (Roux 1964: 288-9; Kuper 1971: 450; Karis and Carter 1987, II: 6-12 and Document 9-15). The restricted normative basis of this cooperative venture, however, is beyond dispute. The African, Coloured and Indian sections of the South African liberation movements exhibited a strong particularistic tendency to fix on the moral norms and principles constitutive of their particular forms of life.

The first clear indications of a transition from the normative to the fourth and final authentic moral stage, as Oser calls it, are to be found in the Non-European Unity Movement which was established in 1934 as a result of close cooperation among the member organizations of the All-African Convention, the Anti-Coloured Affairs Department Movement and dissident branches of the South African Congress as well as white radical intellectuals. Leading roles in this development were played by the radical yet non-Communist Coloured organization, the National Liberation League, set up in 1935, and by the Communist and Trotskyite-inspired Non-European United Front formed in 1938 (Roux 1964: 357-9; Kuper 1971: 456-7; Karis and Carter 1987, II: 107-14 and Documents 65-6). In the wake of the National Party victory in 1948 and the passing of such racially discriminatory and repressive legislation as the Population Registration Act, the Group Areas Act and the Suppression of Communism Act during the first years of government, the whole spectrum of extra-parliamentary opposition groups—whites, Coloureds, Indians and Africans, including the ANC and even such leading members of the exclusive Africanist-oriented ANC Youth League as Oliver Tambo, Walter Sisulu and Nelson Mandela—by the middle of 1950 were ready to enter into mutual relations of cooperation. This new all-encompassing solidarity, expressive of the universalistic principles incorporated into the collective cognitive structures of the South African liberation movement during its authentic moral stage of development, provided the basis not only for the Congress Movement of the years 1953 to 1956, but also for the 'All-in' Conference of March 1961 (Roux 1964: 398-9, 401-2, 423; Kuper 1971: 463-4; Karis and Carter 1987, III: 19-24, 56-73, 349-58 and Documents 9-10 and 55-7). By this time, it has become a typical feature of the ANC style to call for the support of Indians, Coloureds and democratically minded whites. As the basis of this cooperative orientation served the Freedom Charter which was adopted in 1955 at Klipfontein, near Johannesburg, by the Congress of the People, attended by 2884 delegates, including 230 Coloureds, 320 Indians and 112 whites, and subscribed to by the ANC in 1956 as its official policy (Karis and Carter 1987, III: 63-72). In the preamble to the Freedom Charter it is declared 'That South Africa belongs to all who live in it, black and white, and that no government can justly claim authority unless it is based on the will of all the people' (Karis and Carter 1987, III: Document 11: 205).

The most advanced phase in the authentic moral stage of the construction of collective identity of the South African liberation movement was reached, however, when a multi-racial interpretation of universalistic principles, still present in the Freedom Charter through reference to separate 'national groups', was unequivocally replaced by a non-racial interpretation. This was first exemplified by the African People's Democratic Union of South Africa, a short-lived heir of the Non-European Unity Movement, formed in 1961, which in the words of I.B. Tabata stood for 'democracy for all those who accept this country as their home and therefore regard themselves as Africans' (Karis and Carter 1987, III: Document 67: 717). This advance was shortly after incorporated into the mainstream of the liberation movement, as is shown by the self-understanding not only of the African National Congress, but also of the newly formed organizations of the 1980s, the United Democratic Front (1983) and the Congress of South African Trade Unions (1985). The major tensions remaining within the South African liberation movement, especially concerning the nature of the future transformation of South Africa and of the leadership in this process, would themselves seem to be dealt with to a relatively high degree in terms of the requirements of the authentic moral stage of development. This is borne out by the fact that the universalistic principles involved are discussed and criticised from the point of view of different theoretical-philosophical positions and their normative implications.

The schematic reconstruction of the construction of the collective cognitive structures of the South African liberation movement according to Oser's model of cognitive stages of interaction or intersubjectivity can be diagrammatically represented as in Figure 2.

The model of cognitive stages of interaction or intersubjcetivity put forward by Fritz Oser is undoubtedly useful in bringing order into the formation of the collective cognitive structures of the South African liberation movement. Considering the fact that it is a one-dimensional model, specifying four stages in the development of interaction or intersubjectivity without making a clear distinction between the normative structure and the mode of communication characteristic of a collectivity at a particular stage, however, it is a relatively rough theoretical instrument. It is precisely in this respect that the Starnberg model promises to be superior to the Oser model.

The Starnberg Model

In comparison with the Oser model, the Starnberg model is a two-dimensional construct. Instead of distinguishing stages of development

1 FUNCTIONAL	2 ANALYTICAL	3 NORMATIVE	4 AUTHENTIC MORAL
• Imbumba Yama Afrika 1882 • Imvo Zabantsundu 1884 • Native Electoral Association 1884 • Native Education Association 1884 • Ethiopianism 1892 • Bambata Rebellion 1906 • Israelites 1921 • Bondelswarts 1922	• Natal Indian Congress 1894 • SA Native Congress 1902 • African People's Organization 1902 • Natal Native Congress 1902 • Orange River Colony Native Congress 1902 • Native United Political Associations 1902 • S.A Native National Congress 1912	• Industrial Workers of Africa 1917 • Industrial and Commercial Union 1919 • Industrial and Commercial Workers Union of SA 1920 • African National Congress 1923 • All-African Convention 1935 • ANC Youth League 1944 • Pan-Africanist Congress 1959 • Black Consciousness 1968	• Non-European Unity Moment 1943 • Congress Alliance 1955 • SA Council of Trade Unions 1955 • African National Congress mid-1950s on • African People's Democratic Union of SA 1961 • United Democratic Front 1983 • Congress of SA Trade Unions 1985

Fig. 11.2: The Construction of South African Liberation Movement's Collective Identity according to the Oser Model

alone, it proceeds on the basis of the difference between collective norms and principles, on the one hand, and the mode of communication or discourse whereby those normative structures are constructed, on the other (e.g. Habermas 1979a: 1-5; Eder 1985a: 67-74). These two dimensions, which are respectively identified with the principle of universalisation and the principle of discourse, are located at the synchronic and diachronic axes. Discourse exhibits a developmental trajectory on the diachronic axis which passes through clearly identifiable stages—that is, if it does not become blocked along the way due to the interference of authoritarian, ideological or regressive forces (Miller 1986: 428-40).[10] The cognitive—specifically normative—orientation forming the subject of universalisation on the synchronic axis shows a broadening and deepening to the extent that new experiences processed through discourse provide a more adequate basis for the orientation towards the social world. The stages through which discourse develops are designated virtual, formal and real (e.g. Eder 1985a: 77-81; Strydom 1986), indicating the progressively increasing degree to which those involved or affected actually participate and thus have the opportunity to articulate their needs, interests and solidarity. The broadening and deepening of the empirical basis of the normative orientation on the synchronic axis throughout the acquisition of new experiences on the diachronic axis is captured by the graded typology of a normative orientation circumscribed first by a pragmatic or utilitarian-contractual universalisation, second by a rigid principled one and finally by a flexible principled one. This way of explicating the model already suggests an interrelation of the two parametric axes which can in diagrammatic form be expressed by cross-tabulation eventuating in a structural matrix according to which the development of the South African liberation movement could be reconstructed.

A comparison of the Oser and Starnberg models at this point is sufficient to convince one that the latter has a stronger generative thrust than the former without losing the former's strength, namely its structural focus. In addition to the diachronic developmental dimension represented by the principle of discourse, the Starnberg model also incorporates the synchronic structural dimension, in which case the synchronic pragmatic-utilitarian, rigid principled and flexible principled levels of universalisation correspond closely to the functional, normative and the authentic moral stages of the Oser model. As such, the Starnberg model represents a theoretical instrument with a much finer grid than the Oser model for the reconstruction of the formation of the collective identity of a social movement. Applied to the South African liberation movement, the results are as presented in Figure 3.

Normative Orientation \ Stage of Discourse	VIRTUAL	FORMAL	REAL
PRAGMATIC-UTILITARIAN	• Native Electoral Association 1884 • Native Education Association 1884	• Silent majority	• Ethiopianism 1892 • Bambata Rebellion 1906 • Israelites 1921 • Bondelswarts 1922
RIGID PRINCIPLED	• Imvo Zabantsundu 1884	• Natal Indian Congress, 1894 • Native Congress 1902 • African People's Organization 1902 • Natal Native Congress 1902 • Orange River Colony Native Congress 1902 • SA Native National Congress 1912	• ANC Youth League 1944 • Pan-Africanist Congress 1959 • Black Consciousness 1968
FLEXIBLE PRINCIPLED		• Industrial Workers of Africa 1917 • Industrial & Commercial Union 1919 • Industrial & Commercial Workers Union of SA 1920 • ANC 1923 • Non-European Conference 1927, 1930, 1931, 1934 • All-African Convention 1935 • Congress Alliance 1955 • SA Congress of Trade Unions 1955 - - - - - - - - - - • Non-European Unity Movement 1943 • African People's Democratic Union 1961	• ANC, late 50s • United Democratic Front 1983 • Congress of SA Trade Unions 1985

Fig. 11.3: The Construction of the South African Liberation Movement's Collective Identity according to the Starnberg Model

The Starnberg model opens up the possibility of a much more differentiated reconstruction of the formation of the collective identity of the South African liberation movement than Oser's model affords us. With reference to the diachronic and synchronic axes, it is possible to regard the developmental process from the viewpoint of both stages and levels—two things which are synonymous for Oser. The crucial difference between the two models in substantive terms lies in the four categories constituted by the parameters of formal/real discourse and rigid/flexible principled universalisation. The additional differentiation achieved by this refinement might not seem much of a gain from the point of view of the Oser model and the general moral educational task it seeks to serve, yet it is absolutely crucial from the point of view of the theory of social movements, particularly of the politically sensitive critical theoretical variety. It would also seem to be more adequate to the actual history of the South African liberation movement.

Assuming familiarity with the details introduced in the previous subsection, I now propose to identify some of the most crucial turning points in the construction of the collective identity of the South African movement as suggested by the Starnberg model.

To begin with, movements of tribal-traditional resistance and retreat such as Ethiopianism, the Bambata Rebellion, the Israelites and the Bondelswarts as well as movements oriented towards education for and participation in electoral politics such as the Native Electoral and Educational Associations were all of a pragmatic or utilitarian kind. The difference between the two categories is that whereas the former category involved real discourse due to the direct participation of all those affected, the latter presupposed virtual discourse since they acted on behalf of the black population who were neither formally represented nor had the opportunity to participate. What is remarkable, when one moves beyond this stage and level, is that all the organizations serving as bearers of the South African liberation movement prior to the period 1917 to 1920, marked by the founding of such organizations as the Industrial Workers of Africa, the Industrial and Commercial Union and the Industrial and Commercial Workers Union of South Africa, were groupings based on a rigid normative principle. While the newspaper 'Imvo Zabantsundu' identified with and sought entrance to the existing political system, engaging in elitist communication, the more interesting categories are those within which the various congresses, both regional and national fall. The rigid normative principle assumed by these various vehicles of the movement is that of skin pigmentation or colour or better still colour-caste.

The various regional congresses and the South African Native National Congress, called the ANC from 1923, as well as the much later ANC Youth League, the Pan-Africanist Congress and eventually the Black Consciousness Movement founded by Steve Biko, were all without exception colour-based organizations which sought to campaign on behalf of the interests of their own people—the Indians, the Coloureds and the Africans. The difference between the regional congresses and the South African Native National Congress or ANC, on the one hand, and ANC Youth League, the Pan-Africanist Congress and the Black Consciousness Movement, on the other, resides in the fact that, whereas the former group depended only formally on the principle of colour, a particular colour group being merely distinct from others, the latter group actively sought to carry the principle through rigidly and concretely, taking the form of an exclusive and often explicitly anti-white Africanism.

It was for the first time with the founding of the class-based organizations with both a trade union and a political dimension from 1917 onwards, such as the Industrial Workers of Africa, the Industrial and Commercial Union and the Industrial and Commercial Workers Union of South Africa, that this restrictive normative base was at least implicitly questioned and tentatively left behind. The impact this had on the mainstream of the South African liberation movement was that a practice became established according to which some ANC branches, particularly in the Western Cape, accepted also Coloureds and Indians as members. This crucial development in the collective cognitive—more specifically normative—structures of the South African movement, taking the form of a shift from a rigid principled to a flexible principled orientation, made possible the cooperative Non-European Conferences of the late 1920s and early 1930s. It was consolidated, as it were, by the All-African Convention of 1935 which for the first time brought together on a national level Africans from all walks of life and simultaneously admitted both Coloureds and Indians. The culmination point of this development is represented by the founding in 1943 of the Non-European Unity Movement, the very first national organization to leave behind completely the previously accepted colour-bound normative principle. The degree of universalism proclaimed by the Non-European Unity Movement, later to be repeated by its successor, the African People's Democratic Union of South Africa founded in 1961, was not emulated even by the Congress Movement of the 1950s. In the latter, intentionally separate colour-caste organizations, such as the ANC, the Coloured People's Organization, the South African Indian Congress and the white Congress of Democrats, formed the Congress Alliance and undertook to let themselves be guided by the principles of the Freedom Charter.

Characteristic limitations, however, remained. This was the case, to be sure, also with the Non-European Unity Movement and the African People's Democratic Union of South Africa. Whereas the mutual relations within the framework of the Congress Movement, as a rule, did not achieve the universalism formally projected in the Freedom Charter, but rather took the form of strategic cooperation between coloured-bound organizations, the Non-European Unity Movement and the African People's Democratic Union did transcend the implied multi-racial or multi-colour-caste principle in favour of a non-racial or non-colour one (whence the broken line separating them from the other organizations in Figure 3). Yet this was the case more in conception than in fact. The non-racial or non-colour-caste universalistic normative foundation still required to be transposed into the medium of real rather than merely formal discourse. This occurred for the first time when the achievements of the Non-European Unity Movement and the African People's Democratic Union of South Africa became effective in the mainstream of the liberation movement through the ANC since the late 1950s and early 1960s. By the 1980s, this same position was attained by the United Democratic Front (UDF), the South African Communist Party (SACP) and the Congress of South Africa Trade Unions (COSATU).

The most crucial turning point in the formation of the cognitive structures and mode of discourse of the South African liberation movement, and hence in the construction of its collective identity, thus resides in the transition from a formal flexibly principled to a real flexibly principled position. Whether the accomplishment of this transition is a permanent achievement remains an open question. Yet there is no doubt about the fact that the ANC and the SACP, as well as the relatively new organizations, the UDF and COSATU are guided to a significant degree by flexible universalistic principles. These principles allow no distinction among colour groups and seek to give effect to them through open democratic procedures or real discourse within the framework of mass-based organizations which bring together workers, peasants, urban petty bourgeoisie and radical intellectuals.

CONCLUSION

In this essay, I have attempted to make a contribution to the theory of social movements by concentrating on an aspect which seems increasingly worthy of attention, but which nevertheless remains undeveloped to the extent that the appropriate theoretical instruments are still lacking. The general theoretical perspective I have proposed is that of regarding a social movement as a collective learning process, but for present purposes I confined myself to the internal process of construction of the collective identity of a social movement. As regards this question, I introduced a theoretical model deriving from interaction or communication-based genetic-structuralism and tried to show its relevance by employing two different versions—what I called respectively the Oser model and the Starnberg model—for purposes not usually associated with them, namely reconstructing the construction of the collective identity of a social movement. In addition to the theory of social movements in general, I sought at the same time also to make a contribution to the analysis specifically of the South African liberation movement.

The thrust of the theoretical perspective on the construction of the collective identity of a social movement can be summarised briefly. I proposed to consider the formation of a social movement under the aspect of collective learning in order not to register changes purely from the external perspective of the disinterested observer, but rather to reconstruct the process from the internal perspective of the historically acting subjects and their cognitive orientations, yet without falling into the trap of over-identifying with them. The concept of collective learning, it should be pointed out, implies that the internal development of a social movement is not conceived according to Habermas's cognitive psychological theory of the development of moral consciousness, but presupposes the sociologisation of this developmental-logical theory in terms of an interaction or communication theoretical genetic-structuralism which goes beyond his position.[11]

From this point of view, the internal development of a social movement is regarded as showing up in the changes undergone by the cognitive structures underpinning its collective identity, while these structures are accessible in turn through the collective rules and principles as well as the modes of communication characteristic of a movement at various points in time. While the Oser model provided a relatively simple and clear theoretical instrument to approach this task with, the Starnberg model added sophistication to the exercise without any loss of clarity. From the reconstruction of the South African liberation movement by these theoretical means it was established that the crucial turning points in the development of the collective identity of a social movement are three in number: first, from a functionalist (Oser) or pragmatic-utilitarian (Stranberg) orientation to a normative (Oser) or rigid principled (Starnberg) orientation; second, from a normative or rigid principled to an authentic moral (Oser) or flexible principled (Starnberg) orientation; and, finally, from a formal to a real discursive organization of the flexible principled orientation.

From this reconstruction it becomes apparent, then, that the stage-bound modes of communication introduced by the Starnberg model over and above the collective cognitive structures emphasised by the Oser model provide an internally anchored critical perspective we cannot afford to do without in the theoretically informed reconstruction of the formation of social movements.

12

Contemporary Approaches to Collective Identity: A Critical Assessment

Foremost among contemporary approaches concerned with collective identity formation are, first, those dealing with collective identity formation in social movements and, second, those dealing with national identity. The work of Alberto Melucci (1988, 1996) is widely regarded as being paradigmatic of the former category, while the contribution of Shmuel Eisenstadt and Bernhard Giesen (1995; see also Giesen and Junge 1991) represents perhaps the theoretically most interesting example of the latter. Both Melucci and Eisenstadt and Giesen claim to present a theoretical model of identity construction or formation that is of more general significance than just social movement or national identity.

Thus the question is what we are able to learn from these approaches regarding the construction of collective identity in a sense relevant to the constitution and organization of society.

1. PRELIMINARY OUTLINE OF CONTEMPORARY APPROACHES

The Construction of Collective Identity in Social Movements

During the 1980s, Alberto Melucci (1980, 1984, 1985, 1988) made an incisive contribution to the introduction of a constructivist approach to collective identity into sociology, and a decade later he saw fit to restate this same position (1996) in a systematic form.

Inspired by Alain Touraine's action theory, organizational sociology and cognitive social psychology, Melucci conceived of collective identity as the outcome of multiple processes in which actors produce meanings, communicate, negotiate and make decisions. Through these differentiated social processes they define not only themselves, but also their relationship with their situation or environment, including other actors, available resources as well as opportunities and impediments. In Melucci's view, the constructive contribution of the actors to the formation of their collective identity consists of rendering common a cognitive framework, organized along the three axes of ends, means and environment, and translating this into a system of relationships necessary for collective action (1988: 331-33; 1996: 70-77).

In the wake of the perceptive criticism that the cultural dimension is adequately introduced into social movement theory and research only when the constructivist perspective is extended beyond social movements themselves to the structured setting within which they occur (Eder 1993a: 14; see also Strydom 1999c: 73-4, 1999e: 18), Melucci indeed gives special emphasis to what he calls 'the relational dimension of collective identity' in his more recent work (1996: 73) in a manner he neglected earlier. Far from depending on auto-identification alone, he acknowledges, collective identity depends on the identification or recognition granted it by other social and political actors, observers and the rest of the society, whether adversaries, allies or third parties. What is remarkable, however, is that Melucci, notwithstanding this broadening of perspective, continues to confine social constructivist analysis to the self-production of collective action or social movements. Collective identity construction and formation thus remains tied to a lower level than is required to grasp the constitution and organization of society adequately.

Theoretically, Melucci's contribution represents the consolidation of a significant advance, particularly in so far as he incorporates cultural, cognitivist and constructivist insights from a range of social scientific disciplines to formulate a processual theory of collective identity (1988: 345; 1996: 68-70). At best, however, it provides only a starting point, since the theoretical framework for the analysis of the construction of collective identity is not sufficiently embedded in its larger framework.

The Construction of National Collective Identity

In the mid-1990s, Shmuel Eisenstadt and Bernhard Giesen (1995) made an important contribution to the problem of the construction of collective identity. It is of great interest since it presents a general theoretical model that combines symbolic and structural (cognitive classificatory) dimensions to form a macro-constructivist approach.

In terms of Eisenstadt and Giesen's position, collective identity is a social construction that is produced by social carrier groups who act in a particular situation and within the framework of symbolic codes. The central theoretical component is a typology of symbolic codes of collective identity—the major codes of the construction of collective identity being primordiality, civility, and culture. Eisenstadt and Giesen employ these three codes, as ideal types of collective identity, which are then applied in historical case studies to German and Japanese collective identity. Whereas the primordial type of collective identity is anchored in original or unchangeable features such as kinship, ethnicity and race, the civic type depends on familiarity with traditions, routines and institutional or constitutional arrangements and practices in the public arena. The cultural type is constructed with reference to a transcendent realm, whether God, Reason or Progress, and is thus characterised by a universalistic thrust that goes far beyond the naturalism of the primordial type and the communitarianism of the civic type. In Eisenstadt and Giesen's view, Japanese collective identity is exemplary of the primordial ideal type, with a touch of civility, while German collective identity had been constructed historically in accordance with a cultural code, although some elements of primordiality were also present which would later provide a starting point for the construction of a primordial collective identity.

However thought-provoking it might be, and it is a very stimulating contribution, Eisenstadt and Giesen's proposal suffers from various limitations that make it less useful than it at first sight seems. From the current point of view, there is, of course, the transcendent criticism that the authors confine themselves to national collective identity. But then there are also immanent difficulties that make its transfer to a different context implausible. Basically, Eisenstadt and Giesen's theoretical model is less general than they claim it to be. The construction of collective identity is theoretically prejudiced by being formed in the mould of national identity itself. This is borne out not only by their emphasis of such matters as equality, trust and solidarity among insiders, the importance of boundaries marking the processes of inclusion and exclusion, and the centrality of a social carrier group, all of which are too specific and concretistic, but also by their theoretical strategy. The latter, which eventuates in the assertion of the primacy of primordiality, civility and culture, is based on a concretistic interpretation of the 'here', 'now' and 'I' as the 'phenomenal focus of identity' (1995: 75), an arbitrary selection of 'original references of codes' from a wide range of cultural cognitive classificatory systems and schemes (p. 76), and an overhasty move from cultural codes used in the construction of collective identity to ideal types of collective identity (pp. 76-7). Still further in the background lies the theoretical problem of the status of Giesen's (1991; Eisenstadt and Giesen 1995: 77) threefold model of code, process and situation, given that it is based on Popper's 'three-world theory' which suffers from empiricist, ontological and scientistic leanings (Habermas's 1984a: 76-84).

2. THEORY OF COLLECTIVE IDENTITY CONSTRUCTION AND FORMATION

In the discussion of the respective paradigmatic contributions of Melucci and Eisenstadt and Giesen above, difficulties were recorded both in respect of the focal point adopted by the authors and the theoretical position put forward. Despite developing his thinking and showing a predilection for refining his theory of collective identity construction, Melucci not only unwaveringly continued to foster a focus carefully trained on social movements, but he also proved not to have gone far enough in working out the implications of the various new components taken up in his theory. Similarly, Eisenstadt and Giesen resolved to confine their focus to national identity and its historical construction, and theoretically they constructed a framework on premises that cannot be maintained if the focus were to be shifted to the constitution and organization of society. In comparison with Eisenstadt and Giesen's theory of collective identity construction, which is too closely and concretistically tied to their object of study, it is interesting that Melucci's theory is more promising from the point of view of extrapolation to a more general level—and that in spite of the fact that his focus on social movements is much narrower than their one.

To create a basis for a more adequate analysis of collective identity, it is necessary at this stage to establish a more general theoretical model.

Learning from Melucci

To avoid the abortive traditional answer to the problem of sociologically studying collective phenomena, Melucci (1988, 1996) rejects the all too pervasive metaphysical assumption that a collective phenomenon is a unitary empirical datum or ontological essence which is readily accessible either through underlying objective conditions or through inspiring subjective motives. Wishing to account for what had previously simply been taken-for-granted, he draws on multi-disciplinary culturalist, cognitivist and constructivist insights to formulate a processual approach to collective identity.

Theoretically central is his emphasis on the process of social construction of the collective which goes beyond the dualism of structure and agency by mediating between objective conditions and subjective motives and orientations. In general, this constructive process is culturalistically conceived in terms of how social actors make sense of their world through relating to texts, cultural artifacts, social practices and other social actors and thus creating meaning. More penetratingly, however, the process is from the inside regarded from the viewpoint of the formation and reproduction of cognitive frameworks, on the one hand, and of systems of relations necessary for action, on the other. For Melucci, this adds up to the theoretical view that a collective phenomenon is socially constructed through differentiated social processes which combine action orientations, elements of motivation and elements of structure in a variable manner. On this basis, analysis has the task of considering the processes by means of which actors construct something common to them all—that is, a collective identity able to sustain collective action—as well as how the unity of all the elements, orientations, significations, relationships and levels involved is produced or formed and maintained.

As against a pronounced tendency towards the reification of the concept, a tendency that may be strengthened by the link in many minds between identity and permanence, Melucci (1996: 70-2) insists that collective identity is an access route to the sometimes contradictory interaction or communicative processes behind what appears as a stable and coherent definition of collectivity. Collective identity forms part of the process of the construction of an action system. It takes the form of an interactive or communicative and thus shared definition that is negotiated and constructed by a number of individuals or groups to make clear to themselves what the orientations of their action are as well as the field of opportunities and constraints in which the action takes place. Central to the process of the construction of collective identity are 'cognitive definitions' (1996: 70; see also 1988: 332-3) of the actors, the ends, the means and the field of action. Unlike some cognitivists who see the cognitive dimension as necessarily implying unified and coherent frameworks, however, Melucci stresses that it is interactively constructed and comprises different and sometimes even contradictory definitions. Unlike culturalists who focus exclusively on texts or meanings, on the other hand, he regards the process of collective identity construction as involving a continuous reference back to a network of active relationships between actors who are engaged in interaction, communication, mutual influence, negotiation and decision-making. An adequate sociological analysis of the construction of collective identity, therefore, must take into account both the dimension of cognitive frameworks and the dimension of networked active relations.

Melucci's contribution to the theory of the construction of collective identity contains a number of important points that need to be retained for the purposes of developing the theory further. One point concerns his insistence on seeing identity as a process. Identity must not be reified into something given, permanent and static, which also means that a fixation on primordial features and the essentialising of particular historical identities are to be avoided. Identity stands for 'social identification processes' (1996: 157) or processes of identity construction or formation. These processes are of course far from formless. To be able to deal with the structuredness or structuration of these processes, therefore, Melucci introduces—and this is a second important point—the level of 'cognitive frameworks' (1988: 331), 'cognitive frames' (1996: 226) or 'cognitive definitions' (1996: 70), 'symbolic frames' (1996: 349), 'codes' (1996: 357) and 'cultural models' (1996: 359). A further important point stressed by Melucci is that these 'collective frames' (1996: 355) are laboriously constructed by individuals and groups within movements through processes of interaction, communication and negotiation (1996: 355), but also in broader discursive contexts in which collective actors both enter into opposition and conflict with one another and speak the same language in that they define a common field from different points of view (1996: 355-56). It is in the latter context of 'public discourse' (1996: 225-28), to highlight yet another point, that Melucci gives attention to the process of 'challenging codes', as he calls it (1996: title; 356-60). This process involves social movements playing out 'alternative' cultural codes or cultural models (1996: 359) against the 'dominant models' (1996: 357) providing the cultural underpinnings of the technical and instrumental rationality of the techno-scientific, political, and industrial-economic apparatuses and the technocratic power based on them. A final point, which brilliantly expresses an assumption acquired in the preceding decade or so, is that a shift has occurred in social movements and, one could surmise, also in the process of the constitution and organisation of society, 'towards the form of communication' (1996: 141). Not only has the degree of reflexivity in relation to previously taken-for-granted presuppositions increased, one might say, but cultural models themselves have become more discursively available for more deliberate use in processes of collective identity construction which themselves are increasingly organised according to the rules of communication.

While the above five points represent a significant theoretical contribution, they nevertheless leave a wide margin for the further development of the theory of the construction of collective identity. A close and critical inspection quickly shows up a number of limitations that could serve as starting points for the continuation of theoretical reflection. Melucci offers terse theoretical formulations and brief descriptions of the process of collective identity formation both within social movements and within public discourse. What he neglects to do, however, is to analyse those processes in terms implied by the theoretical concepts he introduces along the way. Nowhere does he give a thoroughly theorised analysis of the interaction, communication, negotiation and discourse involved in the construction of identity. What is most conspicuously lacking from a theoretical point of view, however, is an adequate grasp of the structuration or form of these processes. Not only is he not sufficiently clear about the structural quality of identity, but he actually short-circuits his analysis by referring in one part of his work to cognitive frames and in another to symbolic frames, without making any connection between the two or clarifying the relation between them. Whereas the cognitive dimension is adequately introduced at an early stage, it is never employed in the analysis of the process of collective identity formation. What analysis there is, is executed in symbolic terms—an analysis which itself is not pursued far enough either. The problem is moreover exacerbated, despite his warning against fixing on one single omnipotent actor (1996: 226), by the huge cost that the overemphasis on social movements has for constructivist analysis. One cannot assume a relational perspective to the full if one is wedded to one of the actors in the network (see Strydom 1999e: 15-20).

In the final analysis, Melucci fails to exploit the potential of his acute insight into the shift in contemporary society towards the form of communication.

Learning from Eisenstadt and Giesen

Eisenstadt and Giesen's theory of the construction of collective identity seems very promising at first sight. According to them, collective identity is a social construction that is given rise to by a social carrier group who engages in action in a particular situation while drawing on a framework of cultural codes. It is a general theoretical model that can be applied at different levels of abstraction and in different contexts and, in addition, possesses some interesting features. On the one hand, it is a constructivist approach that has a broader sociological appeal than earlier types of constructivism incubated in phenomenology, ethnomethodology and the sociology of scientific knowledge in that it has been given a macro dimension while nevertheless retaining the advantages of methodological situationalism. On the other hand, the central place ascribed to cultural codes as factors playing a structuring role in the process of identity construction adds immensely to its theoretical attractiveness. These latter two features lead one to evaluate their theory as partaking of the momentous and, indeed, historic twofold turn in recent sociology: the cognitive turn, and the transposition of constructivism to the level of society as such. One thus gains the impression of a highly advanced theoretical position that can take the sociological analysis of collective identity construction a significant step forward. Sooner rather than later, however, the devil emerges from the details to destroy this impression together with the accompanying excitement. Once again, one is thrown back to continue the painstaking work of theorising.

The basic problem with Eisenstadt and Giesen's proposal is their particular emphasis. While their theoretical model is supposed to capture the construction of collective identity, that is, the process suggested by the present participle form of 'construction', it actually does not turn out to be a processual model. They indeed regard the task of sociology as being the analysis of the process of construction, yet they insist on the primacy of the latency of the process (1995: 73). This strong theoretical premise leads them to tend to marginalise the process and instead to reify and essentialise collective identity. So, for instance, in their presentation of the proposition that collective identity is not naturally generated but socially constructed (74), they stress the equality, trust and solidarity among insiders rather than construction itself. In extension of this submission, which covers over the differences, negotiations, tensions and conflicts at the heart of the often contradictory process of construction, they regard the construction of collective identity as the establishment of boundaries that simultaneously include some and exclude others. One does not have to deny that identity construction implies difference and distinction to appreciate that Eisenstadt and Giesen's (1995: 74) attempt to give the distinction between in-groups and out-groups the status of a theorem is much too strong. Since the 18th century, at least, this distinction designates a relation that has become a problem. Whereas political ethics was a major way of conceiving of this problem, both the problem and the approach to it have been radicalised in the late 20th century in the wake of the environmental crisis and the process of globalization. Rather than allowing symbolic boundaries to function as theoretical premise, what is required is that they be explained relative to the conditions under which the line is drawn between the inside and the outside. Not even the participants or members any longer simply assume them. Far from just being given, symbolic boundaries are unstable, variable and even the object of contestation among members themselves. Eisenstadt and Giesen thus exhibit a marked and unacceptable tendency towards reification and essentialising or, in a word, ontologising.

This same tendency can also be observed in Eisenstadt and Giesen's treatment of the logic of construction. To begin with, they correctly appreciate the significance of the cultural dimension for the construction process, and they correctly identify the spatial, temporal and reflexive dimensions as the axes providing the basic distinctions—or rather classifications—of which such codes consist. But then they take a number of steps the unjustifiability of which is apparent from their reductive typology of major codes—that is, the threefold typology of primordiality, civility and culture or sacredness (p. 76), which owes something to Edward

Shils. On the one hand, this typology rests on an overly concretistic or essentialist interpretation of the 'here', 'now' and 'I' as the phenomenal foci of identity (p. 75). On the other hand, they combine an arbitrary and one-sidedly emphasised selection of distinctions from the wide range of classification systems and schemata (p. 76). This arbitrariness and one-sidedness is accounted for by the fact that they employed not a general criterion of selection in accordance with the process and logic of construction, but rather one predetermined by their concern with national collective identity (p. 76). To this could be added the fact that they tend to fix on a particular social group serving as carrier of the cultural code which becomes predominant, rather than taking a stronger relational position.

Eisenstadt and Giesen could have avoided these misdirected moves if they took the classificatory problem more seriously by employing a cognitive sociological framework instead for the purposes of formulating the typology—for example, using the distinction among intellectual, normative and aesthetic cognitive structures together with the distinction among the historically transmitted cultural tradition, the institutionally organized social space of intersubjectivity, and the socialisation and individuation of the individual subject and collective. The reductive treatment of the logic of construction that follows from Eisenstadt and Giesen's theoretical strategy becomes apparent as soon as one considers that construction is a much more open and contingent process than being structured by three major codes alone. It is not particular cultural codes that are at the core of the construction process, as they assert, but rather more generally the problem of classification. This is not the end of the tale, however, for the two authors multiply this reductionism when they transform the three codes directly into the ideal types of primordial, civic and cultural collective identity. This theoretical decision in effect gets rid of the logic of the construction process. By way of their three codes, Eisenstadt and Giesen determine beforehand what collective identity amounts to. But what is required, by contrast, is that sociological analysis shows how collective identity is socially constructed through the competition and conflict and, eventually, the synthesis of different codes—in the sense of a practical, provisional normalisation of continuing oppositions—in the medium of communication and discourse.

A Cognitivist Public Discourse Model

In order to avoid the limitations of the respective theoretical proposals made by Melucci and by Eisenstadt and Giesen, a cognitivist public discourse model of the construction of collective identity is envisaged in the present context (e.g. Strydom 2000). In contradistinction to the above-mentioned authors, therefore, three basic theoretical assumptions are explicitly made here.

The first assumption is that the process of construction is best conceived in terms of a communication and discourse theory. The theory adopted here goes back to proposals made by Karl-Otto Apel and Jürgen Habermas and is a development of related ideas introduced by Max Miller (1986, 1992), Klaus Eder (1993a, 1996b) and, more remotely, Ron Eyerman and Andrew Jamison (1991). Although Eisenstadt and Giesen refer to interaction and Melucci to interaction and communication, not one of them thinks it through in a consistent and systematic manner. Melucci who comes closest to it, nevertheless revealingly speaks of contemporary society as an 'information society' rather than a communication society.

The second assumption is that the structuration of the process of construction and hence the structural quality of identity, whether individual or collective, requires an explicitly developed cognitive sociology. On one level, clarity is needed about the components and devices employed by social actors in the construction of collective identity. Neither Melucci nor Eisenstadt and Giesen give any attention to this level of cognitivist analysis. On another level, the theory has to make possible an analysis of the cognitive frames that social actors, whether social movements or other agents, collectively construct for themselves, and in addition it must also allow for the analysis of the symbolic packaging of such frames for the purposes of their strategic communication in public discourse. Once again, neither Melucci nor Eisenstadt and Giesen achieve such refinement in their respective analyses. On yet another level, the theory must in particular give access to collective identity in the sense of the macro-frame that emerges from the competition and conflict of the distinct (meso)-frames communicated by the different participants in public discourse.

The third and final theoretical assumption made in the present context is that the public, over and above the participants, make a decisive contribution to the collective identity that is constructed in and eventually emerges from public discourse (Strydom 1999e). Melucci indeed recognises that 'the consumers of the products of communication participate in moulding public discourse' (1996: 225), but he does not develop this insight far enough to appreciate the epistemic authority and the role of the public in public discourse, nor does he link it to the construction of collective identity—certainly not collective identity in its macro sense.

13

The Challenge of Responsibility for Sociology

Judging from contributions made by the authors such as Emile Durkheim, Max Weber, Talcott Parsons, Arnold Gehlen and Jürgen Habermas, sociologists have always had an appreciation for the concept of responsibility. Besides internalising the social demand of responsibility themselves, they also found ways of fruitfully employing it in sociological analysis.[1] In the postwar period, the 1960s in particular, the sociological interest in responsibility received a boost from the crisis of conscience experienced by physicists, chemists, biologists and sociologists due to the bombing of Japan, the proliferation of chemical and biological weapons, and the exposure of Project Camelot respectively. While the social responsibility of science then became an issue for many, others applied the concept in their investigations in the sociology of science (e.g. Horowitz 1967; Gouldner 1970; Seeley 1970; Rose and Rose 1970). Towards the end of the 1960s, however, a new sense of responsibility started to emerge gradually. It was stimulated, on the one hand, by the cumulative effect of collective activities and man-made disasters harbouring a potentially extensive impact on the environment and future generations and, on the other, by the response of new social movements and the public. In the meantime, the majority of sociologists have probably acquired an awareness of this new sense of responsibility in favour of with such leading philosophers as Karl-Otto Apel (1980, 1988) and Hans Jonas (1973, 1976, 1982, 1984) had been among the first to argue systematically. What sociologists have thus far not yet succeeded in doing, however, is to appropriate this concept for their own purposes, and to make it fruitful for the analysis of the society that is taking shape at present.

The aim of the present essay is to make a contribution to the mitigation of the two-fold deficiency of the sociological response to the new question of responsibility. To achieve this aim, it will be necessary, on the one hand, to briefly clarify the concept of responsibility as it has come to be understood today, and on the other to demonstrate more concretely at least one way in which it can be made fruitful in sociological research. In the first part of the essay, therefore, the recent change in our understanding away from individual responsibility towards collective or, rather, co-responsibility will be briefly reviewed, while indications will also be given of some implications of this change for sociology. The remainder of the essay will be devoted to a more research-oriented sociological development of the problematic of responsibility. In the space opened up by the theoretical analysis, a cultural sociological or socio-cognitivist conception of responsibility as the new macro- or master frame of the late 20th-century discourse about risk is developed and then illustrated with reference to contemporary developments in societal semantics and the environmental field.

1. FROM INDIVIDUAL TO CO-RESPONSIBILITY

A Future Oriented Planetary Macro-Ethics

In their respective attempts to characterise the widely yet vaguely perceived challenge facing the late 20th century, the noted philosophers Jonas (1984) and Apel (1988) provide comparable analyses and diagnoses that are of sociological significance in a number of respects.

Both authors start from the thesis that the promise of modern science-based technology gave rise to a completely new and unprecedented situation when it turned into its opposite: a threat and danger or risk not only to nature and hence human survival, but even to the very nature of human beings. This situation possesses three unique features: socially, it is universal in the sense that it confronts all people with the same problem; spatially, it is planetary or global in the sense that it spans the whole earthly biosphere; and temporally, it is irreversible in the sense that it reaches into the future and potentially affects all future generations of humans, animals and plants.

Both authors agree that the universal, global and irreversible features of the new situation confront humankind today with a moral challenge that requires a novel ethics of responsibility. This ethics can no longer be based on moral norms regulating face-to-face relations and human life in small groups, such as the couple, family, neighbourhood and even the nation, since the range and scope as well as temporal extension of the risks involved demand that it must be appropriate to the macro-dimension of humankind's fragile existence on the finite earth. Whence their respective proposals for a future-oriented, planetary ethics of collective responsibility (Jonas 1984) and a universal, planetary, macro-ethics of co-responsibility (Apel 1987, 1988, 1990, 1991).

From a sociological point of view, the purport of the analysis and diagnosis advanced by Jonas and Apel is twofold. What they achieved, in the first instance, was to demonstrate that a shift has occurred from the traditional emphasis on individual responsibility, which sociologists like Durkheim, Weber, Parsons and even Habermas took for granted, to a new conception of collective or co-responsibility. Second, Jonas and Apel, in effect, established a link between 'risk' and 'responsibility', and thus gave expression to a conceptual pair which plays a key role in the societal semantics of our time.[2]

Collective or Co-Responsibility?

Since the 1980s, a rapidly growing number of sociologists are giving attention to the theme of risk and the risk society. By contrast, only a few sociologists have recognised the simultaneously implied concept of responsibility and the concomitant relativisation of individual responsibility which has occurred as a result of the increasing significance acquired by collective activities and the universal, global and temporal extension of their effects and side-effects. Ulrich Beck's (1992) work is an example of this discrepancy.[3] Wolfgang Schluchter (1991: 333-38), by contrast, seeks to extend Weber's ethic of responsibility in such a way that it includes the moral problems raised by the intensifying exploitation of nature by nuclear and genetic technology. In a brief yet interesting section entitled 'Discourses of Responsibility', Gerard Delanty (1999: 156-57) also acknowledges that challenges faced by society today, which derive from science and technology, the ecological crisis and developments in the knowledge society, no longer admit of being dealt with by recourse to individual responsibility—whence the increasing centrality of collective responsibility or what he also calls 'societal responsibility'.[4]

If one accepts, with authors such as Schluchter and Delanty, the turn away from individual responsibility, interesting sociological questions arise in respect of the way in which sociologists dealt with this problem in the past and the new approach that now has become available. Before touching on this, however, the question of the difference between what many, following Jonas, call 'collective responsibility' and what Apel calls 'co-responsibility'[5] requires some attention.

The expression 'collective responsibility', to begin with, has the advantage of registering unequivocally the recent shift from or, at least, the relativisation of individual responsibility. Yet it is an ambiguous and indeed dubious and misleading expression. Not only does it stimulate the projection of a potentially authoritarian mode of regulation (Bernstein 1994; Hajer 1996: 266), but it also threatens to revive methodological collectivism precisely when sociologists are beginning to see the need for adopting methodological situationalism instead (Knorr-Cetina 1988; Somers 1995b; Eder and Schmidtke 1998). The concept of 'co-responsibility', by contrast, has a different origin and hence meaning. Rather than the metaphysical point of view and ontological idea of humanity preferred by Jonas, it is inspired by Apel's sociology friendly theory of communication and discourse. Responsibility, in these terms, applies to human beings as members of a community of communication and cooperation, and it can be fulfilled only by a worldwide network of formal and informal communications—from discussions and dialogues through round tables and ethics committees to boards and commissions of all kinds at local, national and international level.[6] Thus responsibility, or rather, co-responsibility can be practiced and organized only discursively (Apel, 1987: 27; 1993: 24). This implies that, far from rendering individual responsibility completely redundant, as Delanty (1999: 157) suggests, co-responsibility brings a public level of responsibility for common or shared problems into play without disburdening individuals of their personal responsibility. It stresses the dimension of shared or common problems, but also retains a participatory role for the individual in publicly relevant communication and thus in the discursive shaping and treatment of such problems.

Categories of Responsibility[7]

Considering the sociological treatment of responsibility, the meaning and implications of co-responsibility are best clarified within the framework of a threefold typology of responsibility. It consists of the traditional concept of individual responsibility, as employed by Durkheim (1964) and Parsons (1964), the post-traditional concept of individual responsibility, as exemplified by the work of Habermas (1979a), and, finally, the new concept of co-responsibility.

Individual responsibility first of all in its traditional sense applies within informal pre-institutional contexts. Here it pertains to duties of loyalty incurred within the contexts of friendship, family, kinship and the group or nation. More formal institutional responsibility is also ascribed to the individual within the context of marriage and family, but most typically it extends to occupational roles in a society characterised by the division of labour. It thus presupposes social institutions underpinned by differentiated functional social systems. In this formal case, we are still dealing with a conventional form of individual responsibility in so far as it remains within the normative confines of a given institutional framework.[8]

Post-traditional individual responsibility is post-conventional by nature in that it bursts the limits of pre-institutional and institutional conventions.[9] Duties of responsibility accrue to individuals on this level due to their possession of special knowledge, abilities, judgment, power or influence in particular domains of social life. Rather than observing traditional or conventional limits, they take the initiative to shift the boundaries by assuming individual responsibility for the (re)design and (re)organization of institutions and social systems themselves with a view to the constant monitoring and the reduction or avoidance of negative features and effects. This is of course the classical territory of the sociology of intellectuals,[10] but examples from the second half of the 20th century abound.[11]

The new concept of co-responsibility for which Apel pleads is distinguished by the fact that it admits of being articulated and organized discursively in both a social and political sense, and thus allows the participation of individuals, groups, collective agents and the public. Transcending the post-traditional individual type, it is a mobilisable form of responsibility in that the perception of a practical problem, for instance a hitherto unknown risk, is framed and communicated in such a way that it is assumed that all those whose concern is being raised and whose support is being sought equally bear co-responsibility for the observed consequences and side-effects of collective activity.

Besides protecting the sociologist against unjustifiable political projections and conceptual reductionism, the sociological potential of this threefold typology points in two directions. Not only does the observance of the distinction among different types of responsibility sharpen the sociologist's ability to discriminate between qualitatively different social contexts—the conventional Durkheimian-Parsonian one, the post-conventional Habermasian one, and the currently emerging constructivist one. At the same time, it also opens the way for a sociological analysis of the novel actions in which social actors are increasingly engaging today under the conditions of the new reflexive type of institutions and the nascent communicatively mediated institutional order of our time.

2. RESPONSIBILITY AS NEW MASTER FRAME

Having contrasted past sociological concepts of responsibility with the currently emerging one, we now need to take a further step in order to come to grips with the latter in a more concrete sociological manner. To accomplish this, I propose to make use of a reconstructive methodology.[12] The object of analysis will be what may be variously called a cultural form, model, code or frame that, despite being the outcome of constructive activities, has a discursive existence and exerts a structuring effect on communication and social action and, hence, also on identity formation and institutionalisation. For present purposes, the starting point of this methodology is the interpretation and analysis of social conflicts that are centred round a socially significant problem or issue and are accessible through public communication or debates. The analysis seeks to identify the discursive process at work in this communicative conflict and, in particular, to uncover the structuring features of the discourse that allow the participants to relate to one another. In this sense, the focus will be on the responsibility frame of the late 20th century. For the purposes of the analysis of this master frame, I shall draw on data generated in a number of different research projects conducted during the 1990s.[13] The order of presentation of the material below, however, does not necessarily follow strictly the methodological sequence that had originally been followed in the research process.

Reconstructive Approach to Contemporary Risk Debates

If one considers a historically specific, empirically identifiable set of experiences and their articulation located in space and time, or what is called discourse, it is not necessary to stop at the level of description or even explanation, but it is quite possible by way of a reconstructive approach to unearth and make explicit what lends such a complex its coherence and consistency. Any of a number of examples, either historical or contemporary, could be selected for such purposes. In the context of our present interest in responsibility, however, the focus will be on the various interrelated late 20th-century debates about risks—what is sometimes more narrowly referred to as the 'environmental debate' or more broadly as the 'risk debate' or 'risk discourse' of our time. What needs to be shown by the analysis is the new responsibility frame that is presupposed in these debates and gives them their coherence and consistency, thus structuring them into what more properly may be called 'the responsibility discourse' (Strydom 1999b, 2000).

Description of the Debates

Since the 1960s and in particular the 1970s, a variety of intertwined debates emerged that in one way or another deal with the so-called 'problem of nature' (Moscovici 1968, 1990; Schäfer 1985: 269-70; Eder 1988, 1996a), which means with some aspect of the relation between society and nature, whether external or internal. Among these aspects are many problems that are apparently widely disparate yet are nevertheless closely related to one another. Some of the most pressing of these problems are associated with the late 19th- and 20th-century fusion of science-based technology with industry, and occur in the chemical, pharmaceutical, nuclear and lately the genetic fields. That these developments have grave consequences for the environment are well known, but their ramifications are also to be observed in numerous other areas, such as medicine, agriculture and food, health and welfare policy, insurance, corporate recruitment policy, and so on. But even state economic and development policy, the functioning of the state itself, collective decision-making and collective goods have all proved to be equally problematic with regard to our relation to nature.

As regards internal or human nature, consequences and side-effects have been identified in various areas. Among them are the sexual and quasi-sexual reproduction of human beings, gender in the organization of social relations, the modification of the human genetic inheritance, and the possible creation of clones and transgenic individuals. These problems, and others besides, have given rise to wide-ranging and soul-searching local, national and global debates about our relations to nature in the sense of the ecosphere and the biosphere as well as the human body and emotions.

The Issue of Risk

Although the problem of nature is as old as modern society itself, it was worked up and made into a public and political issue only as late as the second half of the 20th century. In the 1980s, the concept of risk has come to designate the issue implied by the problem of nature. Works such as those of Beck (1992) on the so-called 'risk society', Luhmann (1989, 1995b) on ecological communication and on risk, and Eder (1996a) on the social construction of nature, document this process. The concept of risk proved apt to serve this purpose since it graphically captures the threats, dangers and disadvantages that culturally defined social processes, such as those associated with science, technology, industry and the state, harbour for collective forms of life. That the concept of risk acquired this role is interesting. Initially, it emerged in the rarified context of experts in the nuclear industry in the USA and required both a drastic reformulation and a transposition into the public sphere (Evers and Nowotny 1987), where a widespread awareness of risk is in evidence today. Rather than an actuarial formula, it was required to become a socially meaningful claim, and rather than part of the brief of corporate and state engineers and safety officers, it had to be demonstrated that it was a serious issue that raised moral concern and deserved the necessary support so as to be placed on the public and political agenda. Of great importance in this process of transmutation were undoubtedly the anti-nuclear and environmental movements, yet the making of the problem of nature into the issue of risk, it should be emphasised, was the achievement of a wider discursive process in which various agents participated.

If one considers what an issue is, this becomes clear at once. Lexically, an issue is a dispute between parties in which they join in the hope of arriving at a decision or solution. From a social-theoretical point of view, this means that it is a publicly relevant matter round which antagonistic definitions of the social world and hence social conflicts are organized. The crucial point, however, is that an issue is not something that simply divides people into antagonistic groupings who define the social world in competing or conflicting ways. At the same time, it also coordinates those involved in a manner that goes beyond their particular motivations and social structural characteristics (Miller, 1992a; Eder, 1993a: 191; Strydom 2000: 138, 140-2). A description of the antagonism and conflict generated by an issue is a necessary ingredient yet at best only a first step in a sociological account of the social processes marked by a given issue. In this vein, a description can be offered of the very different ways in which social movements (e.g. the anti-nuclear, environmental and anti-biotechnological patents movements), industry or business, and the state define the issue of risk; the distinct identities they construct and images they present; and consequently the antagonistic relations they maintain in their communication about the issue. But to live up to the aspiration of an adequate account, the sociologist will be required to go beyond the division and separation brought about by the directly observable competition, antagonism and conflict among the contestants towards the other, less observable side of the same process—the coordination of their actions. For far from engaging merely in conflict, the protagonists are focused—albeit in different ways—on one and the same issue, while equally striving to get the matter settled, even if preferably as much in their own favour as possible, in relation to one another and within the field of vision and earshot of the observing, evaluating and commenting public.[14] Focusing on a jointly identified controversial issue, seeking a solution acceptable not only to them but also to the public, and thus assuming a shared universe of discourse, the conflicting parties enter a socially circumscribed situation or structured setting and a discursive process that make room for all and thus transcend their particularities. The coordination of the dissent and conflicting actions of the contenders independently of their particular motives is made possible by the discursively unfolded and generalised situational structures that emerge from yet transcend the choices, values, norms and knowledge initially brought into the situation and communicated by the different actors.

The Responsibility Frame

The central question here concerns these situational structures—comprising, as they do, the object of the reconstructive approach followed here, namely the responsibility frame. To begin with, they are the minimum of what is jointly accepted, often even implicitly, within the domain of what seems to be collectively accepted, largely implicitly, in the form of cultural or lifeworldly knowledge. Within the context of a complex range of—objective, moral and connative—classifications of reality, a variable yet nevertheless relatively small cross-section of cognitive structures and knowledge becomes accepted or rather presupposed by the participants. This shared cognitive component is what codes the situation. As such, it is a set of rules of coordination. It is constantly communicated in the situation and, by being mutually understood, it transcends the motives of the participants and thus relates them to one another and coordinates their conflicting actions. In so far as the coordination effect rests on communication, the rules of coordination are actually structures of discourse. This is why it is possible by means of a reconstructive approach, to a given discourse, to make explicit the rules of the discourse that serve to coordinate the actions of the participants.

Since the reader might take the earlier reference to situational structures and coordinating rules of discourse as indicating a structuralist predilection, it should be recalled that during the 1970s and 80s social theory underwent a significant shift of emphasis (e.g. Eisenstadt 1985) which is presupposed here. This shift was from an emphasis on structure to one on construction and structuration instead. This means that both a comprehensive structural determinism and the notion of a static and immutable structure are eschewed. Characteristic of the new understanding is much rather that there is a close relation between micro-structures and macro-structures, indeed, that they are only different levels of abstraction of one and the same phenomenon (Knorr Cetina 1988; Eder and Schmidtke 1998: 434), that is, relational and coordinating rules or structures. In addition, it is appreciated today that, rather than being given beforehand and remaining unchanged throughout, the structures in question here are contingent and variable discursive structures, which could nevertheless be more or less stable over a particular time-span. Drawn from what is culturally available (Swidler 1986), they are introduced into discourse by the different participants in a varied selection as micro-structures, and are then unfolded, selectively reduced and the remainder generalised in the medium of discourse to a jointly presupposed macro-structure that coordinates the competitive and conflicting actions of the participants. From recent literature it is clear that an attempt is at present under way in sociology to capture their mutable and soft nature by conceiving of them as narrative structures (Somers 1995b; Hajer 1995: 52-8; Eder 1999a). According to this proposal, collectively shared narratives, which are quite unpredictable in the way and the direction in which they change, provide the structural features of social situations and give action a degree of certainty.

The concept of frame, effectively introduced into sociology by Erving Goffman (1986) in 1974, has come to be used to designate the discursively mobilised, developed and changed structural features of social situations (Snow *et al.* 1986; Snow and Benford 1988, 1992; Gamson 1988a, 1988b, 1992; Eder 1996a; McAdam *et al.* 1996). More specifically capturing the cognitive—whether objective, moral or connativè—properties of narratives or story-lines, it refers to the framework that makes possible the perception, experience and interpretation of the social and the natural world, and thus structures action and communication. Frames of this general kind occur at different levels of abstraction and as a rule relate to one another as the micro to the macro and vice versa. American sociologists, however, although having made a significant contribution to the cultural framing literature, tend to restrict the concept of frame or framing processes to the level of collective action. In this context, they emphasise what may be called collective actor or identity frames to the exclusion of the macro-level. A recent work by Dough McAdam, John McCarthy and Mayer Zald (1996) is a good example of this practice.

McAdam *et al.* argue that cumulative scholarship on framing is as yet lacking due, among other things, to conceptual imprecision:

> *'Though Snow and his colleagues meant something quite specific by their use of the term, recent writings have tended to equate the concept with any and all cultural dimensions of social movements. This usage threatens to rob the concept of its coherence and therefore its theoretical utility. In this volume we want to return to David Snow's original conception and define framing rather narrowly as referring to the conscious strategic efforts by groups of people to fashion shared understandings of the world and of themselves that legitimate and motivate collective action'* (*McAdam* et al. *1996: 6*).

The construction of such collective actor frames, of course, involves micro-elements generally referred to as 'framing devices' (Eder, 1996a: 167-69), but how the authors intend to fulfil their major goal of analysing the dynamic relations among opportunities, mobilising structures and framing processes remains obscure. It is simply not possible unless opponents, observers and commentators are studied at one and the same time as the social movement, and attention is specifically given to the macro-level frame that emerges from their competitive or conflicting discursive relations and on the basis of which they then all act. Even when

McAdam *et al.* acknowledge the occurrence of 'intense framing contests' among a social movement, the state and counter-movements, for instance, and see that the filter effect of the media will have a significant impact on 'the outcome of...framing efforts' (McAdam *et al.* 1996: 17), their focus stays fixed on the collective actor frame rather than the macro-level frame that affects the broader structured setting. This, to be sure, is tantamount to the reinforcement of a limitation noted before in the literature: 'only rarely did the [social movement] theoretical perspective go beyond the self-production of collective action. The introduction of a cultural dimension to social movement theory and research, being a recent phenomenon, has opened up the possibility to extend a constructivist perspective regarding the structural context', which means that the emphasis shifts to 'public construction' and the 'historically specific discourse' in which it occurs (Eder, 1993a: 14). When they do move their focus away from the self-production of collective action, McAdam *et al.* return to the micro-level of framing devices to assess 'the cultural impact of the movement in modifying the available tool kit' (McAdam *et al.* 1996: 19) from which the devices were borrowed in the first instance. What remains outside their field of vision, therefore, is the cultural master frame at the macro-level which marks the outcome of the cultural dynamics generated by the relations among the participants in a given discourse.

Now, from a cultural sociological or socio-cognitivist point of view, responsibility is today precisely a new master frame of this kind. It is a cultural model of social practice that has first emerged from the dynamics of the discourse generated by the new social movements, the state and business or industry in the course of antagonistically addressing the issue of risk, and then has become established beyond them at the macro-level. As an established cultural model, the responsibility master frame structures the risk communication of the different participants and hence the discourse thus generated. Since the responsibility frame is the characteristic structuring model of the discourse, the latter may therefore be called the 'responsibility discourse'. As such a pervasive structuring model, the responsibility frame is presupposed by all those participating in the discourse, despite the fact that they typically engage in distinct social practices and communicate risk in competing if not conflicting ways. Since the responsibility frame is not simply a constraining cultural cognitive structure but in particular an enabling one, it admits a wide variation of practices and interpretations. On the one hand, the fact that the responsibility frame has actually emerged and started to exert a structuring effect can be demonstrated by reference to the fundamental change that has taken place in recent years in the semantics of late 20th century societies. On the other hand, the constraining yet enabling force of the responsibility frame can be demonstrated with reference to the general assumption made and the diversity of arguments put forward by the participants in the debates about the risk issue.

3. SOCIETAL SEMANTICS, MASTER FRAMES AND ENABLING STRUCTURES

From Risk Semantics to the Responsibility Master Frame

As regards the establishment of the responsibility frame, it is illuminating to follow the change that has taken place in recent years in the semantics of late 20th century societies. Through his well known work on the risk society, Beck (1992) has of course done more than anyone else to draw our attention to this fundamental semantic shift, but other social scientists such as Moscovici (1968, 1990), Inglehart (1977, 1990) and Luhmann (1989, 1995b) have also made important contributions. The perspective they opened up allows us to appreciate the degree to which a range of new keywords has relativised, if not displaced, traditional political topics in public communication.

Rather than the economic well-being of the individual, for instance, public communication and political rhetoric display an overwhelming concern with collective security or safety in the face of threats or dangers of various kinds, the abstractness and diffuseness of which make them all the more socially explosive. The use of words such as danger, risk, technology assessment, risk management, safety, and so forth have increased dramatically. The shift in societal semantics signalled by the appearance and prevalence of these and other words represents a fundamental change that is of the greatest importance for the analysis of late 20th societies.

Christoph Lau (1989: 418; see also Strydom 2002: 77-8) draws the conclusion that the flood of publications dealing with the issue of risk and the prevalence of the theme in public communication can be taken as indicators that, at a deeper level, reality is to an increasing degree structured and perceived according to the cognitive scheme of safety and danger. This cognitive structuring manifests itself in a generalised consciousness of danger that extends to potentially everything humans make decisions about and have to take responsibility for. Here one could mention a range of matters, from science and technology through food and blood supplies to sexual activity. Elaborating on Lau, it could be pointed out that the scheme of safety and danger, which finds paradigmatic formulation in Beck's treatment of the issue of risk, has relativised schemes that predominated in earlier periods—for instance, the scheme of wealth and poverty encapsulated by Marx in his work on proletarianization, which itself relativised the scheme of order and chaos expressed in Hobbes's concern with early modern violence and disorder.

The central question here, of course, is less than the bare cognitive scheme than the broader master frame or cultural model that became collectively accepted as guiding and giving direction to action or social practices and, hence, as promising a resolution of the issue in question. In the early modern period, when everyone desired order in the face of the chaos of the time, both constitutionalists and republicans as well as absolutists, despite their divergent interpretations, accepted the cultural model of rights. The late 19th and first half of the 20th century, in turn, saw the collective acceptance of the cultural model of justice that coordinated the conflicting interpretations of liberals, conservatives and radicals. Today, the responsibility frame occupies the central place vacated by rights and justice. When Apel (1991: 275) writes that 'Co-responsibility is a principle of ethics that is different from, or goes beyond, the sense of justice', he is entirely correct, but I propose to go a step further still to interpret this statement sociologically in terms of a socially effective, cultural cognitive structure. This means that responsibility or, rather, co-responsibility is a significant new cultural master frame of our time. Perhaps, then, we could say with some justification that at the end of the 20th century we are entering 'another history...[that]...marks the emergence of a new responsibility for all of us' (Moscovici 1990: 14), what may be called the 'era of responsibility' (Corrick 1990: 60).[15]

The Responsibility Master Frame as Enabling Structure

The notion of a collectively accepted cultural frame and, even more, of a normative code of responsibility for the survival of the planet and a sustainable relation to nature advocated by various authors, have a particular implication of which the sociologist must be wary. It amounts to the assumption that everyone is required to assume the same responsibility and, hence, that the responsibility frame is a comprehensively determining or constraining structure. This is not entirely correct, however. It is indeed a collectively accepted or, at least, presupposed cultural frame that coordinates the actions of all the participants at a level beyond their individual motives, yet at the same time it is also an enabling structure. Without giving up the normative reference gained by way of the perspective of coordination, yet renouncing the tendency to regard it as harbouring a complete solution involving the elimination of all conflict, this is where the sociological point of view comes into its own. Rather than simply adopting one particular normative code, that is, one particular interpretation allowed by the cultural frame, it critically takes into account the normative codes communicated by all the participants, namely, all the relevant interpretations of the master frame. For the sociologist, it is not a matter of choosing one normative code or interpretation over the rest, but of showing how the master frame allows divergent, competing and even conflicting ones at one and the same time. Eventually, of course, each one needs to be evaluated critically from the point of view of the cultural structure they all presuppose (Strydom 2000: 87-90).

The enabling force of the responsibility frame can be demonstrated by reference to arguments put forward, for example, in the context of the United Nations Conference on Environment and Development (UNCED) held in Rio de Janeiro in 1992.[16] The major participants included nation-states, business and industry, and finally the social movements. Representing the nation-states were 115 world leaders, such as US President George H. Bush, who spoke on behalf of the North, and Malaysian Prime Minister Mahathir Mohamed, who was the spokesperson for the South. The chairperson of the Business Council for Sustainable Development, the Swiss billionaire Stephan Schmidheiny, represented business and industry. Whereas these participants made official presentations at the plenary session of the UNCED, the non-governmental organizations (NGOs) representing the social movements, Greenpeace from the North and Third World Network from the South, were only allowed to submit reports to the official conference. Consequently, they were compelled to organize their own fringe activities under the banner of the Global Forum. To these various participants could also be added the large number of newspapers that covered the conference. Not only did they make their own contribution to the discourse about risks faced in the environmental field, but they also helped to form public opinion and, hence, the establishment of the new master frame. The question is now: what arguments did each of these participants put forward, what claims did they advance, or what normative codes did they communicate that indicate divergent interpretations of the master frame of responsibility?

The first thing that strikes one on reading a selection of the speeches and reports produced by these various actors is the pervasiveness of the assumption or presupposition of responsibility. The word 'responsibility' is often used in these materials, but even where it is not employed explicitly some circumlocution or reference indicates that this is what is intended. In this vein, the need to care for the environment and to recognise the rights of future generations is taken seriously and mentioned frequently.[17] Without exception, the actors also have an appreciation for the global dimension of these requirements. Leading newspapers such as *The Washington Post*, *The New York Times*, *The Guardian* and *The Times* almost invariably make use of the word 'responsibility', but what they typically do in their editorials is to consider the various participants in their interrelations and thus to give formulation in one way or another to what many simply assume or presuppose.

On the basis of the shared new cultural frame of responsibility, however, the participants put forward divergent and even conflicting interpretations. A brief review of a selection of paradigmatic examples bears this out:

1. President George H. Bush starts from the responsibility that needs to be taken for 'the Earth and the environment' as well as for 'future generations', and acknowledges that this requires 'international cooperation'. On this basis, he then stresses the status of the USA as world leader and superpower that is expected and required to take responsibly for economic development and growth, and is thus willing to take tough decisions based on principles.
2. According to Prime Minister Mahathir Mohamed, Malaysia in particular and the South more generally are concerned about the environment and willing to take responsibility for it in line with what can be expected of them. In fact, he claims, the South maintains a much closer and friendlier relation with the environment than the North. By far the larger proportion of pollution and environmental degradation emanates from industrialisation and economic development in the North. It is therefore inequitable and unfair when the North seeks to use environmental protection as a reason to interfere in and stifle development in the South.
3. Stephan Schmidheiny, spokesperson for business and industry, proceeds from the premise of an unwavering commitment to responsibility on a global scale towards future generations and the environment. Presupposing this, his characteristic concern is the safeguarding of the conditions necessary for an 'eco-efficient' business community as an essential ingredient in the achievement of 'sustainable development' on a global scale.
4. Greenpeace International uses the opportunity offered by its acceptance of the new cultural master frame of a global ethics of responsibility to argue that 'corporate environmentalism' is a 'greenwash' in that transnational corporations, such as DuPont, Shell, Sandoz, General Motors and others, consistently abdicate responsibility by passing the buck. The NGO strongly decries

the persistence of a situation of no public accountability on the part of business and industry.

5. Third World Network, finally, asserts the vital interest of the southern countries in environmental protection and their willingness to take responsibility by committing themselves fully to the environment and adopting environmental policies and environmentally sound production and development. In the view of the NGO, however, the problem is that current levels of environmental degradation and risk generation can be traced back to unsustainable production and consumption patterns in the North and to a constantly reproduced, inequitable and exploitative world order in which the South is the main victim. A sustainable balance between development and the environment can be achieved only on the basis of a drastic reform of the international economy, not when the South is compelled to submit to the vested interests of a North that is unwilling to change.

These examples of actors who are interrelated within the same universe of discourse provide evidence, on the one hand, of the collective acceptance of the new master frame of responsibility and, on the other, their ability nevertheless to articulate their own particular interpretations or definitions of the situation. This is in keeping with their particular forms of life and social practices. The competing and even conflicting nature of their respective positions speaks for itself. Social movements are against corporations, the state and corporations are against the social movements, and the South is against the North. Indeed, the fact that conflict round the issue of risk persists even after the emergence and collective acceptance of the new responsibility frame, indicates that a deep-seated difference is at work here that we might well be wise to regard as an at least 'potential class conflict' (Eder, 1993a: 191, also 119-140). A shared master frame precludes neither the potential nor the reality of such a conflict.

CONCLUSION

In an endeavour to contribute to the sociological appropriation of the late 20th century key concept of responsibility and to make it fruitful for the analysis of contemporary society, I have taken two steps.

In order to show that it is possible to transcend the limits of the social contexts in which sociologists have applied the concept of responsibility in the past, I first offered an outline of a three-fold typology of traditional individual responsibility, post-traditional individual responsibility and, finally, co-responsibility. The argument was that this typology enables the sociologist to open up contemporary forms of action to investigation, unencumbered by the restricting assumptions of traditional sociological concerns (for example, institutional individualism, role theory, the sociology of intellectuals, the development of moral consciousness), yet without denying their relative right.

The focus on co-responsibility rather than collective responsibility encouraged the adoption of a communication and discourse theory according to which society is less a social entity with a core essence than a structured setting accommodating a variety of distinct social actors who maintain different yet changing cultural and institutional relations. On this basis, I investigated, indeed not the social construction of morality as such, but the cultural cognitive structures that result from such a process. Drawing on wide-ranging research experience, but particularly focusing on the participants and discursive process at the UN Earth Summit, an argument was developed in favour of regarding responsibility as an important new master frame of the late 20th century. It is a common, enabling, cultural structure that nevertheless figures as a stake in the conflict between those sharing it.

I am convinced that this concept of the responsibility frame can be of assistance to the sociologist not only in making sense of the conflicts surrounding the issue of risk in contemporary society, but also in getting a glimpse of the probable organization of society in the next number of decades.

14

Risk Communication: World Creation through Collective Learning under Complex Contingent Conditions

By 'risk communication', to begin with, I understand a broad societal phenomenon which is of a historically specific nature. It made its appearance in the late 20th-century risk society as part of the public discourse about risk and responsibility. And, in the meantime, it has become the characteristic feature, the signature as it were, of early 21st-century society. Historically, therefore, it is comparable to the 'poverty communication' of the 19th century and the 'violence communication' of the early modern period (Strydom 1999b, 1999c, 2000, 2002). This means that risk communication is a multi-levelled process that includes all communication, all the different streams or strands of communication, about the central issue of our time: the issue of risk which has increased communication in the past number of decades to an unprecedented degree.

An adequate understanding of risk communication is possible, therefore, only in the context of the risk society and, more specifically, the public discourse about risk and responsibility. What such contextualisation allows one to do, is to appreciate the complexity of the conditions under which risk communication takes place and, hence, also the multi-levelled or differentiated nature of risk communication itself. The unfolding of this discourse during the second half of the 20th century revealed the different streams or strands which go into the makeup of risk communication together with their respective vehicles (Strydom 2002). Whereas risk communication at the outset took the form of closed elite communication about the level of acceptable safety, it later progressively broadened into a form of public communication about the societal production and constitution of risk. In the 1950s, experts in the nuclear industry and regulators were both senders and receivers of risk communication. By the 1970s, however, social movement organizations have entered the ranks of risk communicators and started to address ordinary members of the society. Since then, a significant proportion of the citizenry has become sufficiently concerned and involved to provide the spawning ground of both ideas and organizations feeding into risk communication.

It is remarkable that whereas the discursive logic generated by risk communication for decades sharply divided those affected, even leading to destructive conflict, it has given rise in the course of time to discursive means for the potential coordination of divergent orientations and actions. This suggests that risk communication, in the final analysis, is a cooperative learning process in and through which a communication community arrives at a constructive diagnostic interpretation of its common situation, the challenge it faces, and possible ways of dealing with it, thus creating a form of life for its members.

The social scientific study of risk communication, then, must take into account a number of things: the historically coloured societal conditions of complexity under which it emerged and takes place; the multi-levelled or differentiated nature of the risk communication and the specific character of each of the forms it takes; and, finally, the relations among these different dimensions and the direction taken by their interrelation. To comply with this requirement, I devote this essay to a brief treatment of three topics: first, the complex conditions of risk communication as a multi-levelled process dealt with in terms of the discursive constitution and organization of contemporary society; second, considering the different forms of risk communication from the perspective of the learning processes they harbour such that it becomes possible to determine typical configurations of relations between them and the potential such relations unlock; and finally, reflections on the status and role of normative claims and criteria in the coordination of the different levels of risk communication.

1. COMPLEXITY CONDITIONS OF RISK COMMUNICATION

The complexity of the conditions under which risk communication takes place in contemporary society, including the uncertainty accompanying it, is best clarified by considering the mode of constitution of society and the contribution communication makes to it.

Internal Differentiation of the Multi-levelled Process of Risk Communication

Risk communication is a central component of the communicative-discursive process whereby society—in this case, the 'risk society' (Beck 1992)—is constituted and organized. This process of constitution is characterised by a non-linear social dynamics. The latter rests on the generation of variety by different sources and the selective combination of these contributions into a not fully anticipated or expected outcome. This non-linearity draws our attention to the multi-levelled and internally differentiated nature of risk communication, since the latter is a principal generative source of variety. It is also here that we find an important part of the explanation of the high degree of contingency and uncertainty surrounding risk communication.

Although it may be referring to one and the same object (that is, a risk reality), risk communication draws on a 'culture of contradictions' (Eder 1993a: 194) and is carried and promoted by socially or institutionally distinct agents. For example, state and corporate institutions, on the one hand, and associations, non-governmental organizations (NGOs) and social movements, on the other, while attending to a mutually recognised risk, embody different risk perception and risk communication cultures.[1] They thus entertain different communicative and informative intentions in accordance with their distinct modes of engagement with the world.[2] This provides a basis for introducing a fundamental distinction between the institutional and civic risk communication. Related to these different forms of communication, and reinforcing them, are furthermore corresponding resonance structures[3] to which they are oriented and which make possible both responses to such communications and the forging of connections between them. These structures stretch from institutional resonance to extra-institutional or civil society resonance, both of which implicate cultural resonance. Later, more attention will be given to resonance, at which stage it will be necessary to refer also to public resonance.

From a cognitive perspective,[4] accordingly, risk communication can be said to involve a whole range of related yet different competing and even conflicting cognitive devices, from schemata, operations and scripts—that is, modes of classifying a given risk, making sense of and acting upon it—to cognitive formats for selecting, condensing and generalising relevant information, such as for instance statistics, reports, political analysis and ordinary language. This competitive and potentially conflicting diversity is mirrored, on the other side, by the corresponding resonance structures. Considering these various dimensions, risk communication must thus be regarded in terms of a multi-levelled network in and through which incoming information about a given risk reality is processed in a socially distributed way. Occupying different positions, yet parallel to one another, each of the participating agents frames and communicates the mutually recognised risk in its own particular way and thereby activates resonance structures which allow responses in the form of feedback of one kind or another as well as connections to be forged. And in doing so, each of the participants makes a contribution to the way in which the risk becomes collectively classified, understood and dealt with. Risk communication is thus socially shared, creative cognition or a creative collective cognitive process whereby a community forms and shapes a world for itself.

In contradistinction to contemporary approaches (e.g. Clark 1998; Wertsch 1998) to distributed cognition in networks of situated action which, notwithstanding their commendable highlighting of differences and interdependencies, tend to flatten out different levels and make disjunctions, tensions, contradictions and conflicts unrecognisable, it is vital for an adequate understanding of risk communication not only to stress complexity, but also to keep the concomitant contingency and uncertainty in mind. For this reason, it is imperative to acknowledge that risk communication is not simply a matter of representation, but at the same time also one of signification;[5] not simply one of communicating a position or content in keeping with a communicative and informative intention, but also of contextual references generating meanings going far beyond all intentions; not simply of problem-solving, but also of creating and bringing a world into being.[6]

This brings us to the context or larger intersubjective framework of risk communication—and that means something that duplicates complexity and multiplies uncertainty by imposing a communicatively and discursively mediated yet non-linear social dynamics on risk communication itself.

The Public Communicative Context of Risk Communication

By attracting attention and providing a compelling object of reference, a risk opens a reflexive and communicative moment. Indeed, in conjunction with the schemata, operations and cognitive formats of those affected, risk gives rise to an intersubjective experiential context filled with concern and developing social relations. Individuals, organizations and institutions recognise the consequences of others' decisions and actions potentially affecting them, attribute those consequences to the agents involved, and relate to one another in an effort to collectively define the problem and decide how it could be dealt with. Risk and the cognitive structures[7] corresponding to it not only call forth communication, which in turn activates resonance structures, but also help to forge connections and intensify communication to the point that a larger communicative event takes place and overarching communicative structures come into operation, take effect and develop. Risk communication thus leads to the emergence of a discourse and the establishment of what is called the 'public sphere'.[8] In fact, each of the different forms of risk communication, together with its set of resonance structures, gives rise to a corresponding type of partial public sphere. At a higher level, a more embracing public sphere emerges at the intersection of the different forms of risk communication and resonance structures.

Depending on the conjunction of these strands of risk communication and resonance structures, the public sphere takes on different forms, with four basic types being distinguishable.[9]

Public Sphere at Rest

In Western type societies where certain fundamental arrangements are in place, the backdrop against which activated forms of public sphere appear could be conceived as a 'public sphere at rest' (Habermas 1996a: 379).[10] It is characterised by a low level of constricted risk communication and hence a dearth of resonance. There is indeed an awareness of potential or real risks, but there is no cause for a systematic engagement in risk communication. However, once the perception and recognition of a risk reaches a critical threshold, once risk communication increases and flares up, any of a number of types of public spheres could emerge. This is illustrated by the historical unfolding of the discourse about risk and responsibility since the 1950s and 60s through four phases (Strydom 2002: 11-35)—from a restricted expert and regulator debate about risk calculation and assessment, eventually to a fully fledged public discourse about the societal constitution of risk and its implications for the creation and organization of society.

Institutional Public Sphere

One active type is an elite or institutional public sphere. It is generated by a form of risk communication engaged in by experts such as for example managers, planners, economists, engineers, lawyers, psychologists and regulators representing institutions such as private firms and state administration. Business promotion and political campaigning aimed at mobilising consumers, clients or the citizenry to support some service, product or decision would count as instances of such institutional risk communication. Corresponding to this form of risk communication, institutional resonance is a characteristic structural feature of this type of public sphere. It makes its appearance through the response of such institutions to the perceived needs, demands and criticisms of consumers, clients and citizens.

Liberal or Mass Public Sphere

Another type is the liberal or mass public sphere. The form of risk communication generating this public sphere is borne and promoted by active members of society who are typically organized into consumer groups, neighbourhood groups, voluntary associations, NGOs and social movement organizations. To such civic risk communication corresponds civil society resonance which feeds on the response of active associations, organizations and movements belonging to civil society to political or economic encroachments or problems that their members or others they identify with face in their private life-worlds. Central to this type of public sphere, therefore, are political, social or cultural critique and different forms of protest.

Discursive Public Sphere

A final active type is a mediated or discursive public sphere. This type of public sphere is more general, but also more complex, than the preceding institutional and liberal or mass public spheres. Depending on the degree of development of its defining feature, namely discursive mediation, it could take two related yet distinct forms.

In its first deficient form, it is characterised by the presence of both institutions and civil society. Connections are established and even elaborated between institutional risk communication and resonance, on the one hand, and civic risk communication and resonance, on the other. Although both are affected by sharing a situation in which they face each other, the differences between them are maintained. In some sense or another, institutional and civic risk communication stand over against one another and even get embroiled in contestation and conflict. None of the parties expect and therefore exert themselves to achieve more general agreement and acceptance of the claims it advances. Rather than allowing the full institutionalisation of discourse,[11] the structures of this public sphere facilitate the forgetting or suppression of the bridging potential of communication.

In the case of the enhanced and still more complex form of the discursive public sphere, the crucial difference is made by the incorporation of the public and hence public resonance—which means, the introduction of the third point of view over and above the ego and alter perspectives of the institutional and civil society actors.[12] In such a fully developed public sphere, the participating institutions as well as associations, organizations and movements relate to each other in and through the discursive medium only via a reference to the presence of the non-participating yet nevertheless involved observing, evaluating, judging and commenting public. The epistemic authority coming into play here unequivocally gives priority to the public interest. The publicly embodied third point of view, therefore, has a sobering structuring effect on the self-understanding, self-presentation, mutual sensitivity, mutual understanding and mutual recognition of the active participants and their respective forms of risk communication. This instantiation of the public sphere thus possesses the potential of refining risk communication to the highest degree of legitimacy and hence efficacy possible. But this is possible only under the contingent, uncertain and fragile conditions of the non-linear social dynamics leading to a collective outcome.

This raises the question of what precisely is at stake in risk communication.[13]

2. RISK COMMUNICATION AS LEARNING UNDER CONTINGENT CONDITIONS

The identification of different types of public spheres in which distinct forms of risk communication take place underscores the non-linear dynamic nature of the multi-levelled process of risk communication. Far from simply the transfer of information, risk communication involves the processing of information through its division and recombination, implicating variable configurations of speakers, audiences and others. In turn, such an event implies that learning processes[14] are at work in it. As it takes its course, cognitive structures of different levels and scope, from individual self-understanding to cultural models, undergo a self-organizing transformation resulting in a new classification, reframing and reconstitution of the world. Considering risk communication from this perspective should throw some light on persistent problems and challenges faced by risk communicators, particularly perennial uncertainty, but also on potential opportunities and possibilities for the enhancement of risk communication.

Sociologically, learning processes can take on a variety of different forms, depending on the structure and complexity of the social relations, intersubjective experiential or communicative contexts presupposed. Different configurations of public spheres allow distinct learning processes. The multi-levelled process of risk communication, particularly the impetus driving it forward, cannot be adequately understood unless it is related to these learning processes. For this purpose, some basic as well as composite types of social learning are distinguished below and related to the levels of the risk communication process.[15]

Aggregative Learning

First, aggregative learning at best is possible in a public sphere at rest representing an intersubjective framework characterised by a high level of structural openness and a low level of symbolic complexity. Such learning involves the aggregation of achievements gained through trial and error at the individual levels, whether persons or legal personalities such as institutions. At issue here, therefore, are the individual learning processes of business executives, corporations, politicians and bureaucracies that take place without collective will-formation and, hence, to the exclusion of civil society and the public. It leads to configurations of socio-economic and political or administrative power which give rise to cleavages and class structures as well as associated dynamics of individualisation and social exposure to risk. For example, this type of learning and its consequences were typical of the period prior to the emergence in the 1970s of the concern of social movements and the United Nations with the problem of risk.

Institutional Learning

Second, institutional learning requires an intersubjective experiential context possessing a high level of structural closure and a low level of symbolic complexity such as an elite or institutional public sphere. It involves the kind of learning that different kinds of institutions have to undergo to be able to fulfil their particular missions—for instance, economic institutions (e.g. the corporate sector) to safeguard and further production, distribution and consumption, and political institutions (e.g. the state, the EU) to take care of the population and collective goods. This type of learning assumes the indifference, acquiescence or compliance on the part of the relevant other such as for instance labour, consumers and the citizenry. Thus it typically leads to institutional practices which also have a hierarchical, authoritarian or paternalistic face. In the risk communication of private firms and state institutions, this type of learning is closely allied with and complementary to aggregative learning. Here a form of institutional risk communication prevails which is articulated through a variety of contradictory cultural models. While corporations let themselves be guided by such models as entrepreneurship, profit, smartness, bullishness, risk-taking, customer service and need-fulfilment, and government agencies by such models as reason of state, the common good and public service, both tend to be paternalistic and secretive and therefore readily revert to practices of concealment, denial and cover-up.

Associational Learning

Third, associational learning is made possible by a liberal or mass public sphere which presupposes a configuration of social relations displaying a low level of structural openness and a high level of symbolic complexity.

It involves the coordination and synthesis of the cognitive structures of associating individuals and groups in civil society.[16] Such coordination and synthesis stretch from the construction of a collective identity, via the formation of a collective actor such as a voluntary association, NGOs or social movement. to collective mobilisation and eventually collective action.[17] Involving little or no communication with relevant others, this kind of learning proceeds from the assumption of the opposition of corporations and the state or, at best, their indifference or acquiescence, while hope is pinned to the support of the citizens. Needless to say that this is typical of the contemporary environmental, anti-biotechnology, genetic rights and related movements engaging in civic risk communication. This form of communication, impelled, as it is by associational learning, is guided and given direction by a range of cultural models, including from human and planetary health, through rights, citizenship, sustainability, responsibility, victimology and justice, to global civil society, democracy, cosmopolitanism and ecology.

This brings us to the kind of learning that takes place in a mediated or discursive public sphere which, as we have seen, takes two forms depending on the configuration of the relations involved. In the first case, both institutional and associational learning are present, while in the second the added reference to the public's third point of view gives rise to yet another type of composite learning process well beyond the first. In both contexts, however, we witness the socially or discursively constructed nature of risk communication under conditions of variable contingency which is at the core of the uncertainty enveloping it.

Double Contingency Learning

It is characteristic of institutional learning and associational learning that both involve the erection of boundaries to the exclusion of the other. Where both are present together, we are dealing with what may be called 'collective learning in situations of double contingency' (Trenz and Eder 2004: 12).[18] In such double contingency learning, the parties have a self-referential orientation and are willing and able only to adjust their preferences, accommodate themselves to a certain degree or accept integration up to a certain point under the conditions arising from a confrontation with the other. Given the difference between them yet their sharing of a situation facing each other, institutional and associational learning processes represent what can be regarded as two distinct 'logics of collective action' (Offe and Wiesenthal 1980) which are rather difficult to reconcile. While they could co-evolve, these two logics often do come to stand hard by one another. This involves contestation, resistance and conflict between, for instance, economic and/or political agents, on the one hand, and social movement actors, on the other. It is often unproductive, such as the stalemate between the biotech industry and the genetic rights movement, or it could even be destructive, as in the case of the demise of Monsanto or of the environmental opposition in France. At times, however, it is also productive, as Lewis Coser (1956) argued many years ago with reference to Simmel regarding the integrative function of conflict.[19] The latter is the most positive interpretation of double contingency learning. Through contestation and conflict the parties learn to accommodate one another and to allow a low degree of coordination or even integration.

This kind of learning is obviously central to the risk communication in so far as it involves a process of social or discursive construction which is impelled forward by the competition, contestation and conflict of opposing forces. It marks out the field of experiences familiar to those involved in risk communication. Many of the typical problems, obstacles and frustrations go back to the limits imposed on the relation between institutional and civic risk communication. Often the agents are not merely unable, but in fact obstinately unwilling to generalise their own peculiar frames, cultural models and cognitive formats. Predictably, they thus patently fail to anticipate the resonances elicited by their communications. Consequently, they fall in the trap of one or other of a number of strategies blocking learning (Miller 1986, 2002a): defensively avoiding disagreement; an authoritarian insistence on a predefined consensus; ideologically insisting on an endemic and insurmountable antagonism; and regressively rejecting arguments by disqualifying the people who advance them. Negative phenomena such as paternalism, scientism, technocracy and public relations spin, on the one side, and idealisation, fundamentalism, over-dramatisation and noise, on the other, are well-known manifestations of blocked learning in the risk communication field.[20] Once these blockages are removed or overcome, however, the way is open toward a more demanding, indeed less probable, yet much more promising learning process making possible more efficacious and legitimate risk communication.

Triple Contingency Learning

Societal learning, finally, like the previously discussed composite learning process, presupposes a discursively mediated public sphere in the sense of an intersubjective experiential context characterised by a high level of both structural openness and symbolic complexity. But it is distinct from double contingency learning in that it results from a confrontation and interrelation of the participants before an attentive public. Societal learning is thus a form of discursive learning in which both institutional actors and civil society actors take each other into account via a reference to the observing, evaluating, judging, commenting and thus monitoring public. It is only by passing through the coordinated system of standard setting and 'scorekeeping' (Brandom 1994: 180) perspectives that the participants are at all able to arrive at an understanding of what they have in common and, especially, of what they disagree about. It is this configuration of communicative relations that I have elsewhere called 'triple contingency' (Strydom 1999e) in distinction to the classical sociological concept of double contingency. And by relating learning to it, Trenz and Eder were able to take it yet a step further, conceiving of 'societal learning in situations of triple contingency' or 'collective learning by triple contingency' (2004: 12).

Triple contingency learning represents the collective learning mechanism which brings us closest to the communicative self-constitution and self-organization of society.[21] The threefold set of contingently related communicative relations increases and intensifies public communication and resonance. It draws more participants and observers into the situation and renders cultural models reflexive, autonomous and discursively available, thus activating a plethora of cultural resources for self-reflection, self-problematisation, translation, connectivity and the transformation of self-understanding. And it compels both participants and observers to resonate by making unequivocal options and communicating those options effectively, while either accommodating themselves to the public or anticipating its response. It harbours the 'cosmopolitan' promise of a transformative moment in which a 'creative combination of different forces' (Delanty 2006: 38; also Beck 2005) occurs. The outcome of the multi-levelled process of risk communication, which depends on social construction guided by such discursive learning, is a collective achievement.[22] Risk communication is thus a cooperative collective learning process in which all those involved are required to reach beyond their particular perspectives so as to link up with something larger than themselves and sharable with others.[23]

Such learning is made possible by the emergence of cognitive forms, discourses, public spheres and a public possessing the epistemic authority of observing, evaluating, judging and forming opinion. In turn, public communication—in this case, risk communication—provides the medium for the spatial, temporal and structural expansion of the public sphere as an intersubjective context of learning. In proportion as this context is expanded together with its constitutive public, an improvement in the conditions of both participation and monitoring results. Such improvement facilitates, yet also makes more complex, the achievement of collectively constructed definitions and decisions as well as the enhancement of the conditions of discourse—or 'condensation' as well as 'confirmation', to use Brandom's (1994) terminology. Risk communication in the proper sense of collective learning contributes to both these achievements. Under contemporary conditions, it is crucial not only to the solution of collective problems, but also to the bringing into being of a new world.

3. THE NORMATIVE PROBLEM OF RISK COMMUNICATION

The normative problem connected with risk communication relates to the fact that the latter is the practice of a communication community. The normative aspect concerns the collective evaluative self-definition which a risk community constructs in the guise of a diagnostic interpretation of its common situation, the risk problem it faces, and possible ways of dealing with it. The self-definition expresses the members' agreement or acceptance of that evaluation—that is, agreement or acceptance not in the conventional sense of uniformity of belief and evaluation, but in the post-conventional sense of allowing differences. In turn, the degree of agreement or acceptance gives an indication of the legitimacy of risk communication.

Now, considering the multi-levelled nature of risk communication under complex contemporary conditions, together with the different learning processes and hence rationalities at play in it, it should be readily apparent that there is no one single normative code that could secure agreement and legitimacy without difficulty. Those involved in risk communication distinguish themselves from one another by their distinct engagements with the world, each of which is guided and given direction by a particular conception of the good. Besides the vast difference between institutional and civic risk communication, institutional risk communication alone harbours a variety of conceptions of the good or normative codes, such as those of science, politics, economics, law and so forth. For example, science pursues the truth, but even within science itself there are different and potentially conflicting conceptions of the good, such as microbiology led by rDNA (recombiant DNA) knowledge and ecology by environmental knowledge (Schomberg 1992). And politics or public policy, typically employing a rational decision-making model, seeks to attain the common good. The civic risk communication of associations, NGOs and social movements is likewise guided and directed by the common good, but, by contrast with politics' top-down version, rather a bottom-up one to which moral concern is central.

Due to their being partial, none of these conceptions of the good or normative codes is able to resolve the normative problem entailed by risk communication. Against the background of existing cleavages and class structures, the prevalence of tension as well as competition, contestation and conflict surrounding communication in the risk society bears this out. Endless scientific controversies, irresolvable disagreements among experts, and contested policy options, political decisions and industrial programmes, all demonstrate that the adoption of a partial normative code is fraught with dangers and is therefore unacceptable up to the point of lacking legitimacy. By accepting the truth as expressed by a particular scientific discipline (e.g. microbiology in the case of the release of genetically modified organisms to the exclusion of ecology), we might well diminish our ability to anticipate a future catastrophe or we might even open ourselves to one. However rational, political decisions based on scientific knowledge, while ignoring scientific uncertainty or allowing experts simultaneously to act as advocates, would have a comparable result. But settling for the opposite socially rational arguments of associations, NGOs or social movements alone would also place us in a vulnerable position. We could unwittingly render ourselves vulnerable to collective fictions or illusions which bear little or no relation to reality.

It has become a familiar strategy to criticise the idealism of moral points of view deriving from moral philosophers and articulated by associations, NGOs and social movements. In so far as such agents' implied normative codes are partial and, even more so, if they are reified into unrealisable absolutist or fundamentalist claims, it would indeed be proper to reject them as idealistic. But it is no less idealistic to think that the normative code of science or of rational political decision-making is going to resolve the normative problem raised by risk communication. None of these normative codes by themselves are capable of mobilising sufficient support to establish a legitimate self-definition for a risk community. Such a structural deadlock can be transcended only by fluidising the normative problem communicatively. The tendency of the past decade and a half for public administration to enter into processes of acting out and negotiating with social groups is a response to this requirement. Many see the solution in participation—that is, admitting all those affected to take part in a process of social exchange or mediation of social consensus. That it more often than not eventuates in sub-rational zero-sum games of power and interest conflict, however, suggests that the quality of the outcome of mere participation leaves much to be desired. In situations like this, uncertainty is left to proliferate in an uncontrolled manner.

A major source of uncertainty in the context of risk controversies is the lack of an articulated form staking out who should participate in what way in joint or collective decision-making processes. A promising way of dealing with this deficiency is a discursive one—that is, discursivization through the incorporation of partial rationalities and their associated normative codes in a critical discourse in which situational definitions and norms are jointly or collectively constructed. Discursivization is indeed necessary, but it is by no means sufficient. A further step towards the proceduralisation of such discourse is required (e.g. Apel 1988; Habermas 1996a; Dryzek 1999; Eder 2000c). Over and above institutional and associational learning processes and their sporadic conjunction in situations of double contingency, this would encourage the emergence of more systematic discursive learning processes in which all those involved (both ego and alter) have a rightful place and relate to one another through a reference to the third point of view (namely the Other). In such a situation of triple contingency, all the normative codes are in a justified[24] way incorporated into a larger moral-ethical framework which, in turn, defines and structures the situation in terms of the public interest. Without the reference to the public interest, the participants cannot develop a shared knowledge of their differences, and hence a critical discourse in which the participants collectively learn through the mutual exposure of biases, distortions, half-truths, illusions and rationalisations cannot come about.[25]

It should be noted that the discursively relevant public normative criterion, the public interest,[26] is not simply equivalent to the abstract moral point of view of the moral philosopher, but one emerging from and brought to bear on the particular situation.[27] The alternative to identifying with the normative code of a preferred or favoured agent (e.g. science, the state or the environmental movement) is not to adopt an absolute or abstract moral ideal indicating what ought to be and to hold it up so that participants can see how far short they are falling. It is rather a matter of mobilising and scrutinising all the normative codes—those of ego, alter and the Other—for the purpose of locating starting points for a new constructive learning process which could possibly move us closer to an intact and inclusive communication community.

Even if in this way an evaluative self-definition is attained which is supported by a majority of the risk community's members and, hence, enjoys a high degree of legitimacy, the costs—both rational and moral costs—must be reflected on, acknowledged and justified. Since better grounds or reasons[28] other than those underpinning the justification could conceivably later emerge, openness and a possibility of revision allowing a reconfiguring or minimising of such costs must be retained. Although uncertainty can thus never be eliminated, we do have means to deal with it. Risk communication in the sense of a cooperative collective learning process, as it turns out, is one of the most eminent among the available contemporary means for managing uncertainty. And to the degree that such uncertainty management proves successful and meaningful, risk communication simultaneously helps to bring into being a world possessing its own broadly accepted evaluative self-definition.

15

Cosmopolitanism, Globalization and Learning: Reflections on Delanty's Theory of Cosmopolitanism

In a recent article in *The British Journal of Sociology*, Gerard Delanty (2006) establishes a link between cosmopolitanism and learning. This is an innovative step which both takes further his own work on cosmopolitanism (e.g. 2000, 2003, 2004)[1] and is also of a more general theoretical significance. It introduces a perspective lacking in the existing literature and not only enriches the theory of cosmopolitanism but, more broadly, also promises to improve the theory of globalization—a possibility suggested by his view that, despite being distinct, there is a relation between cosmopolitanism and globalization. Delanty's introduction of the concept of learning and his forging of a relation between cosmopolitanism and learning are highly suggestive and invites explication, extrapolation and development.

A starting point for such explication, extrapolation and development is provided by the theoretical assumptions on which Delanty implicitly draws in his theory of cosmopolitanism. These assumptions derive from the tradition of sociological learning theory or, more generally, cognitive sociology which originally stems from Jürgen Habermas's work of the 1970s,[2] particularly his concern with 'societal learning processes' (1979a: 121), but was decisively redirected, developed and carried forward by Max Miller (1986, 1992a, 2002a, 2002b) and Klaus Eder (1985a, 1988, 1993a, 1999a, 2000a). In the present context, accordingly, Delanty's innovative step is embedded in this more extensive conceptual and theoretical framework and the theoretical implications following from his proposal drawn out. To establish a background for these reflections, Delanty's understanding of the link between cosmopolitanism and learning and of the relation between cosmopolitanism and globalization are first clarified. The remainder of the argument concentrates on the more fundamental question of learning implied by the relation between cosmopolitanism and globalization, involving an explication, extrapolation and extension of Delanty's position. The key component here is a differentiated sociological concept of learning. This discussion culminates in a theoretical account clarifying the relations among cosmopolitanism, globalization and learning which is by no means devoid of empirical significance.

1. COSMOPOLITANISM AND LEARNING

Delanty locates cosmopolitanism in the context of the transformation of the social world. The transformation he has in mind is located at a number of progressively deeper dimensions. Overall, it is characterised by an increase in what he calls 'world openness' (2006: 25). Following indications he gives, the enhancement of world openness could be interpreted in the sense of some degree or other of the opening up of the social world through a broadening of discursive spaces, a reconstitution of self-understandings, an enlargement of the cultural basis of social orientation and action, and an increase in the inclusiveness of social relations. While regarding cosmopolitanism as an integral feature of modernity and being particularly interested in contemporary society in which a global public has attained epistemic authority, he nevertheless sees the emergence of the idea of cosmopolitanism already in ancient times as pointing to the possibility of such transformation occurring under a wide variety of conditions. Characteristic of his position is the insistence that cosmopolitanism does not remain confined to the processes of transformation leading to a global or world society but is also, indeed above all, to be found in contexts at lower, even local, levels. Under modern conditions, however, the mechanism of cosmopolitanism becomes much more visible. Here diversification and pluralisation give rise to tensions which in turn induce not only reflexivity, self-problematisation and self-critique, but also increase communication and, under the gaze of various publics, stimulate discursive transformation.

Delanty regards the opening up of the social world, in the wake of the build-up of tensions, as being achieved through contestation. As the references to pluralisation and reflexivity suggest, not just social forces have a role to play in such contestation but also culture. In fact, he accords a special role to culture. 'Cultural models of world openness' (2006: 25), as he designates them, call forth a process in which competing or conflicting interpretations are contested. Following the cognitive turn in sociology, particularly Habermasian cognitive sociology (Eder 1996a; Strydom 2000, 2002), he conceives of the contestation of alternative interpretations of a cultural model in terms of what he calls 'framing processes' (2006: 25, 31).[3] This implies a sequence of occurrences. First, the problem of world openness is rendered relevant and made into an object of attention by some event or change of conditions. Second, different social actors or agents construct distinct frames in the form of particular cultural models in relation to the issue brought forth by the problematic situation and highlighted by the activated general cultural model of world openness. Through an increase in communication and the resultant practical discourse, third, the different frames are placed in a competitive relation and played out against one another in a discursively mediated cognitive and symbolic contest. From this contestation, finally, there emerges a more general, discursively constructed frame consisting of a synthesis of elements selected from the lower level frames promoted by the competing actors or agents. Here we witness a discursively achieved cultural change, but rather than being something purely cultural it possesses at least potential social significance. The higher level emergent frame represents a new, socially effective interpretation of world openness in so far as it enlarges or broadens the cultural basis of social orientation and action and thus allows an increase in inclusiveness in the sense of establishing relations among social actors or agents and admitting a wider range of them than before.

Delanty, to be sure, adds his own particular twist by interpreting this process as being a matter of 'translation' (2006: 25, 44; see also Delanty 2005). In the process of discursive contestation and construction, relations are established between and among the different competing and conflicting frames in such a way that a more general frame emerges which is communicatively shared by the social actors or agents involved without necessarily obliterating the social structural and cultural differences between them.[4] In the literature, such interrelation and upgrading of frames or cognitive structures is approached according to different models. Social movement theorists think of the interrelation, convergence, overlapping and merging of frames as 'frame alignment' (Snow *et al.* 1986) or 'cognitive adjustment' (Chazel 1997), while social scientists representing a strong cognitivist approach regard the relations among schemata from the point of view of 'connectionism' or schema-connectionist theory (e.g. Turner 2002).[5] Rather than confining it to social movement formation or neuro-physiological processes, Delanty transfers this idea to the higher level and more concrete context of public communication and conceives of it in terms of translation. In doing so, important to note, he emphatically retains the cognitive dimension of the process, but understands it in terms of the Habermasian tradition of a weaker version of cognitive sociology (Strydom 2006a: 224-7, 2007; Eder 2007).

Thus far, I have identified some of the major, progressively deeper levels at which Delanty locates the transformation with which he associates cosmopolitanism. Such transformation is characterised by an increase in world openness which depends on a process of discursive contestation and construction at the centre of which resides a cognitive operation to which he refers as translation. But this does not yet bring us to the end of the line. For at the very core of the process of transformation he locates 'learning' (2006: 39, 41, 44). Once one moves from phenomena such as public communication or discourse, competing cultural models, a process of discursive construction, a reconstituted cultural model, greater inclusiveness and an increased degree of world openness so as to focus on the internal core, then learning comes into view—that is, learning in the sense of 'an internal cognitive transformation' (2006: 41).[6] Delanty assumes that 'culture contains capacities for learning' (2006: 44) or, at least, for making possible learning processes which could feed into the transformation of society. Since it holds in store a multiplicity of cultural models, many of which are strikingly different from one another, opposed and even contradictory, it has the propensity for calling forth, inducing and stimulating competition and conflict not only over their interpretation, but also over their eventual concretisation or realisation through institutionalisation and social action. Learning in a socially significant sense is not possible without such competition and conflict and the discursive construction accompanying them.

2. GLOBALIZATION AND COSMOPOLITANISM

There has been a tendency in the literature to conceive of globalization as a macro-process and to ascribe independent causality and hence explanatory power to it. Considering some of his statements, it would seem as though Delanty himself subscribes to such an interpretation. He writes, for example, that 'globalization...enhance(s)...the dynamic of cosmopolitanism', that 'cosmopolitanism has become relevant today, due not least to the impact of globalization', and he even submits that 'globalization...is the principal motor of modernity' (2006: 38, 43-4). But on closer inspection it becomes clear that this is by no means his position. On the contrary, he criticises various theorists for transposing globalization into the central force driving social transformation which leads them to regard globalization as the primary mechanism of cosmopolitanism, to explain cosmopolitanism by globalization and thus misleadingly to obliterate the distinction between cosmopolitanism and globalization or to reduce the former to the latter. Delanty is emphatic that cosmopolitanism is 'not created by globalization' and, therefore, 'cannot be explained...in terms of globalization', insisting that we should 'distinguish globalization and cosmopolitanism' (2006: 38, 27, 36). At the same time, however, he recognises that there is a 'connection' (2006: 36) between the two. It is here that a theoretically and, eventually, an empirically important question arises—one to which an answer could be extrapolated from Delanty's suggestive remarks. If there is a relation between globalization and cosmopolitanism, and if cosmopolitanism is intrinsically linked to learning, how should we then conceive of globalization? Is there any relation between globalization and learning? Or more fully, what is the relation among cosmopolitanism, globalization and learning?

Attention is first given to Delanty's distinction between globalization and cosmopolitanism and then to the relation linking the two.

Globalization contributes to pluralisation and diversification which intensify relations over an increasingly wider area. By so doing, it creates a range of cultural and social possibilities and establishes a macro-context. Despite regarding the context made available by the process of globalization as an 'unavoidable' one, Delanty diverges from the widespread tendency in the literature to see globalization as the 'primary mechanism' or the 'central dynamic' of societal transformation (2006: 36, 25, 27, 30). As a multi-level process, globalization is 'contingent' and 'indeterminate' (2006: 36). At best, it represents only the 'external' conditions of societal transformation, and therefore it is only when one turns to the 'internal' dimension of societal transformation that cosmopolitanism enters the field of vision (2006: 39). Cosmopolitanism involves the creation and articulation and thus the transformation of cultural models which guide and are given embodiment in social action, institutions and new manifestations of society. It is with such processes, as we have seen, that Delanty associates learning. Solutions to problems given rise to by globalization, therefore, can be expected to be found only on the basis of innovations and achievements attained at this internal level.

As regards the relation between globalization and cosmopolitanism, in Delanty's understanding, it is clear that the external-internal distinction does not imply that cosmopolitanism should be treated as the micro as against globalization as the macro. It is certainly the case that he also approaches globalization as a macro-level process from a micro-perspective, that is, the perspective of the constitution or construction of society, including the generation of the process of globalization. Here 'self-understanding', 'individual agency' and 'social identities' come into play (2006: 41-2). Cosmopolitanism itself, however, does not only have a micro- but also a macro-dimension. The macro aspect of cosmopolitanism concerns 'actual interrelationships of societies' as well as high-level cultural models arising as 'outcome' from such processes (2006: 41). The argument suggests that whereas the context established by globalization can be conceived in macro-realist terms, such cultural models require macro-cognitive and macro-phenomenological conceptualisation instead. The fact that Delanty maintains a relation of 'mediation' (2006: 42) between the micro- and macro-levels prevents the reification of such models on the macro-level. The communicatively and discursively mediated construction, reconstitution and transformation of cultural models are central to his position—which also means that the external-internal distinction is temporally and dynamically overcome.

Delanty's view that cosmopolitanism arises when the interactions of different modernities produce a 'new field of tensions' (2006: 41) sheds more light on the relation between globalization and cosmopolitanism. One could interpret this to mean that, on the one hand, globalisation makes available a context or framework of structural possibilities and constraining effects and, on the other hand, that members of society or citizens respond to these developments by simultaneously grasping opportunities and resisting constraints and the problems they produce in an effort to push the constitution and organization of society in a different direction. In this process, communication mediates the competition, contestation and conflict between the two sides. Theoretically, this is a promising start, while Delanty's suggestions point in the direction of an adequate formulation of the relation. When he deals with the production of the field of tensions, he focuses explicitly on the interrelation of units he conceives in national and civilisational terms, such as French, German, British and American modernities as well as European modernity and the non-European world (2006: 41). But it is what he assumes that adds further clarity to the relation between globalization and cosmopolitanism, particularly as far as learning is concerned.

Besides national and civilisational units, there is a whole range of other forms of modernity that need to be taken into account if one were to relate and align globalization and cosmopolitanism. Of particular importance are the economic, political, legal and civil societal or civic forms, all of which are not only dimensions of the multi-levelled process of globalization but also at stake in cosmopolitanism. A proper grasp of such phenomena as competition, contestation, interaction and mutual interpenetration can be obtained only if these various dimensions of globalization and their alignments with cosmopolitanism are explicitly taken up into the theoretical model. Learning, it should be emphasised, takes place at all these levels. This also implies that a corresponding diversity of cosmopolitan cultural models or models of world openness is constructed. For the purposes of his account, Delanty operates with a general concept of learning, namely internal cognitive transformation, and with a general concept of a plurality of cultural models of world openness. A clarification of the relation between globalization and cosmopolitanism requires a higher level of specificity.

3. GLOBALIZATION AND LEARNING

To adequately embed Delanty's position and to draw out its implications, it is necessary first to establish a baseline understanding of globalization as a multi-level process of transformation, and then to introduce a differentiated concept of learning, correlated with different types of cosmopolitanism, which admits of being aligned with the different dimension of globalization. The establishment of these various connections provides a basis for replacing a spatial by a social account—that is, surrendering the idea of globalization as causal mechanism in favour of focusing on social actors or agents and the discursively mediated processes they activate in the course of their creation and organization of society.

Globalization

What seems to be common to the diverse variety of understandings of globalization in the literature is a developmental thrust beyond what with reference to Habermas's notion of 'the postnational constellation' (2001) could be called the national constellation. Considering the widely accepted view of a multidimensional process, however, globalization is to be conceived in terms of the diverse logics of development which brought modern society into being and now continue from within the national constellation and edges toward the postnational constellation. It is a bundle of distinct economic, political, legal and civil societal dynamic forces, all shot through with culture and presupposing techno-scientific innovation. These dynamic forces, each possessing its own autonomous logic, lead to corresponding not necessarily harmonious institutional outcomes and therefore by no means point in the same direction.

To make sense of the contemporary situation, however, a theoretical strategy is necessary that enables one to get a handle on the relation of tension, contestation, resistance and conflict within the process of globalization between its major logics. This can be done by bundling certain strands so as to distinguish between what may be called functional globalization, the functional form of economic, political and legal globalisation, on the one hand, and communicative globalization, the communicative form of globalization carried by civil society and partially the law, on the other.[7] This gives rise to the following picture: Through accumulation, differentiation, evolution and, eventually, the extension, expansion or enlargement of the economic, political and legal forms of society, functional globalisation opens a social field. Within this open space, which eventually becomes discursively organized, the structuration of society becomes an issue and, indeed, a stake over which different actors and agents compete, conflict and struggle. Economic, political and legal globalization are not just economic, political and legal matters, but they are at the same times factors in the construction or constitution and organization of society. They open and make available opportunity structures or structural possibilities that could, and as a rule do, both foster and inhibit social and collective action. For example, economic, political and legal globalization create conditions or structural possibilities that people could use—say, reflexively transforming self-understanding, forming a social movement, claiming new rights or advancing participatory democracy. But at the same time, functional globalization produces structural effects which constrain people—say, making certain categories of people incapable of participating in politics or joining movements, or reducing people's ability to actually benefit from their rights, for instance, through poverty or exclusion. By generating both structural opportunities and constraining effects, functional globalization gives rise to new cleavages and class relations—indeed, a new transnational social class structure—and thus stimulates struggle over a common stake. The process divides people into different groups or classes who evaluate the structuration of society in different and even antagonistic ways and who thus eventually engage in competition, contestation, resistance and conflict over the mode of creation and organization of society as well as the direction of its development.

What at first glance appears as a two-sided process thus ensues. On the one hand, functional globalisation, given rise to by states, corporations, transnational organizations and legal production regimes, makes available a framework or context of structural possibilities and produces constraining structural effects. On the other hand, members of society or citizens in the guise of social actors, groups, associations, non-governmental organizations (NGOs) and social movements respond to these developments by simultaneously grasping structural opportunities *and* fighting or resisting structural constraints and the problems they produce in an effort to push the creation and organization of society in a different direction. Public communication taking the form of controversies or, more formally, discourses about a variety of serious issues—for example, risk, the environment, capitalist sweatshops, privatisation, free trade, war and peace, arms, stateless business law, social fragmentation, world poverty, rights, citizenship, and so forth—mediates the competition, contestation and conflict between the two sides. The thrust of this discursively mediated process of globalization is clear. Whereas functional globalization tends to give the emerging society at both global and local level a systemically self-regulative character, associations and social movements carrying communicative globalization strive to give rise to a self-organizing society instead which is politically and legally constituted and legitimated in terms of discursive rights.

The Figure 15.1 casts this analysis of globalization in the form of a theoretical model. At the same time, sociological learning theory and cosmopolitanism are incorporated in order to provide a theoretical background for Delanty's innovative step. The argument here, however, is that learning relates not just to cosmopolitanism, but in fact more broadly to globalization also. As a multilevel process, globalization involves different yet interrelated kinds of learning, all of which play a role in the making of the emerging society, both locally and globally. This implies, moreover, that to each of the levels of globalization corresponds a particular type of cosmopolitanism constructing and being guided by its own cultural model of world openness. Delanty distinguishes a number of different types of cosmopolitanism, for instance 'moral', 'political' and 'cultural' types (2006: 28-35), in terms of distinct theories of cosmopolitanism. This proposal could be taken further by locating cosmopolitanism in social reality itself. In this case, both civil societal or civic cosmopolitanism and legal cosmopolitanism could be added.[8] As regards corresponding cosmopolitan cultural models as such, Delanty makes a number of pregnant suggestions: morally, the 'universal human community'; politically, 'world polity', 'cosmopolitan democracy' and 'citizenship'; and culturally, the idea of an 'open…social world' (2006: 28, 29, 32). There is room, therefore, to be both more explicit and systematic. The introduction of sociological learning theory not only in relation to cosmopolitanism, but also in relation to globalization, enables us precisely to be clearer about the range of the types of cosmopolitanism and their particular models of world openness.

Types of Social Learning generating Globalization and Cosmopolitanism

Sociologically, learning processes can take on a variety of different forms, depending on the structure and complexity of the social relations or intersubjective experiential contexts presupposed. Since a number of different configurations of social relations or contexts are involved in the multilevel process of globalization, one can expect it to be impelled forward by a number of distinct social learning processes. In so far as cosmopolitanism correlates with learning, as Delanty proposes, this implies that the different types of cosmopolitanism together with their respective cultural models can be aligned with the various levels of globalization and the learning processes taking place at each. Drawing from and elaborating on Hans-Jörg Trenz and Klaus Eder (2004), who takes up the concept of 'triple contingency' (Strydom 1999e), some basic and composite

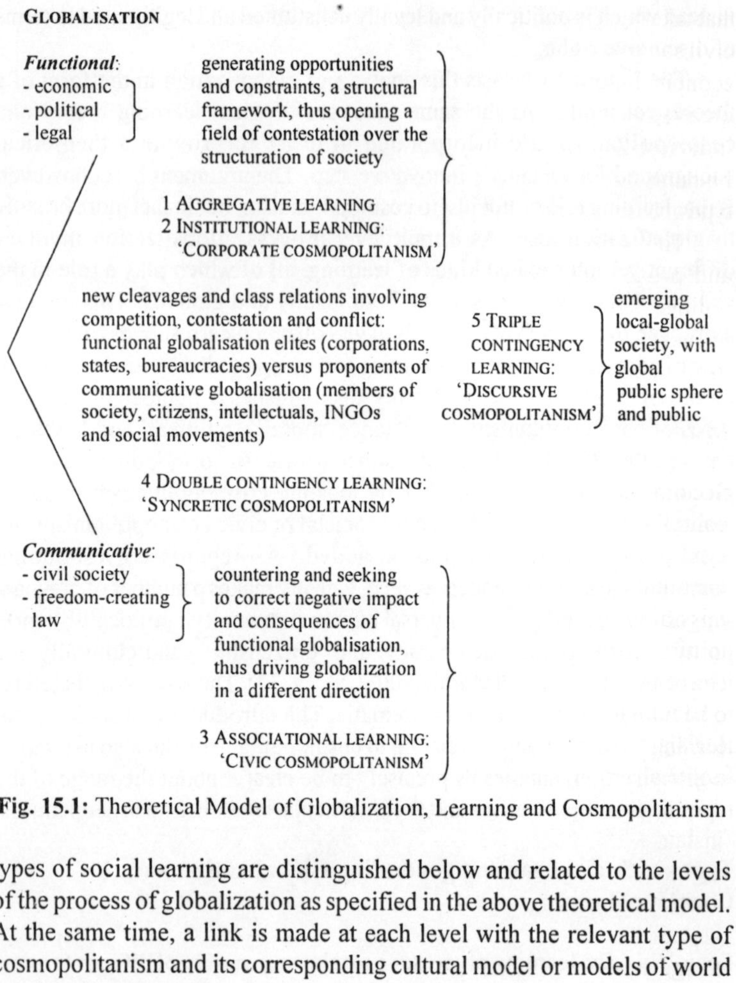

Fig. 15.1: Theoretical Model of Globalization, Learning and Cosmopolitanism

types of social learning are distinguished below and related to the levels of the process of globalization as specified in the above theoretical model. At the same time, a link is made at each level with the relevant type of cosmopolitanism and its corresponding cultural model or models of world openness.

Aggregative Learning

First, aggregative learning, presupposing an intersubjective framework characterised by a high level of structural openness and a low level of symbolic complexity, involves the aggregation of achievements gained through trial and error at the individual level, whether persons or legal personalities. At issue here, therefore, are the individual learning processes of business executives, corporations, politicians, bureaucracies, lawyers and legal firms or 'private governments' (Teubner 2002: 207; also 1997) that take place without collective will-formation and, hence, without taking civil society or the public into account. It leads to configurations of socio-economic and political or administrative power and, consequently, to cleavages and class structures and corresponding dynamics of individualisation (for example, de-socialization, cultural-religious fundamentalism) and social exclusion (for example, world poverty).[9] This type of learning and its consequences are typical of functional globalization.

To aggregative learning corresponds an elitist corporate, bureaucratic and professional type of cosmopolitanism, whether in an economic, political or legal form, which constructs cultural models of freedom or the unencumbered self in relation to cosmopolitan citizenship and then allows itself to be guided by such a model of world openness.[10]

Institutional Learning

Second, institutional learning, presupposing an intersubjective experiential context possessing a high level of structural closure and a low level of symbolic complexity involves the kind of learning that different kinds of institutions have to undergo in order to be able to fulfil their particular missions—for instance, economic institutions (say, the corporate sector) to further production, distribution and consumption; political institutions (for example, the state and the EU) to take care of the population and collective goods; and legal institutions (for example, legal firms, legislatures, the EU, the UN) to provide the necessary rules for economic, political and other activities. This type of learning assumes the indifference, acquiescence or compliance on the part of the relevant 'other' such as for instance labour and consumers, the populous, or the bearers of legally regulated activities. Thus it typically leads to institutional practices which also have a hierarchical, paternalistic or authoritarian side. In functional globalization, this type of learning is closely allied with and complementary to aggregative learning.

Here a form of corporate or institutional cosmopolitanism prevails which is articulated through a variety of cultural models of world openness. Economically, global cosmopolitan—including corporate—citizenship is directed and guided by such models as free trade, mobile production facilities, globally recognised brands and consumerism (see, for instance, World Bank 2002). Politically, the focus on collective goods is oriented by a number of contradictory and even conflicting cultural models, among which the most prominent are a world state or world government, global governance, cosmopolitan democracy and a 'politically constituted world society without world government' (Habermas 2005: 329).[11] Legally, finally, the concern with regulative regimes is today pursued according to conflicting cultural models of world openness, one being 'legal pluralism' (Teubner 2002) which is closely related to the neo-liberal capitalist imaginary, and cosmopolitan law in the sense of a global legal order which, however, itself admits of either an authoritarian or a democratic interpretation.[12] The moral cosmopolitan cultural model of the 'universal human community' mentioned by Delanty (2006: 28), it should be noted, contains a normative thrust—that is, cosmopolitan justice—that is at work not only in some of the political and legal models just listed, but also in the civil societal models to be discussed next.

Associational Learning

Third, associational learning, presupposing a configuration of social relations displaying a low level of structural openness and a high level of symbolic complexity, involves the coordination and synthesis of the cognitive structures of associating individuals and groups in civil society.[13] Such processes stretch from the construction of a collective identity, via the formation of a collective actor or social movement, to collective mobilisation and eventually collective action. In his original conception, Habermas stressed this type, as when he focused on 'social movements as learning processes' (1979a: 125). Processes of this kind assume the indifference, acquiescence, consent or, at least, potential consent on the part of the relevant 'other', for instance the state, the EU, corporations or more generally the public. Needless to say that this type of learning is typical of such contemporary phenomena as the environmental movement and the anti-globalisation movement,[14] the peace movement, the human rights movement and so forth.

The civic type of cosmopolitanism which is related to associational learning takes a variety of contradictory or even conflicting forms, judging by the cultural models of world openness constructed here to guide and give direction to learning processes. On the neo-liberal and legal pluralist side, the model of a global private law society is prominent, while those opposing it invoke the model of a global civil society which is interpreted differently, depending on whether it is regarded as being made up of global institutions such as a reformed United Nations, international governmental organizations, international non-governmental organisations, citizens' groups and social movements, or whether it is seen as communicatively constituted, spanned by a public sphere and remaining rooted in civic communities.[15]

Double Contingency Learning

It is characteristic of institutional learning and associational learning that both involve the erection of boundaries to the exclusion of the 'other', which means that—in the fourth place—we are dealing here with forms of what may be called 'collective learning in situations of double contingency' (Trenz and Eder 2004: 12).[16] In the case of this kind of learning, the parties have a self-referential orientation and are willing and able only to adjust their preferences, accommodate themselves to a certain degree or accept integration up to a certain point under the conditions arising from a confrontation with the other. Given the difference between them yet their sharing of a position vis-à-vis one another, institutional and associational learning processes represent what can be regarded as two distinct 'logics of collective action' (Offe and Wiesenthal 1980) which are rather difficult to reconcile. While they could implicitly co-evolve, these two logics often do come to stand hard by one another. In such a case, it involves the phenomenon of contestation, resistance and conflict between, for instance, economic and/or political agents, on the one hand, and social movement actors, on the other. It is often unproductive, such as the stalemate between the G8 and the anti-globalisation movement or between the West and Iran over nuclear technology, or it could even be destructive, such as in the Israeli-Palestinian case, but at times it is also productive, as Lewis Coser (1956; see also Delanty 1999a; Eder 1999b; Miller 1992b) argued with reference to Simmel regarding conflict many years ago. The latter is the most positive interpretation of double contingency learning. Through contestation and conflict the parties learn to accommodate to one another and to allow a certain degree of coordination or even integration. This kind of learning is obviously central to the process of globalization in so far as it is impelled forward by the contestation, resistance and conflict of functional or capitalist forces, on the one hand, and communicative or democratising forces, on the other.

To dual processes of learning through confrontation corresponds what may be called syncretic cosmopolitanism. Phenomena Delanty discusses in terms of 'societal pluralization', 'networks', 'mobilities' or 'global fluidity', 'hybridity' or 'mixing as a result of cross-fertilization of peoples and cultures' and the interrelation between 'multiple modernities' (2006: 31, 32, 33, 34)—all contain suggestive pointers toward the cultural models of world openness operative in syncretic cosmopolitanism. Different, contradictory and even conflicting interpretations can obviously be attached to these models.

Triple Contingency Learning

Societal learning, finally, presupposing an intersubjective experiential context characterised by a high level of both structural openness and symbolic complexity, is distinct from aggregative, institutional, associational and double contingency learning in that it results from a confrontation and interrelation of the participants in front of an attentive public. Societal learning is thus a form of communicatively mediated or discursive learning in which both institutional actors and civil society actors take each other into account via a reference to the observing, evaluating, judging and thus monitoring public. It is only by passing through the coordinated system of 'scorekeeping' (Brandom 1994) perspectives that the participants are at all able to arrive at an understanding of what they have in common and, by extension, of what they disagree about. It is this configuration of communicative relations that harbours 'triple contingency' (Strydom 1999e) in distinction to the classical sociological concept of double contingency. By relating learning to it, Trenz and Eder were able to take it a step further, conceiving of 'societal learning in situations of triple contingency' or 'collective learning by triple contingency' (2004: 12). Delanty does not mention this concept explicitly, but that the idea is basic to his theory of cosmopolitanism is indicated by his statement that 'cosmopolitanism…is related…to social relations based on contingency' (2005: 34, 36). Not only does he emphasise throughout the constitutive significance of the 'global public' (2006: 27, 31, 32, 35, 36, 37, 40), but concurrently he also insists on consistently bearing in mind the threefold coordinated framework of communicative perspectives embracing the 'self' or 'we', the 'other' and the 'global public' (2006: 30, 37, 40), the latter representing 'the broader context of the world' in which the active participants are constituted as such and thus find themselves. Over and above the competing institutional and civil society actors, then, he sees the global public as the aspect of globalization most pertinent to a theory of cosmopolitanism; as constitutive of the social; as the ever present third point of view or the major resonance which contextualises all public communication and discourse; and as the presence in response to which processes of communicative transformation or learning take place, thus allowing the discursive construction of the social world (2006: 32, 31, 36, 35, 37).

Compared to aggregative, institutional, associational and double contingency collective learning, societal learning taking place under conditions of triple contingency represents the collective learning mechanism which brings us closest to the communicative self-constitution and self-organization of society.[17] It is here that the 'cosmopolitan moment', as Delanty calls it, occurs—which is the transformative moment of the 'creative combination of different forces' (2006: 38). The threefold set of contingently related communicative relations increases and intensifies public communication and resonance. It draws more participants and observers into the situation, and it renders cultural models reflexive, autonomous and discursively available, thus activating a plethora of cultural resources for self-reflection, self-problematisation, translation, connectivity and the transformation of self-understanding. And it compels both participants and observers to resonate by making unequivocal options and communicating these options effectively, while either anticipating the response of the public or accommodating themselves to the public.

Such learning is made possible by the emergence of public spheres from the local to the global level, of discursive forms and discourses, and a public representing the competence to observe, evaluate, judge and to form opinion. In turn, public communication provides the medium for the spatial, temporal and structural expansion of the intersubjective context of learning, right up to the communicatively mediated or discursive public sphere providing the necessary infrastructure for the threefold communicative relations making possible societal learning. In proportion at such a public sphere, together with its constitutive public emerges, an improvement in the conditions of both participation and monitoring results. Such improvement facilitates, yet also makes more complex, the achievement of both collectively constructed definitions and decisions, and the enhancement of the conditions of discourse and hence democratisation. These two achievements, what respectively may be called 'condensation' and 'confirmation' (Brandom 1994), are characteristic features of cosmopolitanism in the proper sense of the word—that is, discursive cosmopolitanism.

CONCLUSION

These reflections sought to take further Gerard Delanty's theory of cosmopolitanism which centrally depends on a connection between cosmopolitanism and learning within the context of the contemporary process of globalization. An attempt was made to do so by embedding his theory in the tradition of sociological learning theory inspired by Habermas by which it is informed and to draw out some of the theoretical implications of his position.

The key insight guiding the reflections was Delanty's establishment of a link between cosmopolitanism and learning whereby he opened up a theoretical perspective for approaching globalization from the inside out. The central step in the argument, therefore, was the differentiation of Delanty's general concept of learning into five types, sociologically distinguished from one another, on the basis of the varying intersubjective, situational contexts in which they transpire. This made it possible, in turn, to proceed to two further dimensions—although this original order of discovery was not mirrored exactly in the order of presentation in the paper. First, not only could Delanty's different types of cosmopolitanism be expanded and theoretically systematised, but they could also be made more concrete by being located in social reality and their guiding cultural models of world openness being specified. Second, it was necessary to decompose the process of globalization into its essential dimensions and to theoretically relate them to one another in such a way that the different types of cosmopolitanism and the respective forms of learning they harbour could be aligned with those dimensions. This analysis prepared the ground for an appreciation of the diversity of learning processes and corresponding cultural models that are brought into play by cosmopolitan processes as they fill out and drive forward the multilevel process of globalization from the inside.

The analysis culminated in the argument that cosmopolitanism in the proper sense of the word as understood by Delanty—the creation and articulation of cultural models in and through a process of communicative mediation resulting in the transformation of self-understandings as well as of society in the direction of greater world openness—coincides with the most demanding, least probable but most adequate kind of learning—societal (triple contingency) learning—which feeds on lower levels of learning and their outcomes and is possible only under conditions where the full threefold structure of communication is in sway.

If the task of this essay—namely, the explication of the relations among cosmopolitanism, globalization and learning—has been accomplished with any degree of success at all, then Delanty's theory of cosmopolitanism should appear as somewhat more theoretically embedded in the tradition of critical theory from which it stems.

Notes

PART I: COLLECTIVE LEARNING

Chapter 1: Collective Learning

1. Vester (1970), Na'aman (1978), Vasquez (1976), Buro (1977, 1982), Mushaben (1985) and Wasmuth (1985).
2. Of particular importance here are Habermas's reconstruction of historical materialism and the Starnberg research programme on the development of moral consciousness and the sociology of law conducted under his direction.
3. Eder (1982, 1985a, 1985b, 1986), Miller (1986), Frankenberg and Rödel (1981), Honneth (1985a), and Wellmer (1986).
4. Accordingly, Miller (1986: 15-22) is able to draw a distinction between 'genetic individualism' and 'genetic interactionism.'
5. This pattern is: (i) individual learning, (ii) enhancement of the collective systems of interpretation, (iii) social movements experimenting with and stabilising new interpretations, and (iv) anchorage of a new level of system differentiation in the new institutional complex. See Habermas (1979a: 98, 111, 121, 125, 144, 154, 165, and 1981, II: 229-93).
6. This deficit provides the reference point of the critiques Miller, Eder, Honneth and Wellmer level against Habermas. See note 3 above.
7. Habermas (1979a: 122), my emphasis. That this is not a problem that can be attributed to the translation is clear from the original text: 'die in Weltbildern bereits ausgebildeten Rationalitätsstrukturen…' (1976b: 37).
8. To the extent that Habermas employs this strategy he may be criticised for 'cognitive idealism' or 'intellectualism.' See Eder (1985a: 56), Honneth (1986) and Schnädelbach (1986).
9. In the construction of this framework, I disagree with Jeffrey Alexander (1982: 65, 114-5) who claims that 'action and order' represent 'the most general basis of social scientific cognition.' The fundamental parameters of social reality and hence the presuppositions of social scientific discourse are, in my opinion, more complex than he would have us believe.
10. I take this change in emphasis as providing the starting point for a new departure, the development of what I call the 'theory of sociation' (*Theorie der Vergesellschaftung*). See Strydom (1986-87).

Chapter 2: The Ontogenetic Fallacy

1. The critique of Habermas's position to be reviewed below applies, in my opinion, with equal force to the work of his colleague, collaborator and friend, Karl-Otto Apel, particularly as represented by his publication of 1988.

2. These critical perspectives include the following arguments:
   - Habermas's theory of socio-cultural evolution, following the classical theories, ultimately gives primacy to natural evolution (Eder 1988: 18);
   - Habermas makes the question of the classification of societies the central question of the theory of socio-cultural evolution, while the central issue is really whether the appropriation of nature is related to learning processes in the dimension of practical reason (1988: 19);
   - Habermas's view of a unilinear and unequivocal process of rationalisation in modern times is unjustified in light of the fact that the modern form of the symbolic appropriation of nature is ambivalent (1988: 23);
   - Habermas's theory of evolution, while correctly emphasising morality, does not radically enough free evolution from natural or universal history, which implies that the location of moral evolution is much more subtle than he would have us believe (1988: 33, 219);
   - Habermas's moralisation of historical materialism places the emphasis on the inner reality of society and as a consequence excludes nature from the theory (1988: 33-4, 51-2) and thus becomes insensitive to the ecological problematic (1988: 36);
   - Habermas operates with an inadequate theory of culture in that he, over and above the rules of productive practices, takes account of the rules of distributive practices by way of moral consciousness, but thereby excludes consumptive practices (1988: 36-7);
   - Habermas's competence theoretical conceptualisation of evolution as the phenotypic manifestation or embodiment of genotypic characteristics betrays a biologistic tendency which leads to a concept of society the emergent properties of which are shifted onto the systemic dimension (1988: 290);
   - Habermas's theory of evolution quarationalistic theory assumes an implicit compulsion towards learning, but what sets it in motion and the social presuppositions of the process are not taken into account (1988: 290-91);
   - Habermas conceives of the theory of evolution as a structural theory of what has been learned, while it should rather be conceived as a structural theory of the practical application of what has been learned (1988: 302);
   - Habermas presents structural models of social formations whereas what is required for the theory of evolution are structural models of praxis (1988: 303);
   - Habermas's theory of evolution, emphasising understanding and cooperation, is not a theory of historical evolutionary processes but a normative theory, a utopian counter-model of modernity (1988: 308);
   - Habermas operates with an affirmative concept of evolution (1988: 309);
   - Habermas seeks to resolve the directional problem in evolution by recourse to developmental logic, but this constitutes nothing less than the ontogenetic fallacy (1988: 310);
   - Habermas constructs ideal stages of evolution rather than identifying real stages (1988: 320);
   - Habermas tries to gauge practical reason and its evolution from ethical systems, but this is possible only with reference to social praxis in which moralisation labour is done, as represented by cultural, political and social movements (1988: 372-3);

- to the extent that Habermas holds to the conception of moral evolution as culminating in modernity, he entertains an evolution-theoretical myth, indeed an ideology which should not be mistaken for a counterfactual (1988: 373);
- Habermas makes correct assumptions about moral learning, but applies them incorrectly: the stages of development do not culminate in modernity, but can be identified in all societies (1988: 375); and finally
- Habermas assumes too close a relationship between learning and evolution (1988: 376).

3. The expression *Vergesellschaftung* runs from such classical authors as Marx, Weber and Simmel through early 20th-century writers such as Lukács and Adorno down to contemporary social theorists like Habermas and Offe. It indeed makes its appearance in English-language literature, yet in such a range of confusing translations that the formation of an awareness of *Vergesellschaftung* as a key concept of social theory was inhibited. Among the translations are the following: socialisation (in both the English-language academic sociological and the Marxist sense), societalisation, sociation, association, appropriation, adaptation and integration. I have provided a preliminary overview in Strydom (1986-87).
4. For several years now I have been engaged in developing a theoretical position which I propose to refer to as 'the theory of sociation'. I have arrived at this position by setting myself off, on the one hand, from Habermas's synchronic-structuralist theory of communicative action and, on the other, from the opposed theory of praxis of his explicit (e.g. Honneth and Eder) and implicit critics (e.g. Touraine and Bourdieu). In strategic respects, it differs sharply from Giddens's rather abstractly named 'theory of structuration'. For one, rather than the duality of structure and agency, it focuses on mediation.

Chapter 3: Sociocultural Evolution or the Evolution of Practical Reason

1. On the by no means fully analysed relation between Habermas and Piaget, see: Oevermann (1976), Harten (1977a, 1977b), Miller (1986: 207-20) and Freitag (1983).
2. Eder never neglects to acknowledge Miller's contribution to the development of his new position, for instance: Eder (1985a: 7, 1985b: 869-90 and 1988: 296).
3. See also Strydom (1987).
4. See Eder (1983) for his initial consideration of Giddens's contribution.
5. Relevant literature and bibliographical details are included in Plotkin (1982) and Mossakowski and Roth (1982).
6. From a certain point of view, to be sure, Habermas's position would seem to be closer to the official genetic than the epigenetic theory: he tries to anticipate the next evolutionary step by imagining the most advantageous modification rather than discovering in the epigenetic system the changes it is capable of producing.
7. A critical investigation into the 'obscure empirical problem' Schmid highlights here has been conducted by Linkenbach (1986). See also Harrison (1991).
8. Habermas initially introduced the idea of a reconstructive theory of social evolution in the context of his controversy with Luhmann, the first stage of which is documented in Habermas and Luhmann (1971). While the Habermas-Luhmann debate proved to be rather wide-ranging and protracted, as shown by later works by both Habermas (1984a, 1987a, 1987b) and Luhmann (1984), the

issue of the theory of social evolution has been an important element of the controversy. See, for instance: Luhmann (1976) and Habermas (1979b) which originally appeared with Luhmann's essay in the journal *Geschichte und Gesellschaft*.

9. In more recent work, Eder introduces legitimating practices, as thematised by Bourdieu, as a mechanism of social evolution in addition to collective learning and class conflict. Over and above the production or constitution of society, it is necessary to take into account the developmental processes transpiring in the cultural representations of society. See Eder (1992, 1989).
10. Eder (1988: 304-5) cites the ritual reversal of a social order and class conflict, in the sense of practices through which the historically specific social order is being dealt with, as examples of structural models of praxis.
11. For a critique of Habermas on the basis of the failure of an attempt by the authors to apply his ontogenetic model to historical material, see Frankenberg and Rödel (1981: 9-31).
12. The position Eder takes here establishes a connection with Lyotard and his critique of Habermas, on which see Frank (1988, 1989). The issue is whether and, if so, how dissensus can be integrated into Habermas's position which emphasises or, rather, over-emphasises consensus. Karl-Otto Apel, friend and colleague of Habermas, has recently in an interview with Rötzer (1987: 70) without any change in his position emphatically insisted on the possibility. Habermas seems to be doing the same in an unpublished manuscript from 1989 entitled 'Individuelle Willensbildung unter den Aspekten des Zweckmässigen, des Guten und des Gerechten, particularly pp. 25-6. Their philosophical stance nevertheless seems to place them in a defensive position when it comes to opening up the problem of the relation between consensus and dissensus. As regards Eder and Lyotard, whereas the latter at least theoretically neglects, if not denies, the relation between morality and rationality, as van Reijen (1987: 567) shows, the latter integrates dissensus while concentrating precisely on this nexus, and he seems to be able to differentiate it in a manner not open to Habermas and Apel. See Eder (1992) in which the significance of contradictions and conflict for communiation and social evolution is of focal concern.
13. Sinha (1988: 78) circumscribes what is called the 'phylocultural complex' as follows: 'the set of assumptions dominating evolutionary and developmental studies at the turn of the century, based upon concepts of parallelism and repetition at different "levels" of biological and cultural organization'.
14. Compare Giddens (1984: 239-42) who lists in general four so-called 'dangers' of evolutionary thought: unilineal compression, homological compression, normative illusion and temporal distortion.
15. Habermas (1987b: 336-67) offers a summary of his position under the title of 'the normative content of modernity'. In the text, I have modified Frederick Lawrence's translation of the original 'Gehalt' by 'content' to 'import' for the reason that Habermas takes pains to emphasise that he is not concerned with orienting contents, but rather with structural possibilities facilitating the rationalisation of action.
16. The use of this expression does not imply that Eder has postmodernist leanings; on the contrary, he argues in favour of 'reflexive modernity'.
17. Touraine (1981: 14) submits that evolutionism forms part of the instrumentarium of self-description of industrial society: '...industrial society...represents itself by the place it occupies in an evolution it describes as progress'.

18. See Dubiel (1988, 1989) for a discussion of the question of whether there are two critical theories or not: Adorno and Horkheimer's 'theory of pure domination' and Habermas's 'theory of abstract emancipation'. Against this background, it may be submitted that Eder's critical theory of the social evolution of practical reason goes some distance beyond these two approaches.
19. The recent past has seen the proliferation of what may be called 'utilisation research' which throws a good deal of light on the problematic addressed by Eder in his theory of the social evolution of practical reason. See, for instance, Evers and Nowotny (1987), Beck and Bonß (1989) and an interesting older work, Wilden (1972).
20. By means of this notion of critique, Eder takes up the theme of a conference held in Frankfurt in 1987 with a view to self-critically inquiring into the continuation of a commitment to enlightenment under the radically changed conditions of the late 20th century. See Rüsen *et al.* (1988).
21. This is a reference to the title of Habermas's collection of political writings, *Die neue Unübersichtlichkeit* (1985b), the title essay of which appeared in English as 'The New Obscurity: The Crisis of the Welfare State and the Exhaustion of Utopian Energies' (1986).

Chapter 4: Critical Theory and the New Social Movements

1. For a systematisation of the various critiques of Habermas's ontogenetically based developmental-logical theory of social evolution, see Strydom (1992; Chapter 2 in this volume).
2. Despite all the positive things she has to say, some too positive, Cohen (1985) argues, first, that the gap between macro social theory and the theory of social movements can be bridged by the hermeneutically accessible concept of civil society, and, second, that Habermas has not yet properly integrated the categories of civil society into his theory, from which follows, thirdly, that she is convinced that he does not yet dispose over a position that is sufficiently sensitive to social movements.
3. White (1988: 91, 97, 102, 124) introduces this latter perspective, but neither develops it nor sees that it remains underdeveloped in Habermas.
4. For example, Cohen (1985) seeks to synthesise resource mobilization theory, the identity oriented paradigm and the Habermasian approach, and Eder (1988: 225-9, 259-61, 264-6) the progressive theory of evolution and the counter-theory according to which 'development turns in circles' (256). A systematic development of such a synthetic theory is presented in Strydom (1988-89).
5. Among the important contributions towards such a concept are, for example: Thompson (1968), Hobsbawm and Rude (1969), Hill (1972), Bürger (1974), Woodcock (1977), Worsley (1984), Schäfer (1985) and Hepp (1987).
6. Although Eder here rejects a maximalist position on meaning interpretation and hence cultural determinism, his dependence on symbolic structuralism nevertheless places him in a somewhat tenuous position.
7. Cohen (1985: 712-5) regards Habermas's sensitivity to ambiguity as a major gain.
8. Since the late 1980s, a concerted effort is underway in critical theory to come to terms with and appropriate the problem of culture without surrendering the achievements of the Enlightenment. See, for example, Rüsen *et al.* (1989).
9. See also Privitera (1990), originally a dissertation completed under Habermas in 1987.

10. Here I diverge sharply from Eder (1988). Since I regard all the dimensions of culture to be underpinned by cognitive-symbolic structures, I isolate one of the three subsets rather that play the symbolic out against the cognitive and the normative, as he does.
11. Here I presuppose the following classification of culture and its institutional and biological-psychological underpinnings:

Cognitive	*Normative*	*Aesthetic/Conative*
Truth	Legitimacy	Truthfulness
Facts	Norms	Experiences
Science/Technology	Morality/Law/Politics	Feeling/Emotion
Intelligence	Conscience	Motivation/Expression

12. I do so with reference to Franz Koppe's (1983: 126, 219) highlighting of the late Greek word 'ἐνδεοητικος' in his discussion of the basic concepts of aesthetics.
13. Eder (1988: 34-5) draws on Marshall Sahlins's (1976) interpretation and critique of Marx's use of this threefold distinction which, in my view, leads to a lack of clarity in his exposition of the relation between the cognitive and symbolic dimensions of culture.
14. Eder (1988: 273-6) develops the idea of an aesthetic or social critique out of Habermas's concept of the validity claim of truthfulness with reference to Bourdieu's 'social critique of the judgement of taste' (1986).
15. Parsons (1978: 320-2) speaks of the 'expressive revolution' as a 'change...in the relative standing of different components of the inherited value system' and thus at least suggests the possibility of an increase in communication based on concrete experience, but then continues to narrow it down by linking it too closely to 'a new religious movement'. Münch (1984: 119-26) offers a voluntaristic interpretation of the expressive revolution. Neither of them, however, establishes a connection with the new social movements and the question of nature. See Strydom (1991) for a more comprehensive overview.
16. Habermas (1987a: 395) himself speaks of the 'new conflicts arising along the seams between system and lifeworld'.

Chapter 5: Contemporary Social Evolutionary Theory

1. A more comprehensive view could have been taken in this essay by including the work of Runciman (1989) also, yet the incorporation of his position in the present account is made difficult by the fact that, by contrast with the German and Swedish schools, he gives little or no weight to interaction, communication, discourse and culture. Due to limitations of space, I also have to forego potentially interesting sociological reflections on the process of convergence in terms of such considerations as theoretical dynamics, the social relations of theorising, communication, friendship, and so forth.
2. For a brief reconstruction of the context of the most recent nodal point in the development of the theory of social evolution, which provides the background of the new European rapprochement, see Strydom (1993: 305-8, Chapter 3 in this volume).
3. Of all the representatives, Eder is the one who has carried forward and transformed the Habermasian theory. Besides Habermas himself, another

representative to whom no attention will be given in the present context is Rainer Döbert (1973, 1981). Max Miller (1986) also proved crucial to Eder's development, yet his own contribution is pitched less at the level of evolution as such.

4. Tom Burns, the leading figure of the Uppsala school, is an American. In later as yet unpublished writings Burns provided me with, such as Burns and Dietz (1997, 1999), references—but no more than only references—are indeed included to both Giesen and Eder.
5. An idea of the self-critical reflection in which Eder engaged in the course of his development of the theory of social evolution can be gathered, for instance, from Eder (1986b: 335; 1988: 33, 66-7, 288-9, 296, 347; and 1996a: 196) and Eder and Schmidtke (1998: 435).
6. Eder raised various critical points: the individualism of Giesen's action-theoretic rationalism (Eder 1988: 44); the naturalism of Giesen's insistence on an independent selection process (Eder 1988: 42); the struggle versus nature as the unquestioned naturalistic presupposition of Giesen's selection-theoretic model (Eder 1988: 44); Giesen's behaviouristic or non-cognitive concept of learning (Eder 1985: 459); Giesen's strategy of adding *ad hoc* assumptions about sociocultural evolution to his Darwinism which betrays the lack of a systematic theory able to deal with cultural phenomena (Eder 1985a: 31).
7. Giesen (1991a: 172, 1991b: 12) explicitly acknowledges Eder's contribution in this respect.
8. In so far as the model of code, process and situation is informed by Karl Popper's three-world theory (Popper 1972; Giesen 1991b: 12), however, a question arises about its adequacy. See, for example, Habermas's (1984a: 76-84) critique of Popper's empiricist attachment and ontological and scientistic leanings. To my knowledge, no one has as yet developed a critique of Giesen along these lines.
9. In so far as Burns and Dietz adopt the Darwinian framework as a general theory for the unification of sociology, their position is similar to that of the German Darwinian school, particularly Giesen.
10. The Uppsala authors' criticism of evolutionism includes a critical mention of Habermas's developmental stage model, but they positively single out his highly relevant conception of discursive processes generating and reshaping culture (Burns and Dietz 1992a: 260; 1997: 3; Dietz and Burns 1992: 188). Curiously enough, they make no reference to Eder who has salvaged this dimension from Habermas's developmental-logical theory and developed it in detail in a series of significant articles and books
11. It is surprising that although they explicitly undertake to give an overview of new theories and the nascent evolutionary paradigm as the context of their own version, the representatives of the Uppsala school do not make any reference in their published work to the substantial contributions of either Giesen or Eder. This is all the more surprising if one considers that Giesen has already earlier worked out a similar position and that Eder disposes over an elaborate theory of the kind of social learning that Burns and Dietz regularly invoke. In 1991, moreover, Burns and Dietz (1992a) presented one of their papers at the Wissenschaftszentrum in Berlin where their attention undoubtedly must have been drawn to the outstanding German contributions to social evolutionary theory. Quite understandably, Giesen on occasion speaks with a note of frustration of the 'remarkable ignorance' (1995: 229) of Burns and Dietz regarding earlier contributions to the new social theory of evolution. References to Giesen and Eder make their appearance for the first time only in later unpublished work (Burns and Dietz 1997, 1999).

12. These rules are conceived as 'schemes' or cognitive frameworks (Dietz and Burns 1992: 197; Burns and Dietz 1997: 12) which as such are to be regarded as Bourdieuian 'structures' (Dietz and Burns 1992: 198).
13. The Uppsala authors accordingly conceive of cultural change as 'a change in the frequency distribution of rules in the population' (Dietz and Burns 1992: 188). In so far as this implies a theory of culture as a social theory of the distribution of knowledge, the question arises as to whether this is not an aggregationist position—which would be unfit adequately to come to terms with the micro-macro problematic (see Strydom 2000: 14).
14. These processes include the social construction of reality through conflicts over definitions and resources (Dietz *et al.* 1989). Burns and Dietz speak of 'bounded constructionism' (1997: 5) in view of the fact that it takes place within the parameters of both environmental and social constraints.
15. The Uppsala authors share with both Eder and Giesen the aspiration that evolutionary sociology should include theoretical reasoning at the level of the micro-macro link.
16. As a rule, Eder speaks not of 'Darwinian' but rather of 'Darwinistic' theory, which can be taken as an indication of his critical stance towards it.
17. It is interesting that while Eder himself takes this alternative route, he distinguishes his own proposal from anti-Darwinian progressivist theories of evolution in sociology which are based on speculation—whether with reference to philosophies of history or to orthogenetic assumptions allowing the nature of the individual organism to fix the potential and direction of evolution (1985a: 22).
18. Judging from his later work, Eder indeed discovered another logic, yet a significantly different one, in which social conflicts are embedded—what he calls 'a logic of separation and coordination' (1993: 191) or, at the evolutionary level, the 'dual logic' of being 'simultaneously chaotic and ordered' which is followed by the change of rule systems (1996a: 195). In the same sense, he conceives of the micro- and macro-dimensions as different levels of abstraction of the same phenomenon, namely rules regulating either the diverging constructive activities of actors or the coordination of those activities (Eder and Schmidtke 1998: 434).
19. Eder initially introduced this concept of conflict in the early 1980s. See, for instance, Eder (1983-84). In the essay of 1973, it was prefigured by his emphasis on operative structures.
20. Three substantial sections, one on the theory of evolution, were left out of the English edition, and another considerably shortened. This abridgement is regrettable, particularly as far as evolution is concerned, but the English edition is considerably enhanced by the addition of a new part on the politics of nature. In its original form, this part played a key role in providing a theoretical basis for an extensive two-year research project conducted in the early 1990s in Italy, Germany, Ireland, Britain and France under the direction of Eder himself. The present author directed the Irish component of this research project. This third part, adds significantly to the fine-tuning of Eder's theory of social evolution.
21. For an earlier, more detailed analysis, see Strydom (1992: 80-83, Chapter 2 in this volume).
22. Despite the fact that they vehemently criticise developmentalism, which presupposes the identity of learning and evolution, the Uppsala authors fail to make clear how they understand the relation between learning and evolution. On occasion, rather surprisingly, their formulations are ambiguous, even seeming as though they might be informed by a developmental perspective—for example:

'Social learning is the cultural analogue of the genetic transmission process. Processes of this kind will lead to changes over time in the prevalence of rules in a culture. As noted above, such changes are cultural evolution' (Dietz and Burns 1992: 190).

23. Strangely enough, Eder uses only the concept of 'ontogenesis' to designate both of these dimensions.
24. See also Dietz *et al.* (1990: 166) on the conflict between explanations based on culture and those based on practical reason, and the possibility of their reconciliation.
25. Eder first toyed with the idea of structural models of practice in a publication dating from 1983, apparently under the influence of Anthony Giddens, but in this context he still defended the idea of developmental logic (Eder 1983: 255). Later these models would be articulated in terms of constructive activity in the medium of public communication in the context of a historically specific discourse. It would be more correct to say that this position emerged from a synthesis of ideas deriving from Habermas, Touraine and Bourdieu.
26. According to a later formulation: 'Evolution is not to be conceived as the change of society or some of its subsystems...but as the change of structures that regulate the construction of the system (and its subsystems)' (Eder 1992: 322).
27. In the present context where the focus is on the new European rapprochement, it is not possible to go into the interesting details of Eder's analysis of institutionalisation. Suffice it to say that he here makes an important contribution to what may be called 'the new cognitive sociology' which is at present in the process of emerging.
28. On those occasions that he does refer positively to Giesen, all originally dating from 1985 (Eder, 1985a: 47; 1993a: 149), it is where Giesen concerns himself with public communication. The works in question are Giesen (1980: 39, 52, 69-70) and Giesen (1983). The latter publication dealing with moral entrepreneurs in public discourse clearly played a decisive role in changing Eder's attitude towards the German Darwinian school. As his concern with public discourse suggests, Giesen here in turn responded to Eder's earlier criticisms by adopting a communication and discourse theory over and above his own Darwinism.
29. In more recent writings, Giesen (1991b: 173) also refers to his position as 'situation oriented' This is more adequate in view of the fact that the addition of a constructive dimension with historical depth not only changes Darwinian selectionist theory, but also goes beyond it toward a new post-classical theory.
30. This cooperation goes back to the 1980s and intensified in the early 1990s around questions of collective identity in general and citizenship in particular in the period during which Eder held a professorship at the European University Institute, Florence. Giesen replaced him there in 1994-95 when he left for the Humboldt University.
31. The particular understanding of interactionism in each of the three strands forms the basis of differences between them that will have to be resolved one way or the other by a coherent formulation of the emerging theory of evolution. Eder (1999b) offers an incisive analysis of some of the issues involved in theorising interactionism.
32. This does not necessarily exclude the acceptance of weak or soft naturalism and hence the possibility of the interference of nature in the sociocultural world (see Strydom 2002). That the new theory of evolution thereby does not fall foul of cultural idealism is demonstrated by its correction of the traditional sociological neglect of the relation between society and nature and, hence, its

ability to come to grips with the current global ecological problem. See, for example, Eder (1988, 1996a), Dietz *et al.* (1990: 167-68) and Burns and Dietz (1992a: 276; 1997: 44-59). Some formulations of the Uppsala school make one wonder, however, whether they do not perhaps lean too strongly in a realist direction. In mitigation of this, however, see Dietz *et al.* (1989) and Burns and Dietz (1997) for the explicit adoption of a constructivist position. The relation between these two positions remains unclear, however.

PART II: TRIPLE CONTINGENCY

Chapter 6: Triple Contingency

1. In a recent paper on object-oriented forms of sociality emerging in postsocial societies, Knorr Cetina (1997) introduces an interesting new perspective but surprisingly remains attached to the traditional sociological thesis of double contingency, albeit without mentioning it explicitly. While she stresses expertise and its 'dehiscence' into society in her theory of 'objectualization', she overlooks the fact that expertise is impossible in public communication. It is precisely in the principle of the public or the 'universality of non-expertise', as Fuller (1993: 285) puts it, that the concept of triple contingency finds its starting point.
2. In this context, 'commerce' refers not simply to economic matters but to all the nascent global forms of intercourse of the time. See Heilbron (1998: 77-106).
3. This was Hannah Arendt's (1971) reason for her infamous attack against the social sciences and her pronounced anti-sociological animus.
4. Curiously enough, Thomas McCarthy (1994: 89) commits a version of this error when he simply equates the third-person perspective with the role of the uninvolved spectator.
5. See also Parsons (1964: 36 and 1977b: 167-8).
6. Alfred Schutz (1967: 170) formulated the problem as follows: 'And these meaning contexts of mine will be "subjective" to the extent that I am attending to your actual conscious experiences themselves and not merely to my own lived experiences of you. Furthermore, as I watch you, I shall see that you are oriented to me, that you are seeking the subjective meanings of my words, my actions, and what I have in mind insofar as you are concerned. And I will in turn take account of the fact that you are thus oriented to me, and this will influence both my intentions with respect to you and how I act toward you. This again you will see, I will see that you have seen it, and so on.' Max Miller (1992a: 10) offers a clear summary statement of double contingency: 'Ego's perspective on ego/alter relationships is contingent on alter's perspective and vice versa. There are two self-other circles that have to be coordinated.' Knorr Cetina (1997: 20, 22) presents a new controversial 'objectual' version focusing on 'social forms binding self and other' based on the 'inter-object-person' relation.
7. Miller (1992a: 10-11) also criticises theories of role-taking or social perspective taking, such as put forward by Piaget, Mead, Flavell, Feffer and Selman, for concentrating on only one side of double contingency: 'They have been interested in ego's and alter's abilities to take multiple roles or perspectives, and they have left open the question of how this taking of multiple roles or perspectives can be coordinated between alter and ego.' Focusing on coordination, as he does, Miller is obviously closer to Habermas than to Luhmann.
8. Although McCarthy (1994: 92, 100) acknowledges the structuring import of a point of view bringing legitimation pressure to bear on actors, he completely

underestimates not only the third-person standpoint which acts as its vehicle but, by way of the critique of the 'oculocentrism' of the traditional subject/object model of knowledge, also the new social scientific understanding of observation. Knorr Cetina (1997: 7-8) incorporates the observational dimension by way of '"other" cultural elements and practices' or the 'alien culture...of knowledge and expertise' which spills over and gets woven into society. Here the third point of view is reduced to the expert and expert cultures.

9. Social scientists are just beginning to appreciate the significance of the observing public at the global level, for example, Hegedus (1990: 263-80), Habermas (1996: 192-236) and Beck (1996). McCarthy (1994: 92-3) stresses the need for the social sciences, critical theory in particular, to adopt a consistently global perspective, but it is unclear how they could achieve this if they are simultaneously required to renounce the third point of view.
10. See, for example, recent critical volumes such as Wellmer (1986), Honneth and Joas (1991), Calhoun (1992), Hoy and McCarthy (1994), Rosenfeld (1996), Rasmussen (1996), and Nancy Fraser (1997).
11. It is only by stressing the communicative process or discourse that it is possible to temporalise, pragmaticise and contextualise communicative rationality without having to surrender transcendence or idealisation, as McCarthy (1994: 72) rightly demands.
12. Lately, both resource mobilisation theory (e.g. McAdam *et al.*, 1996) and rational choice theory (e.g. Esser 1996) have also undergone the cognitive turn.
13. In her recent work, however, Knorr Cetina (1997) understands knowledge and cultural models in terms of the universalisation of expertise rather than of the universality of non-expertise.
14. Various models are available for dealing with the dominant definition of reality: Foucault (1977) provides a model of exclusionary mechanisms and Chomsky (1989) a model of social and cultural control, while a hegemony model is put forward by Gramsci (1985) and followers of his such as Laclau and Mouffe (1985) and Eley (1992).
15. It should be obvious that, despite the employment of the word 'observer', the critique of 'oculocentrism', as articulated by McCarthy (1994: 100) does not apply to the position taken here since use is made of a communication model.
16. The task of bringing out this dimension is bound to loom ever larger as contemporary communication societies are transformed also into knowledge societies. At issue in the latter is not only expert knowledge but in particular taken-for-granted knowledge that frames expert knowledge and, typically, is discursively brought to the level of awareness.
17. In her recent work, for example, Knorr Cetina (1997: 25) submits that: 'sociology...played an important role in bringing about the shift in mentality through which individuals came to be seen as the bearers of personal costs of collective structures'. This is not wrong, of course, but what she overlooks is that sociology only emerged in a cultural space opened up by a broader discourse.
18. The legitimationist position proceeds from the moral criterion of good and bad, evaluates the social actors according to it, and finally identifies with the one it judges to represent the good and hence as being legitimate.

Chapter 7: The Problem of Triple Contingency in Habermas

1. While I borrow the concept of triple contingency from Eder and Schmidtke (1998: 429) who link '*eine dreifache Kontingenz*' to the role of the observer of interaction neglected in classical action theory, I have proposed to develop it in

relation to the role of the public in communication societies (Strydom 1999e, Chapter 6 in this volume). See also the conclusion Delanty (1999b) draw from this proposal.

2. An insightful older critique of Habermas from the point of view of 'the contingency of communication' (Wenzel and Hochmuth 1989), which concentrates on the limitations of his formal pragmatics but operates with an ill-defined concept of contingency, tends in this latter direction. Rather than playing contingency off against Habermas in a transcendent critique, as does contextualism, the present contribution pursues a more theoretically controlled immanent critique. An anonymous referee of *Sociological Theory* brought Wenzel and Hochmuth's article to my attention.
3. For an analysis of some of the theoretical and methodological implications of the theorem of triple contingency, see Strydom (1999e). A substantive analysis of Habermas's treatment of the public would have to take into account publications such as Negt and Kluge (1972), Gerhards and Neidhardt (1990), Cohen and Arato (1992), Calhoun (1992, 1993, 1996), Alexander (1993), Somers (1995a, 1995b), and Fraser 1997).
4. I have put forward some of these theoretical ideas in various writings (e.g. Strydom 1999a, 1999e, 2000, 2002), and at present I am working on a more systematic exposition provisionally called *The New Cognitive Sociology*, in which respect see Strydom (2006a, 2007)
5. An explanation for Parsons's reluctance to mention Schutz might perhaps be found in the misunderstanding that dogged their relationship. See Grathoff (1978).
6. To avoid complicating matters unnecessarily, the overview of Mead, Schutz and Parsons seeks to establish contact points for understanding Habermas's appropriation and use of the classical and neoclassical concept of double contingency. It thus leaves open the more penetrating question of whether these authors themselves went beyond double contingency or not. Mead (1974: 381), for instance, offers a critique of Kant that might be taken to suggest that he observed a higher level of contingency, but this needs investigation. An anonymous referee of *Sociological Theory* urged me to take Mead's critique of Kant into account.
7. Although not mentioning it explicitly, Habermas deals extensively and in detail with double contingency, both in his analysis of Mead's different versions and in his own proposal (Habermas 1987a: 8-9, 11, 13, 26, 35-6, 58-9).
8. For his earlier analysis of Mead, see Habermas (1988a: 63-6).
9. For his earlier analysis of Schutz, see Habermas (1988a: 106-9).
10. Wenzel and Hochmuth (1989: 261) critically focus on Habermas's distinction between lifeworld and situation. While lifeworld is contextually invariant and thus absorbs the threat of contingency, the situation as the site of continuous validity testing accommodates the risk of understanding, thus allowing two possibilities: either the establishment of a shared interpretation or the failure to do so. Although Habermas broaches the second possibility, the authors maintain that he systematically marginalises it, together with the model of communicative action oriented toward working through contextual contingencies.
11. As a crucial constitutive element of the contemporary public sphere, the other being the first- and second-person participants, the public has acquired an unparalleled epistemic authority, that through the resonance it represents, is decisive for determining which participants' influence prevails and what is collectively accepted as socially valid in the wake of a public communication

process. The role of the public is thus observing the participants, evaluating their respective contributions, and determining what is collectively valid and what is not. This role is of course complicated by the inherent pluralism of the public. The fact that it is itself divided into competing counterpublics or supporters, sympathisers, opponents, and bystanders diversifies the dynamics of the process of communicative competition and conflict over the collective validity of different cultural models or frames and makes it difficult to predict which cultural model or combination of models will finally be collectively accepted. For analyses of public communication processes in these terms, see, for example, Eder (1996a) and Strydom (2000, 2002). On the concept of public resonance, see Strydom (2003, Chapter 9 in this volume).

12. As indicated earlier, I assume a cognitive or epistemic theory that not only recognises the central role of the public in societal communication processes, but also seeks to theorise the role of the public in terms of triple contingency in the sense of a level beyond double contingency. The dynamics, unpredictability, and instability brought into communication processes by the public, which is moreover inherently pluralistic, are theoretically conceived in terms of the dynamic interrelation of both micro and macro cognitive or epistemic structures, including cultural models, in societal communication processes. Methodologically, this theoretical position is complemented by methodological situationalism in distinction to both methodological individualism and collectivism. Theoretically decisive for going beyond Habermas, therefore, is the twofold concern with a plurality of cultural models rather than only the one relevant from the moral point of view and with the evolution of situationally specific cultural models or epistemic structures. On this programme, see Strydom (1999a, 1999e, 2000, 2002). See also Delanty (1999b), who draws on these ideas, as well as Eder (1993a, 1996a, 1999a) and Eder and Schmidtke (1998) for related ideas.
13. The difference between Apel and Habermas is that while Apel insists that he is a transcendental philosopher (personal communication, Niedernhausen, Germany, June 20, 1998), Habermas is critical of so-called foundationalism and seeks to accommodate the different perspectives of both the philosopher and the social scientist—a position I heard him spelling out in the academic context. In *Between Facts and Norms* (1996a: 6-7) he tries to make a virtue of this, although his characteristic emphasis is nevertheless conceptual and normative.
14. It is untenable at least in so far as it is given a stronger form than is required to justify engagement in intellectual work.
15. My argument, however, is not intended to be read as being in favour of Rawls, instead.

Chapter 8: Contingency: A Critique of Luhmann

1. For his earlier treatment of contingency in Parsons, see Luhmann (1976). Here he criticises Parsons for tending to bypass the theoretical significance of the problem of contingency, both as general problem and in the form of double contingency. His own proposal is to adopt a thoroughly functionalist approach that from the outset and throughout gives priority to the problem of contingency.
2. This was the case notwithstanding Habermas's own obvious sincerity. See, for example, Habermas and Luhmann 1971; Maciejewski 1973, 1974; Luhmann 1987; Habermas 1987a: 368-85; 1996a: 47-52, 341-51.

3. For a relatively early pertinent suggestion to take a step beyond Luhmann and Habermas on the basis of their commonalities and complementarities, see Arnason (1988: 194-5) and Eder (1988). See now also Miller (2002a).
4. This theory, which is a development of Habermas's, is a cognitive theory, like that of Luhmann himself, but it at the same time restores the sociologically so important normative dimension which Luhmann rejects out of hand.
5. All quotations from German texts are presented in my own translation.
6. In the later development of his work, Parsons extended this solution by his theory of symbolic media of interchange, as for instance in Parsons (1977b: 204-69). Thus Luhmann was able in his early assessment of Parsons to develop a position according to which media such as truth, love, money and power are 'a way of coping with double contingency on the level of the social system of society' (1976: 515).
7. A basic assumption that Parsons made here and was shared by many others besides, which accounts for the traditional sociological integrationist or harmonious concept of culture, is that language as such already involves symbolic generalisation. Luhmann (1992b: 379) is also aware of this. Be that as it may, the short circuit that makes possible this problematic conception can be traced to the missing distinction between cultural structures of a cognitive and symbolic kind—two dimensions which stand in a variable and dynamic relation.
8. It is untypical of Luhmann to make such admissions, and therefore it is unsurprising that he presents this one somewhat inconspicuously in a sub-clause.
9. Luhmann introduces important considerations relevant to contemporary methodological situationalism in his discussion of selection and selection contexts (1984: 188). On methodological situationalism, see for instance Knorr-Cetina (1988), Eder and Schmidtke (1998) and Boltanski and Thévenot (1999). Constructivism is a theme with which Luhmann deals in detail in *Die Wissenschaft der Gesellschaft* (1992a). For a general overview of constructivism, including Luhmann, see for example Delanty (1997).
10. It is at this juncture that Luhmann sees a relation between double contingency and self-reference: 'When ego experiences alter as an alter ego and acts within the same context of experience, then every determination that ego imposes on his or her own action refers back to himself or herself' (1984: 182).
11. It should be pointed out that although the subtitle of his main work, documenting his shift to autopoietic systems theory, leaves the impression of an aspiration towards a theory of social systems as a general theory, Luhmann has emphatically stated that his concern is with a 'sociological theory which aims to consolidate disciplinary relations' (1984: 11). The particular angle from which he wants to reconstitute sociology becomes apparent when one reads 'functional system' instead wherever he writes 'social system'.
12. For an analysis of the increasing differentiation and organization of communication processes, see, for instance, Luhmann (1984: 551-92); Gerhards and Neidhardt (1990); Habermas (1996a: 360-6); Strydom (1999e: 3-6).
13. See, for instance, Habermas's (1997b: 133-4) pertinent critique of dialogical philosophy. Here I wish to qualify, however, that in his analysis of the structure of communication Habermas himself fails to thematise the third person adequately. Emphasising 'the third person orientation toward something in the objective world' (134), he overlooks the fact that in communication the third-person point of view is embodied by the audience or public. This is peculiar for an author who has made an unparalleled contribution to the sociology of the public sphere (Habermas 1989, 1996a; Calhoun 1992). For a critical analysis of Habermas, see Strydom (1999d, 1999e, 2001).

14. Intended here is Peirce's threefold concept of the sign rather than Saussure's twofold concept. See, for example, Apel (1981), Rochberg-Halton (1982) and Joas (1992a).
15. 'Semantic mediation' can here be taken to refer to the semantics of social systems deriving from their functionally specific binary codes and programmes (Luhmann 1984: 602-3, 432-3), for instance, payment/non-payment and prices in the economic system; legal/illegal and laws in the legal system; truth/falsity and theories in the scientific system, and so forth.
16. Theoretically, one could, of course, interpret this quantitative concept in connectionist or network terms, but this still leaves a higher level of contingency relevant to social situations unaccounted for.
17. Miller apparently overlooks Luhmann's postulation of double contingency as basic theorem, however, since he focuses on Luhmann's concept of meaning and regards his assumption of the basic mutualistic organization of social systems or double contingency as a derivative assumption (1987: 197).
18. Luhmann himself makes communication central to his theory, as when he submits that 'communication is the autopoietic process of social systems' (1984: 530), but he treats it in a narrowly cognitivist (and eventually functionalist) manner without reintroducing, as he should do, the sociologically important social dimension embracing higher-level cognitive-symbolic, including normative, qualities. This leads to some critics describing his position not entirely unjustifiably yet somewhat inappropriately as 'behaviouristic' (e.g. Krawietz 1992: 19).
19. Elsewhere, Miller makes use of the concept 'intersystemic discourse' in distinction not only to Luhmann's 'functionally specific communication', but also Habermas's 'lifeworld communication' (1994: 109, 112). His own concept is, of course, an extension and development of Habermas's concept of discourse.
20. He presents detailed empirical analyses of this kind in Miller (1986).
21. Miller has an acute awareness of 'collective acceptance' and 'collective validity' (1986: 258-80; 1987: 187, 188, 200, 202; 1994: 116), but he treats it in such an abstract manner that he does not see it as the source of the limitation of too expansive openness or of the determination of the undetermined. In his critique of Luhmann's concept of double contingency, in other words, he does not pursue the problem of contingency to the end but takes a different track instead. The communication and discourse theoretical direction he takes is by no means mistaken or unfruitful, yet the theoretical question of contingency remains. At the more concrete level, Miller's (e.g. 1994: 111) work contains references to 'the public' and suggestions regarding the role it plays in communication processes, but it is never reflected upon in its own right, developed, and taken up in the context of the theoretical problem of contingency.
22. Luhmann's work indeed contains interesting formulations, such as for example: 'In the norm, acting is fitted to motivational foundations, and this means nothing less than being thematised in the context of observations of the second order. Observations of the second order are the operative basis for the structural differentiation of certain social systems. This means that society can conduct observations only in the form of communications' (1998: 57). Nevertheless, I am less positive than Eder and Schmidtke. In Luhmann, second order observation is tied to a bare naturalistic cognitivist or informational concept of communication. While the cognitive turn in sociology is doubtless of fundamental importance and not sufficiently appreciated in the discipline, an adequate conceptualisation of the third point of view requires not a narrow but a broad cognitive (embracing not only theoretical-empirical knowledge but also

moral-practical and aesthetic-practical knowledge) communication and discourse theory that allows the reintroduction of the reconstituted normative approach within its context (eg. Strydom 2007).

23. When Eder and Schmidtke (1998: 429) originally introduced the term '*dreifache Kontingenz*', they laboured under two limitations: they understood it exclusively in terms of observation and located it at the level of elementary social processes. Instead, I locate it within the context of societal communication processes and link it to the role of the public in such communications. An adequate theoretical explication of triple contingency would require that attention be given to what Miller calls 'collective acceptance' and 'collective validity' from the point of view of contingency. In addition, such theoretical explication needs to be related to methodological situationalism. The confines that methodological collectivism and moral philosophy traditionally impose on such questions must be transcended.
24. Different approaches toward conceiving such cultural models are emerging in contemporary sociology, but all of them presuppose a post-classical theory according to which culture is no longer seen as an overall framework, but rather as a repository of increasingly reflexive and autonomous resources or devices that are used in strategic ways by actors according to the demands of specific situations. Contemporary examples, not mentioning older authors such as Touraine or Bourdieu, are: Swidler's (1986) 'toolbox'; Gamson's 'cultural themes and counter-themes' (1988: 166), or Boltanski and Trévenot's (1991, 1999) different repertoires of evaluation or justification invoking different 'orders of worth'.
25. For example, Strydom (2008). Besides politics, examples from other fields readily come to mind, such as the establishment of the collective or co-responsibility frame (Strydom 1999c) in the environmental field, and Deutsche Bank and Monsanto's eventual acceptance of the European public's rejection of genetically modified foodstuffs (Strydom 2002: 117-21).
26. Habermas on the one hand correctly recognises that the public is an abstract phenomenon that is constituted for the first time only at the level of highly complex and organized communication processes, but on the other he tends, under the sway of moral philosophy, to extrapolate a univocal normative code from the public. In the latter respect, he adopts a legitimationist approach rather than the required constructivist one (Strydom 1999e, 2001).
27. In particular, Luhmann replaces the value-theoretical concept of culture with a communication or informational concept.
28. At this juncture, Miller would introduce his concept of 'coordinated dissent' (1987: 203-9).
29. Formally modelling triple contingency, Loet Leydesdorff (2007; see also 2009) recently confirmed that a formal analysis of Luhmann's position shows that a further level of contingency than he is willing to acknowledge is necessary for system formation: 'In Chapter 3 of *Soziale Systeme*, Luhmann discussed "double contingency" as central to the emergence of social systems. Borrowing the concept from Parsons, he provides it with a completely new solution. In my opinion, the simulations in terms of expectations accord with this solution...[But]...Luhmann moves fast in this chapter from 'double contingency' towards the emergence of social systems without a specification of the mechanism...According to Luhmann, the social system would 'emerge' from double contingency (in the singular!). I guess that a double contingency can go on forever when no third party comes into play. Piet Strydom used the term

"triple contingency" for explaining the emergence of a modern communication society in the 16th and 17th century. The third party becomes abstracted as a public. In principle, one could model a triple contingency analogously, using:

$$x(t) = a\,(1 - x(t+1))\,(1 - x(t+1))\,(1 - x(t+1))$$

One interpretation would be that triple interactions provide a short-term window for organization (decision-making) to step into the system. The relation between interaction and organization would then be conditional for the emergence of the social system' (Leydesdorff 2009).

Chapter 9: Resonance

1. Alberto Melucci clearly expresses this insight which has arisen in social theory in the late 20th century with reference to a shift that has occurred in social movements, that is, a shift 'towards the form of communication' (1996: 141). This shift, however, does not remain confined to social movements, but applies also to the process of the constitution and organization of society. Not only has the degree of reflexivity in relation to previously taken-for-granted presuppositions increased, but cultural models themselves have become more discursively available for more deliberate use in processes of constitution which themselves are increasingly organized according to the rules of communication.
2. This critique has to be qualified. Eder indeed does not differentiate between levels of critical resonance so as to recognise public resonance in its own terms. Yet in 1998 I originally drew the concept of 'triple contingency' ('*dreifache Kontingenz*') from Trenz and Eder's (2004) work. What I did over and above them, was to link the concept not simply to observation, but rather to the public and its role in communication societies. In the meantime, Eder *et al.* (2002) has developed a theory of communicative situations in which the public plays a prominent role.
3. On the relations of mediation implied here, see for instance Schutz (1967: 118-9, 131) and D'Andrade (1995: 179) and, more generally, on the threefold sign-relation, Apel (1981).
4. For a critique of Habermas, see Strydom (1999d, 1999e, 2001, 2006b).
5. As regards Eder, see the qualification in note 2 above.
6. Bourdieu is criticised by Eder (1989) and Habermas by Wenzel and Hochmuth (1989) as well as Strydom (2001).

Chapter 10: Intersubjectivity—Interactionist or Discursive

1. It is interesting to note that Pierre Bourdieu's (1990: 59, note 8) analysis of dance as a model of social integration involving the 'synchronization of the homogeneous and orchestration of the heterogeneous' indirectly supports Brandom's example of Fred Astaire and Ginger Rogers dancing to illustrate how different things are being done at the same time as the participants are engaged in a shared practice. He outlined this example in a letter to Habermas (2003b: 165, 309) who interprets it as proof of an objectivistic, methodological individualist position. Where Bourdieu and, I think, Brandom see a shared situational structure or, rather, a structuring practice which allows participants nevertheless to execute different yet coordinated actions, Habermas insists that the participants are at best engaged in 'mutual observation' and that this excludes 'the possibility for them to converge in their intersubjective recognition of the

same validity claim and [to] share knowledge in the strict sense of the term' (2003b: 165).

2. Here we witness an insistence on 'convergence' and 'sharing' which leads Habermas, as intimated in the previous note, to a foreshortened analysis of intersubjectivity—foreshortened in the sense of a lack of attention to both the mode of structuration and the temporal dimension of communication. Below, I return in more detail to this problem.
3. The interactionist or dialogical intersubjectivism extracted from Habermas's critique of Brandom and characterised in this paragraph has been an object of criticism from various sides. Ulrich Oevermann (e.g. 1983; Oevermann and Habermas 1979), the minimally published yet enormously influential Frankfurt sociological colleague of Habermas who partially under Theodor Adorno's impact founded 'objective hermeneutics', was perhaps the first to highlight the limits of this position. Niklas Luhmann (1987, 1995a) was also a dogged critic whose 'systems theoretical concept of communication' deriving from Norbert Wiener's cybernetics became a model for authors inspired by him, such as for example Karl Hörning, Daniela Ahrens and Anette Gerhard (1997), Tilmann Sutter and Michael Charlton (1999) and Loet Leydesdorff (2000). The problem with Luhmann's position is that he conceives of communication as the unity of information, utterance and understanding to the exclusion of the acceptance or rejection of what is understood (1995a: 147). The most interesting recent development that is critical of Habermas is represented by a group of authors who adopt Luhmann's concept of communication yet seek to build Oevermann's objective hermeneutics into it, for example, the authors collected in Tilmann Sutter (1997). Also here, however, the concept of system is so strong that it hardly allows discourse. Apart from the outside, however, critique has been developed over many years also by authors inspired by Habermas himself. This immanent critique was first coherently formulated by Max Miller (1986, 1992a) who drew on authors such as Jean Piaget and Lev Vygotsky, but was also influenced by Oevermann and Luhmann and who in turn, played some role in the merging of the latter two. In effect, Miller showed that whoever engages in communicative action necessarily enters into a social relationship possessing structural features that are presupposed by the participants. Against this background, it became apparent that Habermas's abiding attachment to an individualist approach to social reality is accompanied by his neglect of the structural nature of social relations. His latest statement of position is to be found in Miller (2002a). Pursuing this suggestion, but also borrowing from Alain Touraine, Bourdieu and even Luhmann, Klaus Eder (1988, 1996a) since the mid-1980s sought to identify structural models of practice and to make them amenable to empirical research—that is, without giving up communicative reason in favour of practical reason. Recently, Eder has restated both his critique of Habermas's tendential psychologism and individualism and his own attempt to theorise the dimension of structuration (1999a, 2000a).
4. The theory of signs in question here is Charles Sanders Peirce's threefold semiotic version as distinct from the twofold structuralist (or semiological) version of Ferdinand de Saussure and his followers. On Peirce, see for example Karl-Otto Apel (1981), and on the distinction between semiotic and structuralist theories, see for example Eugene Rochberg-Halton (1982) and Hans Joas (1992a). In addition to intersubjectivity, Luhmann (1995a: 146-7) also rejects a theory of signs as irrelevant for understanding communication, but what he has in mind is Jacques Derrida's semiology. In this dispute, interestingly, we witness the symptoms of a slowly emerging battle in the current post-disciplinary situation

over the most appropriate trans-discipline of our time: systems theory (or cybernetics), information theory or semiotics.

5. Compare my critique of Habermas in terms of the concept of resonance in Strydom (2003, Chapter 9 in this volume).
6. Not only Habermas is disadvantaged by the retention of this traditional concept, but so too are Luhmann (1992b: 378-9; 1995a: 103-36) and his followers (e.g. Sutter 1997: 303-36).
7. See also Hans-Jörg Trenz and Eder's (2004) creative analytical use of the concept of triple contingency. Here, however, a cautionary note should be sounded against a purely functionalist theory of democracy.
8. One of the most persistent theorists of collective learning processes, Klaus Eder, has recently again pointed out that Habermas's assumption of the centrality of the cognitively competent individual militates against an adequate understanding of learning which, instead, requires recognition of the fact that the actor ultimately is only the medium for the action-directing cultural models representing society. It is 'less the actor's competence than the script followed by the actor' (2000a: 223) that is of importance in collective learning. If this argument covers the discursive moment of structure formation and the structuration of the process of communication, however, then the next step in the temporal sequence, namely the different interpretations of the discursive outcome and their coordination under given situational conditions, is still left open.
9. For comparable elaborations of this complex theoretical premise and corresponding critically oriented empirical analyses in diverse fields, see Eder (1996a, 1999b), Delanty (1999a) and Strydom (2000, 2002).

PART III: APPLICATIONS

Chapter 11: The Construction of Collective Identity

1. For a critique, see Strydom (1987 and 1992, Chapters 1 and 2 in this volume).
2. An overview of the two positions and the controversy they have been engaged in since the late 1960s is offered by Harrison Wright (1977).
3. Piaget (1967: 29): 'un système de rapports dont chacun engendre, en tant que rapport même, une transformation des termes qui'il relie'.
4. It is interesting to note that Habermas (1979a: 154-5) distinguishes 'three stages of communication'—a position not taken into account by Oser, although he makes reference to Habermas. On the other hand, Habermas does decline explicitly the deal with 'the cognitive aspects of this communicative development'.
5. It should be noted that complex communicative processes do not require a consensus on goals since the realisation of diverse and indeed changeable goals is made possible by shared interpretations. See, for example, Piaget (1968: 385) and Klaus Japp (1984: 324). The relevance of Habermas's category of 'action oriented towards understanding and agreement' becomes apparent here.
6. Oser (1981: 99) slightly modified.
7. See also Roux (1964: 125): 'Socialists and Labour men in Britain have at all times found difficulty in grasping the attitude of South African Labour on the colour question'.
8. Legassick (1976) offers an overview of South African liberalism which reveals its close relationship with segregation and a defensive reaction to demands for democratisation.

9. Records of three of these conferences are documented in Karis and Carter (1972: 257-90).
10. My own proposal—originally developed in 1986—for the identification of blocked collective learning processes, which is a central task of critical theory, differs somewhat from that of Miller. Building on Habermas's (1979a: 2-3; 1984a: 38-40) distinction of four validity claims, it is presented in the following theoretical scheme:

Blocked Learning Processes

Pathological Process	*Domain of Reciprocity*	*Principle of Reciprocity*	*Content of Reciprocity*	*Blockage*
Authoritarian	objectivity	truth	free information	prevention/ limitation
Ideological	normativity	legitimacy	legality publicity plurality	prevention/ limitation
Repressive	subjectivity	truthfulness	endeetics/ needs articulation	repression
Regressive/ Self-Destructive	intersubjectivity	comprehensibility	communication	destruction

11. For a critique of Habermas and indications pointing beyond his position, see for example Eder (1985a), Miller (1986) and Strydom (1987, 1990a, 1992).

Chapter 13: The Challenge of Responsibility for Sociology

1. Durkheim (1964) focused on responsibility in the context of organic solidarity and linked it to institutional individualism; Weber (1970) analysed social action according to whether it was normatively guided by either an ethic of conviction or an ethic of responsibility; both Parsons (1964) and his German counterpart Gehlen (1969) investigated responsibility in the institutional context of social, occupational and professional roles; Habermas (1979a), by contrast, related it to the development of post-conventional moral consciousness and hence the acquisition and generalisation of the ability to take a critical attitude toward operating norms and institutions.
2. That the concepts 'risk' and 'responsibility' occur together is no coincidence. They are complementary concepts based on the important contemporary socio-cognitive scheme of 'safety and danger'.
3. While his main theme is risk, Beck largely neglects the question of responsibility, notwithstanding the fact that Lash (1994: 201) is of the opinion that responsibility is the key to his work. That Beck in fact overlooked the shift from individual to collective or co-responsibility in *Risk Society* is apparent from his energetic elaboration of the theory of individualisation. In a more recent article, Beck (1996) for the first time began touching on the new concept of responsibility.
4. The present author led a team that did sociological research on responsibility (Strydom and Skillington 1994; Mullally 1996), gave a lecture course that explicitly linked risk and responsibility (Strydom 1995-96), and subsequently published various materials on the topic (Strydom 1999b, 2000, 2002).

5. In a conversation with the present author in 1998, Apel signalled his strong opposition to the concept of 'collective responsibility' and instead insisted on 'co-responsibility'.
6. This communicative dimension carried by a flexible and even fleeting institutional infrastructure is what Eder (1993b), Beck (1994: 28) and Lash (1994: 201) refer to as the new type of 'reflexive institutions'. This is undoubtedly a major new topic for sociological theory and research.
7. In distinguishing the dimensions of the concept, I am following much appreciated advice of Mike Featherstone. For analytical purposes, I draw on Apel's theory of responsibility, particularly Apel (1998).
8. Both Durkheim's (1964: 42-3) idea of institutional individualism and neo-classical role theory in sociology, such as represented by Parsons (1964: 41-2, 95, 272, 323), are obviously in accord with this conventional conception. Gehlen (1969) assumed a comparable position.
9. Habermas (1979a: 69-94, particularly 82) argues for the recognition of such a post-conventional viewpoint when he criticises Parsonian role theory and, more generally, the traditional sociological emphasis on socialisation to the neglect or even exclusion of the complementary phenomenon of individuation.
10. Eyerman and Jamison (1991: 94-119) offer an interesting new version of this old problem with their concept of the contemporary 'movement intellectual', and thus open up an area within which the new concept of responsibility can be sociologically investigated.
11. For example, Robert McNamara, who, when moving from the US defence department to the World Bank, unexpectedly changed position by adopting the position of critic of the world economic system and World Bank policy (Apel 1998); and Nelson Mandela or Bram Fischer who were willing personally to pay the cost of publicly speaking out or acting against the apartheid regime in South Africa.
12. This reconstructive methodology, which is cognitivist by nature, was developed by Habermas (1979a: 1-68) and Apel (1984). It takes the form of the uncovering and analysis of necessary structural presuppositions or rules of communication, the making explicit of what is implicitly presupposed. According to both authors, critical sociology at its deepest level is possible only as reconstructive sociology. In my understanding, however, it forms only one side of a broader methodology, the other side being constructivist by nature (see, for example, Strydom 1999a, 2000).
13. They are all collaborative EU projects of which the present author was the responsible scientist at the Centre for European Social Research while being a director of the latter institution. They include: 'Framing and Communicating Environmental Issues' coordinated by Klaus Eder, 'Extended Producer Responsibility' coordinated by Aiveen Henry, and 'Environmental Sustainability and Institutional Innovation' coordinated by Patrick O'Mahony. In this context, Gerard Mullally and Tracey Skillington carried a heavy research burden. See O'Mahony (1999), Mullally (1996) and Skillington (1997). A PhD project undertaken by Marie Mater (1998) in close conjunction with this research should also be mentioned.
14. On the significance of the public, see Strydom (1999e).
15. Corrick's graphic expression is apt, although his argumentation leaves much to be desired. Marie Mater brought his piece to my attention.
16. For the empirical basis of my account, I fall back on texts presented in Mater (1998), which were originally drawn from International Development Centre (1993a, 1993b) and the media, and the analysis she brought to bear on them.

The present interpretation, however, is largely based on a rereading of the relevant texts.

17. To reduce this concern with responsibility simply to ideology would tantamount to repeating the erroneous treatment of culture by both functionalism and Marxism. This does not prejudice, of course, the need for a critical approach.

Chapter 14: Risk Communication

1. Douglas and Wildavsky (1982) made an important theoretical contribution to the conceptualisation of social and institutional differences, but, having done so from an unhistorical structuralist Durkheimian perspective, they neglected the crucial pragmatic-communicative dimension (e.g. Apel 1988; Habermas 1996a; Boltanski and Thévenot 1991; Eder 1996a; Strydom 2002, 2005, 2006a). In addition, also the differentiation of modern society into function systems (Luhmann 1995a) has to be taken into account.
2. Habermas (1979a: 41-2) identifies the 'double structure of speech', embracing the 'level of intersubjectivity' and the 'propositional content', to which corresponds Sperber and Wilson's (1986) conceptual pair of 'communicative intention' and 'informative intention'. Thévenot (1998, 2001, 2007) distinguishes different modes of engagement with the world and corresponding cognitive formats.
3. Different authors focus on distinct aspect of resonance—e.g., Gamson (1988): cultural resonance; Luhmann (1989): system resonance; Habermas (1989, 1996a): civil society resonance; Eder (2000b): institutional resonance and extra-institutional resonance. An overview leading to a first attempt at systematisation is offered in Strydom (2003, Chapter 9 in this volume) in which, in addition, I introduce the concept of public resonance distinct from civil society and extra-institutional resonance.
4. Some relevant cognitivist literature would include: Cicourel (1990); Conein (2005); D'Andrade (1995); Eder (1996a, 2007); Saferstein (1998, 2007); Strydom (2000, 2002, 2006a, 2007); Thévenot (1998, 2001, 2007).
5. See, for example, Sinha (1988) for a discussion of the distinction between representation and signification.
6. Drawing on phenomenological and non-Western ideas, but obviously lacking an adequate knowledge of the social sciences, Varela *et al.* (1991) interestingly attempt to introduce the perspective of collective world creation or 'enactivism' into the cognitive sciences.
7. Elsewhere I proposed to consider the currently characteristic cognitive order and organization of society in terms of the cognitive scheme of safety and danger (Strydom 2002: 77-8).
8. On two occasions, Habermas critically reflected on the concept of the public sphere which he originally introduced in 1962: a conference held upon the publication of *The Structural Transformation of the Public Sphere* (1989a) in English and the preparation of a new German edition (1990), while shortly after he returned to the topic to update it more thoroughly (1996a).
9. The following analysis builds on Habermas (1989a, 1990a, 1996a), Trenz and Eder (2004) and Eder (2006).
10. To allow for the dynamic circulation of power, Habermas (1996a) draws a basic distinction between two states of the public sphere. While a public sphere at rest is characterised by a normal or routine mode of problem-solving, an activated public sphere proceeds by an extraordinary mode of posing and solving problems, fuelled by heightened public attention, crisis consciousness, and an intensified

search for solutions. It should be added that it is the latter state in which the counterfactual force of communicative reason enters actual social relations which allows world creation. Risk is an issue which typically gives rise to crisis consciousness and activates the public sphere, the implication being that risk communication is a lightening rod directing latent counterfactual considerations into everyday communication.

11. On the institutionalisation of discourse, and hence self-legislation, and the role of communicative reason in such a configuration, see Brunkhorst (1993).
12. An awareness of the importance of the third point of view or third party reference goes back, among others, to Adam Smith's 'sympathy' or 'impartial spectator' (1982: I.i.1, I.i.5.8), Kant's 'sensus communis' (1972: § 40), Mead's 'taking the attitudes of others toward oneself' leading to the 'generalised other' (1974: 90), Piaget's 'placing oneself in reciprocal relation' leading to 'ideal norms at the back of all rules' (1968: 383, 385) and Habermas's 'public...constitutive for...the public sphere' (1996a: 364) as well as 'the moral point of view' (1999a: 84), and it is shared by various contemporary authors, including for example Miller (1986, 1992a), Giesen (1991), Boltanski and Thévenot (1991), Chazel (1997), Thévenot (2001) and Eder *et al.* (2002). The elemental insight preserved in this tradition suffers from a lack of clarity, however, due to its implicit or explicit attachment to the traditional social-theoretical concept of 'double contingency' and its interpretation from one-sided or cross-cutting objectivist, conventionalist and cognitivist perspectives. For some analysis, see Strydom (1999e).
13. Philosophically, we are encouraged to search for what is at stake in communication in the rationality structures transported in it (e.g. Apel and Kettner 1996; Wingert and Günther 2001). Without by any means denying the relevance of this, I propose more social scientifically to focus on the closely related cognitive structures and learning processes. As the later discussion of normative criteria suggests, however, it is impossible nevertheless to circumvent the question of rationality.
14. A cognitivist theory according to which learning is conceived as the self-organizing transformation of cognitive structures of different levels and scope which, in favourable cases, brings forth something structurally new is to be found in, for example, Miller (1986, 2002a), Eder (1996a; 1999a) and Strydom (2000). At the intersection between cognitive structures and social or communicative-discursive processes, a rule-governed transformation takes place which leads from a previous state of the world to a newly constructed one, involving the reorganization of cognitive classifications of reality and thus the reframing of the world. A good example is Eder's (1996a) analysis of the communication and framing or the making of the environment into an issue and the consequent institutionalisation of the environmental movement. In the course of such a learning process, the cognitive structures of social actors—e.g. social movement spokespersons, business executives, politicians—undergo change at the same time as the transformation of organizational—e.g. social movement, corporate, governmental—frames and, at a still higher level, cultural models of very wide scope—e.g. ecology taking the place of industrialism. The outcome of the process was thus the establishment of a new cultural model, a new kind of politics and a new kind of institutional order—in the form, respectively, of ecology, the politics of nature, and post-corporatism. Simultaneously, of course, all these levels imply a transformed self-understanding on the part of the actors involved.
15. I do so by drawing from and elaborating on Miller (1986, 1992a, 2002a) as well as Trenz and Eder (2004), who take up the concept of 'triple contingency' I

introduced elsewhere (Strydom 1999e). See also Eder *et al.*'s (2002: 104-8) theory of 'communicative situations'.

16. This is the theme of the wide-ranging literature on collective identity formation and the constitution of collective action in social movements. On the problem of coordination and synthesis as such, see for example Eder (1993a), Miller (2002a) and Strydom (2000, 2006b). Also of relevance is Engel's (1997) distinction among collective representations, collective beliefs and collective judgements.
17. In his original conception, Habermas stressed this type, as when he focused on 'social movements as learning processes' (1979a: 125). There he also envisaged that what was thus learned could be transposed to the level of society.
18. Parsons formalised this classical idea by introducing the 'proposition of double contingency', circumscribing it as follows: 'There is a *double contingency* inherent in interaction. On the one hand, ego's gratifications are contingent on his selection among available alternatives. But in turn, alter's reaction will be contingent on ego's selection and will result from a complementary selection on alter's part' (Parsons and Shils 1951: 16). Luhmann (1984, 1995a) and even Habermas (1992, 1996a) adopt the concept as being central to sociology. Strydom (1999e, 2001) offers a detailed overview and critique.
19. For similar arguments, see also Miller (1992a) and Eder (1999b).
20. Blockages in learning go back largely to power. On the basis of bringing together the complementary approaches of Habermas and Foucault, I have elsewhere analysed different ways in which power enters into discourse (Strydom 2000, particularly 50-2). See also Eder (2006).
21. The core insight encapsulated here is the one from which both Apel and Habermas single-mindedly proceed throughout their writings, yet inconsistencies are apparent. For critical analyses, see for example Wellmer (1986), Brunkhorst (1993), Miller (2002a), and Strydom (2001, 2006b).
22. This collective achievement is a socio-cognitive construct which brings together convincing, credible, justified and therefore acceptable claims with elements of qualified authority and normatively recognised power in a way that inspires trust and legitimacy (Honneth 1991; Boltanski and Thévenot 1991; Habermas 1996a; Engel 1997; Strydom 2000, 2002).
23. Turner (1994) has severely criticised the widely accepted social scientific assumption of sharing, but what is meant by 'sharable' here, by contrast, Piaget captured years ago: rather than subjecting 'each personality to rules that have a common content, it simply obliges individuals to place themselves in reciprocal relation with each other without letting the laws of perspective resultant upon this reciprocity destroy their individual points of view' (1968: 385).
24. The problem of justification is central to Apel and Habermas's discourse ethics and related work, but it has been taken up also into the new French 'pragmatic sociology' (Boltanski and Thévenot 1991).
25. See Strydom (2000, 2002) for the related concept of socio-cognitive critique.
26. On the common good or public interest, see for example Boltanski and Thévenot (1991) and Offe (2001). In a penetrating analysis of the contemporary renaissance of the concept, Offe submits that the field of public interest evaluation, judgement and argumentation lies between the formal sphere of legally sanctioned obligation and the informal sphere of legally allowed freedom, with the implication that it represents a third kind of criterion or norm. When he asks after the social reference of the concept of public interest, however, he does not raise the possibility of the third point of view beyond organized corporate actors—who, according to him, are tempted to misuse it for authoritarian-paternalistic

purposes—and unorganized associations—whose micro-politics, he thinks, appeals to it without contradiction.

27. The key insight here is Habermas's insistence right up to his latest publication on 'the *factual* role of performatively presupposed *counterfactual* assumptions' (2005: 30, my translation). See, for example, Eder's (2006) defence of it against criticisms. One rationale for the introduction the concept of 'triple contingency' (Strydom 1999e) was to attempt to capture the relation between the counterfactual and the factual in a way amenable to empirical research. In the present case, the public interest is a counterfactual assumption which takes actual effect in social life through the orientations and actions of the participants and, in particular, through the impact its embodiment in the public's reaction to the participants has on the conditions of their actions.
28. On grounds or reasons, see Kettner (1996).

Chapter 15: Cosmopolitanism, Globalization, and Collective Learning

1. Learning theoretical assumptions inform form a range of Delanty's writings (e.g. Delanty 1999; O'Mahony and Delanty 1998; Delanty and O'Mahony 2002).
2. Proceeding from the assumption of a 'mechanism of not-being-able-not-to-learn' (1979a: 147) drawn from Jean Piaget and Serge Moscovici, Habermas regularly calls on 'learning processes' throughout his writings right up to his most recent publications (e.g. 2005), yet he has never developed his learning theory systematically.
3. In the background here stand cognitively oriented sociologists like Erving Goffman (1986), David Snow *et al.* (1986) and William Gamson (1988).
4. The intention here is to shift the emphasis from the traditional understanding focusing on sharing in the sense of grasping a common meaning to cooperating in a social activity involving the coordination of social perspectives via a third point of view. See Piaget (1968: 385) and Brandom (1994: 497, 485).
5. For the distinction between strong and weak cognitivism, see Dan Sperber (1997). For a general overview of types of cognitive sociology, see Strydom (2007).
6. Miller (e.g. 1986), Eder (e.g. 1996a) and Strydom (e.g. 2000) all represent a cognitivist learning theory according to which learning is conceived as the self-organizing transformation of cognitive structures of different levels and scope which, in favourable cases, brings forth something structurally new. At the intersection between cognitive structures and social or communicative-discursive processes, a rule-governed transformation takes place which leads from a previous state of the world to a newly constructed one. This process takes place in the form of learning in the sense of the reorganization of cognitive classifications of reality and thus the reframing of the world. A good example is Eder's (1996a) analysis of the communication and framing or the making of the environment into an issue and the consequent institutionalisation of the environmental movement. There he showed how, in the course of such a learning process, the cognitive structures of social actors—for example, social movement spokespersons, business executives, politicians—undergo change at the same time as the transformation of organizational—for example, social movement, corporate, governmental—frames and, at a still higher level, cultural models of very wide scope—for example, ecology taking the place of industrialism. The outcome of the process was thus the establishment of a new cultural model, a new kind of politics and a new kind of institutional order—in the form, respectively, of ecology, the politics of nature, and post-corporatism.

Simultaneously, all these levels imply a transformed self-understanding on the part of the actors involved.

7. The proposed strategy is in accord with Delanty's own earlier distinction between the 'dual forces of capitalism and democracy' as the 'two dynamics' of globalization (2000: 89-92). Hauke Brunkhorst, a member of the generation succeeding Habermas, speaks of the 'globalization of functionally differentiated society' as distinct from the 'globalization of democratic solidarity', the latter of which he also circumscribes as 'egalitarian and self-determined solidarity' and 'communicative solidarity' (2005: xxiv, 76, 96). There is also a more direct suggestion of 'communicative globalization' in the original German edition of his book, as when he speaks of a 'kommunikativer Globalisierungsgewinn' (2002: 215).
8. In an earlier work, Delanty (2000) did give some attention to legal globalization and stressed what he then called 'civic cosmopolitanism'. In the article under discussion, the latter functions as a diffuse guiding idea.
9. See Brunkhorst (2005) on the reproduction of typically modern inclusion problems at the global level.
10. Craig Calhoun (2003) offers an exploration of this type of cosmopolitanism.
11. Danilo Zolo (1997) extensively criticizes the world state, world government or global governance model, while David Held (1996) advocates cosmopolitan democracy. Initially, Habermas (2001) linked global governance and cosmopolitan democracy, but in his more recent work (e.g. 2005) the new formulation cited in the text frequently recurs.
12. Both Held's (1996) critique of 'geogovernance' and Zolo's (1997) critique of the 'new Holy Alliance' target such authoritarian legalism. Habermas (2001, 2005) offers a democratic interpretation of the global legal order. On the latter, see also Tomuschat (1997) and Lukashuk (1997).
13. On this problem of coordination and synthesis, see Eder (1993a), Miller (2002a) and Strydom (2006b).
14. Alain Touraine's successor, François Dubet, identifies the 'alter-globalization movement' (2004: 705) as the sociologically more interesting phenomenon.
15. Mary Kaldor (2003) puts forward the former interpretation, while Delanty's own preference is for the latter which, in his earlier work, he sought to capture by means of the concept of 'civic cosmopolitanism' (2000).
16. Talcott Parsons formalised this classical idea by introducing the 'proposition of double contingency', circumscribing it as follows: 'There is a *double contingency* inherent in interaction. On the one hand, ego's gratifications are contingent on his selection among available alternatives. But in turn, alter's reaction will be contingent on ego's selection and will result from a complementary selection on alter's part' (Parsons and Shils 1951: 16). Although not explicitly named, the idea is also to be found in well-articulated form in Alfred Schutz (e.g. 1967: 170). Luhmann (1984, 1995a) and even Habermas (1992, 1996a) adopt the concept as being central to sociology.
17. The core insight implied here is the one from which Habermas single-mindedly proceeds throughout his work, yet not without some inconsistency. See, for instance, Strydom (2001, 2006b).

References

Abercrombie, N. (1972) 'Evolutionary Theories Again', *Sociological Analysis* 2: 47-51.

Adorno, Theodor (1972) *Gesammelte Schriften*, Vol. VIII: *Soziologische Schriften*. Frankfurt: Suhrkamp.

—— (1981) *Prisms*. Cambridge, MA: MIT.

Alexander, Jeffrey (1982) *Theoretical Logic in Sociology*, Vol. I. London: Routledge & Kegan Paul.

—— (1993) 'The Return of Civil Society', *Contemporary Sociology* 22: 797-803.

Apel, Karl-Otto ed. *(1976) Sprachpragmatik und Philosophie*. Frankfurt: Suhrkamp.

—— (1978) 'Der Ansatz von Apel', in W. Oeluller (ed.) *Materialien zur Normendiskussion*, Vol. I. Paderborn: Schöningh, pp. 160-203.

—— (1980 [1973]) *Towards a Transformation of Philosophy*. London: Routledge & Kegan Paul.

—— (1981) *Charles S. Peirce: From Pragmatism to Pragmaticism*. Amherst, MA: University of Massachusetts Press.

—— (1984) *Understanding and Explanation: A Transcendental-Pragmatic Perspective*. Cambridge, MA: MIT Press.

—— (1987) 'The Problem of a Macroethic of Responsibility to the Future in the Crisis of Technological Civilization: An Attempt to Come to Terms with Hans Jonas' "Principle of Responsibility",' *Man and World* 20: 3-40.

—— (1988) *Diskurs und Verantwortung: Das Problem des Übergangs zur postkonventionellen Moral*. Frankfurt: Suhrkamp.

—— (1990) 'The Problem of a Universalistic Macroethics of Co-Responsibility,' in S. Griffioen (ed.) *What Right does Ethics have*? Amsterdam: VU University Press, pp. 23-40.

—— (1991) 'A Planetary Macroethics for Mankind: The Need, the Apparent Difficulty, and the Eventual Possibility,' in E. Deutsch (ed.) *Culture and Modernity: East-West Philosophical Perspectives*. Honolulu: University of Hawai Press, pp. 261-78.

—— (1993) 'How to Ground a Universalistic Ethics of Co-Responsibility for the Effects of Collective Actions and Activities,' *Philosophica* 52(2): 9-29.

—— (1998) 'First Things First: Zur Begründung einer planetaren Makroethik primordialer Mit-Verantwortung,' in M. Kettner (ed.) *Angewandte Ethik als Politikum*. Frankfurt: Suhrkamp.

—— *et al.* (1971) *Hermeneutik und Ideologiekritik*. Frankfurt: Suhrkamp.

—— and Kettner, Matthias, eds. (1992) *Zur Anwendung der Diskursethik in Politik, Recht und Wissenschaft*. Frankfurt: Suhrkamp.

—— and Kettner, Matthias, eds. (1996) *Die eine Vernunft und die vielen Rationalitäten*. Frankfurt: Suhrkamp.

Arendt, Hannah (1971) *The Human Condition*. Chicago: University of Chicago Press.

Arnason, Johann P. (1979) 'Review of Jürgen Habermas, Zur Rekonstruktion des historischen Materialismus,' *Telos* 39: 201-18.

—— (1980) 'Marx and Habermas,' in A. Honneth and U. Jaeggi (eds.) *Arbeit, Handlung, Normativität: Theorien des historischen Materialismus*, Vol. II. Frankfurt: Suhrkamp.

—— (1988) *Praxis und Interpretation: Sozialphilosophische Studien*. Frankfurt: Suhrkamp.
Beck, Ulrich (1988) *Gegengifte: Die organisierte Unverantwortlichkeit*. Frankfurt: Suhrkamp.
—— (1992 [1986]) *Risk Society: Towards a New Modernity*. London: Sage.
—— (1994) 'The Reinvention of Politics: Towards a Theory of Reflexive Modernization,' in U. Beck, A. Giddens and S. Lash, *Reflexive Modernization: Politics, Tradition and Aesthetics in the Modern Social Order*. Cambridge: Polity Press, pp. 1-55.
—— (1996) 'World Risk Society as Cosmopolitan Society? Ecological Questions in a Framework of Manufactured Uncertainties,' *Theory, Culture and Society* 13(4): 1-32.
—— (1997) *The Reinvention of Politics*. Cambridge: Polity.
—— and Bonß, Wolfgang eds. (1989) *Weder Sozialtechnologie noch Aufklärung?* Frankfurt: Suhrkamp.
—— and Grande, Edgar (2005) *Das kosmopolitische Europa*. Frankfurt: Suhrkamp.
Benjamin, Walter (1980) *Illuminationen: Ausgewälte Schriften*. Frankfurt: Suhrkamp.
Berger, Peter L. and Luckmann, Thomas (1967) *The Social Construction of Reality*. Harmondsworth: Penguin.
Berger, Peter L. *et al.* (1974) *The Homeless Mind: Modernization and Consciousness*. Penguin: Harmondsworth.
Berkowitz, Marvin (1981) 'A Critical Appraisal of the Educational and Psychological Perspectives on Moral Discussion,' *Journal of Educational Thought* 15: 20-33.
Bernstein, Richard J. (1994) 'Rethinking Responsibility,' *Social Research* 61(4): 833-52.
Blatt, Moshe and Kohlberg, Lawrence (1975) 'The Effects of Classroom Moral Discussion upon Children's Level of Moral Judgement,' *Journal of Moral Education* 4: 129-61.
Bock, K. (1978) 'Theories of Progress, Development, Evolution', in T. Bottomore and R. Nisbet (eds.) *A History of Sociological Analysis*. London: Heinemann, pp. 39-80.
Böhme, Gernot (1997) *Einführung in die Philosophie*. Frankfurt: Suhrkamp.
Boltanski, Luc and Thévenot, Laurent (1991) *De la justification: Les economies de la grandeur*. Paris: Gallimard.
—— (1999) 'Sociology of Critical Capacity', *European Journal of Social Theory* 2(3): 359-77.
Bourdieu, Pierre (1977) *Outline of a Theory of Practice*. Cambridge: Cambridge University Press.
—— (1986) *Distinction: A Social Critique of the Judgement of Taste*. London: Routledge & Kegan Paul.
—— (1987) *Sozialer Sinn*. Frankfurt: Suhrkamp.
—— (1990) *The Logic of Practice*. Cambridge, UK: Polity Press.
Brand, Karl-Werner (1982) *Neue soziale Bewegungen: Entstehung, Funktion und Perspektive neuer Protestpotentiale*. Opladen: Westdeutscher Verlag.
Brandom, Robert B. (1994) *Making It Explicit: Reasoning, Representing, and Discursive Commitment*. Cambridge, MA: Harvard University Press.
Brunkhorst, Hauke (1993) 'Zur Dialektik von realer und idealer Kommunikationsgemeinschaft', in A. Dorschel, M. Kettner, W. Kuhlmann und M. Niquet (eds.) *Transzendalpragmatik*. Frankfurt: Suhrkamp, pp. 342-58.
—— (2002) *Solidarität: Von der Bürgergesellschaft zur globalen Rechtsgenossenschaft*. Frankfurt: Suhrkamp.
—— (2005) *Solidarity: From Civic Friendship to a Global Legal Community*. Cambridge, MA: MIT Press.
Bürger, Peter (1974) *Theorie der Avantgarde*. Suhrkamp: Frankfurt.
Burns, Tom (1986) 'Actors, Transactions and Social Structure', in U. Himmelstrand (ed.) *Sociology: From Crisis to Science?*, Vol. II: *The Social Reproduction of Organization and Culture*. London: Sage, pp. 8-37.

—— (1999) 'The Evolution of Parliaments and Societies in Europe: Challenges and Prospects', *European Journal of Social Theory* 2: 167-94.

Burns, Tom and Dietz, Thomas (1992a) 'Cultural Evolution: Social Rule Systems, Selection and Human Agency', *International Sociology* 7: 259-83.

—— (1992b) 'Institutionelle Dynamik: Ein evolutionärer Ansatz', *Journal für Sozialforschung* 32: 283-306.

—— (1997) 'Evolutionary Sociology: Selective Environments, Human Agency, and Institutional Dynamics'. Paper read at ISA conference on 'Sociological Theory and the Environment', Zeist, the Netherlands.

—— (1999) 'Revolution: An Evolutionary Perspective'. Unpublished paper.

Burns, Tom and Flam, Helena (1986) *The Shaping of Social Organization: Social Rule System Theory and Its Applications*. London: Sage.

Burns, Tom *et al.* (1985) *Man, Decisions and Society*. London: Gordon and Breach.

Buro, Andreas (1977) 'Die Entstehung der Ostermarsch-Bewegung als Beispiel für die Entfaltung von Massenlernprozessen,' *Friedenanalysen*, 4. Frankfurt: Suhrkamp, pp. 50-78.

—— (1982)'Kann die "neue" vom der "alten" Friedensbewegung lernen?' *Friedenanalysen*, 16. Frankfurt: Suhrkamp, pp. 401-17.

Calhoun, Craig ed. (1992) *Habermas and the Public Sphere*. Cambridge, MA: MIT.

—— (1993) 'Civil Society and the Public Sphere', *Public Culture* 5: 267-80.

—— (1996) 'Social Theory and the Public Sphere', B.S. Turner (ed.) *The Blackwell Companion to Social Theory*. Oxford: Blackwell, pp. 429-70.

—— (2003) 'The Class Consciousness of Frequent Travellers: Towards a Critique of Actually Existing Cosmopolitanism' in D. Archibugi (ed.) *Debating Comopolitics*. London: Verso.

Campbell, Donald T. (1974) 'Evolutionary Epistemology', in P.A. Schilpp (ed.) *The Philosophy of Karl Popper*, Vol I. La Salle: Open Court, pp. 413-63

Chazel, François (1997) 'Les ajustements cognitifs dans les mobilisations collectives', in R. Boudon, A. Bouvier and F. Chazel (eds.), *Cognition et Sciences Sociales*. Paris: Presses Universitaires de France, pp. 193-206.

Childe, V.G (1947) *History*. London: Watts & Co.

—— (1951) *Social Evolution*. London: Watts & Co.

Chomsky, Noam (1989) *Necessary Illusions*. Boston: South End Press.

Cicourel, Aaron V. (1990) 'The Integration of Distributed Knowledge in Collaborative Medical Diagnosis', in J. Galegher, R.E. Kraut and C. Egido (eds.) *Intellectual Teamwork*. Hillsdale, NJ: Erlbaum.

Clark, Andy (1998) 'Embodied, Situated, and Distributed Cognition', in W. Bechtel and G Graham (eds.) *A Companion to Cognitive Science*. Oxford: Blackwell, pp. 506-17.

Cobb, R., Ross, J.-K. and Ross, M.H. (1976) 'Agenda Building as a Comparative Political Process', *American Political Science Review* 70: 126-38.

Cohen, Jean (1982) *Class and Civil Society: The Limits of Marxian Critical Theory*. Amherst: University of Massachusetts Press.

—— (1985) 'Strategy or Identity: New Theoretical Paradigms and Contemporary Social Movements,' *Social Research* 52: 663-716.

—— and Arato, Andrew (1992) *Civil Society and Political Theory*. Cambridge, MA: MIT.

Conein, Bernard (2005) *Les sens sociaux: Trois essays de sociologie cognitive*. Paris: Economica.

Corrick, B.J. (1990) 'An Era of Responsibility,' *The Futurist*, 24(2): 60.

Coser, Lewis A. (1956) *The Functions of Social Conflict*. Glencoe, NJ: Free Press.

D'Andrade, Roy (1995) *The Development of Cognitive Anthropology*. Cambridge: Cambridge University Press.

Delanty, Gerard (1997) *Social Science: Beyond Constructivism and Realism*. Buckingham: Open University Press.

—— (1999a) 'Die Transformation nationaler Identität und die kulturelle Ambivalenz europäischer Identität', in R. Viehoff and R.T. Segers (eds.) *Kultur, Identität, Europa*. Frankfurt: Suhrkamp, pp. 267-88.

—— (1999b) *Social Theory in a Changing World: Conceptions of Modernity*. Cambridge: Polity Press.

—— (2000) *Citizenship in a Global Age: Society, Culture, Politics*. Buckingham: Open University Press.

—— (2003) *Community*. London: Routledge.

—— (2005) 'Cultural Translations and European Modernity' in E. Ben-Rafael and Y. Sternberg (eds.) *Comparing Modern Civilizations: Pluralism versus Homogeneity*. Leiden: Brill.

—— (2006) 'The Cosmopolitan Imagination: Critical Cosmopolitanism and Social Theory', *The British Journal of Sociology* 57(1): 25-47.

—— (2004) 'Cosmopolitanism', in R. Robertson and J.A. Scholte (eds.) *Encyclopedia of Globalization*. New York: Grolier Academic Publishers.

—— and O'Mahony, Patrick (2002) *Nationalism and Social Theory: Modernity and the Recalcitrance of the Nation*, London: Sage.

Dietz, Thomas and Burns, Tom (1992) 'Human Agency and the Evolutionary Dynamics of Culture', *Acta Sociologica* 35: 187-200.

Dietz, Thomas *et al.* (1989) 'Definitions of Conflict and the Legitimation of Resources: The Case of Environmental Risk', *Sociological Forum* 4: 47-70.

—— (1990) 'Evolutionary Theory in Sociology: An Examination of Current Thinking', *Sociological Forum* 5: 155-71.

Döbert, Rainer (1973) *Systemtheorie und die Entwicklung religiöser Deutungssysteme*. Frankfurt: Suhrkamp.

—— (1981) 'The Role of Stage Models within a Theory of Social Evolution, illustrated by the European Witch Craze', in U.J. Jensen and R. Harré (eds.) *The Philosophy of Evolution*. Brighton: Harverster Press.

Douglas, Mary and Wildavsky, Aaron (1982) *Risk and Culture: An Essay on the Selection of Technical and Environmental Dangers*. Berkeley, CA: University of California Press.

Dryzek, John S. (1999) *Discursive Democracy: Politics, Policy, and Political Science*. Cambridge: Cambridge University Press.

Dubet, F. (2004) 'Between a Defence of the Subject and a Politics of the Subject: The Specificity of Today's Social Movements', *Current Sociology* 52(4): 693-716.

Dubiel, Helmut (1988) *Kritische Theorie der Gesellschaft*. Weinheim/Munich: Juventa.

—— (1989) 'Herrschaft oder Emanzipation: Der Streit um die Erbschaft der Kritischen Theorie, in A. Honneth *et al.* (eds.) *Zwischenbetrachtungen: Im Prozeß der Aufklärung-J. Habermas zum 60. Geburtstag*. Frankfurt: Suhrkamp, pp. 504-18.

Dubow, Saul (1987) 'Race, Civilization and Culture: An Elaboration of Segregationist Discourse in the Interwar Years,' in S. Marks and S. Trapido (eds.) *The Politics of Race, Class and Naitonalism in Twentieth Century South Africa*. London: Longman, pp. 71-94.

Durkheim, E. (1964 [1893]) *The Division of Labour in Society*. New York: Free Press.

—— (1976 [1912]) *The Elementary Forms of the Religious Life*. London: Allen & Unwin.

Eder, Klaus (1973) 'Komplexität, Evolution und Geschichte', in F. Maciejewski (ed.) *Theorie der Gesellschaft oder Sozialitechnologie: Beiträge zur Habermas-Luhmann-Diskussion*. Frankfurt: Suhrkamp, pp. 9-42.

—— (1976) *Die Entstehung staatlich organisierter Gesellschaften*. Frankfurt: Suhrkamp.

—— (1977) 'Zum Problem der logischen Periodisierung von Produktionsweisen: Ein Beitrag zu einer evolutionstheoretischen Rekonstruktion des historischen Materialismus', in U. Jaeggi and A. Honneth (eds.) *Theorien des historischen Materialismus*. Frankfurt: Suhrkamp, pp. 501-23.

—— (1982) 'Kollektive Lernprozesse und Geschichte,' *Saeculum* 33: 116-32.

—— (1983) 'Strukturen kollektiver Praxis: Die Theorie der sozialen Evolution revisited', postscript to P.A. Berger, *Herrschaftsform Stadt*. Munich: Academic, pp. 243-58.

—— (1983-84) 'Collective Learning Processes and Social Evolution: Towards a Theory of Class Conflict in Modern Society'. *Tidskrift för Rättssociologi* 1: 23-36.

—— (1984) 'On the Cultural Origins and the Historical Formation of the Traditional State: Some Theoretical Considerations', in W. Dostal (ed.) *On Social Evolution*. Vienna: Berger & Sons, pp. 110-40.

—— (1985a) *Geschichte als Lernprozeß? Zur Pathogenese politischer Modernität in Deutschland*. Frankfurt: Suhrkamp.

—— (1985b) 'The "New Social Movements": Moral Crusades, Political Pressure Groups, or Social Movements,' *Social Research* 52: 869-90.

—— (1986a) 'Prozedurale Rationalität', *Zeitschrift für Rechtssoziologie* 7: 1-30.

—— (1986b) 'Soziale Bewegung und kulturelle Evolution: Überlegungen zur Rolle der neuen sozialen Bewegungen in der kulturellen Evolution der Moderne', in J. Berger (ed.) *Die Moderne: Kontinuitäten und Zäsuren*. Gottingen: Schwartz, pp. 335-57.

—— (1987) 'Learning and the Evolution of Social Systems', in M. Schmid and F.M. Wuketits (eds.) *Evolutionary Theory in the Social Sciences*. Dordrecht: Reidel, pp. 100-25.

—— (1988) *Die Vergesellschaftung der Natur: Studien zur sozialen Evolution der praktischen Venunft*. Frankfurt: Suhrkamp.

—— ed. (1989a) *Klassenlage, Lebensstil und kulturelle Praxis*. Frankfurt: Suhrkamp.

—— (1989b) 'Politik und Kultur: Zur kultursoziologischen Analyse politischer Partizipation', in A. Honneth *et al.* (eds.) *Zwischenbetrachtungen*. Frankfurt: Suhrkamp, pp. 519-48.

—— (1990a) 'Countercultural Movements against Modernity: Nature as a New Field of Class Struggle', *Theory, Culture and Society* 7: 21-47.

—— (1990b) 'The Cultural Code of Modernity and the Problem of Nature: A Critique of the Naturalistic Notion of Progress', in J. Alexander and P. Sztompka (eds.) *Rethinking Progress: Movements, Forces and Ideas at the End of the Twentieth Century*. London: Unwin Hyman, pp. 67-87.

—— (1992) 'Contradictions and Social Evolution: A Theory of the Social Evolution of Modernity', in H. Haferkamp and N.J. Smelser (eds.) *Social Change and Modernity*. Berkeley/Oxford: University of California Press, pp. 320-49.

—— (1993a) *The New Politics of Class: Social Movements and Cultural Dynamics in Advanced Societies*. London: Sage.

—— (1993b) 'Reflexive Institutionen: Eine Untersuchung zur Herausbildung eines neuen Typus institutioneller Reglung im Umweltbereich,' Unpublished Research Design. Florence: European University Institute.

—— (1995) 'Die Institutionalisierung sozialer Bewegungen: Zur Beschleunigung von Wandelungsprozessen in fortgeschnittenen Industriegesellschaften', in H.-P. Müller and M. Schmid (eds.) *Sozialer Wandel*. Frankfurt: Suhrkamp, pp. 267-90.

—— (1996a) *The Social Construction of Nature: A Sociology of Ecological Enlightenment*. London: Sage.

—— (1996b) 'The Institutionalisation of Environmentalism: Ecological Discourse and the Second Transformation of the Public Sphere', in S. Lash, B. Szerszynski and B. Wynne (eds.) *Risk, Environment and Modernity*. London: Sage, pp. 203-23.

—— (1999a) 'Societies Learn and yet the World is Hard to Change', *European Journal of Social Theory* 2(2): 195-215.

—— (1999b) 'Integration durch Kultur? Das Paradox der Suche nach einer europäische Identität, in R. Viehoff and R.T. Segers (eds.) *Kultur, Identität', Europa.* Frankfurt: Suhrkamp, pp. 147-79.

—— (2000a) *Kulturelle Identität zwischen Tradition und Utopie*. Frankfurt: Campus.

—— (2000b) 'Zur Transformation nationalstaatlicher Öffentlichkeit in Europa: Von der Sprachgemeinschaft zur issuespezifischen Kommunikationsgemeinschaft', *Berliner Journal für Soziologie* 10(2): 167-84.

—— (2000c) 'Taming Risks through Dialogues: The Rationality and Functionality of Discursive Institutions in Risk Society', in M.J. Cohen (ed.) *Risk in the Modern Age: Social Theory, Science and Environmental Decision-Making*. Houndsmills: Palgrave, pp. 225-48.

—— (2001) 'Sustainability as a Discursive Device for Mobilizing European Politics', in K. Eder and M. Kousis (eds.) *Environmental Politics in Southern Europe*. Dordrecht: Kluwer. pp. 25-52.

—— (2006) 'Making Sense of the Public Sphere', in G. Delanty (ed.) *Handbook of Contemporary European Social Theory*. London: Routledge, pp. 333-46.

—— (2007) 'Cognitive Sociology and the Theory of Communicative Action: The Role of Communication and Language in the Making of the Social Bond', *European Journal of Social Theory* 10(3): 389-408.

—— Giesen, Bernhard, Schmidtke, Oliver and Tambini, Damian (2002) *Collective Identities in Action*. Aldershot: Ashgate.

—— and Kantner, Cathlene (2001) 'Transnationale Resonanzstrukturen in Europa: Eine Kritik der Rede von Öffentlichkeitsdefizit', in Mauricio Bach (ed.) *Die Europäisierung nationaler Gesellschaften*. Opladen: Westdeutscher Verlag, pp. 306-31.

—— and Rödel, Ulrich (1978) 'Handlungstheoretische Implikationen des historischen Materialismus', in K.O. Hondrich and J. Mattes (eds.) *Theorievergleich in den Sozialwissenschaften*. Darmstadt: Luchterhand, pp. 140-5.

—— and Schmidtke, Oliver (1997) 'Jenseits des ptolemäischen Weltbildes der Soziologie: Auch ein Beitrag zur Kritik neuerer Theorien ethnischer Mobilisierung'. Draft version of Eder and Schmidtke 1998.

—— and Schmidtke, Oliver (1998) 'Ethnische Mobilisierung und die Logik von Identitätskämpfen: Eine situationstheoretische Perspektive jenseits von "Rational Choice"', *Zeitschrift für Soziologie* 27: 418-37.

Eisenstadt, Shmuel N. (1985) 'Macro-Sociological Analysis-Background, Development and Indications,' in Eisenstadt and H.J. Helle (eds.) *Macro-Sociological Theory: Perspectives on Sociological Theory*, Vol. I. London: Sage, pp. 1-10.

—— and Giesen, Bernhard (1995) 'The Construction of Collective Identity', *European Journal of Sociology* 36: 72-102.

Eley, Geoff (1992) 'Nations, Publics, and Political Cultures', in C. Calhoun (ed.) *Habermas and the Public Sphere*. Cambridge, Mass.: Cambridge University Press, pp. 289-339.

Engel, Pascal (1997) 'Croyances collectives et acceptations collectives', in R. Boudon, A. Bouvier and F. Chazel (eds.), *Cognition et Sciences Sociales*. Paris: Presses Universitaires de France, pp. 155-73.

Esser, Hartmuth (1996) 'Die Definition der Situation', *Kölner Zeitschrift für Soziologie und Sozialpsychologie* 48: 1-34.

Evers, A. and Nowotny, H. (1987) *Über den Umgang mit Unsicherheit: Die Entdeckung der Gestaltbarkeit von Gesellschaft*. Frankfurt: Suhrkamp.

Eyerman, R. and Jamison, A. (1991) *Social Movements: A Cognitive Approach*. Cambridge: Polity Press.

Fink-Eitel, Heinrich (1993) 'Innerweltliche Transszendenz: Zum gegenwärtige Stand Gesellschaftstheorie', *Merkur* 47(3): 237-45.

Flew, Anthony (1984) *Darwinian Evolution*. London: Paladin.

Forman, Lionel (1959) *Chapters in the History of the March to Freedom*. Cape Town: Real Printing and Publishing Co.

Foucault, Michel (1977) *Discipline and Punish*. Harmondsworth: Penguin.

—— (1980) *Power/Knowledge*. Brighton: Harvester Press.

Francis, E.K. (1981) 'Darwins Evolutionstheorie und der Sozialdarwinismus', *Kölner Zeitschrift für Soziologie und Sozialpsychologie* 33: 209-228.

Frank, Manfred (1988) *Die Grenzen der Verständigung*. Frankfurt: Suhrkamp.

—— (1989) *Das Sagbare und das Unsagbare*. Frankfurt: Suhrkamp.

Frankenberg, Günter and Rödel, Ulrich (1981) *Von der Volkssouveränität zum Minderheitenschutz*. Frankfurt: Europäische Verlagsanstalt.

Fraser, Nancy (1997) *Justice Interruptus*. New York: Routledge.

—— and Honneth, Axel (2003) *Redistribution or Recognition?* London: Verso.

Freitag, Barbara (1983) 'Theorie des kommunikativen Handelns und genetische Psychologie', *Kölner Zeitschrift für Soziologie und Sozialpsychologie* 35(1): 555-76.

Fuller, Steve (1984) 'The Cognitive Turn in Sociology', *Erkenntnis* 21: 439-50.

—— (1993) *Philosophy, Rhetoric, and the End of Knowledge*. Madison: University of Wisconsin Press.

Gamson, W.A. (1988a) 'A Constructionist Approach to Mass Media and Public Opinion', *Symbolic Interaction* 11(2): 161-74.

—— (1988b) 'Politicai Discourse and Collective Action,' in B. Klandermans *et al.* (eds.). *From Structure to Action: Comparing Social Movement Research Across Cultures*. Greenwich, CT: JAI Press, 219-44.

—— (1992) *Talking Politics*. Cambridge/New York: Cambridge University Press.

—— Croteau, D., Hoynes, W. and Sasson, T. (1992) 'Media Images and the Social Construction of Reality', *Annual Review of Sociology* 18: 373-93

—— and Lasch, K. (1983) 'The Political Culture of Social Welfare Policy', in Shimon E, Spiro and Ephraim Yuchtman-Yaar (eds.) *Evaluating the Welfare State*. New York/ London: Academic Press, pp. 397-415.

—— and Modigliani, A. (1987) 'The Changing Culture of Affirmative Action', in R.D. and M.M. Braungart (eds.) *Research in Political Sociology*, Vol. 3. Greenwich, CT: JAI Press, pp. 137-77.

—— and Stuart, D. (1992) 'Media Discourse as Symbolic Contest: The Bomb in Political Cartoons', *Sociological Forum* 7(1): 55-85.

Gehlen, A. (1969) *Moral und Hypermoral*. Frankfurt: Metzner.

Gerhards, Jürgen and Neidhardt, Frieldhelm (1990) *Strukturen und Funktionen modernen Öffentlichkeit*, FS III 90-101. Berlin: Wissenschaftszentrum Berlin für Sozialforschung.

Giddens, Anthony (1979) *Central Problems in Social Theory*. London: Macmillan.

—— (1984) *The Constitution of Society: Outline of the Theory of Structuration*. Cambridge: Polity.

Giesen, Bernard (1980a) *Makrosoziologie: Eine evolutionstheoretische Einführung*. Hamburg: Hoffmann und Campe.

—— (1980b) 'Gesellschaftliche Identität und Evolution: Ein Vergleich soziologischer Theorietraditionen', *Soziale Welt* 31: 311-32.

—— (1983) 'Moralische Unternehmer und öffentliche Diskussion: Überlegungen zur gesellschaftliche Thematisierung sozialer Probleme', *Kölner Zeitschrift für Soziologie und Sozialpsychologie* 35: 230-54.

—— (1987) 'Media and Markets', in M. Schmid and F.M. Wuketits (eds.) *Evolutionary Theory in Social Science*. Dordrecht: Reidel, pp. 171-94.

—— (1991a) 'Code, Process and Situation in Cultural Selection', *Cultural Dynamics* 4: 172-85.

—— (1991b) *Die Entdinglichung des Sozialen: Eine evolutionstheoretische Perspektive auf die Postmoderne*. Frankfurt: Suhrkamp.

—— (1993) *Die Intellektuellen und die Nation: Eine deutsche Achsenzeit*. Frankfurt: Suhrkamp.

—— (1995) 'Code und Situation: Das selektionstheoretische Programm einer Analyse sozialen Wandels—illustriert an der Genese des deutschen Nationalbewußtseins', in H.-P. Müller and M. Schmid (eds.) *Sozialer Wandel*. Frankfurt: Suhrkamp, pp. 228-66.

—— and Junge, K. (1991) 'Vom Patriotismus zum Nationalismus: Zur Evolution der "Deutschen Kulturnation"', in B. Giesen (ed.) *Nationale und kulturelle Identität: Studien zur Entwicklung des kollektiven Bewußtseins in der Neuzeit*. Frankfurt: Suhrkamp, pp. 255-303.

—— and Lau, Christophe (1981) 'Zur Anwendung darwinistischer Erklärungsstrategien in der Soziologie', *Kölner Zeitschrift für Soziologie und Sozialpsychologie* 33(2): 229-56.

—— and Schmid, Michael (1975) 'System und Evolution: Metatheoretische Vorbemerkungen zu einer soziologischen Evolutionstheorie', *Soziale Welt* 26: 385-413.

—— *et al.* (1998) *Intellectuals and the Nation*. Cambridge: Cambridge University Press.

Ginsberg, Morris (1956) *Essays in Sociology and Social Philosophy,* Vol. III. London: Heinemann.

—— (1970) 'L.T. Hobhouse', in T. Raison (ed.) *The Founding Fathers of Social Science*. Harmondsworth: Penguin, pp. 154-61.

Goffman, Erving (1961) *Encounters*. Indianapolis: Bobbs-Merrill.

—— (1986) *Frame Analysis: An Essay on the Organization of Experience*. Boston: Northeastern University Press.

Gouldner, A. (1970) 'Anti-Minotaur: The Myth of a Value-Free Sociology,' in J.D. Douglas (ed.) *The Relevance of Sociology*. New York: Appleton-Century-Crofts, pp. 64-84.

Gramsci, Antonio (1985) *Selections from the Cultural Writings*. London: Lawrence & Wishart.

Granovetter, M. (1979) 'The Idea of "Advancement" in Theories of Social Evolution and Development', *American Journal of Sociology* 85: 489-515.

Grathoff, Richard, ed. (1978) *The Theory of Action: The Correspondence of Alfred Schutz and Talcott Parsons*. Bloomington: Indiana University Press.

Habermas, Jürgen (1962) *Strukturwandel der Öffentlichkeit*. Neuwied: Luchterhand.

—— (1971a) *Toward a Rational Society*. London: Heinemann.

—— (1972a) *Knowledge and Human Interests*. London: Heinemann.

—— (1972b) *Kultur und Kritik*. Frankfurt: Suhrkamp.

—— (1973) 'Wahrheitstheorien', in H. Fahrenbach (ed.) *Wirklichkeit und Reflexion*. Pfullingen: Neske, pp. 24-65.

—— (1974) *Theory and Practice*. London: Heinemann.

—— (1976a) *Legitimation Crisis*. London: Heinemann.

—— (1976b) *Zur Rekonstruktion des Historischen Materialismus*. Frankfurt: Suhrkamp.

—— (1978) 'Der Ansatz von Habermas', in W. Oelmuller (ed.) *Materialien zur Normendiskussion*, Vol. I. Paderborn: Schöningh, pp. 123-59.

—— (1979a) *Communication and the Evolution of Society*. London: Heinemann.

—— (1979b) 'History and Evolution', *Telos* 39: 5-44.

—— (1981a) *Theorie des kommunikativen Handelns*, Vol. I-II. Frankfurt: Suhrkamp Verlag.

—— (1981b) 'New Social Movements', in *Telos* 49: 33-7.

—— (1982) 'A Reply to my Critics,' in J.B. Thompson and D. Held (eds.) *Habermas: Critical Debates*. London: Macmillan, pp. 219-83.
—— (1983) *Moralbewusstsein und kommunikatives Handeln*. Frankfurt: Suhrkamp.
—— (1984a) *The Theory of Communicative Action*, Vol. I. London: Heinemann.
—— (1984b) 'Über Moralität und Sittlichkeit: Was macht eine Lebensform "rational"?', in H. Schnädelbach (ed.) *Rationalität*. Frankfurt: Suhrkamp, pp. 218-35.
—— (1984c) *Vorstudien und Ergänzungen zur Theorie des kommunikativen Handelns*. Frankfurt: Suhrkamp.
—— (1985a) *Der philosophische Diskurs der Moderne*. Frankfurt: Suhrlamp.
—— (1985b) *Die neue Unübersichtlichkeit*. Frankfurt: Suhrkamp.
—— (1986a) 'Entgegnung', in A. Honneth and H. Joas (eds.) *Kommunikatives Handeln*. Frankfurt: Suhrkamp, pp. 327-405.
—— (1986b) 'Moralität und Sittlichkeit: Treffen Hegels Einwände gegen Kant auch auf die Diskursethik zu?', in W. Kuhlmann (ed.) *Moralität und Sittlichkeit*. Frankfurt: Suhrkamp, pp. 16-37.
—— (1986c) 'The New Obscurity: The Crisis of the Welfare State and the Exhaustion of Utopian Energies', *Philosophy and Social Criticism* 11(2): 1-19.
—— (1987a) *The Theory of Communicative Action*, Vol. II. Cambridge: Polity.
—— (1987b) *The Philosophical Discourse of Modernity*. Cambridge: Polity.
—— (1987c) *Eine Art Schadenabwicklung*. Frankfurt: Suhrkamp.
—— (1988a) *On the Logic of the Social Sciences*. Cambridge: Polity Press.
—— (1988b) *Nachmetaphysisches Denken*. Frankfurt: Suhrkamp.
—— (1988c) 'Die neue Intimität zwischen Politik und Kultur', in J. Rüsen *et al.* (eds.) *Die Zukunft der Aufklärung*. Suhrkamp: Frankfurt, pp. 59-68.
—— (1989a) *The Structural Transformation of the Public Sphere*. Cambridge: Polity.
—— (1989b) 'Individuelle Willensbildung unter den Aspekten des Zweckmässigen, des Guten und des Gerechten', Frankfurt: Unpublished Manuscript.
—— (1990a [1962]) *Strukturwandel der Öffentlichkeit*. Frankfurt: Suhrkamp.
—— (1990b) *Die nachholende Revolution*. Suhrkamp: Frankfurt.
—— (1991) 'Charles S. Peirce über Kommunikation', in Habermas, *Texte und Kontexte*. Frankfurt: Suhrkamp, pp. 9-33.
—— (1992) *Faktizität und Geltung*. Frankfurt: Suhrkamp Verlag.
—— (1996a) *Between Facts and Norms: Contributions to a Discourse Theory of Law and Democracy*. Cambridge: Polity.
—— (1996b) *Die Einbeziehung des Anderen*. Frankfurt: Suhrkamp Verlag.
—— (1997a) 'Kommunikative Freiheit und negative Theologie: Fragen an Michael Theunissen', in Habermas, *Von sinnlichen Eindruck zum symbolischen Ausdruck*. Frankfurt: Suhrkamp, pp. 112-35.
—— (1997b) *Vom sinnlichen Eindruck zum symbolischen Ausdruck*. Frankfurt: Suhrkamp.
—— (1999a) *The Inclusion of the Other: Studies in Political Theory*. Cambridge: Polity.
—— (1999b) 'Von Kant zu Hegel: Zu Robert Brandom's Sprachpragmatik', in *Wahrheit und Rechtfertigung*. Frankfurt: Suhrkamp, pp. 138-85.
—— (1999c) *Wahrheit und Rechtfertigung*. Frankfurt: Suhrkamp.
—— (2001) 'Robert Brandom: *Making It Explicit*', in J. Habermas, *Zeit der Übergänge*. Frankfurt: Suhrkamp, pp. 166-70.
—— (2001) *The Postnational Constellation: Political Essays*, Cambridge: Polity.
—— (2003a) *Truth and Justification*. Cambridge : Polity Press.
—— (2003b) 'From Kant to Hegel: On Robert Brandom's Pragmatic Philosophy of Language', in *Truth and Justification*. Cambridge, UK: Polity Press, pp. 131-73.
—— (2005) *Zwischen Naturalismus und Religion: Philosophische Aufsätze*. Frankfurt: Suhrkamp.

—— and Luhmann, Niklas (1971) *Theorie der Gesellschaft oder Sozialtechnologie—Was leistet die Systemforschung?* Frankfurt: Suhrkamp.
—— and Oevermann, Ulrich (1979) 'Streitgespräch,' Unpublished transcript of a debate, University of Frankfurt, 14.2.1979.
Hajer, M.A. (1995) *The Politics of Environmental Discourse: Ecological Modernization and the Policy Process*. Oxford: Clarendon Press.
—— (1996) 'Ecological Modernization as Cultural Politics,' in S. Lash, B. Szerszinski and B. Wynne (eds.) *Risk, Environment and Modernity: Towards a New Ecology*. London: Sage, pp. 246-68.
Hansen, A. (1991) 'The Media and the Social Construction of the Environment', *Media, Culture and Society* 13: 443-58.
Harris, M. (1979) *Cultural Materialism*. New York: Random House.
Harrison, P.R. (1991) 'Habermas and the Problem of Archaic Societies', *Thesis Eleven* 28: 127-31.
Harten, Hans-Christian (1977a) *Vernünftiger Organismus: oder gesellschaftliche Evolution der Vernunft*. Frankfurt: Syndikat.
—— (1977b) *Kognitive Sozialisation und politische Erkenntnis*. Weinheim/Basel: Belz.
Hauser, Arnold (1951) *The Social History of Art*, Vol. II. New York: Vintage.
Hegedus, Zsuzsa (1990) 'Social Movements and Social Change in Self-Creative Society', in M. Albrow and E. King (eds.) *Globalization*. London: Sage, pp. 263-80
Held, David (1980) *Introduction to Critical Theory*. London: Hutchinson.
—— (1996) *Models of Democracy*. Cambridge: Polity Press.
Heidegger, Martin (1967) *Being and Time*. Oxford: Blackwell.
Heilbron, Johan (1998) 'French Moralists and the Anthropology of the Modern Era', in J. Heilbron *et al.* (eds.) *The Rise of the Social Sciences and the Formation of Modernity*. Dordrecht: Kluwer, pp. 77-106.
Hepp, Corona (1987) *Avantgarde: Moderne Kunst, Kulturkritik und Reformbewegungen nach der Jahrhundertwende*. Munich: Deutscher Taschenbuch Verlag.
Hill, Christopher (1972) *The World Turned Upside Down: Radical Ideas During the English Revolution*. Penguin: Harmondsworth.
Ho, Mae-Wan and Saunders, Peter (1979) 'Beyond Neo-Darwinism: An Epigenetic Approach to Evolution,' *Journal of Theoretical Biology* 78: 573-91.
—— (1982) 'An Epigenetic Approach to the Evolution of Organisms: With Notes on the Relevance to Social and Cultural Evolution,' in H.C. Plotkin (ed.) *Learning, Development and Culture*. Chichester/New York: Wiley.
Hobsbawm, Eric J. and Rude, George (1972) *Captain Swing*. Penguin: Harmondsworth.
Hofstadter, R. (1955) *Social Darwinism in American Thought*. Boston: Beacon Press.
Honneth, Axel (1981a) 'Eine unabgeschlossenes Kapitel kritische Gesellschaftstheorie,' *Aesthetik und Kommunikation* 12: 162-70.
—— (1981b) 'Moralbewusstsein und Klassenherrschaft,' *Leviathan* 9: 556-70.
—— (1982) 'Moral Consciousness and Class Domination,' *Praxis International* 2: 12-25.
—— (1983) 'Moralischer Konsens und Ungerechtigkeitsempfindung,' in *Almanach: Suhrkamp Wissenschaft Weisses Program*. Frankfurt: Suhrkamp, pp. 108-14.
—— (1985) *Kritik der Macht: Reflexionsstufen einer kritischen Gesellschaftstheorie*. Frankfurt: Suhrkamp.
—— (1986) 'Diskursethik und implizites Gerechtigkeitskonzept,' in W. Kuhlmann (ed.) *Moralität und Sittlichkeit*. Frankfurt: Suhrkamp, pp. 183-93.
—— (1989) 'Moralische Entwicklung und sozialer Kampf: Sozialphilosophische Lehren aus Hegels Früwerk,' in A. Honneth *et al.* (eds.) *Zwischenbetrachtungen: Im Prozess der Aufklärung: Jürgen Habermas zum 60. Geburtstag*. Frankfurt: Suhrkamp, pp. 549-73.
—— (1990) *Die zerrissene Welt des Sozialen*. Frankfurt: Suhrkamp.

—— (1991) *Critique of Power*. Cambridge, MA: MIT.

—— (1992) *Kampf um Anerkennung*. Frankfurt: Suhrkamp.

—— (2000) *Das Andere der Gerechtigkeit*. Frankfurt: Suhrkamp.

—— and Joas, Hans (1980) *Soziales Handeln und menschliche Natur*. Frankfurt: Campus Verlag.

—— and Hans Joas eds. (1986) *Kommunikatives Handeln*. Frankfurt: Suhrkamp.

—— and Joas, Hans (1988) *Social Action and Human Nature*. Cambridge: Cambridge University Press.

Horkheimer, Max (1972) *Traditionelle und kritische Theorie*. Frankfurt: Fischer.

—— (1974) *Critique of Instrumental Reason*. New York: Seabury.

—— and Adorno, Theodor (1972 [1944]) *Dialectic of Enlightenment*. New York: Herder and Herder.

Hörning, Karl H., Ahrens, Daniela and Gerhard, Anette (1997) *Zeitpraktiken*. Frankfurt: Suhrkamp.

Horowitz, I.L. (1967) *The Rise and Fall of Project Camelot*. Cambridge, MA: MIT.

Inglehart, R. (1977) *The Silent Revolution*. Princeton, NJ: Princeton University Press.

—— (1990) *Culture Shift in Advanced Industrial Society*. Princeton, NJ: Princeton University Press.

International Development Centre (1993a) *The Earth Summit CD-ROM*. Ottawa: United Nations and Canadian Centre for Occupational Health and Safety.

—— (1993b) *The Earth Summit NGO CD-ROM*. Ottawa: United Nations and Canadian Centre for Occupational Health and Safety.

Japp, Klaus (1984) 'Selbsterzeugung oder Fremdverschulden: Thesen zum Rationalismus in den Theorien sozialer Bewegungen,' *Soziale Welt* 35: 313-29.

Joas, Hans (1986a) 'Die unglückliche Ehe von Hermeneutik und Funktionalismus,' in A. Honneth and H. Joas (eds.) *Kommunikatives Handeln*. Frankfurt: Suhrkamp, pp. 144-75.

—— (1986b) 'Eine soziologische Transformation der Praxisphilosophie-Giddens' Theorie der Strukturierung', *Zeitschrift für Soziologie*, 15: 237-85.

—— (1992a) *Pragmatismus und Gesellschaftstheorie*. Frankfurt: Suhrkamp.

—— (1992b) *Die Kreativität des Handelns*. Frankfurt: Suhrkamp.

Jonas, H. (1973) 'Technology and Responsibility: Reflections on the New Tasks of Ethics,' *Social Research* 40(1): 31-54.

—— (1976) 'Responsibility Today: The Ethics of an Endangered Future,' *Social Research* 43(1): 77-97.

—— (1982), 'Technology as a Subject for Ethics,' *Social Research* 49: 891-98.

—— (1984 [1979]) *The Imperative of Responsibility: In Search of an Ethics for the Technological Age*. Chicago: University of Chicago Press.

Jones, G. (1980) *Social Darwinism and English Thought*. Sussex: Harvester.

Kant, Immanuel (1972 [1790]) *Critique of Judgement*. New York: Hafner.

Karis, Thomas and Carter, Gwendolen eds. (1987) *From Protest to Challenge: A Documentary History of African Politics in South Africa, 1882-1964*, Vol. I-IV. Stanford: Hoover Institute Press.

Kettner, Matthias (1992) 'Über einige Dilemmata angewandter Ethik', in K.-O. Apel and M. Kettner (eds.) *Zur Anwendung der Diskursethik in Politik, Recht und Wissenschaft*. Frankfurt: Suhrkamp, pp. 9-28.

—— (1996) 'Gute Gründe: Thesen zur diskursiven Vernunft', in K.-O. Apel and M. Kettner of (eds.) *Die eine Vernunft und die vielen Rationalitäten*. Frankfurt: Suhrkamp, pp. 424-64.

Knorr Cetina, Karin (1979) 'Sociality with Objects', *Theory, Culture and Society* 14: 1-30.

—— (1981) *The Manufacture of Knowledge*. Oxford: Pergamon.

—— (1988) 'The Micro-Social Order: Towards a Reconception', in N.G. Fielding (ed.) *Actions and Structure: Research Methods and Social Theory*. London: Sage, pp. 20-53.

—— and Cicourel, Aaron V. eds. (1981), *Advances in Social Theory and Methodology*. Boston: Routledge & Kegan Paul.

Kohlberg, Lawrence (1976) 'The Moral Atmosphere of the School,' in D. Purpel and Kevin Ryan (eds.) *Moral Education*. Berkeley: McCutchan, pp. 196-220.

—— (1985) 'The Just Community Approach to Moral Education in Theory and Practice,' in M. Berkowitz and F. Oser (eds.) *Moral Education: Theory and Application*. Hillsdale, N.J./London: Erlbaum, pp. 27-87.

—— (1986) 'A Current Statement on Some Theoretical Issues,' in S. and C. Modgil (eds.) *Lawrence Kohlberg: Consensus and Controversy*. Philadelphia/London: Falmer, pp. 485-546.

Koppe, Franz (1983) *Grundbegriffe der Ästhetik*. Frankfurt: Suhrkamp.

Krawietz, Werner (1992) 'Zur Einleitung: Neue Sequenzierung der Theoriebildung und Kritik der allgemenine Theorie soziale Systems', in W. Krawietz and M. Welker (eds.) *Kritik der Theorie sozialer Systeme: Auseinandersetzungen mit Luhmanns Hauptwerk*. Frankfurt: Suhrkamp,, pp. 14-42.

Kuper, Leo (1971) 'African Nationalism in South Africa, 1910-1964,' in M. Wilson and L. Thompson (eds.) *The Oxford History of South Africa*, Vol. 2. Oxford: Clarendon Press, pp. 424-76.

Laclau, Ernesto and Mouffe, Chantal (1985) *Hegemony and Socialist Strategies*. London: Verso.

Lakatos, Imre (1970) 'Falsification and the Methodology of Scientific Research Programmes', in I. Lakatos and A. Musgrave (eds.) *Criticism and the Growth of Knowledge*. Cambridge: Cambridge University Press, pp. 173-7.

Lash, S. (1994) 'Expert-Systems or Situated Interpretation? Culture and Institutions in Disorganized Capitalism,' in U. Beck, A. Giddens and S. Lash, *Reflexive Modernization: Politics, Tradition and Aesthetics in the Modern Social Order*. Cambridge: Polity Press, pp. 198-215.

Lau, Christophe (1981) *Gesellschaftliche Evolution als kollektiver Lernprozeß*. Berlin: Duncker und Humblot.

—— (1989) 'Risikodiskurse: Gesellschaftliche Auseinandersetzungen um die Definition von Risiken,' *Soziale Welt* 3: 418-36.

Legassick, Martin (1976) 'Race, Industrialization and Social Change: The Case of R.F.A. Hoernle,' *African Affairs* 75: 224-39.

Leydesdorff, Loet (2000) 'Luhmann, Habermas, and the Theory of Communication', *Systems Research and Behavioural Science* 17: 273-88.

—— (2007) 'The Communication of Meaning in Anticipatory Systems: A Simulation Study of the Dynamics of Intentionality in Social Interactions', Vice-Presidential Address, 8th International Conference of *Computing Anticipatory Systems (CASYS07)*, Liège, Belgium, 6-11 August 2007, *Proceedings of the American Institute of Physics* (forthcoming), available as a preprint version at http://www.leydesdorff.net/casys07

—— (2009) 'Modelling "Triple Contingency"', in S. Ó'Tuama (ed.) *Critical Turns in Critical Theory: New Directions in Social and Political Theory (Festschrift in Honour of Piet Strydom)*. London: Tauris Academic Studies.

Lichtenberg, Judith ed. (1990) *Democracy and the Mass Media*. Cambridge: Cambridge University Press.

Linkenbach, Antje (1986) *Opake Gestalten des Denkens: Jürgen Habermas und die Rationalität fremder Lebensformen*. Munich: Fink.

LiPuma, E. (1993) 'Culture and the Concept of Culture in a Theory of Practice', in Craig Calhoun *et al.* (eds.) *Bourdieu: Critical Perspectives*. Cambridge: Polity, pp. 14-34.

Lopreato, J. (1984) *Human Natural and Biocultural Evolution*. Boston: Unwin Hyman.
—— (1990) 'From Social Evolutionism to Biocultural Evolutionism', *Sociological Forum* 5: 187-212.
Lovtrup, Soren (1974) *Epigenetics*. London/New York: Wiley.
Luhmann, Niklas (1976) 'Generalized Media and the Problem of Contingency', in J.J. Loubser *et al.* (eds.) *Explorations in General Theory in Social Science: Essays in Honour of Talcott Parsons*, Vol. II. New York: Free Press, pp. 503-32.
—— (1976) 'Geschichte und Evolution', *Geschichte und Gesellschaft* 2: 284-309.
—— (1978) 'Geschichte als Prozess und die Theorie soziokultureller Evolution', in K.-G. Faber and C. Meier (eds.) *Historische Prozesse*. Munich: DTV, pp. 413-40
—— (1982) *The Differentiation of Society*. New York: Columbia University Press.
—— (1984) *Soziale Systeme: Grundriss einer allgemeine Theorie*. Frankfurt: Suhrkamp.
—— (1986) *Ökologische Kommunikation*. Opladen: Westdeutscher Verlag.
—— (1987) 'Intersubjektivität oder Kommunikation: Unterschiedliche Ausgangspunkte soziologischer Theoriebildung', *Diskurs* 1(2): 24-33.
—— (1989) *Ecological Communication*. Cambridge: Polity.
—— (1992a) *Die Wissenschaft der Gesellschaft*. Frankfurt: Suhrkamp.
—— (1992b) 'Stellungname', in W. Krawietz and M. Welker (eds.) *Kritik der Theorie sozialer Systeme: Auseinandersetzungen mit Luhmanns Hauptwerk*. Frankfurt: Suhrkamp, pp. 371-86.
—— (1995a [1984]) *Social Systems*. Stanford, CA: Stanford University Press.
—— (1995b) *Risk: A Sociological Theory*. Berlin/New York: de Gruyter.
—— (1998) *Observations on Modernity*. Stanford, CA: Stanford University Press.
—— (1999) 'Öffentliche Meinung und Demokratie', in R. Maresch and N. Werber (eds.) *Kommunikation, Medien, Macht*. Frankfurt: Suhrkamp, pp. 19-34.
Lukács, Georg (1971 [1923]) *History and Class Consciousness*. London: Merlin.
Lukashuk, I. (1997) 'The Law of the International Community', in International Law Commission *International Law on the Eve of the Twenty-First Century: Views from the International Law Commission*. New York: United Nations.
Lyotard, Jean-François (1984) *The Postmodern Condition*. Minneapolis: University of Minnesota.
Maciejewski, Franz ed. (1973) *Theorie der Gesellschaft oder Sozialtechnologie: Beiträge zur Habermas-Luhmann-Diskussion*. Frankfurt: Suhrkamp.
—— (1974) *Theorie der Gesellschaft oder Sozialtechnologie: Neue Beiträge zur Habermas-Luhmann-Diskussion*. Frankfurt: Suhrkamp.
Mannheim, Karl (1972) *Ideology and Utopia*. London: Routledge and Kegan Paul.
Marcuse, Herbert (1972) *Negations: Essays in Critical Theory*. Harmondsworth: Penguin.
Marks, Shula (1970) *Reluctant Rebellion: The 1906-1908 Disturbances in Natal*. Oxford: Clarendon Press.
Marx, Karl (1974) *Grundrisse: Foundations of the Critique of Political Economy*. Harmondsworth: Penguin.
—— (1976) *Capital*. Harmondsworth: Penguin.
Mater, Marie A. (1998) *Environmental Discourse between North and South: A Theory of Discourse for a Global Public Sphere*. Unpublished PhD Thesis, National University of Ireland.
McAdam, D., McCarthy, J.D. and Zald, M.N. eds. (1996) *Comparative Perspectives on Social Movements: Political Opportunities, Mobilizing Structures, and Cultural Framings*. New York: Cambridge University Press.
McCarthy, Thomas (1978) *The Critical Theory of Jürgen Habermas*. London: Hutchinson.
—— (1979) 'Translator's Introduction', in J. Habermas, *Communication and the Evolution of Society*. London: Heinemann, pp. vii-xxi.

—— (1994) 'On the Pragmatics of Communicative Reason', in D. Couzens Hoy and T. McCarthy, *Critical Theory*. Oxford: Blackwell, pp. 63-100.

McIver, R.M. and Page, C.H. (1949) *Society: An Introductory Analysis*. New York: Rinehart.

Mead, George Herbert (1974 [1934]) *Mind, Self and Society*. Chicago: University of Chicago Press.

Melucci, Alberto (1980) 'The New Social Movements: A Theoretical Approach,' *Social Science Information* 19: 199-226.

—— (1984) 'An End to Social Movements?,' *Social Science Information* 23: 819-35.

—— (1985) 'The Symbolic Challenge of Contemporary Movements,' *Social Research* 52: 789-816.

—— (1988) 'Getting Involved: Identity and Mobilization in Social Movements', in B. Klandermans, H. Kriesi and S. Tarrow (eds.) *From Structure to Action*. Greenwich, CT: JAI Press, pp. 329-48.

—— (1995) 'The New Social Movements', in L. Maheu (ed.) *Social Movements and Social Classes*. London: Sage, pp. 107-19.

—— (1996) *Challenging Codes: Collective Action in the Information Age*. Cambridge: Cambridge University Press.

—— (1986) *Kollektive Lernprozesse: Studien zur Grundlegung einer soziologischen Lerntheorie*. Frankfurt: Suhrkamp.

—— (1992a) 'Discourse and Morality: Two Case Studies of Social Conflicts in a Segmentary and a Functionally Differentiated Society', *Archives Européennes de Sociologie* 33(1): 3-38.

—— (1992b) 'Rationaler Dissens: Zur gesellschaftlichen Funktion sozialer Konflikte' in H.-J. Giegel (ed.) *Kommunikation und Konsens in modernen Gesellschaften*, Frankfurt: Suhrkamp, pp. 31-58.

—— (1994) 'Intersystemic Discourse and Coordinated Dissent: A Critique of Luhmann's Concept of Ecological Discourse', *Theory, Culture and Society* 11: 101-21.

—— (2002a) 'Some Theoretical Aspects of Systemic Learning', *Sozialer Sinn* 3: 379-421.

—— (2002b) 'Who Conducts a Discourse? A Reply to My Commentators', *Sozialer Sinn* 3: 461-68.

Miller, David (1982) 'Introduction,' in G.H. Mead, *The Individual and the Social Self.* Chicago: University of Chicago Press, pp. 1-26.

Miller, Max (1987) 'Selbstreferenz und Differenzerfahrung: Einige Überlegungen zu Luhmann's Theorie sozialer Systeme', in H. Haferkamp and M. Schmid (eds.) *Sinn, Kommunikation und soziale Differenzierung: Beiträge zu Luhmann's Theorie sozialer Systeme*. Frankfurt: Suhrkamp, pp. 187-211.

Mills, C. Wright (1956) *The Power Elite*. New York: Oxford.

Moscovici, Serge (1968) *Essai sur l'histoire humaine de la nature*. Paris: Flammarion.

—— (1990) 'Questions for the Twenty-First Century,' *Theory, Culture and Society*. 7: 1-19.

Mossakowski, D. and Roth, G. eds. (1982) *Environmental Adaptation and Evolution*. Stuttgart/New York: Fischer.

Mullally, G. (1996) 'Extended Producer Responsibility,' Unpublished Research Report, EU Project EXPRESS. Cork: Centre for European Social Research, University College Cork.

Münch, Richard (1984) *Die Struktur der Moderne*. Frankfurt: Suhrkamp.

Mushaben, Joyce (1985) 'Cycles of Peace Protest in West Germany,' *West European Politics* 8: 24-40.

Na'aman, Shlomo (1978) *Zur Entstehung der deutschen Arbeiterbewegung*. Hannover: SOAK.

Negt, Oskar and Kluge, Alexander (1972) *Öffentlichkeit und Erfahrung: Zur Organisationsanalyse von bürgerlicher und proletarischer Öffentilichkeit.* Frankfurt: Suhrkamp.

Neidhart, Friedhelm and Rucht, Dieter (1991) 'The Analysis of Social Movements', in Dieter Rucht (ed.) *Research on Social Movements.* Frankfurt/Boulder: Campus Verlag/ Westview Press, pp. 421-64.

Nelson, R.R. and Winter, S.G. (1982) *An Evolutionary Theory of Economic Change.* Cambridge, MA: Harvard University Press.

Oberdorfer, Bernd (1992) 'Einschränkung von Beliebigkeit? Systemische Selbstreproduktion und gesellschaftlicher Strukturaufbau', in W. Krawietz and M. Welker (eds.) *Kritik der Theorie sozialer Systeme: Auseinandersetzungen mit Luhmanns Hauptwerk.* Frankfurt: Suhrkamp, pp. 302-26.

Oevermann, Ulrich (1976) 'Piagets Bedeutung für die Soziologie,' in *Hommage á Jean Piaget zum 80. Geburtstag.* Stuttgart: Klett, pp. 36-41.

—— (1983) 'Zur Sache: Die Bedeutung von Adornos methodologischem Selbsverständnis für die Begründung einer materialen soziologischen Strukturanalyse', in L. von Friedeburg and J. Habermas (eds.) *Adorno-Konferenz 1983.* Frankfurt: Suhrkamp, pp. 234-89.

—— and Habermas, Jürgen (1979) 'Streitgespräch', Unpublished transcript of a debate, University of Frankfurt, 14.2.1979.

Offe, Claus (2001) 'Wessen Wohl ist das Gemeinwohl?', in L. Wingert and K. Günther (eds.) *Die Öffentlichkeit der Vernunft und die Vernunft der Öffentlichkeit.* Frankfurt: Suhrkamp, pp. 459-88.

—— and Wiesenthal, Helmut (1980) 'Two Logics of Collective Action', in M. Zeitlin (ed.) *Political Power and Social Theory.* Greenwich, CT: JAI Press, pp. 112-28.

Ogorek, R. (1987) 'Review of Klaus Eder, "Geschichte als Lernprozeß?"', *Kölner Zeitschrift für Soziologie und Sozialpsychologie* 39: 813-16.

O'Mahony, Patrick and Delanty, Gerard (1998) *Rethinking Irish History: Nationalism, Identity and Ideology.* Houndsmills: Palgrave.

Oser, Fritz (1981) *Moralisches Urteil in Gruppen, Soziales Handeln, Verteilungsgerechtigkeit.* Frankfurt: Suhrkamp.

—— (1984) 'Cognitive Stages of Interaction in Moral Discourse,' in W. Kurtines and J. Gewirtz (eds.) *Morality, Moral Behaviour and Moral Development.* New York: Wiley, pp. 159-74.

Parsons, Talcott (1961) 'Some Considerations on the Theory of Social Change', *Rural Sociology* 26: 219-39.

—— (1964a) *The Social System.* New York: Free Press.

—— (1964b) 'Evolutionary Universals in Society' *American Sociological Review* 29: 339-57.

—— (1966) *Societies: Evolutionary and Comparative Perspectives.* Englewood Cliffs: Prentice-Hall.

—— (1971) *The System of Modern Societies.* Englewood Cliffs: Prentice-Hall.

—— (1977a) *The Evolution of Societies.* Englewood Cliffs: Prentice-Hall.

—— (1977b) *Social Systems and the Evolution of Action Theory.* New York: Free Press.

—— (1978) *Action Theory and the Human Condition.* Free Press: New York.

—— and Shils, Edward A., eds. (1951) *Towards a General Theory of Action.* Cambridge, MA: Harvard University Press.

Piaget, Jean (1967) *Etudes Sociologiques.* Geneva: Librairie Droz.

—— (1968 [1932]) *The Moral Judgement of the Child.* Harmondsworth: Penguin.

Plotkin, H.C. ed. (1982) *Learning, Development and Culture.* Chichester/New York: Wiley.

Popper, Karl R. (1972) *Objective Knowledge.* Oxford: Oxford University Press.

Power, Clark (1981) 'Moral Education Through the Development of the Moral Atmosphere of the School,' *The Journal of Educational Thought* 15: 4-19.

—— and Reimer, Joseph (1978) 'Moral Atmosphere: An Educational Bridge Between Moral Judgement and Moral Action,' in W. Damon (ed.) *New Directions for Child Development*, Vol.II: *Moral Development*. San Francisco: Jossy-Bass.

Privitera, Walter (1990) *Stilprobleme: Zur Epistemologie Michel Foucaults*. Meisenheim: Anton Hain.

Rasmussen, David M. ed. (1996) *Handbook of Critical Theory*. Oxford: Blackwell.

Rochberg-Halton, Eugene (1982) 'Situation, Structure and the Context of Meaning', *The Sociological Quarterly* 23: 455-76.

Rödel, Ulrich, Frankenberg, Günter and Dubiel, Helmut (1989) *Die demokratische Frage: Ein Essay*. Suhrkamp: Frankfurt.

Rose, H. and Rose, S. (1970) *Science and Society*. Harmondsworth: Penguin.

Rosenberg, Bernard and White, David M. eds. (1957) *Mass Culture*. New York: Free Press.

Rosenfeld, Michel ed. (1996), Special Issues on: 'Habermas on Law and Democracy', *Cardoso Law Review* 17(4-5).

Rötzer, F. ed. (1989) *Denken, das an der Zeit ist*. Frankfurt: Suhrkamp.

Roux, Edward (1964) *Time Longer than Rope: A History of the Black Man's Struggle for Freedom in South Africa*. Madison: University of Wisconsin Press.

Runciman, W.G. (1989) *A Treatise on Social Theory: Substantive Social Theory*, Vol. II. Cambridge: Cambridge University Press.

Rusch, Gebhard (1999) 'Kommunikation der Wirklichkeit der Media der Wirklichkeit der Komunikation', in G. Rusch and S.J. Schmidt (eds.) *Konstruktivismus in der Medien- und Kommunikationswissenschaft*. Frankfurt: Suhrkamp, pp. 7-12.

Rüsen, J. *et al.* eds. (1988) *Die Zukunft der Aufklärung*. Frankfurt: Suhrkamp.

Saferstein, Barry (1998) 'Ethnomethodology', in W. Bechtel and G. Graham (eds.) *A Companion to Cognitive Science*. Oxford: Blackwell, pp. 391-401.

—— (2007) 'Process Narratives, Grey Boxes, and Discourse Frameworks: Cognition, Interaction, and Constraint in Understanding Genetics and Medicine', *European Journal of Social Theory* 10(3): 424-47.

Sahlins, Marshall (1976) *Culture and Practical Reason*. Chicago/London: University of Chicago Press.

—— (1985) *Islands of History*. Chicago: University of Chicago Press.

Saretzki, Thomas (1988) 'Collective Action vs. Functionalism: Some Remarks on Joas' Critique,' *Praxis International* 8: 52-72.

Schäfer, W. (1985) *Die unvertraute Moderne: Historische Umrisse einer anderen Natur- und Sozialgeschichte*. Frankfurt: Fischer.

Schluchter, Wolfgang (1991) *Religion und Lebensführung*, Vol. I: *Studien zu Webers Kultur- und Werttheorie*. Frankfurt: Suhrkamp.

Schmid, Michael (1982a) 'Habermas's Theory of Social Evolution,' in J.B. Thompson and D. Held (eds.) *Habermas: Critical Debates*. London: Macmillan, pp. 162-80.

—— (1982b) *Theorien sozialen Wandels*. Opladen: Westdeutscher Verlag.

—— (1987) 'Collective Action and the Selection of Rules: Some Notes on the Evolutionary Paradigm in Social Theory,' in M. Schmid and F.M. Wuketits (eds.) *Evolutionary Theory in Social Science*. Dordrecht: Reidel, pp. 79-100.

—— and Wuketits, F.M. eds. (1987) *Evolutionary Theory in Social Science*. Dordrecht: Reidel.

Schmidt, Siegfried J. (1999) 'Blickwechsel: Umrisse einer Medienepistemologie', in G. Rusch and S.J. Schmidt (eds.) *Konstruktivismus in der Medien- und Kommunikationswissenschaft*. Frankfurt: Suhrkamp, pp. 119-45.

Schnädelbach, Herbert (1986) 'Was ist Neoaristotelismus?,' in W. Kuhlmann (ed.) *Moralität und Sittlichkeit*. Frankfurt: Suhrkamp, pp. 38-63.

Schöfthaler, T. and Goldschmidt, D. eds. (1984) *Soziale Struktur und Vernunft*. Frankfurt: Suhrkamp.

Schomberg, René von (1992) 'Argumentation im Kontext wissenschaftlicher Kontroversen', in K.-O. Apel and M. Kettner (eds.) *Zur Anwendung der Diskursethik in Politik, Recht und Wissenschaft*. Frankfurt: Suhrkamp, pp. 260-77.

Schutz, Alfred (1967) *The Phenomenology of the Social World*. London: Heinemann.

Seeley, J.R. (1970) 'The Making and Taking of Problems: Toward an Ethical Stance,' in J.D. Douglas (ed.) *The Relevance of Sociology*. New York: Appleton-Century-Crofts, pp. 85-95.

Shepperson, George (1953) 'Ethiopianism and African Nationalism,' *Phylon* 14: 9-18.

Sinha, Chris (1988) *Language and Representation: A Socio-Naturalistic Approach to Human Development*. Hemel Hempstead: Harvester Wheatsheaf.

Sizwe, No (1979) *One Azania, One Nation: The National Question in South Africa*. London: Zed Press.

Skillington, Tracey (1997) 'Politics and the Struggle to Define: A Discourse Analysis of the Framing Strategies of Competing Actors in a "New" Participatory Forum', *The British Journal of Sociology* 48(3): 493-513.

Smith, Adam (1982 [1759]) *The Theory of Moral Sentiments*. Indianapolis: Liberty Fund.

Snow, D.A. and Benford, R.D. (1988) 'Ideology, Frame Resonance, and Participant Mobilization,' in B. Klandermans *et al.* (eds.) *From Structure to Action: Comparing Social Movement Research Across Cultures*. Greenwich, CT: JAI Press, pp. 197-217.

—— (1992) 'Master Frames and Cycles of Protest,' in A.D. Morris and C.M. Mueller (eds.) *Frontiers in Social Movement Theory*. New Haven, CT: Yale University Press, pp. 133-55.

—— Rochford, E.B., Worden, S.K. and Benford, R.D. (1986) 'Frame Alignment Processes, Micro-Mobilization and Movement Participation', *American Sociological Review* 51(4): 464-81.

Somers, Margaret (1994) 'Rights, Rationality, and Membership', *Law and Social Inquiry* 19: 63-112.

—— (1995a) 'What's Political or Cultural about Political Culture and the Public Sphere? Toward an Historical Sociology of Concept Formation', *Sociological Theory* 13: 113-44.

—— (1995b) 'Narrating and Naturalizing Civil Society and Citizenship Theory: The Place of Political Culture and the Public Sphere,' *Sociological Theory* 13(3): 229-74.

Spencer, Herbert (1893) *The Inadequacy of "Natural Selection"*. London: Williams and Norgate.

Sperber, Dan (1997) 'Individualisme méthodologique et cognitivisme' in R. Boudon, A. Bouvier and F. Chazel (eds.) *Cognition et sciences sociales*, Paris: PUF, pp. 123-36.

—— and Wilson, Deirdre (1986) *Relevance: Communication and Cognition*. Oxford: Blackwell.

Strydom, Piet (1986) 'On the Principle of Freedom of Speech', Paper presented to the philosophical society Cogito, University College Cork, Ireland, 25.4.1986.

—— (1986-87) 'Institutionalisation in Critical Theoretical Perspective,' Protocol of Graduate Seminar, Department of Sociology, University College Cork, Ireland.

—— (1987) 'Collective Learning: Habermas's Concessions and Their Theoretical Implications,' *Philosophy and Social Criticism* 13(3): 265-81. [Chapter 1 in this volume]

—— (1988-89) 'Contemporary Culture and the New Social Movements', Unpublished lecture course. Cork: University College Cork.

—— (1990a) 'Habermas and New Social Movements', *Telos* 85: 156-64. [Chapter 4 in this volume contains an expanded version]

—— (1990b) 'Metacritical Observations on a Reductive Approach to Critical Theory', *Political Studies* 38(3): 534-42.

—— (1991) 'Freedom of Speech and the Expressive Revolution: On the Latest Shift in the Foundation of Rights', Lecture delivered at Janus Pannonius University, Pécs, Hungary 27.3.1991, Centre for European Social Research, Cork, Working Paper No. 7.

—— (1992) 'The Ontogenetic Fallacy: The Immanent Critique of Habermas' Developmental Logical Theory of Evolution', *Theory, Culture and Society* 9(3): 65-93. [Chapter 2 in this volume]

—— (1993) 'Sociocultural Evolution or the Social Evolution of Practical Reason: Eder's Critique of Habermas', *Praxis International* 13(3): 304-22. [Chapter 3 in this volume]

—— (1995-96) 'Sociology of Risk and Responsibility,' Unpublished lecture course. Cork: University College Cork.

—— (1999a) 'Hermeneutic Culturalism and its Double: A Key Problem in the Reflexive Modernization Debate,' *European Journal of Social Theory* 2(1): 45-69.

—— (1999b) 'The Civilisation of the Gene: Biotechnological Risk Framed in the Responsibility Discourse', in P. O'Mahony (ed.) *Nature, Risk and Responsibility*. London: Macmillan, pp. 21-36.

—— (1999c) 'The Challenge of Responsibility for Sociology', *Current Sociology* 74(3): 65-82. [Chapter 13 in this volume]

—— (1999d) 'The Contemporary Habermas: Towards Triple Contingency?' *European Journal of Social Theory* 2(2): 253-63.

—— (1999e) 'Triple Contingency: The Theoretical Problem of the Public in Communication Societies', *Philosophy and Social Criticism* 25(2): 1-25. [Chapter 6 in this volume]

—— (2000) *Discourse and Knowledge*. Liverpool: Liverpool University Press.

—— (2001) 'The Problem of Triple Contingency in Habermas', *Sociological Theory* 19(2): 165-86. [Chapter 7 in this volume]

—— (2002) *Risk, Environment and Society*. Buckingham/Philadelphia: Open University Press.

—— (2003) 'Resonance: Triggering a Dormant Dimension of the Public Sphere', in V. Kultygin and V. Zhukov (eds.) *European Social Theory: Sources and Challenges*. Moscow: European Sociological Association, pp. 83-99. [Chapter 9 in the volume]

—— (2005) 'Risk', in S. Restivo (ed.) *Science, Technology, and Society: An Encyclopedia*. New York: Oxford University Press, pp. 474-76.

—— (2006a) 'Contemporary European Cognitive Social Theory', in G. Delanty (ed.) *Handbook of Contemporary European Social Theory*. London: Routledge, pp. 218-29.

—— (2006b) 'Intersubjectivity—Interactionist or Discursive? Reflections on Habermas' Critique of Brandom', *Philosophy and Social Criticism* 32(2): 155-72. [Chapter 10 in this volume]

—— (2006c) 'Cognitivism', in A. Harrington, B.L. Marshall and H.-P. Müller (eds.) *Encyclopedia of Social Theory*. London: Routledge.

—— (2006d) 'Framing', in A. Harrington, B.L. Marshall and H. P. Müller (eds.) *Encyclopedia of Social Theory*. London: Routledge.

—— (2007) 'Introduction: A Cartography of Contemporary Cognitive Social Theory', *European Journal of social Theory* 10(3): 339-56.

—— (2008) 'In Search of Structures of Cooperation: The Discursive Construction of Morality in the Land Reform Dispute in Post-Apartheid South Africa', in Ananta Kumar Giri (ed.) *The Modern Prince and the Modern Sage: Transforming Power and Freedom*. New Delhi: Sage.

—— (2009) 'On Naturalism and Realism in Social Science: Critical Theory and Critical Realism', in S. Ó'Tuama (ed.) *Critical Turns in Critical Theory: New Directions in*

Social and Political Thought' (Festschrift in Honour of Piet Strydom). London: Tauris Academic Studies.

—— and Skillington, Tracey (1994) 'Outline of Research on Extended Producer Responsibility,' Unpublished Research Design, EU Project EXPRESS. Cork: Centre for European Social Research, University College Cork.

Sutter, Tilmann ed. (1997) *Beobachtung verstehen, Verstehen beobachten*. Opladen: Westdeutscher Verlag.

—— and Charlton, Michael (1999) 'Die Bedeutung einer konstruktivistische Theorie sozialen Handelns für die Medienforschung', in G. Rusch and S.J. Schmidt (eds.) *Konstruktivismus in der Medien- und Kommunikationswissenschaft*. Frankfurt: Suhrkamp, pp. 79-113.

Swidler, A. (1986) 'Culture in Action: Symbols and Strategies,' *American Sociological Review* 51: 273-86.

Teubner, Gunther ed. (1997) *Global Law without a State*. Aldershot: Ashgate.

—— (2002) 'Breaking Frames: Economic Globalization and the Emergence of *lex mercatoria*', *European Journal of Social Theory* 5(2): 199-217.

Thévenot, Laurent (1998) 'Pragmatiques de la connaissance', in A. Borzeix, A. Bouvier and P. Pharo (eds.) *Sociologie et connaissance: Nouvelles\approches cognitives*. Paris: CNRS, pp. 101-39.

—— (2001) 'Pragmatic Regimes Governing the Engagement with the World', in T.R. Schatzki, K. Knorr Cetina and E. von Savigny (eds.) *The Practice Turn in Contemporary Theory*. London: Routledge, pp. 56-73.

—— (2007) 'The Plurality of Cognitive Formats and Engagements: Moving between the Familiar and the Public', *European Journal of Social Theory* 10(3): 409-23.

Thompson, E.P. (1968) *The Making of the English Working Class*. Harmondsworth: Penguin.

Thompson, Leonard (1969) *African Societies in Southern Africa*. London: Heinemann.

Tomuschat, C. (1997), 'International Law as the Constitution of Mankind', in International Law Commission *International Law on the Eve of the Twenty-First Century: Views from the International Law Commission*, New York: United Nations.

Toulmin, Stephen (1972) *Human Understanding*. Oxford: Clarendon Press.

Touraine, Alain (1971) *The Post-Industrial Society*. New York: Random House.

—— (1977) *The Self-Production of Society*. Chicago: Chicago University Press.

—— (1981) *The Voice and the Eye*. London: Cambridge University Press.

Trenz, Hans-Jörg and Klaus Eder (2004) 'The Democratizing Dynamics of a European Public Sphere: Towards a Theory of Democratic Functionalism', *European Journal of Social Theory* 7(1): 5-25.

Tugendhat, Ernst (1980) 'Zur Entwicklung von moralischen Begrundungsstrukturen im modernen Recht,' *Archiv fur Rechts- und Sozialphilosophie*, Special Issue 14: 1-20.

Turner, Stephen (1994) *The Social Theory of Practices: Tradition, Tacit Knowledge and Presuppositions*. Cambridge: Polity.

—— (2002) *Brains/Practices/Relativism: Social Theory after Cognitive Science*. Chicago: University of Chicago Press.

Van den Daele, Wolfgang (1977) 'The Social Construction of Science', in E. Mendelsohn *et al.* (eds.) *The Social Production of Scientific Knowledge*. Dordrecht: Reidel, pp. 27-54.

Van den Berghe, Pierre (1978) *Man in Society: A Biosocial View*. New York: Elsevier.

—— (1990) 'Evolutionary Theory in Sociology: An Examination of Current Thinking', *Sociological Forum* 5: 155-85.

Van Parys, P. (1981) *Evolutionary Explanation in the Social Sciences*. Totowa, NJ: Rowman and Littlefield.

Van Reijen, W. (1987) 'Miss Marx, Terminals und Grands Recrits oder: Kratzt Habermas, wo es nicht juckt?', in D. Kamper and W. van Reijen (eds.) *Die unvollendete Vernunft*. Frankfurt: Suhrkamp.

Varela, Francisco J., Thompson, Evan and Rosch, Eleanor, eds. (1991) *The Embodied Mind: Cognitive Science and Human Experience*. Cambridge, MA: MIT.

Vasquez, John (1976) 'A Learning Theory of the American Anti-Vietnam War Movement,' *Journal of Peace Research* 13: 299-314.

Vester, Michael (1970) *Die Entstehung des Proletariats als Lernprozess*. Frankfurt: Europäische Verlagsanstalt.

Wasmuth, Ulrike (1985) 'Ist die Friedensbewegung tot? Zur Analyse von Protestzyklen,' *Vierteljahresschrift für Sicherheit und Frieden* 3: 138-46.

Weber, M. (1970) 'Politics as Vocation,' in H.H. Gerth and C. Wright Mills (eds.) *From Max Weber: Essays in Sociology*. London: Routledge and Kegan Paul, 77-128.

Weick, K.E. (1979) *Social Psychology of Organizing*. New York: Addison Wesley.

Welker, Michael (1992) 'Einfache oder multiple doppelte Kontingenz? Minimalbedingungen der Beschreibung von Religion und emergenten Strukturen sozialer Systeme', in W. Krawietz and M. Welker (eds.) *Kritik der Theorie sozialer Systeme: Auseinandersetzungen mit Luhmanns Hauptwerk*. Frankfurt: Suhrkamp, pp. 355-70.

Wellmer, Albrecht (1986) *Ethik und Dialog: Elemente des moralischen Urteils bei Kant und in der Diskursethik*. Frankfurt: Suhrkamp.

Wenzel, Harald and Hochmuth, Uwe (1989) 'Die Kontingenz von Kommunikation: Zu kritischen Theorie des kommunikativen Handelns von Jürgen Habermas', *Kölner Zeitschrift für Soziologie und Sozialpsychologie* 41: 241-69.

Wertsch, James V. (1998) 'Mediated Action', in W. Bechtel and G. Graham (eds.) *A Companion to Cognitive Science*. Oxford: Blackwell, pp. 518-25.

White, L.A. (1959) *The Evolution of Culture*. New York: McGraw-Hill.

White, Stephen K. (1988) *The Recent Work of Jürgen Habermas: Reason, Justice and Modernity*. Cambridge: Cambridge University Press.

Wilden, Anthony (1972) *System and Structure*. London: Tavistock.

Wilson, B.S. (1985) 'Morality in the Evolution of the Modern Social System', *British Journal of Sociology* 36(3): 315-32.

Wingert, Lutz and Günther, Klaus eds. (2000) *Die Öffentlichkeit der Vernunft und die Vernunft der Öffentlichkeit: Festschrift für Jürgen Habermas*. Frankfurt: Suhrkamp.

Woodcock, George ed. (1977) *The Anarchist Reader*. Fontana: Glasgow.

World Bank (2002) *Globalization, Growth and Poverty: Building an Inclusive World Economy*. Washington, DC: World Bank.

Worsley, Peter (1984) *The Three Worlds: Culture and World Development*. London: Weidenfeld and Nicolson.

Wright, Harrison (1977) *The Burden of the Present: Liberal-Radical Controversy over Southern African History*. Cape Town: David Philip.

Wynne, Brian (1988) 'Unruly Technology', *Social Studies of Science* 18: 147-67.

—— (1989) 'Building Public Concern into Risk Management' in J. Brown (ed.) *Environmental Threats*. London: Belhaven.

Zolo, Danilo (1997) *Cosmopolis: Prospects for World Government*. Cambridge: Polity Press.

Index